SCOTTISH HISTORY SOCIETY
FOURTH SERIES
VOLUME 15

Papers on Peter May
Land Surveyor

PAPERS ON
PETER MAY
LAND SURVEYOR
1749-1793

edited by Ian H. Adams, PH.D.

★

★

EDINBURGH
printed for the Scottish History Society *by*
T. AND A. CONSTABLE LTD
1979

ISBN 0 906245 05 2

Printed in Great Britain

PREFACE

When I started editing the *Descriptive List of Plans in the Scottish Record Office* in August 1964, it was clear even then that I was privileged to be close to a major historical source. At the time, however, supporting documentary evidence appeared to be sparse indeed. The turning point came with the deposit of the Seafield papers, one of the truly remarkable archives in the Scottish Record Office. The handlisting of this collection was in the hands of Mr Andrew Anderson, then assistant keeper and now curator, and without his kindness in bringing my attention to many of the documents now reproduced in this volume, this work could never have been envisaged. Work on Peter May's papers was made even more pleasurable by sharing a common interest with Dr Ian Grant, and together we have created indexes which not only have given us both wider access to information, but which we have also been able to share with a growing band of scholars studying eighteenth-century change. Over the years there has not been a single member of the staff of the Scottish Record Office who has not afforded me some assistance; thus I dedicate my thanks to all the staff of the Scottish Record Office, 1964-79.

In these times of economic stringency considerable cuts have been made. About twenty-five per cent of the material collected has not been used, and many footnotes have been curtailed; much of the guidance in this came from Dr T. I. Rae, to whom I give my thanks. Miss Catherine Armet, archivist at Mount Stuart, transcribed several of the documents from the Bute collection, and Mrs Meredyth Somerville and Mr George Fortune both gave assistance at a critical time in transcribing and checking material. The two diagrams in the introduction were drawn by Miss Grace Foster, cartographer in the Department of Geography, University of Edinburgh.

I am indebted to the Earl of Seafield and the Seafield Trustees for their permission to publish extensive extracts from the Seafield muniments now housed in the Scottish Record Office, Edinburgh. The Marquis of Bute has given his gracious permission to quote from his family papers at Mount Stuart, Rothesay. To the Trustees of the National Library of Scotland I give my thanks for permission to quote from the Brown papers. Extracts from the Exchequer records appear by permission of the Controller of H.M. Stationery Office. Finally, items appear from the records of the British Fishery Society, Crown Commissioners, Court of Session, Register of Deeds, Register of Sasines, Gordon Castle muniments and Rose of Kilravoch papers with the approval of the Keeper of the Records of Scotland.

Edinburgh
January, 1979

IAN ADAMS

A generous contribution from the
Carnegie Trust for the Universities of Scotland
towards the cost of producing this volume
is gratefully acknowledged by the
Council of the Society

CONTENTS

Introduction

THE DAWN OF SCOTTISH LAND SURVEYING

PETER MAY is not the kind of person you find in the *Dictionary of National Biography*: neither an Oxford cleric, nor a minor poet, he was a land surveyor and estate factor, whose life spanned nearly the whole of the second half of the eighteenth century, an important participant in the Agricultural Revolution in Scotland. Some scholars might wince at the term Agricultural Revolution, but I am convinced that an economic event of such a description did occur in Scotland. It is what W. W. Rostow has called 'take-off'; the period in which the concept of economic growth is not only seen to be normal, but indeed becomes instilled in the minds of the leaders of society.[1] As Peter May saw it in 1779, 'Every branch of business, whether commerce, agriculture or manufacture that is once established on a proper foundation, is not only of consequence to the adventurers, but the whole community derive benefit from it'.[2] Although the letters and papers of Peter May represent strong evidence for revolutionary changes, it is possible to measure these changes in an even more objective manner. My own researches have included quantitative analysis of division of commonties, building of planned villages and the activity of land surveyors.[3] Other scholars have been developing similar methods: in the fields of agricultural change, land management, forest exploitation, planned villages, the statistical basis of agrarian change, changes in the culti-

[1] W. W. Rostow, *Stages of Economic Growth*, Cambridge University Press, 1960. The Rostovian model identifies societies in their economic dimensions as lying within one of five categories: the traditional society, the pre-conditions for take-off, the take-off, the drive to maturity, and the age of high mass-consumption.

[2] See below, p. 209.

[3] I. H. Adams, Economic process and the Scottish land surveyor, *Imago Mundi*, vol. 27, 1975, pp. 13–18.

vation fringe, landownership and agrarian society in the seventeenth century.[1] These have given a firm foundation to our understanding of change in the eighteenth century. Now the concept of agricultural revolution has undergone considerable revision in England, but it would be foolish to take the revised positions as applying to Scotland for all the parameters of change – historical, social, political, legal, economic, cultural and one could even say geographical – were totally different in Scotland and even more markedly so as the Union in many ways had not yet made its mark.[2] There is no question that the adoption of innovations, such as liming and clover, was widespread in the old agrarian system, but what was missing was the overwhelming conviction that the land was a productive machine to be harnessed for profit, attainable only by increasing output *per capita*. When that became the social as well as the economic goal, and the fruits of Newtonian science applied to the same objective, then society was ready for rapid transformation: that is what we now call the Agricultural Revolution. Nearly all the

[1] Respectively: R. A. Dodgshon, Agricultural change in Roxburghshire and Berwickshire, 1700–1815, unpubl. PH.D., University of Liverpool, 1969; Ian D. Grant, Landlords and land management in North-Eastern Scotland 1750–1850, unpubl. PH.D., University of Edinburgh, 1979; James Lindsay, Forest land use in Argyllshire and Perthshire, unpubl. PH.D., University of Edinburgh, 1974; Douglas Lockhart, Planned villages of North-east Scotland, unpubl. PH.D., University of Dundee, 1975; Valerie Morgan, The First Statistical Account as a basis for studying the agrarian geography of late eighteenth-century Scotland, unpubl. PH.D., University of Cambridge, 1969; Martin Parry, The fluctuating cultivation fringe of the Lammermuirs, 1580–1900, unpubl. PH.D., University of Edinburgh, 1972; Lorretta Timperley, Landownership in Scotland, c. 1770, unpubl. PH.D., University of Edinburgh, 1978; I. D. Whyte, Agrarian change in Lowland Scotland in the seventeenth century, unpubl. PH.D., University of Edinburgh, 1974.

[2] The traditional English view, enunciated by Lord Ernle and still held by some scholars for example Mingay, places it firmly in the period 1760 to 1843. Another view put forward by Kerridge is that the Agricultural Revolution dominated the period between 1560 and 1767 and that its main achievements occurred before 1720, most of them before 1673, and many of them earlier still. Finally, there is a body of scholarly opinion, the gradualist school, that sees the spread of agricultural change over such a wide time span that the concept of revolution is not really tenable. The same debate has been taken up in Scotland where it remains an open question until more work can be produced. *See* G. Whittington, Was there a Scottish Agricultural Revolution, *Area*, vol. 7, 1975, No. 3, pp. 204–6; and correspondence relating thereto by D. Mills and M. Parry, ibid., vol. 8, 1976, No. 3, pp. 237–9. And in reply, I. H. Adams, The Agricultural Revolution in Scotland, a contribution to the debate, ibid., vol. 10, No. 3, 1978, pp. 198–203; and I. D. Whyte ibid., pp. 203–5.

methods they applied were already well known, but the revolution lay in their simultaneous use across almost the entire face of the country.

Considerable influence could be exercised by the great landowners of Scotland to forward or thwart agricultural improvement. Very few participated in any large-scale enclosure before the 1760s and those who did often found themselves bankrupt. 'This was an age of fast-rising rents, but it was also an age of insolvent landlords.'[1] The landowner could control the pace of enclosure through the system of leases or tacks, and it has even been suggested that the annual lease was a symptom of backwardness prior to enclosure.[2] However, this is not entirely the case, for the annual lease could be the mark of a *progressive* estate. From the seventeenth century farmers had been accustomed to leases of seven or nine years;[3] but when major rearrangement of an estate was envisaged, each lease as it ran out was continued on an annual basis until all leases had come in. At this point the estate could be remodelled and all the farmers would be put on long leases simultaneously; these could of course expire together, enabling the landlord to carry out any *future* remodelling without the problems entailed by varying lengths of lease. Thus the annual lease in this circumstance was an example, not of rapacious, but of far-sighted landlordism.[4] The enthusiasm for wide-scale expiry of leases at the same period diminished in the time of agricultural depression when landowners found that it could be difficult to find tenants for many farms which were becoming vacant simultaneously.

Generally one can say that the speed and comprehensiveness of Scottish improvements stemmed from the landowners demanding maximum returns to support their conspicuous consumption. The modest castle gave way to the grandiose mansion house: William Duff, 1st Earl Fife is reported as having spent, between 1740 and 1745, some £70,000 building Duff House. To give the aristocrats

[1] E. Cregeen, *Argyll Estate Instructions, 1771–1805*, Scottish History Society, Edinburgh, 1964, p. xi.

[2] D. Mills letter, *Area*, vol. 8, 1976, No. 3, p. 237.

[3] I. D. Whyte, The development of written leases and their impact on Scottish agriculture in the seventeenth century (forthcoming).

[4] An example of these can be found on the Hopetoun estates, *see* I. H. Adams, *The mapping of a Scottish estate*, Educational Studies Dept., University of Edinburgh, 1971.

privacy the towns of Fochabers and Cullen were torn down and rebuilt on completely new sites. As time went on capital expenditure diminished, but it was replaced by the obligation of maintaining an absentee landownership. From the following pages we can see monies flowing to Europe to keep the embarrassing 7th Earl of Findlater out of the country, and to London to support the Bute family. In the latter case some £4,000 per annum was leaving the island of Bute. These were but the dues of Union, a ceaseless, debilitating flow of capital out of Scotland that turned into a flood in the nineteenth century.

Yet the irony was that the clear-headed efficiency demanded in running their far-off Scottish estates created an agricultural system second to none. The success of this agrarian movement had been conceived on the battlefield of Culloden, for here fell not only Highland manhood, but also any hope of an alternative to the Union with England. One avenue of national progress was closed, yet another opened. Whatever their political hue, Scots (there were prominent exceptions) found it difficult to make a political career at Westminster. The Hanoverian Scot was swept up with the Jacobite in the Rebellion's aftermath. Thus a generation of talented aristocratic Scots was forced to turn to things economic, not unlike the post-Second World War Germans and Japanese, and to expend their energies on things Scottish of which the beneficiaries were the Trustees of the Boards of Manufacturers, the Board of the Annexed Estates, and their own estates. Several men, such as the 5th Duke of Argyll, the 4th Duke of Gordon, the 6th Earl of Findlater, the 2nd Earl of Hopetoun, Sir Archibald Grant of Monymusk, and Sir James Grant of Grant, gave their unstinting energies to the improvement of Scotland. And they had influence over a much wider region than the narrow, although very substantial, confines of their own estates. Relatives and neighbours were bombarded with advice, often unsolicited; questionnaires were sent to the successful to elicit the secrets of their success; servants and professional men with the desired expertise were exchanged from estate to estate. There were no geographical barriers to the rapid diffusion of information that was required to bring about the massive agrarian changes of the age. Men could gain immense prestige by their improvements; to Lord Deskford, later the 6th Earl of Findlater and Seafield, could be attributed, 'the exclusive merit of introducing into the north of Scotland those improvements in agriculture and manufactures, and all kinds of useful industry, which in the space of a few years raised his country from a state of semi-barbarism to a degree of civilisation equal to that of the most improved districts of the south'[1].

The great landlords found it difficult to find the right kind of men to implement the new ideas in agriculture and estate management. With their English upbringing men like James Stuart Mackenzie could be forgiven for their jaundiced view of the Scottish scene: 'I observe there is hardly such a thing as what they call in England a land steward, regularly bred to that service; what is called a factor here seems to be only a sort of agent and receiver, which is a mighty small part indeed of an English land steward's business, who does not employ three days in the year receiving rents, but his great and material business is attending to the proper laying out of farms, and instructing the tenants in the cultivation of their lands, directing the making and keeping in repair all fences and inclosures, valuing woods, timber, etc., directing the regular cutting of it. In these and many other works he is constantly on horseback going about the estate of which he has the management so as to see everything that is going forward among the tenants. By what I have heard, there are not half a dozen such land stewards in all Scotland.'[2] Mackenzie was well aware that under Findlater's patronage Peter May had trained men as close to the English ideal as they could expect and in the end he poached Peter May from the Findlater interest into his own Bute interest. The Earl of Rosebery experienced a similar problem, for we find him writing to Findlater on 15 October 1770 (a few days before Findlater died) requesting an opinion on one John Home who had replied to the following advertisement:

> AN OVERSEER WANTED (In a place of Trust, and where caution will be required). His business will be (amongst other things) to buy and sell cattle, to pay and oversee workmen, to receive and pay money in general, and to keep regular Accounts,

[1] Quoted in Sir James Balfour Paul, *The Scots Peerage*, Edinburgh, 1907, vol. 4, pp. 39-40.

[2] See below, p. 161.

> Books, and Journals; to contrive and line out Fences, Plantations, and Pleasure-Grounds; to agree for the execution thereof, and to calculate and measure the contents and value of most kinds of work. In short, he must be fit to superintend the works of one who has a great farm, is a great grazier, incloser, planter and builder. He must therefore be active, sober, steady, and of undoubted integrity. His encouragement will be in proportion to his abilities. . . .[1]

James Stuart Mackenzie's remarks were unfair for he failed to recognise that the existing structure of estate management in Scotland was very different from that in England. In the typical large Scottish estate in the mid-eighteenth century the rents were collected by a local factor, giving part-time attendance only to his duties. On a number of estates, for instance those of the Duke of Buccleuch, such officials were known not as factors, but as 'chamberlains'. Remittances might be made by these factors directly to the owner, who would also audit their accounts, but more commonly they passed to his Edinburgh-based *doer* or law-agent. In some estates the factor with responsibility for the area surrounding the principal mansion house also acted as the general receiver, taking remittances from the other factors and acting as *primus inter pares*. Where a proprietor was abroad or in minority, overall supervision was often exercised by commissioners, appointed from among the relations, friends and advisors of the owner; though sometimes commissioners were appointed for more limited purposes, such as set (lease) of a part of the estates. In some instances the auditing function exercised by the owner or his doer passed to the general receiver or commissioners, as happened in the case of Bute's estates, but the century from 1750 saw the general adoption of independent audit by accountants. Their professional training owed much to Alexander Farquharson, who succeeded William Laidlaw as Clerk of Accounts to the great Buccleuch estates in the minority of Henry, 3rd Duke of Buccleuch, and whose pupils ultimately became responsible for audit on almost all the great estates. Lower down the scale were the clerk, ground officer, land surveyor, farm grieve, forester, gardener, as well as the household staff. Duties could be combined

[1] SRO. GD248/3408/6.

and designations of various posts were by no means consistent. However, there existed a structure which was to evolve into a modern system of estate management that ultimately outshone many an English great estate.[1] From the ranks of estate servants, writers, clerks, land surveyors, schoolmasters and army officers, young Scots gained the necessary experience in the second half of the eighteenth century to create a cadre of worthy, reliable officials who, in later generations, became the butlers of the British Empire. The camaradarie that existed between Peter May and Lord Deskford (the 6th Earl of Findlater) was lost after the succession of the absentee 7th Earl. The latter's truculent adieu to May's departure for Bute for an extra £50 per annum clearly displays the mixed up attitudes of the ruling class.[2] Complaining of May's disloyalty after years of intensive effort raising the rents to pay for the Earl's exile, shows little appreciation of his own lack of responsibility to his native land.

PETER MAY

The quality of May's work, where little of similar sophistication had been earlier seen in Scotland, and a reference by James E. Handley to Lord Deskford's English overseer led me to suppose that Peter May was this man.[3] It was always the easy answer to look southwards for solutions to awkward questions of origins in Scotland. It is, however, becoming clear that in many fields the Scots were capable of developing expertise on relatively slender foundations, and themselves played a dominant role in the recording of the Scottish countryside during the second half of the eighteenth century.

Peter May was born sometime between 1724 and 1733, probably

[1] For a masterly account of the evolution of estate management in Scotland, *see* Ian D. Grant, Landlords and land management in North-Eastern Scotland 1750-1850, unpubl. PH.D., University of Edinburgh, 1979.

[2] Below, p. 201.

[3] James E. Handley, *Scottish farming in the eighteenth century*, Faber, London, 1953, p. 165; my statement that he was probably English appeared in, The land surveyor and his influence on the Scottish rural landscape, *Scottish Geographical Magazine*, vol. 84 pt. 3, 1968, p. 250. Unfortunately one's errors can be perpetuated, e.g. in that excellent work by Ian S. Ross, *Lord Kames and the Scotland of his day*, Clarendon Press, Oxford, 1972, p. 322.

in Moray or Aberdeenshire. Of his parents we know little: of his mother there is not a word and one must assume she had died by 1754. His father James, from the parish of Turriff, was an arboriculturist of some kind, for there survives a statement in a letter to the Earl of Findlater and Seafield by Peter May's brother James,[1] that 'my father . . . has been a long practitioner of that business'.[2] His death at Aberdeen on 17 June 1778 at the reputed age of 103 is the only other piece of information we have of this man.

Of Peter May's schooling we know nothing, although from the evidence encompassed in these pages he was highly numerate, had a clear grasp of scientific agriculture, was at home with basic principles of civil engineering especially matters of drainage, had a good grasp of spelling, wrote with a neat hand, but was totally devoid of the smart classical asides which were so fashionable at the time.

Where Peter May gained his undoubted professional skills is another mystery, but it is incumbent upon one to speculate a little. May's cartographic style shows every sign of a modern professional training – good linework, neat appropriate lettering, illustrated key, attractive but neat compass rose, table of contents – although he used the already somewhat old fashioned symbol of houses in perspective rather than in plan. Most of these characteristics were to be found in plans made by the land surveyors of the Northeast. These surveyors fall into two groups; those that we know were trained by Peter May, and the rest (Fig. 2). The rest, comprising David Aitken, William Crawford and sons, John Home, and Alexander and John Sangster, share with Peter May a style of such similarity that one is forced to speculate that there must be a considerable likelihood of a common training. As it can be proved that Alexander Sangster trained David Aitken and John Home trained William Crawford the net draws closer around the remainder. One other surveyor has an identical style to May's and he is William Urquhart who was trained by John Forbes.

[1] James May first appears on 17 Jan. 1749 as the gardener to Captain John Urquhart of Craigston and Cromarty (1696–1756). He bought the latter estate in 1741. Urquhart's son William sold Cromarty in 1763 to Patrick, Lord Elibank, and James May returned to the estate to measure it for him on 8 Sept. 1769.

[2] Seafield muniments (SRO. GD248/982/2).

John Forbes, estate factor, was born in 1711 at Kildrummy in Moray, and appears professionally as a servant to the Earl of Findlater in 1745.[1] The Earl's housekeeper, Jean Dalrymple, married Forbes and a short time later, around 1747 or 1748, the Earl recommended him for the position of factor to Keith Urquhart of Meldrum. The question arises, did this man, whose contribution to the cartographic record is modest, have the skills to train this great school of land surveyors? Only one plan, dated 1753, can be found in the huge Scottish Record Office collection, 'Plan of the town of Bannon heritably belonging to Alexander Duff of Hatton . . .'.[2] The cartographic style is neat with correctly drawn cartographic elements such as title, scale, table of contents and a functional border. The lettering, probably the most difficult skill to master, is neat and constant. Furthermore he had some legal training for he drew up and prepared a number of feu charters for Old Meldrum. That he had the respect of the landowners in the Northeast for his surveying skills is without doubt, for he made several plans for division of mosses which required not only cartographic skill, but also implied respect for his personal integrity.[3] This is born out when he was named as one of the surveyors authorised on 1 March 1758 to make a plan of the salmon fishings in the Water of Findhorn. In the end Forbes did not undertake the commission in this very important legal battle, leaving Peter May to face legal manoeuvrings which included calling his professional skills into question.[4] Again, the evidence shows that Forbes had prospered for in 1752 he lent his former employer, the Earl of Findlater, £312 sterling.[5] He was active for many more years, training William Urquhart in 1768,[6]

[1] He witnessed 2 May 1745 docquet to accounts crop 1743 of John Munro, one of the Earl's factors (SRO. GD248/1468).

[2] RHP. 2527.

[3] Duff of Meldrum papers (NRA (Scot.) survey 508, p. 5); Carnegie of Crimonmogate papers (NRA (Scot.) survey 64, p. 4).

[4] Sir William Dunbar of Durn and others *contra* Alexander Brodie of Lethen and others (SRO. CS29 6/1/1762). In Feb. 1765 an appeal to House of Lords against the decision in the original case was dismissed (SRO. GD247/70/34). Because of limitations of space documents relating to this case have been omitted from this volume. He was also involved in a case involving the Spey fishings.

[5] SRO. GD248/1389.

[6] Particular Register of Sasines, Aberdeen and Kincardine (SRO. RS8/29, part 2, fo. 206).

making a plan of the Longhill at Crimonmogate in 1770–1,[1] and in his factorship in the 1770s.[2]

Thus, to speculate, I would suggest that Peter May with his brother James was trained by John Forbes in the mid-1740s whilst in the service of the Earl of Findlater (thus the basis for Lord Deskford's later patronage). The Findlater connection is confirmed in a letter of 25 June 1766 when after giving a detailed description of May's method of surveying an estate and presenting the findings in the form of a book May writes, 'I was laid to this practice by My Lord Findlater and have found it the most useful application of my business . . .'. This was before he began his massive survey of Findlater's estates, for he stated in 1757, 'This method I follow with all large estates, and I find it gives general satisfaction. The Earls of Erroll and Findlater are to have all their lands done in the book way . . .'.

To continue the speculation, when Forbes left Findlater's service to become factor at Meldrum, Peter May went to Aberdeen where he became clerk to Andrew Logie, a baillie of the burgh. More importantly the baillie could also draw maps: few samples of his work survive, the most significant being *A survey of the Cities of New and Old Aberdeen, the Harbour and Country adjacent*, which is to be found in the British Museum.[3] On a more mundane level Logie was active in surveying parcels of ground within Aberdeen itself. The disposal of Aberdeen's lands to individuals amongst the magistrates and town council had had a long tradition, there was a spate of such dubious disposals in the 1740s and 50s, and clearly Baillie Logie was central to several of these deals. On 11 April 1749 Aberdeen Town Council 'appointed Baillie Logie and the clerk to

[1] Erroll muniments at Crimonmogate (NRA (Scot.) survey 64, p. 4).

[2] Forbes's son James was born in 1763 and succeeded him in his factorship. Later James became factor to General Gordon Cumming Skene of Dyce and was involved in 1817 in founding a planned village at Dyce (*Aberdeen Journal*, 26 Feb. 1817).

[3] Unfortunately the antecedents of this plan are somewhat messy: the manuscript is a copy, but with corrections, of *A survey of Old & New Aberdeen, with ye adjacent country between ye Rivers Dee and Don inscribed to ye Rt. Honourable D. Forbes Esq., Ld. President of ye Sessions in Scotland.* By G. & W. Paterson. Sold by J. Millan, bookseller, next Scotland Yard, Whitehall, 1746. A nineteenth-century photolitho copy was published by W. & A. K. Johnston (RHP6416/2). Paterson's plan was itself a copy of one by James Gordon made around 1661. There is a copy of Logie's plan in the Scottish Record Office (RHP6308/3).

measure the said lots' of the lands of Gilcomston.[1] Again in January 1751, 'the Council nominate and appointed Provost Alexander Robertson, Baillie Logie, Convenor Auldjo, and the clerk or any two of them as a Committee of Council for dividing the lands of Old Ferryhill into lots and preparing the same for being feued out, with power to them to call for skilfull persons to assist them to put up the said tack of Old Ferryhill in lots, and mark out proper cart roads, and appoints them to report, which being done and agreed to be the Council they agreed that Baillie Logie should make a draught of it.'[2] Yet when a feu charter was drawn up on 29 June 1757 it is quite clear who made the plan; 'all and whole those parts of the lands of Old Ferryhill marked and designed upon the plan and survey thereof made out by Peter May . . .'.[3] Finally, when Peter May required a 'Certificate of Loyalty' it was subscribed by the magistrates of Aberdeen, who asserted he had 'been employed by us and our predecessors in surveying and planning the Town's lands . . .'.[4]

In fact Peter May makes his first appearance in the records on 25 February 1752 when the magistrates of Aberdeen appointed him 'or any other sufficient land measurer' to lay out lots in the division of the Gilcomston lands. Clearly by this time he was fully trained and getting commissions on his own merit, for the following year he surveyed Gordon's Burgh (Fort William) for the Duke of Gordon.[5] The longstanding patronage by James Ogilvy, Lord Deskford (later 6th Earl of Findlater and 3rd Earl of Seafield) emerges from the pages of a curious account from Lord Deskford's day book of November 1754. Apparently May was in Edinburgh with Lord Deskford who was meeting the future commissioners of the Annexed Estates, the Earl of Hopetoun, William Grant, Lord Prestongrange and brother of Sir Archibald Grant of Monymusk, and General Humphrey Bland, commander-in-chief of the armed forces in Scotland.

[1] Aberdeen Council Register, vol. 61, p. 384: below p. 1. [2] Ibid., pp. 528-9.

[3] Particular Register of Sasines, Aberdeen and Kincardine (SRO. RS8/26/1, fos. 192*r*-193*v*).

[4] Below, p. 3.

[5] The plan is missing, but the list of inhabitants to accompany it has survived (SRO. RHP35982). Payment for this survey is recorded among Gordon Castle muniments (SRO. GD44/152/32).

In many ways the Board of the Annexed Estates was the vital catalyst that set alight the spirit of improvement that was to sweep through Scotland for the next generation. The Annexed Estates comprised the thirteen largest of the fifty-three estates originally forfeited to the Crown by the attainder for treason of owners implicated in the 1745 Rebellion. Ardsheal, Arnprior, Barrisdale, Callart, Cluny, Cromarty, Kinlochmoidart, Lochgarry, Lochiel, Lovat, Monaltry, Perth and Struan were singled out for special attention as part of the Government's scheme to eliminate the threat of Jacobitism by removing some of the basic causes of discontent and disaffection in the Highlands. The Annexing Act of 1752 (25 Geo. II c. 41) expressly empowered the commissioners to have the lands surveyed and plans made 'setting forth the extent and different qualities of the grounds, the several advantages and disadvantages arising from their situation and what improvements may be made upon the same'. Though there was some delay in appointing the Commissioners under the Act, once appointed they wasted no time before applying themselves to this very question. One of the Commissioners, Lieutenant-Colonel David Watson, who had already been in charge of William Roy on his military survey from 1747 to 1755, laid before their first meeting on 23 June 1755 a paper entitled 'Instructions to the surveyors to be employed in surveying the Forfeited Estates', which was amended and approved at the next meeting on 30 June.[1] This proved to be one of the most important documents in the history of Scottish surveying, for the Commissioners included twenty of Scotland's leading landed proprietors and its terms were to be echoed repeatedly in the instructions given by individual landowners to their own surveyors over the next few years.[2]

It fell to Colonel Watson to propose that Peter May, land surveyor in Aberdeen, should survey the Lovat estate. May had offered to undertake this with five assistants and one theodolite at a rate of 13s. a day whilst in the field and 7s. for himself whilst at home drawing a fair copy. His offer was accepted on 14 July 1755 and a small committee, made up of Lord Deskford, Colonel Watson and

[1] SRO. E721/1, pp. 12, 14.

[2] *See* Duke of Gordon's instructions to Alexander Taylor in 1770 printed in I. H. Adams, *List of Plans in the Scottish Record Office*, vol. 2, pp. ix-x.

Sir Gilbert Elliot of Minto, drafted instructions to be forwarded to the factor, Captain John Forbes of New.

The record of Peter May's activities becomes clear and almost unbroken from July 1755, and henceforth the intricacies of his professional life can be followed step by step. Here we can see the Agricultural Revolution as portrayed in the working life of one of its main protagonists. For most of his life we can see the guiding hand of the 6th Earl of Findlater: as Commissioner of the Annexed Estates he enabled May to benefit from the commission to survey Lovat and Cromarty; as uncle of James Grant of Grant he recommended May as 'the best land surveyor in Scotland'; and finally he gave May the factorship of his property in the parishes of Elgin, Birnie, St Andrews and Spynie. His patronage introduced May to the foremost improvers of the day including Lord Kames, Lord Kinnoull, Robert Barclay of Ury, Sir Archibald Grant of Monymusk and James Stuart Mackenzie. Throughout, Peter May sat at table with these great men.

Peter May rose to command the greatest respect from men in very high places. This is clearly born out by the words of James Stuart Mackenzie, Lord Privy Seal of Scotland, to his brother the Earl of Bute, former Prime Minister of Britain: 'I more and more approve of Mr May's method of going to work. He has great temper in treating with the many absurd heads he has to deal with. He shows great judgement in forming his plans of future improvements. He is most active and assiduous in whatever he undertakes, and it is surprising to see what insight he has already acquired, not only into the land in Bute, but likewise into the turn and genius of the people there; to this I may add that he has a liberal way of thinking. . . .'[1] This last point is shown in a statement by May about excessive rents, 'I acknowledge in the most ingenuous manner that I am more apprehensive of exceeding the real and adequate value of the lands, than being under that standard. I am aware of the dangerous consequences that always attend the over-renting lands. A bankrupt estate occasioned by injudicious management is the most dismal situation both for the landlord and the tenantry.'[2]

As to Peter May's personality and relationships to family and

[1] Below, p. 202. [2] Below, p. 205.

friends we have plenty of evidence throughout his correspondence that he gave and received faithful friendship from a wide circle. Probably the most important letters in this category are those to his nephew George Brown whose life and career mirrored his own. For example Peter May's attitude towards money in his letters to Brown reflects a combination of Lowland Scot's canniness and middle class frugality, attitudes which have nurtured two centuries of Scottish bankers, civil servants and colonial administrators. 'By what I have said', he wrote to his 25-year-old nephew, 'I would not have you apprehend that I mean to enforce your being a miser. I only mean to recommend economy and that too in a very decent manner, and the earlier that this is implanted it takes root the better.' George Brown took his uncle's advice for he left £17,526 14s. 3½d. at his death in 1816.[1]

In marked contrast his own son turned out to be far less worthy, although there is never a hint of less than complete support for him however outrageous his adventures. Alexander (Sandy) was Peter and Euphemia's only child, although they virtually adopted one of brother James's daughters, Barbara. May trained his son in the art of land surveying and gave him the fruits of his own experience in estate management. Time and again we find him leaving Sandy with quite heavy responsibilities. On their move to Bute, May intended from the start only a short career there before retiring and settling his son in the factorship. At first Sandy impressed James Stuart Mackenzie, who wrote to the Earl of Bute: 'by the bye, I like [him] mightily, for I think him a treasure to you'. After May's retiral in 1789, Alexander succeeded his father and continued to run the estate. Lord Bute's dissatisfaction with Alexander May eventually began to appear, and in February 1799 he wrote that he had not heard from May for several months, and, shortly afterwards, that he could no longer trust him. Alexander's drinking habits finally led Lord Bute to dismiss him in May 1803. Of his later career we know little, but on 18 December 1804 it was reported that May had gone to England to survey an estate. Later he was back in Greenock in the partnership of Still, May and Company, merchants, which went bankrupt around 1807.[2] In 1810 he prepared a plan of the new town of

[1] SRO. Moray Testaments (CC16/4/10) and Moray Inventory (CC16/5/2, p. 267).
[2] Renfrewshire Sasine Abridgements, 1st series, No. 8877.

Largs,[1] and was postmaster in Greenock till his death in September 1823.

Peter May retired from the service of the Earl of Bute probably with the settlement of crop 1789. Thus as the 1790s started, the long-held wish to return and settle among friends in the north could have been fulfilled. But this did not happen, for we find him in Edinburgh in 1791 for the marriage of his adopted daughter Barbara to William Beveridge, Writer to the Signet.[2] Apart from that we know little of his first three years of retirement, but it is clear that by the summer of 1793 something had gone wrong with his ambition, for May had settled in the New Town of Edinburgh in the fashionable St Andrew's Square. This would have kept him near Barbara; and he may also have had doubts as to his son's competence and thus felt it imperative to settle strategically between him in Bute and the Earl's Commissioners in Edinburgh. The record does not tell us. Whatever the reason, he stayed in St Andrew's Square for just a year, for the *Edinburgh Directory* records a move to No 4 St James Square from July 1794 to July 1795. The last document in his hand is dated 8 January 1794, and according to the *Scots Magazine*, May died on 25 June 1795.[3] From July 1795 Mrs May is to be found living at No 55 Princes Street.[4]

THE NORTHEAST SCHOOL OF SCOTTISH LAND SURVEYORS

It was no accident that a vigorous school of land surveyors and agricultural consultants flourished in northeast Scotland, for here was the region where many of the changes associated with the Agricultural Revolution were first carried out on a wide scale. The enclosure of whole estates such as those of the Duke of Gordon, Earl of Findlater and Seafield, Earl Fife, Grant of Grant and many others affected vast areas reflecting the pattern of massive land holdings.[5] The planned village movement had its roots and most

[1] Messrs Mitchell, Johnston & Co. (NRA (Scot.) survey 623, p. 20).
[2] Edinburgh Marriage Register, 22 Nov. 1791.
[3] *Scots Mag.*, vol. 57, p. 411.
[4] There is registered a discharge Mr James May and others to the Trustees of the late [Peter, the entry being erroneously entered as Robert] May dated 22 Dec. 1795 (SRO. Register of Deeds Dur. vol. 272, pp. 484-7).
[5] L. Timperley, Landownership in Scotland in the eighteenth century, unpublished PH.D., University of Edinburgh, 1977.

vigorous expression in the area.[1] Estate management was taken to its limits of efficiency by removing people from the agrarian sector whilst maintaining very high rent rolls. Indeed from the estate records of this area we can construct a network of personnel, information and ideas that amounts to an economic revolution capable of changing the old agrarian orders of society.

The daunting prospect of the unimproved Aberdeenshire countryside must have forced Archibald Grant of Monymusk to question the wisdom of his agricultural ambitions. Where was he to get the professional assistance, for example in land surveying, in a country where no one with such skills was available. In March 1719 he purchased 'compass and rule' for £3 and a 'theodolite and chain' for the astronomical sum of £50 8s. sterling.[2] Even when Grant's English expert, Thomas Winter, arrived at Monymusk in 1726 the necessary cartographic instruments were not available: 'I should by this time have given you a plane of your house and gardens as they now are: allso have shewn you what alterations and improvements may be made, but have no instruments to doe it with. Please send me down as soon as possible a case of drawing instruments with a brass scale rule in . . .'.[3] Winter settled to the unenviable task of introducing the new ideas to a sullen tenantry and he farmed and held the position of baron baillie in the estate to 1742. His son Thomas arrived with his father in Scotland in 1726 for as Thomas senior wrote to Sir Archibald, 'I could wish my boy was 4 or 5 years older I should be glad to accept your offer for him'.[4] Thomas junior made his first survey in 1736 on the Monymusk estate, but two years later he obtained a commission from the Duke of Gordon.[5] In 1747 Winter went to Castle Grant to make a 'Plan for a new little garden and terraced walks at Castle Grant' for Sir Ludovic Grant.[6] Henceforth commissions rolled in, but increasingly they took

[1] D. Lockhart's unpublished PH.D. op. cit.; and his paper 'The planned villages of Aberdeenshire: the evidence from newspaper advertisements', *Scottish Geographical Magazine*, vol. 94, No. 2, Sept., 1978, pp. 95-102; and G. A. Dixon, 1978, op. cit.

[2] Henry Hamilton, *Selections from the Monymusk papers, 1713-1755*, Scottish History Society, 1945, p. lxix.

[3] Ibid. pp. 104-5.

[4] Ibid. pp. 110-11.

[5] Henry Hamilton, *Life and Labour on an Aberdeenshire Estate, 1735-50*, 3rd Spalding Club, 1946, p. 128; and receipt from Gordon Castle papers (SRO. GD44/51/379).

[6] RHP. 8946.

Thomas, who is joined by Archibald, Peter and William (their relationships are not too clear), southwards to Perthshire where he settled at Muthill in 1749 and at Culdies near Crieff from 1758 until the last reference to him in 1761. The work of the Winters records the unenclosed landscape of several lowland estates.[1] On the evidence so far they cannot be said to have played a major role in setting up the Northeast School of Land Surveyors.

As stated earlier I think the genesis must be found in the work of someone like John Forbes, and if the surmise is correct then there is a strong possibility he trained such men as Alexander Sangster, who was the gardener to Lord Ross at Balnagown Castle, Ross-shire, and who occasionally ventured outwith that estate to make plans. For instance he was commissioned several times to make plans to settle disputes before the Court of Session. In 1748 he surveyed the disputed mosses around Loch Eye, in Easter Ross.[2] Again, he was called upon to draw a map of the lands of Tain in a dispute between the burgh and the litigious laird of Cadboll.[3] With Charles Ross in 1759 he drew judicial plans in Fearn, and four years later made a plan, engraved by Hector Gavin, of a river dispute at Dingwall. What is clear from Sangster's career is that his essays in surveying would not have provided a basis for a career spanning 1748 to 1763 without his position as a gardener.

Alexander Sangster was also the father-in-law to another land surveyor, David Aitken, whose style is very close to May's. Aitken made many surveys from 1763 to 1804 mainly in Ross and Cromarty, Sutherland, Orkney, Caithness and Inverness. He was from 1763 to 1771 gardener on the Annexed Estate of Ross at the Milton of Newtarbat: it was reported to the Commissioners on 15 December 1763, 'that the said David Aitken intends to raise thorns and nurseries of all kinds and is in other respects an useful man. Board agreed to give a house and 3 acres of ground to David Aitken upon

[1] For example Blair Atholl estates (Blair Atholl muniments, map D. 3); Glamis estates (NRA (Scot.) survey 885, p. 125); Earl of Morton's estates (RHP1021); John Ramsay of Ochtertyre (RHP13495); Taymouth for Earl of Breadalbane (RHP961/3); Rosyth for Earl of Hopetoun (Hopetoun mss., photocopy RHP9274); and others to be found in the SRO.

[2] SRO. Court of Session Misc. documents (RH9/16).

[3] RHP10128; *See* R. W. Munro and Jean Munro, *Tain through the centuries*, Tain Town Council, 1966, p. 89.

the farm of New Tarbet . . . and also two acres of ground of the said farm rent free for a nursery garden'.[1] John Sangster, whose relationship with Alexander is not known, made a series of estate, commonty and road plans mainly in Aberdeenshire, where he resided at St Fergus from 1769 to 1785.[2]

The man who made the greatest contribution to the foundation of the 'Northeast School' was Peter May (see Fig. 2). Not only did his own work change the face of the countryside, but he trained a series of apprentices who carried his influence much wider afield. Indeed, four of them – the brothers Alexander and George Taylor, Thomas Milne and George Brown – were to carve careers in land surveying, cartography and civil engineering which were landmarks in their day.

Thomas Milne

Thomas Milne gained his first surveying experience with Peter May in the early 1760s, and had gone to work for Earl Fife in April 1768. The spirit of improvement had begun to stir on the Gordon Castle estates and in 1769 James Ross, the chamberlain at Gordon Castle, wrote to Peter May asking him for a suitable man. May suggested George Brown, but already Brown was inundated with work on a freelance basis and was reluctant to take on a full-time position. Thus in June 1770 Thomas Milne engaged to survey the Gordon Castle estates and remained in the Duke's service until 1785. From 1770 to 1776 Milne was joined by Alexander Taylor and occasionally by George Brown. From August 1776 to 1783 Milne continued to work alone. In the autumn of 1776 he surveyed parts of Strathaven, Rhynie, Enzie and Gartly. Thereafter he leased a small farm from the Duke in Enzie, close to Gordon Castle, and spent more time farming than surveying. From April 1780 Milne was rejoined by Alexander Taylor, but the major part of the surveyor's task was over in the Gordon Castle estate and in 1785 Milne left Scotland to begin a residence of twenty-one years in England.[3]

[1] SRO. E721/7, p. 155.
[2] Plans in SRO. (RHP2528, 3568, 13296); and SRO. RS8/29, fo. 114.
[3] For his early career, *see* I. H. Adams, *Descriptive List of Plans in the Scottish Record Office*, H.M.S.O., Edinburgh, vol. 2, 1970, pp. viii–xv.

There was really very little in Milne's career as an estate surveyor in Scotland to suggest future eminence in the field of cartography. But in England he advertised himself as 'an artist in the lines of civil engineering, surveying, valuing, dividing and draining land, picturesque gardening, engraving and dialing'. At first he participated in the great trigonometrical surveys of English counties, which had been stimulated by £100 premiums offered by the Society of Arts for any original county survey upon a scale of one inch to one mile.[1] One must assume that he must have extended his skills in the years 1785 to 1788, probably with William Faden in London, for he made a map of Hampshire between 1788 and 1790 for Faden to publish.[2] Thereafter he worked with Thomas Donald to make the county map of Norfolk, published in 1794. By this time Milne had gained a considerable reputation, for in a book published in 1791 he is described as 'one of the most able and expert surveyors of the present day', with a special aptitude in the use of the theodolite.[3] This appears to have been recognised by his peers, for he was elected in 1793 a member of the Society of Civil Engineers. He was now ready to undertake his most ambitious work, of making a land use map of such sophistication as not to be repeated until Dudley Stamp started the Land Utilization Survey of Britain in the 1930s. Milne's map, on a scale of two inches to one mile and engraved on six plates, bears the title *Milne's Plan of the Cities of London and Westminster, circumadjacent Towns and Parishes etc, laid down from a Trigonometrical Survey taken in the Years 1795–9. Printed for and Published by Thomas Milne, No. 7 New-street, Knightsbridge as the Act directs; 11th March 1800*. The map records the use of each field by means of an inserted letter and an overpainted colour. It is possible to distinguish seventeen categories of land use.[4] The influence of this map was slight, however, for few seem to have been printed and only one

[1] J. B. Harley, The Society of Arts and the surveys of English counties, 1759–1809, *Journal of the Royal Society of Arts*, vol. 112, pp. 43–6, 119–24, 269–75, 538–43.

[2] J. B. Harley, The re-mapping of England, 1750–1800, *Imago Mundi*, vol. 19, pp. 56–67.

[3] George Adams, *Geometrical and Graphical Essays*, 1791 (2nd ed. 1797), in which Milne contributed chapters entitled 'Mr Milne's Method of Surveying' and 'Observations on Plotting'. Quoted in G. B. G. Bull, Thomas Milne's land utilization map of the London area in 1800, *The Geographical Journal*, vol. 122, pt. 1, Mar. 1956, p. 26.

[4] John H. Harvey, The nurseries on Milne's land-use map, *Transactions of the London and Middlesex Archaelogical Society*, vol. 24, 1973, pp. 177–98.

complete copy of the six sheets is known to have survived.[1] Of his later years we know little, but he returned to Scotland in 1809 to reside at Mr Hall's, Frederick Street, Aberdeen.

The brothers Taylor

Of the three brothers Taylor – Alexander, George and William – all but William became eminent land surveyors. The first reference to them appears on 3 November 1766, when May wrote to Alexander instructing him in the matter of reduction by squares, and to set his brother William drawing ridges and shading round fields. It is possible that the Taylor brothers were the sons of William Taylor, surveyor at Fort George, who was working in the northeast from 1756 to 1766.[2] His sudden disappearance from the records in 1766, and a reference by Peter May in April 1767, in his proposals to survey James Grant of Grant's estates on Speyside, that 'the surveyor has a couple of lads who are bred to the business and can measure land by themselves', lead to this conclusion. On May's recommendation, Alexander Taylor applied to Grant of Grant early in 1768 to engage as a salaried surveyor. One of his first tasks that year was to make 'A Plan of New Grantown with the lands of Kylentra, Easter and Wester Driggy, etc., now appropriate for its accommodation belonging heritably to James Grant of Grant, Esq.'[3] In June 1770 he moved on to work for the Duke of Gordon for a salary of £35 per annum, and his place with Grant of Grant was taken by brother George.[4] George completed the survey of Speyside and Abernethy which was bound into a volume of thirty-two

[1] King George III's Topographical Collection, British Library; this has been reproduced by G. B. G. Bull (ed.), London Topographical Society, 1975-6.

[2] The first reference to William Taylor relates to his making a plan for Sir Robert Gordon of Gordonstoun in 1756 (RHP31). In 1762 he was described as a surveyor in Fort George (RHP1428). He had a brother John who was the roads overseer at Fort George.

[3] RHP. 13911; a considerable body of literature has appeared with regard to this plan and the founding of Grantown-on-Spey: A. Geddes, The foundation of Grantown-on-Spey, 1765, *Scottish Geographical Magazine*, vol. 61, 1945, pp. 19-22; Heather Woolmer, Grantown-on-Spey: an eighteenth-century new town, *Town Planning Review*, vol. 41 No. 3, July 1970, pp. 237-49; and a series of authoritative articles by George A. Dixon on various aspects of early Grantown-on-Spey have appeared from 9 Apr. 1965 to 5 May 1972 in the *Strathspey and Badenoch Herald*.

[4] I. H. Adams, George Taylor, a surveyor o' pairts, *Imago Mundi*, vol. 27, 1975, 55-64.

splendid plans.[1] As George Taylor's work at Castle Grant was coming to an end, he seems to have canvassed Grant's relatives and neighbours for work. With James Grant of Ballindalloch, governor of East Florida, he found unwelcome competition, 'I am told the Governour has employed a lad of the name of Brebner from Rothes, who led the chain to Mr Home for some months, to survey his lands and that there is a Taylor just now employed at Ballendalloch to equip him. I suppose that is one of the Governour's frugal plans, and I wish he may be served in proportion, and of which I have not the least manner of doubt.'[2] William, about this time, decided to take himself off to a more attractive sphere. He went first to London, hoping to secure a cadetship in the East India Company, in which, he was led to believe, he 'could not fail of success in India in the business which I had learned'.[3] For two years running he failed in his ambition, and in sheer desperation he worked for James Macpherson ('Ossian'), for his keep only without wages, transcribing documents for Macpherson's *Original papers containing the secret history of Great Britain, 1660–1714*.[4]

By April 1775 George Taylor had moved to Edinburgh and, with Andrew Skinner, formulated proposals for a book of plans of Scotland's roads.[5] Taylor appealed to Sir James Grant of Grant to use his influence on their behalf:

> 'I take the liberty to send you a copy of the proposals for publishing a book of plans of the Scotch roads. You will pardon the trouble I so often give you, as gentlemen on the highway are obliged to lay aside all delicacy. By means of Lord Gardenston and Mr Barclay of Ury I have reason to hope something will be procured from the Commissioners of the Annexed Estates, and the Trustees for Manufactures, towards encouraging the undertaking. Lord Gardenston has ordered petitions to be presented, which will be done tomorrow. He mentioned fifty or sixty pounds. I would therefore beg you

[1] RHP. 3964. [2] SRO. GD248/201/2. [3] SRO. GD248/462/4.

[4] William appears to have given up land surveying completely, for by 1781 he had become joint manager, with Sheridan, of the Opera House, London (Letter from Marian Grant to Lady Grant, 18 Aug. 1781, SRO. GD248/518/1).

[5] Andrew Skinner remains an enigma; nothing is known of him except the linking of his name to Taylor's in several cartographic works.

> would be so good as write some of the Commissioners in our favour, sensible it would have its due weight. . . .'[1]

Grant of Grant ignored this and a further request for help, but Taylor and Skinner's petition was read by the Commissioners on 12 July 1775.[2] Financial help was not immediately forthcoming but the Commissioners approved the undertaking and ordered the secretary to 'signify that as individuals they will be disposed to encourage the petitioners'.[3] They published the *Maps of the Roads of North Britain* on 8 February 1776 and in the following July reminded the Commissioners of their promise and were rewarded with a grant of 100 guineas. Still with a deficit of £300 they went again to the Commissioners, and their plea was heard by Lord Kames, Lord Gardenston, Lord Stonefield, George Clerk Maxwell, Sir Adolphus Oughton, Lord Ankerville and the Solicitor General. An award of £50 was decided upon, but they 'resolved that no further sum shall be granted'.[4]

It was in the autumn of 1776 that Taylor and Skinner advertised their scheme to map the roads of Ireland.[5] Operations started in February 1777 and with the assistance of two other surveyors and sixteen assistants they completed the bulk of the work that season. The following year was spent surveying the county of Louth and they published that map on 28 September 1778.

Taylor and Skinner probably left Ireland for America in the spring of 1779, and Taylor was commissioned in a Provincial Regiment of Foot (Cumberland's Regiment). Of his military career we know little, but he accompanied the expedition to capture Charleston which set out from New York on 23 December 1779, and, after an overlong voyage wracked by gales, arrived exhausted at James Island on 11 February 1780.[6] A letter from his brother William to Sir James Grant of Grant reported George's appointment as Assistant Engineer during the siege of Charleston.[7] In 1781

[1] SRO. GD248/244. [2] SRO. E728/53/1.
[3] SRO. E721/11, p. 148. [4] SRO. E721/11, p. 200-1.
[5] J. H. Andrews (ed.), *Maps of the Roads of Ireland*, Irish University Press, Shannon, 1969, p. v.
[6] For the story of this convoy and chart of voyage, *see* I. H. Adams, The complicity of climate with the American cause, *New Edinburgh Review*, Nos. 35 and 36, 1976, pp. 49-56.
[7] SRO. GD248/510/1.

Taylor and Skinner made a *Map of New York and Staten Islands, and part of Long Island* which had been ordered by General Sir Henry Clinton, K.B. With the collapse of the British the two surveyors departed for Jamaica in the autumn of 1782.

Alexander Taylor remained in the employment of the Duke of Gordon until August 1776, and thereafter did some work for Sir James Grant of Grant. Work associated with agricultural improvements became scarce in Scotland in the early 1780s, principally because of the poor harvest in 1782 and the very depressed year that followed. In 1783, Alexander was in Ireland making a map of county Kildare. Later he became one of Ireland's leading cartographers, and died there in 1828. George in the meantime had returned to Scotland and, in 1785, produced an exquisite manuscript copy of his *Sketches of the roads in Scotland*.[1] From 1787 to 1796 he resided at Annfield (otherwise Forresterhill) in Aberdeenshire. During this period he obtained a few land surveying commissions. In 1790 he was employed by Aberdeen Town Council to ascertain the boundary between the town's lands and Pitfoddels.[2] Three years later, along with Colin Innes and John Home, he made a plan of the salmon fishings of the River North Esk,[3] and in the same year also made a survey for the proposed Aberdeenshire Canal.[4] After this in 1796 he again forsook Scotland and returned to Ireland, where he worked on the improvement of the Dublin-Kilcullen road.

George Brown

Peter May's sister, Barbara Brown, had a son George in 1747 who was, above everyone, to carry on the May school of land surveying in northern Scotland. George Brown started his apprenticeship with his uncle about the age of thirteen and it seems it was a period in which he learned not only his professional skills but also a degree of bitterness. He wrote on 11 July 1795 shortly after his uncle's death, 'I have at last got a copy of Mr May's settlements which is full upon my part equal to my expectations and some of my other friends

[1] University Library, Cambridge; *see* Roger H. Fairclough, 'Sketches of the Roads in Scotland, 1785': the manuscript road book of George Taylor, *Imago Mundi*, vol. 27, 1975, pp. 65-72.

[2] Court of Session process (SRO. CS34/4/54).

[3] Court of Session process (SRO. CS. 181 Misc. bdle. 12).

[4] Sir John Sinclair, *Statistical Account of Scotland*, vol. 19, 1797, p. 226 [*OSA*].

may say that he has been too liberal towards me, but any man who will consider that I wrought hard to him for nine years and during that time or since never had a shilling, even clothes to my back or shoes to my feet, and in good measure contributed a little to making part of the money, will not think I am overpaid'.[1] He appears in the records surveying the estates of James Grant of Grant on Speyside in the summer of 1767. From the beginning Brown had plenty of commissions and when the Duke of Gordon approached him in 1769 to engage on a salaried basis George would have none of it. 'I was recommended by Mr May to Brodie, and Brodie recommended me to some of the neighbouring gentlemen, so that I have found plenty of business even in my first outset. I find I am now under engagements for eight or nine months at least, and I have reason to believe that more will cast up in time, and this turns out greatly more advantageous than any engagement I can get by the year.'[2] From 9 April 1770, when he advertised in the *Aberdeen Journal* that he intended to settle in Aberdeen, to 1778, he conducted an ever-growing land surveying business. Much of his work was done for the landowners of the Northeast: in 1771 for Lord Forbes at Pittodrie; in 1772 for Lord Saltoun in Buchan; in 1774 for Grant of Monymusk; in 1776 for Craigievar estate. Occasionally he ventured further afield as in 1771 when he surveyed an estate for Sir Alexander Ramsay recently purchased from George Dempster of Dunnichen. With Peter May's departure for Bute, George Brown succeeded not only to the factorship in Elgin but also took over the farm at Linkwood.[3]

Brown's factorship was somewhat stormy and on at least two occasions, one in 1784 and the other in 1790, he nearly left his job and Linkwood. Having been deeply offended by the Earl of Findlater he wrote on 4 April 1784, '. . . I left an exceedingly good business when I sat down here, which I did at the desire of Mr May and much against the advice and opinion of many other friends, but from the friendship and attention shown me by my Lord Findlater when last in the country, I had little notion of moving while that

[1] SRO. GD248/3423/2. [2] Below, p. 165.

[3] Below p. 233, n. for a description by Alexander Wight of Linkwood under Brown's management; for a detailed examination of Brown's career, *see* Ian D. Grant, op. cit., pp. 228–244.

continued. From what his Lordship said to me that seems at an end and I am therefore resolved to give up the business immediately and leave this part of the country . . .'.[1]

It was not to be, for he had many fruitful years ahead at Linkwood. He married Margaret Clark and their first child, Marjory was born there in May 1779, and there followed nine children with eighteenth-century regularity.[2] His political interests on behalf of his employer led him to be elected as burgess of Elgin in 1780, town councillor in 1781, and provost seven times between 1782 and 1815; furthermore, he was several times burgh treasurer. Brown also inherited from Peter May the factorship of Cosmo Gordon's estate of Buckie. If this was not enough he supplemented his income by being postmaster in Elgin, Assistant Quartermaster for Scotland, agent for the Aberdeen Bank, a linen manufacturer, brewer, farmer, nurseryman, civil engineer, as well as continuing private practice land surveying in most of the counties in the north and northeast.

The opening up of the Highlands by means of a network of roads had long been the ambition of the British Government. General Wade made the first sustained attempt by building 250 miles of 'Military Road' between 1725 and 1736.[3] In George Brown's opinion it had been a pretty disastrous effort: 'I need not mention your Lordship the rugged country both these lines of road passes through, but particularly the line from Inverness to Bernera, a great part whereof was originally formed as a Military road, but without exception the worst conducted that I ever saw, for it seems to have been the wish of the Engineer to go over every steep precipice in the way.'[4] Towards the end of the century pressure was brought to bear on the Government by the British Fisheries Society and the Highland Society to rectify this situation. George Brown was commissioned to make a number of surveys between 1790 and 1799, and found that about 1,000 miles of road were needed at a cost of

[1] SRO. GD248/3406/12.

[2] Parochial Registers, Elgin, births 1776–1819 (GRO. OPR 135/5).

[3] William Taylor, *The Military Roads of Scotland*, David & Charles, Newton Abbot, 1976.

[4] Letter from George Brown to Lord Adam Gordon reporting Brown's progress of surveying the Highland roads. This letter was passed on to Henry Dundas (SRO. RH2/4/64).

£150,000. The immediate result of his work was the building of a road from Contin near Dingwall to the newly established fishing settlement at Ullapool.[1] Most important, however, was the influence of his work towards the setting up of the 'Commission for making Roads and building Bridges in the Highlands of Scotland' which was set up by Act of Parliament in 1803.[2] When they started their task in July 1803 they were presented with the fruits of Brown's work which saved them a considerable amount of time and labour. Brown continued to give service to the Commission undertaking various enterprises including writing for Thomas Telford a detailed paper on setting up fishing villages using his experience as factor on Cosmo Gordon's estate of Buckie.[3]

Training land surveyors was another sphere in which Brown played an important role. His varied and extensive business required large numbers of assistants who could in later life capitalise on their Brown connection. One of his first apprentices was Robert Johnston whom he inherited from Peter May. Thereafter he trained Colin Innes and Robert Shand (1781),[4] James Chapman (1784), William Matthew (1785), William Mackay (1796), John Innes (1799), Alexander Warren (1803), Thomas Shier and John Sim (1804), George Johnston and George McWilliam (1808), John Tait (*c.* 1815) and David Steinson (1816). His own son Peter, who was born in 1791, took some training from his father, but upon taking over the factorship at Linkwood established a reputation as an agriculturalist, stockbreeder and valuator, and handed over most of the surveying side of his father's business to George McWilliam.[5]

George Brown left northeast Scotland a very different place when he died on 19 June 1816, for the numerous plans he left behind were the blueprints for our present-day landscape. Peter May, George Brown and their many followers were the unseen hands that created the human landscape of Scotland.

[1] For the story of the building of Ullapool 1792–1798, *see* Jean Dunlop, *The British Fisheries Society, 1786–1893*, John Donald, Edinburgh, 1977. It is not generally recognised that Peter May made a plan for a settlement there in August 1756, below, p. 12.
[2] A. R. B. Haldane, *New Ways through the Glens*, Nelson, Edinburgh, 1962, pp. 44–45.
[3] British Fisheries Society papers, letter March 1808 (SRO. GD9/306/2).
[4] The dates given represent the first documentary evidence of their surveying land; one can assume they began their training some time before the given date.
[5] Peter Brown remained at Linkwood until his death in 1868.

John Home

Finally, another surveyor of a calibre comparable to May's to emerge in the northeast during this period was John Home (sometimes Hume). Similarity of cartographic style and career as nurseryman, land surveyor and farmer, provides circumstantial evidence of a common master, but no documentary evidence has as yet been discovered linking them. John Home was born in 1733-4. Of his training we know nothing, but before becoming a full-time surveyor he possessed a small nursery garden adjoining the farm of Colleonard near Banff. The earliest reference to him is to be found in an advertisement in the *Aberdeen Journal* in 1760 offering a variety of plants for sale. An advertisement in the *Caledonian Mercury* of 7 March 1763, announces his resolve to give up the nursery business and apply himself 'to the business of laying out and surveying of grounds which he has practised with approbation'.[1] He wanted to dispose of all his stock, including a wide variety of exotic trees, at reduced rates. The business was taken over by Thomas Reid under whom it flourished to the extent of him being able to supply Garden of Troup with 1,900,000 trees in a period of three or four years.[2]

The first known plan by Home was of the lands of Tilliesnaught, property of Thomas Forbes, in the parish of Birse, Aberdeenshire.[3] The plan was surveyed in 1762 and 1764, spanning the period when he disposed of his nursery. In February 1766 he made a survey of the moss and lands of Mosstowie, Hillside and Greens for the magistrates of Elgin and Earl Fife. John Home was to go on and have a considerable, but all too often turbulent, career in land surveying. From 1763 to 1772 he concentrated his business in and around Aberdeenshire, then in 1772 or early 1773 he moved to Edinburgh. However, in November 1773 he was recruited to take up the recently deceased John Kirk's commission to survey the Countess of Sutherland's estate of Assynt.[4] For the next two years he was engaged in this exacting work, after which he returned south to make

[1] Quoted by M. L. Anderson, *A History of Scottish Forestry*, vol. 1, pp. 576, 600-1.
[2] *OSA*, vol. 20, pp. 331-2.
[3] Nicol of Ballogie papers (NRA(Scot.) survey 60, p. 3).
[4] R. J. Adam, *John Home's survey of Assynt*, Scottish History Society, Edinburgh, 1968.

a living from farming and land surveying at Liberton, near Edinburgh. But one must conclude that success eluded him, for a second marriage to Elizabeth Knox in 8 June 1783[1] and a removal a year later to the vicinity of Stonehaven in Kincardineshire to take up the tenancy of a farm, did not prevent him by 1787 being 'by misfortunes reduced to the most indigent situation'.[2] He returned home and obtained from Earl Fife a lease of nineteen years of the farm of Pluscarden, six miles southwest of Elgin, to commence at Whitsunday 1788. Home's return was the result of his old friend William Rose of Balivat's compassion on hearing of his misfortunes.[3] Rose had a good opinion of his abilities and accuracy as a land surveyor, and his offer of the small but adequate farm of Pluscarden should have provided more than sufficient opportunity to provide a base to exercise his profession. 'But he was not long settled in his farm', reported Rose, 'before he proved himself to be one of those unhappy people who are never satisfied, and who reckon themselves oppressed whenever they are deprived of their own will in any particular.'[4] Rose went on in the evidence to support Home's eviction: 'He quarrelled with all his neighbours; and, instead of behaving with that civility and discretion which would have induced the gentlemen of the country to employ him as a land surveyor, he made them all shun him, to get free of his clamour and complaints'. Home told Rose that he had been promised by Mr MacKenzie of Seaton a comfortable settlement on his estate in East Lothian, and consequently offered to remove from Pluscarden. Rose felt doubly let down because he had also commissioned Home to make surveys of the Earl's lands of Pluscarden. Indeed, Rose went so far as to advance the total cost of the survey, £57, before he had a plan in his hands; and they remained unmade. In the ensuing unsavoury legal dispute over meliorations Home was very lucky to be awarded £25.[5]

[1] There is a bit of a mystery about this marriage for the *Edinburgh Marriage Register, 1751–1800* records Home marrying an Elizabeth Knox in Old Kirk parish on 8 June 1783 (p. 352), and again the same lady in St Andrews parish on 20 Dec. 1792 (p. 359).

[2] Petition by William Rose 17 June 1794 (SRO. RH15/483, p. 2).

[3] Factor and Commissioner for Earl Fife.

[4] Petition by William Rose cited.

[5] Court of Session process, Rose *v.* Home (SRO. CS236 R/7/3).

After this unhappy episode Home returned south to write the *General View of the Agriculture of Berwickshire* which was published in 1797. John Ainslie, a man of considerable humanity and Scotland's premier cartographer, was driven to distraction by this man: 'I have been much plagued with John Home who is writing the Report of Berwickshire. Without exception he is the most troublesome man I ever had anything to do for, and so very particular about trifles that I have lost all patience with him.'[1] Decline continued, for in 1804 he was residing in St Ann's yards, the haven for Edinburgh's bankrupts. He was listed in the *Edinburgh Directory* as living at Gosford's Close, Lawnmarket, when he died around 1809.

For all his irrascibility John Home was a capable man, and bequeathed his skills to William Crawford, who in turn passed them on to his sons (Fig. 1). The Crawfords made a significant contribution to Scottish land surveying. William Crawford senior first appears in the cartographic record in 1774;[2] thereafter his activities covered most of the counties between Sutherland and Dumfries, and he produced a one inch to the mile map of Dumfriesshire in 1804. He operated from various Edinburgh addresses between 1789 and 1820 (Cameron Bank 1793, Buccleuch Entry 1810, St Patrick's Square 1820). He was joined by his sons William in 1793 and David from 1812. William senior was last heard of in 1828. William junior carried on the business until his death in 1843, going into partnership with William Brooke in 1839. David died on 26 May 1829 having been one of the first railway surveyors in Scotland.

Thus from 1750 to 1850, on the eve of the Ordnance Survey's entry to Scottish mapping, a small band of land surveyors served not only their own region's need but also produced some talented cartographers at a national level. It was a critical service they rendered to a nation undergoing agricultural, industrial and transport revolutions. That so many came from the northeast is indicative of the great part played by the men of that region in changing the face of Scotland. Not least was the role of King's and Marischal

[1] Letter to Rev. Dr Douglas, author of *General View of Agriculture in the county of Roxburgh*, dated 15 Aug. 1797 (NLS. MS3117 fo. 23).

[2] He first appears on 7 June 1774 as assistant to John Home on the survey of Assynt (R. J. Adam, op. cit., p. 58).

Colleges in Aberdeen which, without examining, were in the forefront of mathematical teaching and had a pervasive influence on many who were to be the estate managers of the late eighteenth and early nineteenth centuries.

SOURCES

Land surveyors had little time to keep a diary, a privilege which belonged to the leisured classes. Even when ordinary people did keep a diary the chances of its survival were slim, for few outwith the landed gentry preserved the everyday papers of earlier generations. George Brown kept a day-book which is now in the National Library of Scotland. The papers of William Kyle, a prominent land surveyor in Glasgow, are preserved in the Strathclyde Regional Archives. For Peter May, for whom no such record has survived, one is forced to gather together all scraps of information and piece them together in the hope of forming at least a partial picture of the life of a professional man. Fortunately, in the case of Peter May, there is an exceptional abundance of records, for the muniments of his employers – the Dukes of Gordon, the Earls of Findlater, the Earls of Bute, and James Grant of Grant – have been carefully preserved. In compiling this volume items have been incorporated from:

Scottish Record Office

British Fishery Society papers (GD. 9).
Crown Commissioners records including Duke of Gordon papers (CR. 8).
Court of Session processes (CS. various).
Exchequer Records (Forfeited Estates papers) (E. 700–788).
Gordon Castle muniments (GD. 44).
Register House plans (RHP).
Register of Deeds (RD).
Register of Sasines (RS).
Rose of Kilravock papers (GD. 125).
Seafield muniments, including Grant of Grant and Cullen House papers (GD. 248).

National Library of Scotland

Brown papers (MSS. 3258–76).

Signet Library

Session papers.

Other Muniments

Aberdeen burgh records.

Bute muniments, Mount Stuart, Rothesay.

A strict chronological arrangement of the documents selected has been adhered to. While certain subjects like the Annexed Estates might have benefited from an analytic arrangement, the overall *pattern* of May's life would then have been lost. What we are able to see is a professional man grappling with a myriad of problems. As the documentary record reflects the accidents of survival, there is necessarily a degree of unevenness in the narrative; for example, the years 1768 to 1771 are covered with a wealth of information while those from 1774 to 1778 are frustratingly bare. Little editing of the text was required for May expressed himself clearly, spelt accurately, and wrote in a neat hand; surprisingly few words of Scots intruded into his language. Spelling has been modernised throughout, punctuation supplied where necessary, and modern conventions of capitalisation have been adhered to. Identifiable place-names have been rendered in their modern form, but names now lost, such as former muirs and mosses, are given as they appear in the documents. The heading to each document gives the names of the correspondents and occasionally a brief description, the date of writing and place. The exact archival reference number is given. Opening salutations, extended compliments and farewells, and irrelevant personal passages have been omitted.

As individual documents May's letters, spread as they are through several archives, do not have exceptional impact, but when assembled together it is possible to trace the actions and ideas from which we have derived much of today's human landscape. In these pages we can see the introduction of agrarian change across the face of Scotland from the island of Bute to the Moray Firth, while in May's participation in the setting up of the first cotton mill in Scotland, he unwittingly was present at the birth of an industry which was to epitomize the industrial revolution. In the end one is left with a great deal of admiration for a man working in a society undergoing radical change. As he grappled with complex problems, overcame disappointments, working all the time in difficult conditions with poor communications, he retained a sense of humanity that captured the affection of his contemporaries. I hope that this volume will reward him with a small niche in the story of the great geographic and economic changes that Scotland witnessed in the second half of the eighteenth century.

Peter
(1791 - 1868)

= Helen
Leslie

Elizabeth
(1796-)

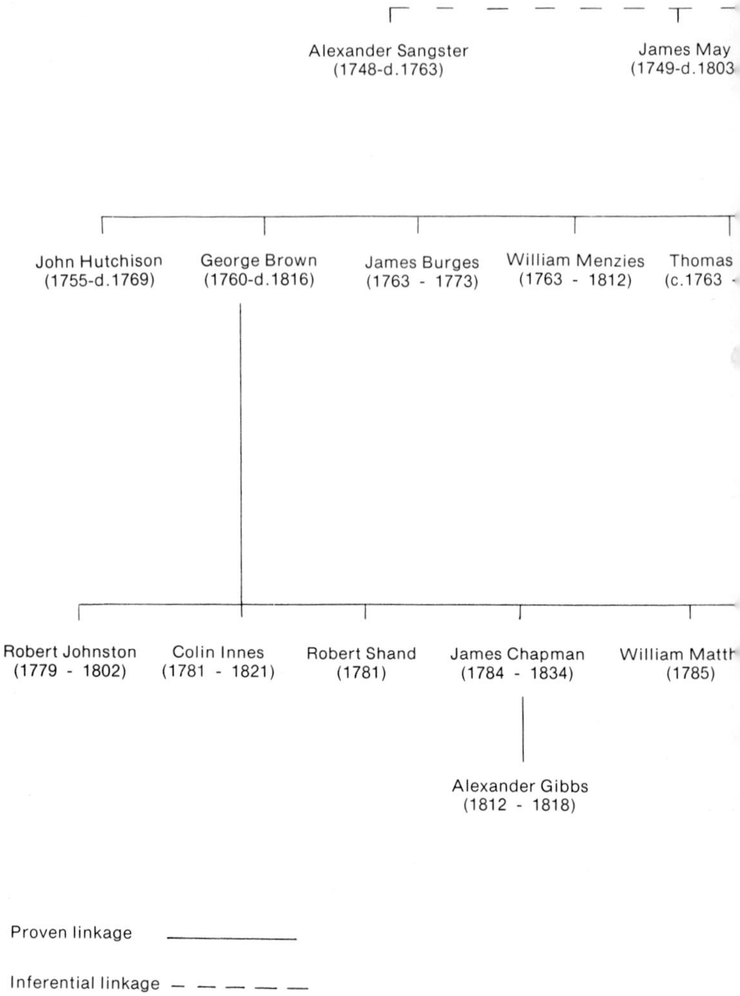

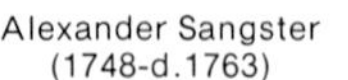

Alexander Sangster
(1748-d.1763)

James May
(1749-d.1803

John Hutchison
(1755-d.1769)

George Brown
(1760-d.1816)

James Burges
(1763 - 1773)

William Menzies
(1763 - 1812)

Thomas
(c.1763 -

Robert Johnston
(1779 - 1802)

Colin Innes
(1781 - 1821)

Robert Shand
(1781)

James Chapman
(1784 - 1834)

William Matth
(1785)

Alexander Gibbs
(1812 - 1818)

Proven linkage ————————

Inferential linkage — — — — —

The Northeast School of land surveyors: the passage of professional skills through a master/trainee relationships for 120 years of Scottish land surveying. N.B. the da present the span of professional careers unless otherwise stated.

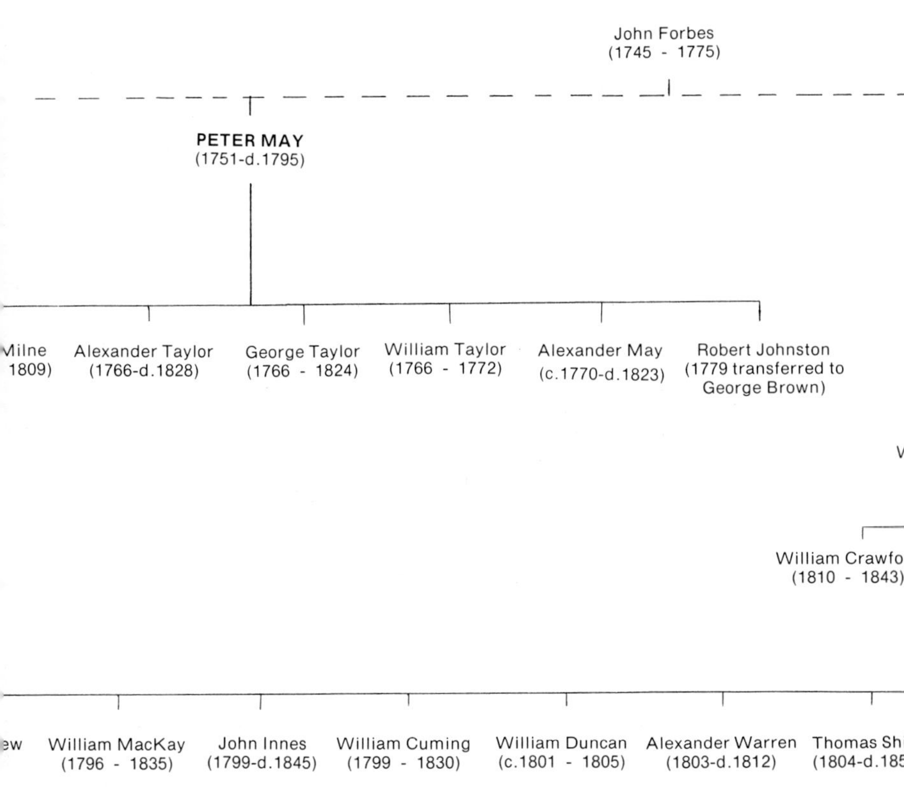

George
(1

Alexander Duncan
(1830 - 1865)

roven

es re-

= [?]
'78)
Barbara
(- 1793)
= ? Brown
Elizabeth
3 children
George
(1747 - 1816)
= Margaret
Clerk
(-1808)
Isobel
Elizabeth
Margaret
John
Colonel
rjory
79-)
James Ogilvie
(1780-)
John
(1783-)
Euphemia
(1784-)
Mary
(1786-)
= Col.Wm.
Stewart
Barbara
(1787-)
Ann
(1788-)
George
(1790 - 1865)
Maj. Gen. Sir
= Maria
Macdonell

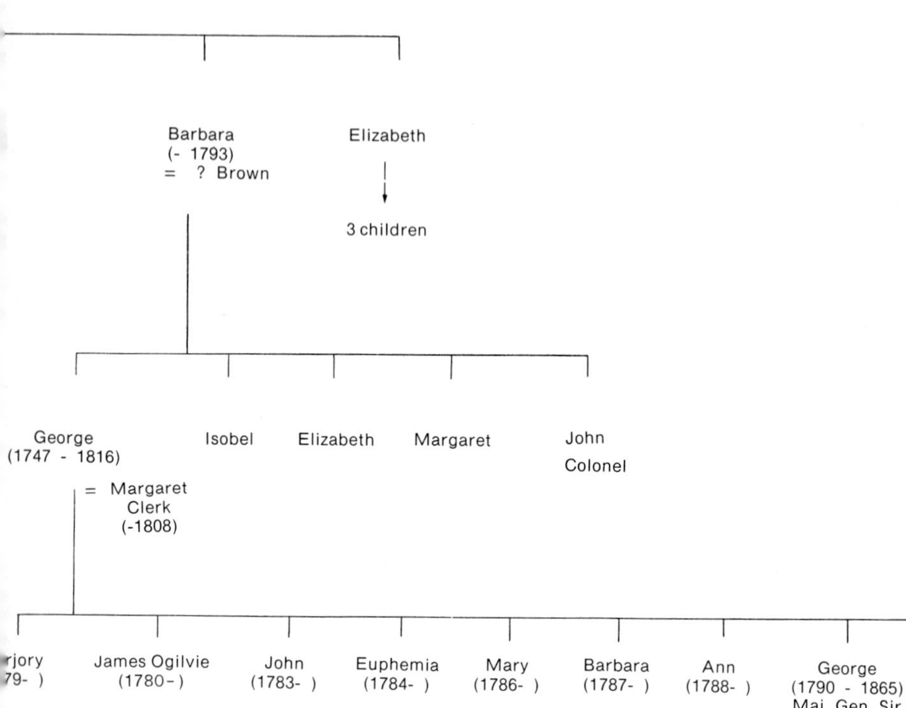

je

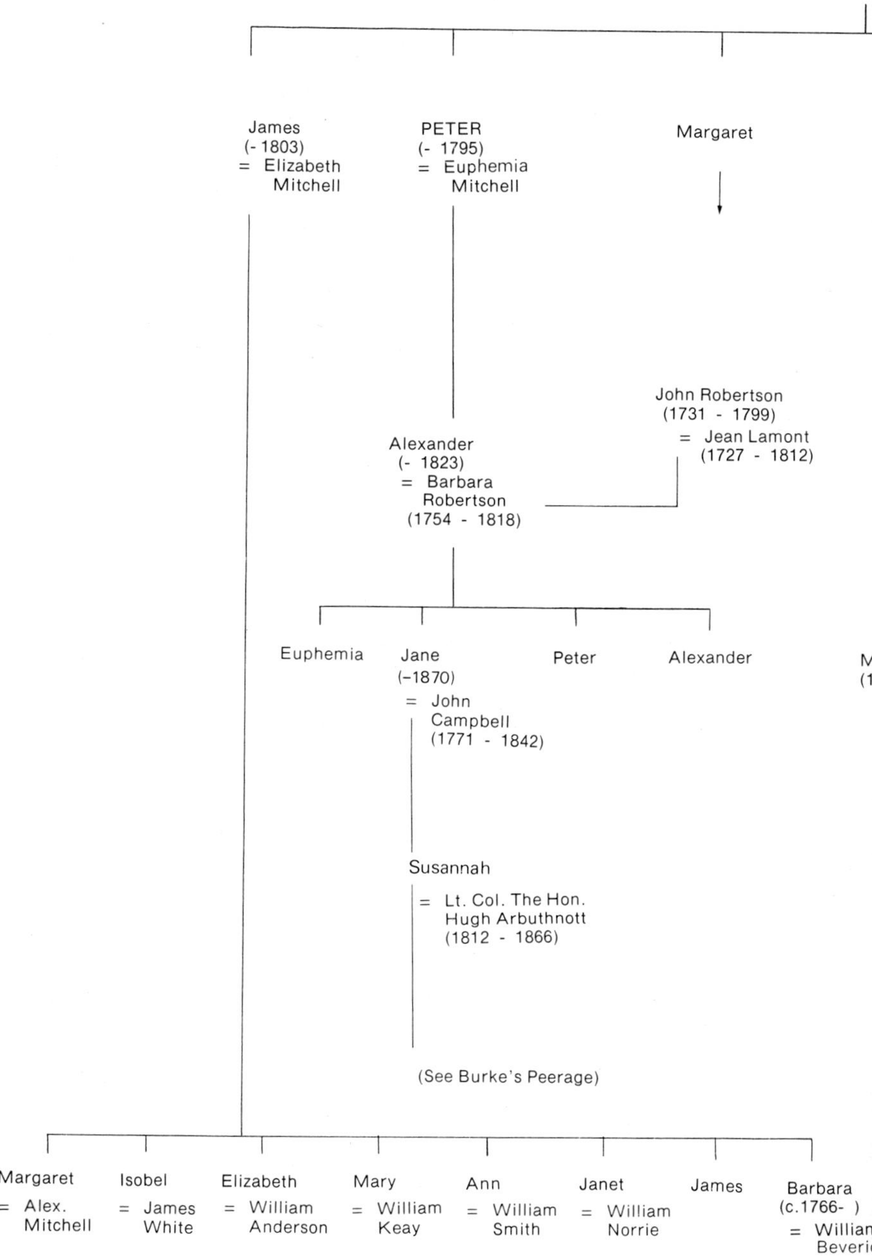

Peter May's family tree

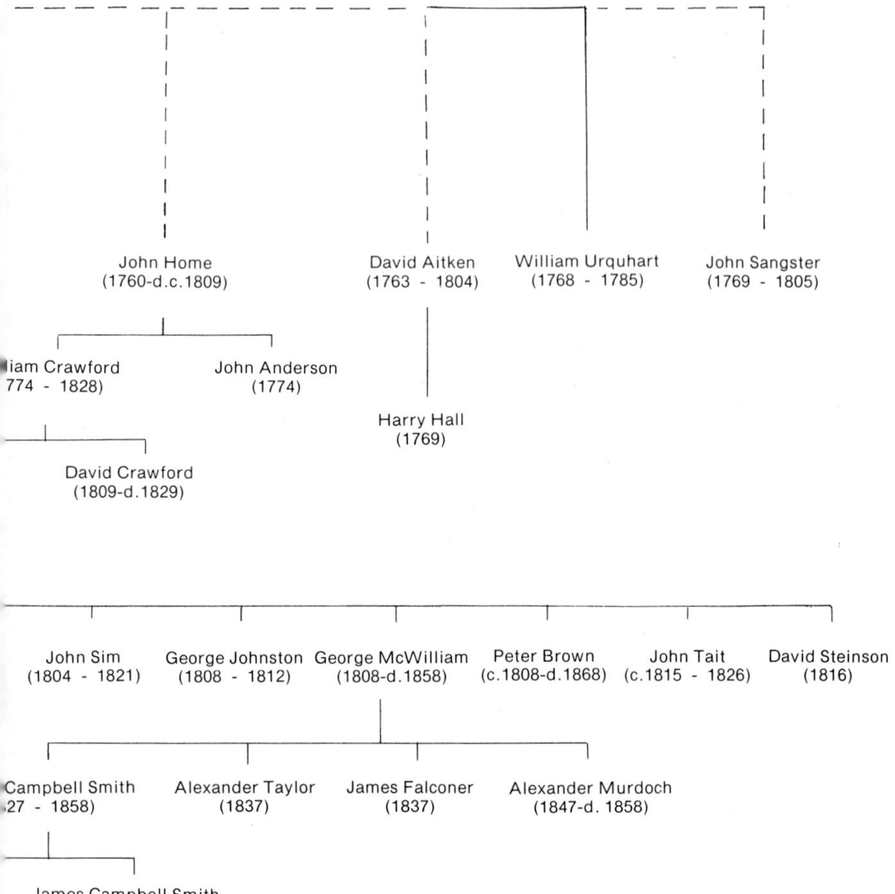
John Home
(1760-d.c.1809)
David Aitken
(1763 - 1804)
William Urquhart
(1768 - 1785)
John Sangster
(1769 - 1805)
iam Crawford
774 - 1828)
John Anderson
(1774)
Harry Hall
(1769)
David Crawford
(1809-d.1829)
John Sim
(1804 - 1821)
George Johnston
(1808 - 1812)
George McWilliam
(1808-d.1858)
Peter Brown
(c.1808-d.1868)
John Tait
(c.1815 - 1826)
David Steinson
(1816)
Campbell Smith
27 - 1858)
Alexander Taylor
(1837)
James Falconer
(1837)
Alexander Murdoch
(1847-d. 1858)
James Campbell Smith

1749—1767

LAND SURVEYOR: ANNEXED ESTATES COMMISSIONERS AND OTHER CLIENTS

Aberdeen Council Register vol. 61, p. 384

Aberdeen, 11 April 1749

... The said day the Provost presented to the council a scheme of division of the lands of Gilcomston into twelve lots, being the report of the committee formerly named for dividing the same. Which being seen and considered by the council they approved thereof and agreed thereto, and appointed Baillie Logie and the clerk to measure the said lots, and to distinguish them one from another by props, and appointed Baillie Logie to draw a plan of the whole, having regard to the course of the pipes and fountains, and reserving six foot on the south side of the miln lead of Gilcomston all along the same for upholding the lead, and for a walk to the inhabitants.

vol. 61, pp. 599-600

Aberdeen, 25 February 1752

... The Provost represented, that the feuars of Gilcomston had delayed taking out their charters on account that they were uncertain of their measures and had not proper allowance for roads, etc. Therefore the council agreed that the feuars might be called and enquired if they were satisfied with the measures conform to the plan, which if they were not then the council appointed Peter May or any other sufficient land measurer to be called by the magistrates and put upon oath, who was to measure all the controverted lots, and who was to give allowance of three foot round each lot for inclosing the same, and this measure hereafter to be the rule for ascertaining the feu duty in time coming, but no allowance for subdivision dykes.

List of the inhabitants in Gordon's Burgh [Fort William] with the number and dimensions of their houses and yards as they presently possess them taken from a regular survey made by Peter May

RHP. 35982

September 1753

	Feet	Total Feet	A.R.F.[1]	£	s.	d.
Mr George Douglas, Sheriff, a store house	76					
ditto, an office house beside his garden	50	126	2		10	
ditto, a pretty little garden			2	1		
Dougal McLachlan, a dwelling house	33	67				
ditto, slaughter house and byre	34				5	7
ditto, for a yard			16		5	
William Stalker, merchant, house and shop	41	54				
ditto, for ⅓ of ane house	13				4	6
Mr Hugh Glass, innkeeper, for 2 houses	108					
ditto, for a peat house and stable	53	188			15	8
ditto, for a byre	27					
ditto, for 3 gardens			1 6		10	
Board of Ordnance 4 divisions but one house		130			10	10
			Total	£4	1s.	7d.
There follows 200 entries of a similar nature, in total				£33	13s.	5d.
			Total	£37	15s.	0d.

Extract of Lord Deskford's day book, kept by Peter May, 6 November–29 November 1754

SRO. GD248/1068

Discharge Peter May from 18th November

Nov.		£	s.	d.
18th	Paid for 8 cart load of coals at 5s. per load	2	0	0
	Paid to a caddie to seek Provost Aberdeen			2
19th	Paid for do. to seek Mr Brebner			1
	Paid to a workman for wheeling away the rubbish and dirt from the back of little house		1	0
	Paid for black, oil and tar for greasing the chaise, viz. a chopin oil at 1s., and 8d. for black and sixpence for tar		2	2
20th	Paid for a table of postages and post days that the posts come in and go out to Edinburgh which is put up in my Lord's room per his order			6

[1] Acres, roods and falls Scots measure: 40 falls = 1 rood; 4 roods = 1 acre.

Nov.		£	s.	d.
21st	Paid to the chairman that brought my Lord from Lord Prestongrange[1]		1	0
22nd	Paid to a gardener for cutting the walk to the meadow and come past the forecourt as per my Lord's orders		1	3
23rd	Paid to the chairman that brought my Lord from General Bland's[2]		5	0
	Sum of this week's expenses	£2	11	2

CERTIFICATE OF LOYALTY

We the Magistrates of the City of Aberdeen subscriving do hereby certify and attest that the bearer Peter May, land surveyor, who has been employed by us and our predecessors in surveying and planning the town's lands, and with whom we are personally acquainted, is a person of good fame and character and of undoubted loyalty and true affection to His Majesty's person and government both in Church and State, and we can recommend him as a sober and diligent man, and deserving encouragement in his business, in testimony whereof we have not only subscrived these presents but also caused the Seal of our City to be hereto affixed at Aberdeen the ninth day of July one thousand seven hundred and fifty five years.[3]

Alexander Osborne, Baillie and J.P.
James Abernethy, Baillie and J.P.

Aberdeen July 9th, 1755, attested by John Ogilvie, minister at Aberdeen[4]
Thomas Forbes, minister at Aberdeen[5]

[1] William Grant of Prestongrange, judge in Court of Session. One of the future commissioners of Annexed Estates.

[2] General Humphrey Bland, commander-in-chief of the forces in Scotland, also a future commissioner of Annexed Estates. Presumably they were undertaking preliminary discussions prior to setting up the Commission.

[3] The certificate (SRO. E731/34) was given to the Board of Commissioners by Lord Deskford on 4 Aug. 1755 (SRO. E721/1).

[4] John Ogilvie (1732-1813), minister in Aberdeen, author of many works; but he was 'an able man lost. His intellectual wealth and industry were wasted in huge and unhappy speculations.' To him was addressed one of Samuel Johnson's notorious remarks, 'Let me tell you the noblest prospect which a Scotsman ever sees is the high road which leads him to England.' (Hugh Scott, *Fasti Ecclesiae Scoticanae*, Edinburgh, 1926, vol. 6, p. 108).

[5] Thomas Forbes, minister at Aberdeen, called 20 Sept. 1733 to the parish of Slains and Forvie, transferred to third charge at Aberdeen in 1749.

Edinburgh 12 July, 1755. The above facts are attested to be true by
William Mowat, Provost of Aberdeen

Minutes of Commissioners of Annexed Estates

SRO. E721/1, pp. 1, 11

Edinburgh, 14 July 1755

Sederunt: John, Marquis of Tweeddale; John, Earl of Hopetoun; James Ogilvie, Lord Deskford; James, Lord Somerville of Drum; Robert Craigie, the Lord President of the Court of Session; John Idle, the Lord Chief Baron of the Court of Exchequer; Charles Erskine, the Lord Justice Clerk; John Maule of Inverkeillor, one of the Barons of Exchequer; William Grant, Lord Prestongrange; Robert Dundas of Arniston, the Lord Advocate; General Bland, commander-in-chief of forces in Scotland; James Oswald; Gilbert Elliot of Minto; William Alexander, provost of Glasgow; George Drummond, provost of Edinburgh; Colonel David Watson, in charge of the military survey of Scotland; and Mansfeldt Cardonnel, Alexander Le Grand, and Joseph Tudor, commissioners of customs.

Colonel Watson represented to the meeting that Peter May, land surveyor at Aberdeen, offered to undertake to survey the estates of Lovat and Cromarty, with five assistants and one theodolite, at a rate of thirteen shillings a day for himself and the five assistants while he is out upon his survey, and seven shillings a day for himself after his return home during the time he is drawing out the fair plan.

The meeting agreed to the proposal and appointed the said Peter May to proceed to survey the estates of Lovat and Cromarty, and appointed Lord Deskford, Colonel Watson and Mr Elliot to draw up instructions to the factor on these two estates, in relation to this matter, and particularly with respect to the subsistence money to be advanced to the surveyor and the men working under him, similar to those given to the factor on the estate of Perth, and likewise directions about finding proper guides, payment to whom is to be made by the factor, exclusive of the thirteen shillings a day, a copy of which instructions to be laid before next meeting.

Letter of instructions to Captain Forbes of New, factor on the estates of Lovat and Cromarty SRO. E721/1, p. 4

Edinburgh, 14 July 1755

The Commissioners for managing the Forfeited Estates in Scotland, annexed to the Crown, have this day directed us, Lord Deskford, Colonel Watson and Mr Elliot of Minto, as their committee, to acquaint you that they have appointed Peter May, land surveyor at Aberdeen, forthwith to proceed to make up a survey and proper plans of the estates of Lovat and Cromarty, as directed by the Annexing Act.[1] To guide him in which survey they have given him instructions which he will communicate to you. They have likewise directed us to order you to give him all the assistance in your power for perfecting his survey and that you should furnish him with the requisite number of guides, well skilled in the marches of the estates and of the different farms thereupon in each barony respectively.

The Commissioners have agreed to allow thirty shillings a week for subsistence money to the surveyor and his five assistants, to be advanced by you upon his receipt to account of his wages of thirteen shillings a day for himself and the five assistants while he is out upon his survey, and seven shillings a day for himself after his return home during the time that he is drawing out his fair plan. You are hereby directed and required to advance and pay the said subsistence money to the surveyor accordingly, and to pay the guides such wages as in your judgement they may deserve. You are likewise to take particular care that the surveyor and assistants be well used and furnished with provisions and necessaries at the common prices of the country. You are further directed to inform the Commissioners of the day when the surveyor arrives and begins his survey, and of the day he leaves off or ends surveying these estates. The Commissioners likeways expect that you shall from time to time inform them how the said Peter May goes on with his work and if he attends to it with diligence.

[1] 25 Geo. II, cap. 41, 'An Act for annexing certain Forfeited Estates in Scotland to the Crown unalienably; and for making Satisfaction to the lawful Creditors thereupon; and to establish a Method of managing the same; and applying the Rents and Profits thereof for the better civilizing and improving the Highlands of Scotland, and preventing Disorders there for the future.' 1752.

Peter May to Lord Deskford SRO. E746/78/1

Castle Leod, 10 November 1755

I came to this country the first of August and had then some weeks of indifferent good weather but have been very unlucky ever since. We have scarce had two good days together without snow or rain which has interrupted my business much. I have surveyed the barony of Castle Leod and am now at New Tarbet, which I believe will take me a month yet to finish it, and is all I can propose to do this season. In the course of my survey I made memorandums upon the farms and observations upon the soil, which I have classed under these three characters, viz.: all the arable land under good, indifferent and bad, and the barren ground under improvable and not improvable, whereby I mean to give the Commissioners some idea of the real value of the farms, which they would still judge better of if these farms were made in separate plans and bound up in a book like an atlas, and done to a large scale with proper observations, which would make them more intelligible than it is possible for them to be when they are all put upon the same plan, which my instructions bids me do. And in the estate of Castle Leod a farm will not be so large as a quarto of paper and yet the plan is very bulky as it contains upwards of 15,000 acres, whereof there is only 2,000 arable. This I would willingly suggest to Colonel Watson, but I am afraid he would think I did it in order to procure myself more work which is not at all my meaning.

The tenantry here are the poorest people I ever saw; they have neither meat nor clothes. The reason of this I apprehend is partly owing to the small possessions they occupy, partly to the oppressive way they have been used by the landlords, but most of all by their own indolence and laziness. They don't work nor do their business in season, and the women they in general can do nothing but spin a thread at the 'rock in the bossom'. What I think another great loss to the country people is the habit they have of distilling whisky and drinking it in drams; there is scarce a house where they don't brew their barley and sell in spirits. By this means they spend a great deal of time drinking and the price of barley does not turn out to near so good an account as if it were sold to the merchant. You'll see by the rentals the people here are very numerous especially a sort called meallers, which are bodies that have only a house, and some of them yards, for which they pay no other rent but services to the proprietor.

New Tarbet is a very pretty place, but the house and gardens are already gone into great disorder and the young trees and nurseries, of which there is great plenty, are all neglected and abused. They stand so thick in the wilderness quarters that they are killing one another. It is a pity they are not sold or planted out. The tenant's yards might consume so many of them, which they have need of as it is a very naked country. The tenants here are in a better way than the barony of Castle Leod, though I don't think them well in comparison with Banffshire.

Capt. John Forbes of New, factor for His Majesty's Annexed Estates of Lovat and Cromarty Dr. to Peter May, land surveyor

SRO. E787/14/3

November 1755

To my subsistence money from the 1st of Aug. 1755 to the 17th Dec. thereafter being 20 weeks at £1 10s. per week as allowed by the Commissioners for myself and assistants	£30	0	0
To my guides who showed me the marches and explained the languages per allowance of the Commissioners and the agreement with Capt. Forbes viz.			
To Charles Matheson for 7 weeks at 8d. per day	£1	8	0
To John Garve and John McPhaill for guiding me in Weaves and other hilly parts of the estate being 9 days, each at 8d. per day		12	0
To William McOwny, my guide at New Tarbet for 6 weeks at 8d. per day	£1	4	0
	£33	4s.	od.

Minutes of Commissioners of Annexed Estates

SRO. E721/1, pp. 47-48

Edinburgh, 8 December 1755

A letter to Lord Deskford of date the tenth ulto. from Peter May, land surveyor, was laid before the Board and read, giving an account of his proceedings, and taking notice that it would be more convenient that separate plans of the different farms were made and bound up in a book, etc. That the house and gardens of New Tarbet were gone into disorder, and that some of the young trees ought to be planted out etc., *Ordered:* That the said Peter May do observe his instructions with respect to making plans and that he have it in his eyes to make out particular plans afterwards, in case the Board shall think fit to order it, and with respect to the gardens of New Tarbet, *Ordered:* That the factor on the estates of Lovat and Cromarty do employ a gardener or other fit person in the most frugal manner he can to take care of the planting and nurseries at New Tarbet, and that the factor after advising with the said Peter May do cause to be planted out such of the young trees as shall be thought proper about the tenants' yards in the neighbourhood where he shall judge it convenient.

Alexander Williamson to Peter May SRO. E726/1, p. 38

Edinburgh, 17 April 1756

By order of the Commissioners for managing his Majesty's Annexed Estates, I am to acquaint you that they direct that you go on with your survey of the estates of Lovat and Cromarty as soon as the season will permit, and inform the Board from time to time of your proceedings, and that you do finish the same as soon as you can accurately. They likewise direct that you distinguish in the plans the possessions of the subtenants, and Captain Forbes will mark their respective rents.

Alexander Williamson to Peter May SRO. E726/1

Edinburgh, 8 May 1756

I received your letter of the 25th ulto. and have laid the same before the Commissioners for managing his Majesty's Annexed Estates, and I am ordered to acquaint you that they direct, with respect to the plans of the estate of Lovat and Cromarty that are finished, that you put the same carefully up in a box and send them by carrier to the office here. With respect to the assistant surveyor the Commissioners agree to allow you one upon the same terms and conditions with the assistant surveyors employed in the other estates, viz. five shillings a day during the time of the survey. As to your account you may send it or not as you think proper.

Alexander Williamson to Capt. John Forbes SRO. E726/1

Edinburgh, 11 May 1756

I have received yours of the 6th current desiring to know whether the land surveyor should proceed to survey the barony of Coigach before he shall begin with the estate of Lovat, etc., and have laid the same before the Commissioners for managing his Majesty's Annexed Estates, and they direct that he do proceed to survey the barony of Coigach first, in order that the same may be done in the summer season, and he may go on with the estate of Lovat afterwards. This you will please communicate to Mr May the surveyor.

A Plan of the Coast and other remarkable Places between the Rivers Dee and Don surveyed Anno 1756 by Peter May RHP. 6308/2

Aberdeen, 16 June 1756

Compeared Peter May, land surveyor, who being solemnly sworn made oath that in obedience to the magistrates of Aberdeen he made a true and faithful survey of the harbour and entry thereof with adjacent coast between the Rivers Dee and Don, and that this plan is a just and accurate description of the premises surveyed by him the deponent, containing the whole bearings and distances as therein described together with the high and low water marks both at spring and neap tides, all which is marked locally on the plan as they were at the time of the survey which was taken on the fourteenth day of June current all which he declares to be true as he shall answer to GOD.

(signed) James Reid J.P. Peter May, surveyor.

This is an exact copy of the original but contracted to a smaller size which is likewise attested by the said Peter May.

Minutes of Commissioners of Annexed Estates

SRO. E726/1, pp. 112-14, 117-18

Edinburgh, 16 June 1756

Another letter from the said Peter May of date 25th ulto. transmitting the plans of such part of the said estates as are already surveyed, and also transmitting his account for making the said surveys and desiring payment of the same, etc. and the said letters and accounts being read, *Resolved:* That a committee be appointed to consider the said account and report to the Board. And Mr Baron Maule and Lord Prestongrange were appointed accordingly.

Edinburgh, 28 June 1756

A report of the Committee appointed to consider the account transmitted by Peter May . . . read and approved. *Ordered:* That the factor on the said estates do inform himself of the number of days that the said surveyor was out upon the said survey, and that he certify the same to the Board.

And with respect to the time to be allowed for drawing out the plans of the said survey, *Remitted* the same to Lord Milton to be considered, and to report his opinion to the Board.

Peter May to Commissioners of Annexed Estates SRO. E746/78/2

Coigach, 21 July 1756

I am now surveying at Coigach, part of the Cromarty estate, and have orders to measure the subtenants' possessions separately from the principal tacksmen, to do which distinctly is almost impossible as they are so interwoven with one another and run-ridged on sundry farms with the tenants themselves, and these ridges are only patches that they dig up with a crooked spade, and so very small that there will be above 100 ridges in an acre scattered up and down like easie [lazy] beds of potatoes. Where they are at a side or lie by themselves I shall measure them separately, but where they are intermixed as above there can be no such thing done with exactness.

The estate of Coigach is a very large country, and the subject difficult and tedious to measure, being little else but high mountains with scattered woods, steep rocky places, and a number of lochs in the valleys, which with the great distance there is between houses makes me obliged to sleep in the open fields for several nights together, which is dangerous in a climate where so much rain falls. I wish the Commissioners would condescend to allow me a tent or otherwise I'll have great difficulty to go through. There is no such thing as sleeping in their houses in the summer time, they are so full of vermin. Everything is scarce and dear, my living costs me more here than it does in Aberdeen although I can scarcely get bear bannocks. I pay my people eight pence a day and with difficulty I can get them at any rate. Captain Forbes can certify you anent this. I wish you could spare me a line either by Captain Forbes or by post, and advise me if the Commissioners have yet examined my plans or how my account is sustained.

Advertisement for the tenants on Annexed Estates SRO. E729/7

July 1756

The Hon. Commissioners for the Annexed estates having resolved that their tenants should be visited and an opportunity given them for some conversation. Their Lordships were pleased to appoint Mr Francis Grant for that purpose who will be a day at each of the following places on Lovat estate at Castle Dounie and Kirk of Dores, and Cromarty estate at Ullapool, Ardmair, New Tarbet and Castle Leod in the end of July.

Report of Mr Francis Grant, General Riding Officer and Inspector SRO. E729/7

1756

Accordingly I kept my appointment and summoned all the tenants to meet me . . . I began talking to them and had an interpreter for those that did not understand English. . . .

Then I endeavoured to demonstrate the particular benefit to themselves as well as to the nation by inclosing and sowing grass for hay which might save many of their cattle's lives, planting trees, potatoes, liming, sowing hemp and flax and manufacturing the same, etc. Also the manner of searching for the appearances of mines, the great consequences from them, giving labour and good wages to numbers of people, making a ready market and good prices for the product of the country, and the whole produce is so much additional wealth to the kingdom.

Then we talked of various things and grievances . . . villages and townships being the most considerable article I shall begin with them, of which I take Ullapool to be the first, lies on north side of Loch Broom about ten miles long and about one quarter way from the mouth of it is a peninsula of plain ground above one mile circumference jutting into the loch and makes fine natural harbours on both sides . . . I desired Mr May to survey and measure the peninsula itself and mark out the place for a township also to make a regular plan of it with ground behind the houses for gardens. . . .

A Survey and design for a Village at Ullapool RHP. 3400

Undated

A FEW OBSERVATIONS

This part of the farm of Ullapool of which the above is a plan, lies upon the Firth of Loch Broom and near the southeast side of the estate. It forms a kind of peninsula, having the River of Ullapool upon the north with the coast upon the west and south sides. I have designed and marked upon the plan a village just opposite to that part of the Firth called Kirk Bay with one street and rows of houses on each hand and in the middle a kirk, tolbooth or court house with an avenue northwards which divides the fields and also may serve for an entry from that side. I have also marked out gardens behind the said houses which contains at an average one third of an acre the piece, and can be subdivided afterwards as succession requires. Behind the town and gardens the ground is divided into regular enclosures containing about five and a half acres one with another.

The present natural situation of Ullapool is that the whole field including moss, bare ground and cornfields that lie on the southmost side of the river is very level and free from stones and bog, but the greatest part at present is moss from 4 to 6 feet deep, which appears to lie upon a bottom of white . . . [hereafter a significant proportion of the account is illegible].

Minutes of Commissioners of Annexed Estates

SRO. E721/1, pp. 132–3

Edinburgh, 12 August 1756

A letter from Peter May, land surveyor, of date the 21st ulto. being read . . . *Ordered:* That the factor on the said estate do provide the said land surveyor with such a tent as he shall find proper and necessary; *Ordered:* That the said factor do advance and pay the said

Peter May the sum of fifty pounds sterling on account of his wages for making surveys on the estate of Cromarty.

Edinburgh, 25 October 1756

A letter from Peter May, land surveyor on the estates of Lovat and Cromarty of date 23rd ulto. being read, giving an account of his proceedings, and desiring payment of the balance of his account for surveys made by him, etc., *Ordered:* That the factor on the said estates of Lovat and Cromarty do advance and pay to the said Peter May, upon his receipt to account of his wages, over and above the subsistence money formerly ordered by the Board, such a sum as will be sufficient to pay off the assistants employed by him the said Peter May in surveying the said estates.

A Survey of Little-Gruinard, etc. RHP. 3401

[summer 1756]

A FEW OBSERVATIONS

The farm of Little Gruinard whereof the above is a plan lies in the parish of Lochbroom disjoined from the barony of Coigach about seven miles, having both the Meikle and Little Loch Brooms between them, with steep rocky hills almost inaccessible. It is bounded on the east by the lands of Mungostone, on the south and west by Dundonald's lands, and on the north by the coast; all which boundings are marked locally upon the plan as they lie upon the ground. Where we find very little arable land and that bad of the kind, being full of stones and rocks which obliges them to dig it with a spade, yet as the most of it lies along the coast, where they have plenty of dung, it yields large returns from twelve to sixteen bolls increase after one bolls sowing is not thought extraordinary, which is almost incredible to a stranger but would be much more so if he saw the subject when the crop is off the ground, where rocks and stones seem more than half, yet when we look over their method of tillage the relation will gain more credit.

Their method of culture here and over all the west country I have yet surveyed, is in general to dig up their land with a spade in this manner, viz.: every third year they give the land a large dunging, and that year the ridges are dressed in the very same way they make what we call lazy beds for potatoes, that is the one half of the ridge is turned above the other, which leaves from four to about six foot of trenches waste between the ridges for that year. After these trenches are thus cast up on the ridges, the whole again gets a slight dunging which is spread and harrowed in with the seed. The second year the ground is likewise digged over once and in the digging is levelled down considerably to the furrows that was emptied the year before. The third year the same operation is again repeated as it was for the second, and the ground is quite levelled down save only open furrows. This last two crops is generally oats or pease, and such as is well near the coast they often give them a dunging between. By this method of tillage they have generally large returns but at the same time it is worth noticing they have little more than one half of the land under seed at least the year it is dunged.

The farm of Little Gruinard is but a very middling one, and would make a poor subsistence living, being little else but hills and rocks with very bad pasture either on the farm or at the shieling, were it not that the fishing is annexed to it upon which the bulk of the living depends. And which I think is the best farm and might be considerably improved by thinning the mouth of the river from the great stones that lie so thick and interrupt the fish in going up especially when the river is small. The creaves are also very insufficient and lie at too great a distance up the river, which hurts the fishing much tho' there is great opportunities for stell fishings here, as it is a bottom of beach on each side of the river's mouth. Yet as far as I could learn, nothing of that kind was done; they content themselves with looking to the creaves and only fishing a little in the mouth of the river, and even in that way I was told they got from a last, to a last and a half, of fish yearly, but often find difficulty in disposing of them as it is a very out of the way place.

There is a stell fishing belonging to Mr Mackenzie of Gruinard which is disputed, and which I had instructions from Captain Forbes to survey and mark the distance it was from the Little Water of Gruinard, where there are creaves belonging to this farm. Which I accordingly did, and have marked the same locally upon the plan, where it is noted to be Gruinard's stell fishing, bearing south from the said water 54 chains or one thousand and three hundred ells from the foresaid Little Water which is a considerable distance. But it may be observed from the plan that the bay where the water runs into [damaged], and has also a stell fishing of Dundonald's upon the very opposite side to Gruinard's, that lies only from the said creaves at the distance of fifty-six chains coastwise, and only thirty-one the nearest way by water. . . .

Peter May to Commissioners of Annexed Estates SRO. E746/78/4

Undated [*c.* 2 November 1756]

I have done with Coigach a fortnight ago and am now begun at the Aird of Lovat, where I intend to continue for a month if the weather continues good. Coigach is a large extensive country with little corns, but plenty of pasturage, and in many places cover of wood which makes it convenient for grazing and breeding cattle, upon which the bulk of their stock and living depends; though I think there might be other improvements made, as there is plenty of limestone quarries upon sundry farms, and that near the middle of the estate, with moss very contiguous to them; yet as far as I know or could be informed there was never one boll burnt upon the estate. Watering would likewise be of great service to them, and is done at easy expense, and might be practised upon many farms here, as there is great command of water which will be seen from the survey. I have not seen a country where poor people might live more comfortably than here, fish of all kinds in plenty, butter and cheese the same, with moss and firing upon every farm in great abundance, which is of no small consequence to them. The poorest sort of people here may be well employed either to themselves or to the tacksman in improving and taking in ground. I often recommended it to them to make up small yards near their houses for cabbages and turnips, and to plant potatoes in the fields where they have in sundry places ware and fern, which would make fine manure for them, and these crops would not be hurt by a wet season as corns are. But they all answered in one voice that as they had no lease they would never propose to improve upon an uncertainty. The tacksmen and sub-tenants are now in a civil war; formerly I have reason to believe there was ground for complaints, but now the case is quite otherwise and they want to balance accounts with them, so that at present there is a bad neighbourhood among them, to prevent which the best plan would be to break some farms and fill them entirely with the present sub-tenants, or detach them to remote corners at some distance from the principal tacksmen. These things with other proper observations I shall suggest along with the plans.

I wrote some time ago begging the Commissioners to enlarge my allowance when I am upon the survey as I have an assistant along with me to whom I pay a crown a day beside the five day labourers that are allowed for stationing and chaining, and to these I paid eight pence a day during my survey in Coigach which Captain Forbes very well knows. And as neither his nor their payments depend upon the plans being given in but are paid weekly, I must therefore entreat the Commissioners would give me an order upon Captain Forbes for their payments, which is per week to my assistant at a crown a day £1 10 0
To five day labourers at 8d. per day is per week £1 0 0

£2 10s. 0d.

I have only got £50 of last year's account which is already pretty much spent in the above payments. I therefore beg the Commissioners would look over that account, and either pay me accordingly to the days given in which I shall declare upon oath, or according to the worth of the work, for I cannot afford to lay out of my money.

Minutes of Commissioners of Annexed Estates

SRO. E721/1, pp. 151–2

Edinburgh, 12 November 1756

A letter from Peter May, land surveyor on the estates of Lovat and Cromarty without date . . . being read, *Ordered:* Deferred the consideration of the said Peter May's remarks on the barony of Coigach till he shall transmit the plans of his surveys.

As to the payment of the balance of his account, *Deferred* the consideration thereof till his survey is finished.

Edinburgh, 29 November 1756

A letter from the factor on the estates of Lovat and Cromarty of date 9th current being read . . . desiring to be informed of the bargain with Peter May, land surveyor, with respect to the wages to be paid to his assistants and guides, *Ordered:* That the secretary do acquaint the said factor to the terms of the agreement made with Peter May with respect to the wages to be paid to his assistants and guides.[1]

Estimate anent repairing the creaves on River Conon, Cromarty estate SRO. E787/18/2

Castle Dounie, 30 November 1756

The Water of Conon ran entirely into the east or right-hand channel upon the plan formerly, but for several years bygone it has been making eruptions to the left, and by a spate in September last it has gone all that way, so that one can walk quite dry over many places where the old course was. This accident must ruin the creave fishing until some proper method be taken either to bring the water to its former channel or remove the creaves to the channel of water, for which purpose Captain Forbes desired me to survey and make a plan[2] of both the old and new course as above and at the same time to mark down what appeared the most effectual method to repair the creaves and if possible to prevent breaches for the future.

The creaves at present stand opposite to the corf house[3] as may be seen on the plan and have been very sufficiently made and are still good. There is likewise sundry pools below the creaves where they fish well with the net, which I suppose will be a considerable inducement to the tacksman to have the water brought and continued if possible into the former channel. But from the situation of the water on the plan we may see that the new channel is by much the straightest, as also the deepest. On both these accounts I apprehend it will be ready to make eruptions, especially as it runs upon a loose gravelly bottom that easily washes down with spates. The old course very nigh where it divides runs upon a rotten gritty rock tho' hard enough to resist water and I suspect would be troublesome to deepen.

[1] Capt. Forbes of New had written to the Commissioners on this point on 9 Nov., and the Secretary sent him the Board's instructions immediately after the meeting on the 29th.

[2] A Survey of the Creaves (SRO. E787/18/2).

[3] A house or shed for curing salmon and for keeping nets in during the close season.

For these reasons I think it the most eligible scheme to remove the creaves to the place where the water divides and instead of the dyke that stands presently across the river marked A – A, I rather think the dyke should be begun from the bend marked B and go slanting along with the course of the water, something like the lines B C D on the plan. Which dyke so made will resist the stream and force off the water much better than if it were made more across, and at the same time would answer either or both channels of the water as there might be chests on both. This ought to be the plan whether it be for the creaves or only to keep the water in the old channel, and the dimensions should not be less than twenty feet broad at the foundation and raised up on both sides ending in the top like a very narrow causeway something like the section on the margin.[1]

What will be the expense of making such a dyke is very difficult to calculate as it entirely depends upon the materials being contiguous or easily got, neither of which is the case here. There is a quarry opposite to creaves where stones may be had, but the road to carry them is bad and will be expensive, for which reasons I cannot pretend to make an exact estimate and therefore shall only mention that the length of the dyke will be about two hundred and eighty yards and in the middle of the river will be from six to eight foot high and not less than twenty foot at bottom.

As I have already observed whether the creaves be continued whether here they are, the greatest part of the dyke must be made and the gravel thrown away that the spates have choked up, so as to give some of the water access into its old channel which can only be done in frosty weather or when the river is very small. But at any rate this last operation of clearing away the gravel ought to be gone about before the fishing begin. It is common on other creaves, and it would be extremely prudent here, to have some stones lying on the river side to be at hand either to prevent eruptions or to mend breaches when they happen.

After writing the above I was called upon by the factor and concerting with him and the tacksman we agreed that it was absolutely necessary to keep up the old creaves as they are so very good and stand in a place where spates can never hurt them. They likewise insisted upon my saying something anent the expense of the new

[1] No section was drawn in the margin.

proposed dyke as above which I can't pretend to do with exactness and therefore instead of an estimate can only venture to give my opinion. And in order to make that as clear as I can, shall first see how many stones may be sufficient to make one ell at the above dimensions, viz. twenty foot wide at the bottom and at an average six foot high. Upon this plan we suppose the dyke to end in a point which will make a wall six feet high, but only ten feet thick including both top and bottom. Thus every ell here is equal to four ells of a stone dyke two and a half thick and six feet high, which could cost in my opinion not less than two shillings at the distance the stones are at. Ergo every ell of the new dyke will cost four times that, which is eight shillings, and there will be wanted about two hundred and forty ells as forty may be added from the above in account of the river having access the old way. Upon the whole if I were living in the neighbourhood, I would not undertake it for a hundred pound, but as this is only no more than my humble opinion I do not lay it down as an estimate.

Capt. John Forbes of New, factor for His Majesty's Annexed Estates of Lovat and Cromarty Dr. to Peter May, land surveyor.

SRO. E787/14/2

Received, Castle Leod, 4 December 1756

To cash in part of the account for last year's survey as by order of the Commissioners	£50	0	0
To my subsistence from the 24th of June to the 4th of December, both inclusive, making 23½ weeks at £1 10s. per week as allowed by the Commissioners	35	5	0
To John Hutcheson, my assistant surveyor, from the 1st of August to the 28th of Novr. both inclusive makes 17 weeks and 1 day at 5s. for himself per day and 3s. per day to 5 men for stationing and chaining in all £2 8s. per week, viz. 17 weeks and a day incl.	41	4	0
To extraordinary expense for boats surveying the Summer Islands and parts of the coast that was inaccessible by land as per particular account	2	6	6
	£128	15s.	6d.

Account of debursements for guides and other necessary expense when surveying the Annexed Estates of Lovat and Cromarty, Summer 1756

SRO. E787/14/2

Received, Castle Leod, 4 December 1756

	£	s.	d.
To John McKenzie, ground officer, for guiding me in Coigach from the 24th June to the 18th Octr. both inclusive at 8d. per day or 4s. per week being 16 weeks and 5 days	£3	7	4
Paid to Findlay Matheson as guide by my assistant surveyor from the 1st of Augt. to the 23rd Octr., being 12 weeks at 4s. per week	2	8	0
Paid for extraordinary guides when I was reconnoitring the marches and surveying the wadsetts of Achtaskyle and Gruinard with the disputable fishings		19	6
Paid for 2 guides, viz, one for myself and one for my assistant, when surveying that part of the Estate of Lovat lying in the parish of Kirkhill from the 26th Octr. to 28th Novr. inclusive, being 5 weeks at 4s. per week each	2	0	0
	£8	14s.	10d.

	£	s.	d.
Paid to a boat and crew when surveying the Summer Islands being 4 days at a crown per day for said boat and crew	1	0	0
Paid ditto when I was surveying along the coast of Kerrowgarve and Cashbrecky 2 days, it being inaccessible by land		10	0
Paid do. for a day surveying Island Gruinard		5	0
Paid for a boat from Baddenscaly to Gruinard		4	0
Paid for a boat from Gruinard to Dundonald		2	6
Paid for a boat and crew surveying Island Martin and the coast along Craigmore it being inaccessible by land		5	0
Extraordinary expense	£2	6s.	6d.

Peter May to Commissioners of Annexed Estates SRO. E746/78/5

Aberdeen, 21 December 1756

I have just now yours with instructions from the Honourable Commissioners anent remitting accounts and making out the plans, the contents whereof I shall obey. Only allow me to observe, that if both doubles are to be illuminate as I did last years it will take a very considerable time, for which I cannot produce vouchers from anybody, nor do I know how to certify the Board about that part of the work, unless they think it right that the time for drawing out the plans be ascertained by oath, or otherwise according to the worth of the work. Either or both these ways the Honourable Board may have.

The plan of Coigach will swell to a large size or otherwise must be drawn to a small scale. How would it do to make it in three or four separate plans that could join or not as they thought convenient?

I shall endeavour to make my observations the truth, and as distinct as possible.

Minutes of Commissioners of Annexed Estates SRO. E721/2

Edinburgh, 10 January 1757

A letter from Peter May, land surveyor on the estates of Lovat and Cromarty, of the 21st ulto. . . . being read, *Ordered:* Deferred, The consideration of so much of the said letter as relates to the surveyor's payment for making out the plans till the plans shall be sent up; and with respect to the surveys of Coigach, *Ordered:* That the same be drawn out in three separate plans to join together.

Petition by Peter May to Commissioners of Annexed Estates
SRO. E787/14/1

Undated, read 4 July 1757

Humbly sheweth, That the Honourable Commissioners were pleased to appoint me to make a survey and proper plans of the estates of Lovat and Cromarty as directed by the Annexing Act, conform to your Honours' instructions then delivered me and communicated to the factor upon these estates. And for making this survey it was agreed that your petitioner should be paid at the rate of 13 shillings a day for myself and five assistants while out upon the survey, and 7 shillings a day for myself upon my return home during the time I am employed in making out the plans. And the Honourable Board were then pleased to order Captain Forbes of New, factor on these estates, to advance to your petitioner 30 shillings a week for subsistence money when upon the survey and to accompt of said wages of 13 shillings a day;

That the Estates of Lovat and Cromarty were greatly more extensive than your petitioner at first imagined, and therefore found it necessary to apply for an assistant, and upon application your Honours were pleased by your secretary to acquaint that you had agreed to allow me an assistant upon the same conditions with the others, viz. 5 shillings a day for himself during the survey;

That your petitioner has proceeded so far in the said survey and has herewith lodged an accompt expressing the different periods he has been employed in making the survey and drawing out the plans, and charging for himself, this assistant, and the men for stationing and chaining conform to the above-mentioned agreement, on the other hand giving credit for such sums as have been advanced by your Honours' factor to accompt of subsistence money or otherwise as by your directions, and upon this accompt ther remains due to your petitioner a balance of £183 5s. 6d. sterling;

That in May 1756 your petitioner sent up plans of the baronies of Castle Leod and New Tarbet belonging to the Cromarty estate, and he has now lodged in the office such plans of the estates of Lovat and Cromarty as are finished, viz. the wadsetts of Achtaskyle and Gruinard with the disputable fishings there, and a design for a village at Ullapool, and all the lands of Lovat in the parish of Kirkhill with duplicates of each plan for last years survey. Your petitioner has likewise completed the survey of Coigach, which is the last part of the Cromarty estate, but the plans are not yet drawen out fair. With these plans there are separate books wherein are engrossed the measures and particular observations on every farm, describing their advantages and disadvantages, and at the same time noticing when they are too large and would bear a division or when small to adjoin them with some others so as to make them commodious and afford a comfortable living to the possessors. By the plans the Honourable Commissioners will see the situation and boundings of every farm, with the arable and barren grounds distinctly marked, and the names and contents of every field wrote within itself.

Your petitioner humbly begs leave to observe to the Honourable Commissioners that the marches of the farms on the Annexed Estates, at least such of them as have come under my survey, are very irregular and discontiguous, the arable lands frequently run ridg'd, and the principal tacksmen and subtenants interfere with one another, whereby they are troublesome to themselves, to the factors, and to the Honourable Board. To remedy that, your petitioner would humbly propose to divide and parcel out the farms of such a size as one with industry may live comfortably upon them, which they cannot from such small farms as a number of them occupy at present although they were rent free. Then to accommodate these little farmers, crofters or subtenants, I would humbly mean to take one or two farms upon a barony and divide them in small crofts among these poor people, and also settle some of them upon improvable ground that lies near the moss or otherwise convenient firing, with premiums to be distribute according to their industry and progress of taking in land. And if some sensible man were to shew them an example, especially for raising potatoes, cabbages, or turnips, which are crops that would thrive well in the Highlands, and would be extremely useful, especially where grain is so uncertain and at best makes but a small part of their living. If these people were thus accommodate they might be useful either to work at manufactures, or be employed as day labourers to the neighbouring farmers, by which they would be constantly in business, and so earn a more comfortable living, promote industry, and be more useful to themselves and others in that way than they ever will so long as they continue to occupy small possessions upon which every man yokes his plough.

Your petitioner will be forgiven for stating these things to the Honourable Board as they could not escape his notice in making the survey, and therefore thought it his duty to mention them, but are more particular in the Book of Observations upon the different farms.

May it therefore please the Honourable Commissioners to take the premises under their consideration, and to approve of the petitioner's account and order payment of the balance due thereon with such other instructions as your Honours shall see meet. . . .

Peter May to Stamp Brooksbank, Secretary to the Annexed Estates Commissioners SRO. E746/78/6

Edinburgh, 5 July 1757[1]

The time I am out upon the survey is attested by the factor, who likewise can advise whether I have attended thereto with diligence. But you have been pleased to observe that it is necessary for the Honourable Board to have some kind of certificate as to the time I am employed drawing out the plans. For that part of the work I

[1] On 4 July May appeared before the Commissioners who ordered him to take his accounts to the secretary, Stamp Brooksbank for examination. The main problem was that they had no idea as to the painstaking effort required to produce plans (SRO. E721/2, pp. 91-92).

must beg leave to observe that drawing out the plans fair, casting up the contents of every separate field, and writing upon the plans, together with the book of observations, is tedious and really requires more time than one would imagine or than I have charged, upon which I can make oath if the Honourable Commissioners require it. But to satisfy them and also exonerate myself, let the plans be perused by the Commissioners and the remarks thereon, or by any other judge they shall think proper to appoint, and whatever shall be determined in that case shall fully satisfy me. This is the only voucher I can think of with respect to the time charged for making out the plans, which I hope will be sustained by the Honourable Board. . . .

Peter May to Stamp Brooksbank SRO. E746/78/7

Undated

You advised me the other day that it was the Commissioners' pleasure to know what would be the expense of copying over all the plans of the Annexed Estates that have been yet surveyed. This, sir, I am difficulted to do, nor can I pretend to make an estimate so distinctly as that the sum shall be neither more or less than the exact worth of the work. It was necessary to draw the plans at first to a large scale in order to get the fields and their contents accurately cast up, but this has swelled the plans to such a size as makes them unwieldy. It would therefore in my humble opinion be necessary in copying them over to contract them to a smaller size. This would make them more manageable, and help to remove the clumsy appearance they make on such large sheets, but at the same time I must observe that these contractions will be more tedious than if the duplicates were drawn the same size with the originals.

The best and only way I can propose to guess what they may be done for is from my own accounts as given in upon oath and sustained by the Honourable Board, viz:

May 1756. To drawing plans of the baronies of Castle Leod and New Tarbet, part of the Cromarty Estate as per account £44 2

June 1757. To plans of the wadsets of Gruinard, Auchtascailt, with the disputable fishings, and a design for a village at Ullapool, with that part of the lands of Lovat lying in the parish of Kirkhill, per account £41 4

To plans yet to deliver to the Board, viz., the baronies of Coigach (part of the Cromarty Estate), of Stratherrick, of Glen Strathfarrar, with all

the lands lying in the parishes of Kilmorack and Kiltarlity, belonging to the Lovat Estate. This will be at least double to the plans already given in, but as they are not quite finished cannot make a precise calculation, but am certain they will not be under	£140
	£225 6s.
Then if I am right to suppose the Estates of Lovat and Cromarty equal to the Perth and Strowan Estates there is nothing more to do than double this sum, viz.	£225 6
	£450 12s.

If it were not too late, and that I might take the liberty to offer my humble opinion to the Honourable Board anent the surveys and plans of these estates, I should blame myself and the other surveyors that they were not more useful than it appears they are or can be from such a method as has been followed. In the very beginning of my work I suggested to Captain Forbes, the factor, and before I delinate any of the plans wrote up my humble opinion, which was: That in order to make the surveys useful and the plans manageable it would be necessary to have a large book like an atlas wherein to engross the plans after this manner, viz.,

In the beginning a draught of the estate ought to have been drawn to a very small scale; the principal use of this general map was to shew the contiguousness of the farms, and how their marches lay or interfered with one another; also on this chart the boundings of the estate and all the conterminous heritors' grounds, and lines of marches distinctly marked, with disputable places, which are often met with where the grounds are hilly and of little consequence. Then I proposed separate plans done to a large scale, where the farms were large suppose one upon a sheet, when small from one, two or three; opposite to each of these plans was to be full and proper explanations of their situation, of the extent of the farms and all the different fields, the quality of the land expressed as much as could be learned from observation or information, with every remarkable occurrence that happened in the course of the survey. At the end of this book an index was to be made, where any farm on the barony as engrossed therein was shewn at once, and without the present difficulty of perusing a plan, some of which are as large as a carpet.

This method I follow with all large estates, and I find it gives general satisfaction. The Earls of Eroll and Findlater are to have all their lands done in the book way, and propose to make new rentals from these actual surveys, which always turns out to their account, which is a material point with most gentlemen, and nothing contributes more thereto than an accurate and distinct survey.

Minutes of Commissioners of Annexed Estates

SRO. E721/2, pp. 154–5

Edinburgh, 16 August 1757

The Secretary having reported that in pursuance of a minute of the Board of the fourth day of July last he had examined the account of Peter May, land surveyor, for surveying the Annexed Estates of Lovat and Cromarty in the years 1755 and 1756, whereby it appears that the factor on the said estate has paid to the said Peter May for himself and assistants £156 9s. of subsistence money and £14 5s. 4d. for guides to show the marches of the different farms and other incidental charges, and that there is a balance due still to Peter May of £183 15s. 6d. And that the several sums in the said account corresponding to the number of days he and assistants were employed upon the survey conform to his agreement with the Board are justly calculated, But the Secretary can say nothing with regard to the time stated by Peter May as employed by him in protracting the plans, And the said factor having also reported that it is consistent with his knowledge that the surveyor and his assistants were employed for the number of days in surveying the estates and the guides paid as charged in the account and that he thinks the account fairly stated, only he is no judge of the time necessary for protracting the plans.

And the said Peter May in his letter dated the 5th of July last addressed to the Secretary offering to make affidavit with regard to the truth of the article stated by him for the time employed in protracting the plans, *Ordered:* That the factor do acquaint the said Peter May to make affidavit upon the truth of his account before a Justice of the Peace or other competent judge, and that the factor do transmit the said affidavit to the Board, whereupon an order will be made for payment to the said Peter May of the balance due to him by his said account.

Minutes of Commissioners of Annexed Estates

SRO. E721/4, pp. 2-3

Edinburgh, 21 November 1757

A letter from the factor upon the annexed estates of Lovat and Cromarty dated 11th October last being read, transmitting an affidavit by Peter May, land surveyor, upon the truth of the accounts given in by him for surveying part of the annexed estates of Lovat and Cromarty in the years 1755 and 1756 as directed by a minute of the Board of the 16th of August last, by which accounts it appears there is a balance of £183 15s. 6d. sterling due to the said Peter May, and the said affidavit being likewise read, *Ordered:* That the said factor do pay the said balance of £183 15s. 6d. sterling to the said Peter May.

Minutes of Commissioners of Annexed Estates

SRO. E721/4, p. 231

Edinburgh, 14 August 1759

The Board having again taken into consideration the petition of the tenants of Garthmore and Garthbeg upon the Annexed Estate of Lovat and of Thomas Fraser, wadsetter of Gorthleck [Gortulegg] concerning the damage done to the grounds of their farms by the over-flowing of Loch Garth and the waters that run into it and out of it, with the factor's report thereupon, and an estimate of the expense it would cost to prevent such damage for the future. The Board before coming to any resolution thereupon, *Ordered:* That the factor on the said estate do commune with Mr Fraser of Gorthleck and the other tenants of the said farms and know from them what they are willing to contribute to the reparation of the damage done to the grounds of their farms by the said Loch and waters, and for preventing the like in time coming agreeable to the plan and estimate made thereof by Peter May, land surveyor, each of them according to their respective interests and the value it will be of to them, And report an account of the same, with his opinion thereon, to the Board.

Minutes of Commissioners of Annexed Estates

SRO. E721/4, pp. 236–7

Edinburgh, 7 January 1760

A Petition from Peter May, land surveyor, being read, setting forth that he has now completed the surveys of the Annexed Estates of Lovat and Cromarty which took up more time than he at first imagined as the Estate of Cromarty lies very much scattered and disjoined. That by the fatigue he underwent in the said survey he has contracted an indisposition which has prevented his giving in the plans of the said survey, and in the mean time praying the Commissioners would order payment to him of the balance of his account for the actual survey, amounting to £112 5s. sterling according to an account presented with the said petition, or what part of the said balance should to them appear proper, and that when the plans are finished he will lay the same with proper remarks before the Board. *Referred:* To Mr Baron Maule and George Drummond, Esqr., to examine the said account and to report, And in the meantime, *Ordered:* That a precept be made out upon the Receiver General for paying £50 sterling to the said Peter May in part of the said balance of his account.

Minutes of Commissioners of Annexed Estates

SRO. E721/4, pp. 265–6

Edinburgh, 14 March 1760

Mr Drummond, to whom it was referred to examine the account of Peter May, land surveyor, for surveying part of the estate of Lovat in summers 1757 and 1758, *Reported:* That he had examined the said account with the vouchers, and that the same appeared to be justly stated, and that the balance now resting of the said account to Peter May is £62 5s. sterling after deducting the £50 paid him by precept the 7th of January last, *Ordered:* That a precept be made out upon the Receiver General for paying to the said Peter May the said sum of £62 5s. sterling.

Minutes of Commissioners of Annexed Estates

SRO. E721/5, pp. 25-6

Edinburgh, 11 August 1760

Proposals by Thomas Fraser of Gorthleck and the tenants of Garthbeg upon the Annexed Estate of Lovat in pursuance of a minute of the Board of the 14th of August 1759 concerning the draining of Loch Garth[1] and widening the channel of the Water of Dee to prevent their grounds from being overflowed, being read, setting forth: that with respect to Garthbeg it is certainly true that these lands are chiefly hurt by the overflowings of the Water of Dee, and for these five years past the tenants have suffered considerable losses by their corn and pasture ground being overflowed; that the tacksman is in America, a Lieutenant in Colonel Fraser's Regiment, and his wife and eight children are at home upon the possession; and in these circumstances its not to be supposed that any contribution worth while can be had from the tacksman's wife, but as there is a necessity for preventing these overflowings of the Water of Dee she is willing to contribute £10 sterling for that purpose upon condition of having the lease of the said farm renewed in her husband's name; that the proprietors of the Estate of Lovat were always in use of being at the expense of securing the grounds of the said farm from being overflowed and destroyed by the said Water; and if at any time any damage was done to the farm thereby the tenants got allowance in their rents to the extent of such damage; that the intention of draining some part of Loch Garth and making an outlet from it is for the benefit of the farms of Gorthleck and North Miggavie; that the tenants of North Miggavie are so miserably poor no assistance can be expected from them, and Mr Fraser is willing to contribute £5 sterling which is the full of his proportion.

And the factor on the said estate having reported that he thinks the said proposals not unreasonable; that the possessors of North Miggavie are extremely poor and nothing can be expected from them; that in his opinion Lieut. McTavish, whose lease of Garthbeg is near expired, may have it renewed, or the Commissioners may repeat the £10 sterling to him in case he is removed; that it is quite necessary

[1] Now part of Loch Mhor.

to carry the plan for draining of Loch Garth and widening the channel of Dee into execution, but the factor begs leave to suggest that as that part of the country is at such a distance from his place of residence that he cannot attend the overseeing of the work himself, in his opinion, therefore, Mr Fraser of Gorthleck and Mr McTavish, brother to Lieut. McTavish, should be obliged to execute the work in the most substantial manner according to Mr May's plan, and they should not be entitled to draw any part of the money which the Commissioners shall agree to supply for that purpose but in proportion as the work advances and as the factor shall find it necessary.

And the Board having read and considered Mr May's plan whereby it appears that it will take £46 13s. 4d. sterling for altering and widening the channel of the Water of Dee and erecting bulwarks so as to secure the grounds of the farm of Garthbeg from being overflowed and damaged, and £25 sterling for draining Loch Garth for the benefit of the farms of Gorthleck and North Miggavie, and considering the necessity that appears for having the said work executed,

The Board agree that the same shall be accordingly done and accept of the contributions offered as above by the tacksman of Garthbeg and Gorthleck, and appoint the saids Thomas Fraser and Mr McTavish, brother to Lieut. McTavish to cause the said work to be executed, and *Ordered:* That as the work advances and provided that the same shall be properly and substantially executed agreeable to Mr May's plan, That the factor on the said estate do pay to them the money that shall be expended by them thereupon to the extent of the balance remaining after the said respective contributions shall have been exhausted, the said balance then being, according to the estimate of the expense made by Mr May, Fifty six pounds thirteen shillings and four pence sterling; And recommend it to the factor to take care that the work be sufficiently done so as to answer the purpose intended.

And, The Board do further agree and Resolve that in case of Lieut. McTavish's being removed from Garthbeg without obtaining a new lease, that the above ten pounds contributed by him for the said work shall be allowed him by the factor in his rents for Garthbeg at his removal.

Lord Deskford to James Grant of Grant SRO. GD248/672/4

Castle of Banff, 22 February 1761

I had by last post the pleasure of yours of February 14th, and was extremely glad to hear from you. I think it is a good custom for you to write sometimes, even though the correspondence you carry on should not be very entertaining . . . I consider money laid out by a gentleman to promote industry upon his estate as being really laid out at more than common interest, but I refer all these matters till we meet in Strathspey, where, besides thinking of improving the country you should this summer begin to think of the disposition of your grounds and plantations. Trees take a great while to grow, and nobody repents of having begun to plant early, especially in this country where everything must be raised from the seed, whereas about London by the help of nurserymen one can transplant into his grounds a full grown plantation at once. You should talk to the Duke of Argyll about trees, for in that matter he must be allowed to have merit, even by those who might think it indecent for them to allow him merit as a statesman.

It would be right likewise for you to make acquaintance with Miller at the Physick Garden at Chelsea, and you should see Mr Gray's nursery at Fulham, and Gordon's at Milend. And, if you have not done it already, it would be right before you come down to make a tour for two or three days through some of the best disposed gardens in the neighbourhood of London. . . .

You don't write a word of news, and to us country gentlemen that silence may not be improper, for if Europe should be turned topsy turvey we can't help it a bit. But as a friend to Palladio you might have told me what palaces the king meditates. How Mr Adams or Mr Chambers stand in favour? How the English painters appear to you just come out of Italy? What poetry is going forward, and how the taste of the Court is in these matters? Does a million of English money reconcile the people of England to my lord Bute? Does the sunshine of royal favour reconcile his uncle to him? As all things are changeable under the sun, especially at Courts, what does Lord Bute do in the way of making hay while the sun shines? Who is to be member for Inverness-shire? I don't expect an answer to all these queries, but do let me know when you intend to be down. . . .

Lord Deskford to James Grant, younger of Grant

SRO. GD248/672/4

Castle of Banff, 12 April 1761

I am told you have been sometime in the country, but we have not heard a word of you. I don't think this quite right, but however, I am to be at Gordon Castle upon Sunday next, would it not be right for you to come there that day to dinner.

I intend to be at Castle Grant this year when you form your plan for laying out your ground within sight of the house. If you fix upon your time for that purpose, it would be right to have a surveyor there, to put what you resolve upon paper; and if I know the time soon, I can appoint Peter May, the best surveyor in Scotland, to be there. Sir Archibald Grant has a very good fancy in these things. . . .[1]

Old Machar parish register New Register House, Edinburgh

13 June 1761

Peter May, land surveyor at Aberdeen, signified his purpose of marriage with Miss Euphemia Mitchell,[2] daughter of the Reverend Mr James Mitchell, minister of the gospel in this parish, the said Mr Mitchell being cautioner for both parties. Whereupon, without consigning pledges, they were three several time proclaimed and married on the eighteenth of June by Mr Partick Duff.

Lord Deskford to Peter May SRO. GD248/904/bundle 1760–1

Castle of Banff, 14 October 1761

To surveying and planning the farms of Buchragie, Craigherbs, and Collynard	£3	3
To Peter Cushny for a case of mathematical pocket instruments as per discharge	£1	0
To Hugh Gordon for mending a theodolite and Robert Brands, cutler, for cleaning instruments as per receipt		7
	£4	10s.

[1] Sir Archibald Grant of Monymusk wrote a long letter to James Grant, younger of Grant, entitled 'Friendly Hints and Suggestions' giving detailed instructions on how to improve an estate (Sir William Fraser, *The Chiefs of Grant*, 1883, vol. 2, pp. 438–43).

[2] Born 16 Feb. 1734 (*Fasti Ecclesiae Scoticanae*, vol. 6, p. 20).

Received payment of the above account and the same discharged by Peter May.

Peter May to Capt. John Forbes of New, factor on Annexed Estate of Lovat SRO E769/83/1

1762

The other complaint is from Gorthleck and North Miggavie setting furth that the Loch Garth has of late years swelled above the usual height, as is already observed in the explanation of the plan. To cure this a new outlet is proposed to be made at the west end of the said Loch Garth cutting through a moss, viz. from E to C, but there will only want to be cast from E to H which is 500 yards; the deepest place of this channel will require from 11 to 12 feet but at the loch side no more than four, which makes 8 feet for a medium. Breadth of this 16 and as it is all a moss may in my opinion be cast for 1s. per yard so the 500 yards will cost £25. A new outlet as here proposed would be of great service to the farms of Gorthleck and North Miggavie as it would lower the surface of Loch Garth from three or four feet and that in my opinion would effectually drain all the low grounds on each side of the burn called Loanmore which is the ground of their complaint and is at present an entire morass. I would willingly have made this outlet to have served another purpose. Instead of making a new channel for the Water of Dee, as marked upon the plan, I intend to bring it all into the Loch Garth and then made this new outlet serve for all, which it would have done very well, and been executed for two thirds of the expense in the above estimate as the declivity was greatly to that side. But the tacksman of the foresaid Garthbeg objected to that and said it would hurt his farm much to turn the water into the Loch, as by that course most of his arable lands would lie on the other side, which would make it extremely difficult for him to carry dung or even crop it but seldom in winter. This memorandum I have put to the plan of the ground and both together. I hope they may be of some use.

Thomas Fraser of Gorthleck to Commissioners of Annexed Estates
SRO. E769/83/2

3 August 1762

I have these 20 days ago begun the outlet from Loch Garth and after being out of pocket about £9 or £10 I am now assured by those of the best skill that see it that it cannot be executed under £40 or £50 sterling. I have begun at the wester end, where for about 40 yards where no more depth was necessary than from 2 to 4 foot the work appeared practicable enough. But as they proceeded 9 or 10 yards more and came to the depth of 6, 7 and 8 feet in order to be 4 feet below the level of the loch according to Mr May's plan, I say after going six feet deep all below that of the moss is quagmire, so very soft and brittle that it cannot be got out of the ditch but with great difficulty as what is above this depth thrown out to both sides of the Channel adds greatly to the height as it is directed to be 16 feet broad at the top, so all that is below this depth must be thrown out in boxes made for that purpose, which takes a great deal of time and consequently adds considerably to the expense. But, what is still worse, when it is brought to the proper depth, and this rubbish thrown out on the banks of the outlet, as there is no solid bottom the weight of it sinks down the banks. By that means the bottom of the Channel left in the evening of a proper level will next morning be 2½ feet or 3 feet higher, occasioned I suppose by the weight of the rubbish on the banks which sinks them as they have no proper bottom or channel. And by the pressure of the banks on both sides the bottom of the channel bulges up two or three foot in 24 hours, for this moss appears to be a crust above a body of water that lies stagnant, for the deeper you go the softer. Yet if this outlet is followed it must be sunk to 12 feet deep before you come to the summit of the moss from which there will be yet the distance of 100 yards and followed to that depth near 200 yards before a declivity begins towards the loch: that and the rubbish thrown out to make the channel will be a great height. I have struggled with the workmen these 10 or 12 days past against the opinion of my operator there, and you know an ingenious enough fellow, to see if the moss turned anyhow drier as they proceeded, and get to any thing of a solid bottom. But in place of that it's rather turned more wet. He came to me last night after sounding the moss in different parts with poles 15 or 16 feet long at the bottom of what is made of the channel and in other parts of the moss where he was to proceed and declares he could find no bottom and that the deeper he sunk it the softer. And declared to me if I did not resolve to launch out to the expense of at least £50 that it will be imprudent to go on further without such an allowance. That the 100 yards or near it already done, of which about forty the easiest part of the work, has cost about £8 or £9 and that near 300 yards yet before the declivity towards the loch must in proportion cost a good deal more, and the depth of this 300 yards must be from 8 to 12 feet and the other 150 feet declining from 10 till 4 being the depth proposed below the surface of the loch. If the plan is followed out, as indeed I humbly think it should, the rubbish to be taken out of the channel must be carried some distance from the top of the bank to prevent the bad effect of the weight of it I have formerly mentioned. And barrows to carry off this wet rubbish must be got and hands employed to drive it at some distance which will add considerably to the expense.

As this is the case, which I wish I may have made intelligible enough, I am determined to be at no further expense nor follow it out any longer until I hear from you after laying the matter before the Commissioners. If they will prosecute the scheme, as certainly they should, I will lay out their money as frugally as I can or if they will think proper to drop it I hope they will order to repay me my outlays deducting a fifth part as I have agreed to bear that proportion of £25, the sum estimate by Mr May, the land surveyor, to make this outlet.

PS. I am resolved to keep some few at work to save appearances until I hear from you. As the plan and estimate was done by Mr May at the desire as would appear of his employers, I hope the Commissioners will not see me a loser for what I have laid out as I have attempted to execute it not from any skill or judgement I had of such an affair myself but in consequence of their deliverance upon the petition relative to it and the notion I had of Mr May's skill to make a proper estimate. But it seems he had not time to consider the nature and quality of the moss and the bottom it has, for every man that works it after digging 6 feet must have a floor of deals to support him and these will sink 2 and sometimes 3 feet before he is any time at work.

Minutes of Commissioners of Annexed Estates SRO. E721/6, p. 345

Edinburgh, 23 December 1762

A letter from Thomas Fraser of Gorthleck being read, importing that he had succeeded in making the drain from Loch Garth through a moss, agreeable to May, the surveyor's, plan, at an expense of £33 1s. 9d., that the farms adjacent to the loch have already been benefited by the said drain, and he is of opinion that the whole of the loch may be drained, by which means a considerable extent of country would be gained, the loch being about five miles in circumference, *Referred:* To Mr Montgomery to give the proper directions to Gorthleck for sounding the loch and taking the level so as that from his report the Board may be satisfied whether the drain is practicable. And in the meantime, *Ordered:* That a precept be made out upon the Receiver General for paying to James Fraser, Writer to the Signet, for the behoof of Thomas Fraser of Gorthleck his father, the sum of £40 sterling to account of the expense of draining the said loch.

Report by Peter May with respect to the draining Loch Garth in Stratherrick SRO. E769/12

22 July 1763

When Mr May was employed surveying that part of the Lovat Annexed Estate called Stratherrick it was represented to him by Thomas Fraser of Gorthleck that Loch Garth had for several years backward made encroachments on and overflowed the contiguous lands about the sides of the loch, particularly a meadow lying towards the east end of it which was now almost under water or turned into an inaccessible morass and this increase of Loch Garth was said to be owing to the Water of Dick's bringing down shingle and gravel and discharging it into the Burn of Loan which is the ordinary outlet of Loch Garth.

The surveyor at that time made a plan of the said loch together with the contiguous grounds and local channels of the said Waters of

Dick and Loan to be laid before the Honourable Board, and at the same time with the assistance of Mr Fraser it was projected that a new channel or outlet should be made in a different place for draining Loch Garth, or at least for bringing it to its old standard and also preventing the bad effects that would be occasioned from shingle and gravel brought down by the Water of Dick through its having a communication with the said loch or burn of Loan.

Along with this plan the surveyor thinks he gave in a note of the levels together with an estimate of the expense for cutting the new channel or outlet from Loch Garth, which at that time was thought to be a work of no great expense as the subject where the channel was intended and now made appeared to be moss as far down as could be reached. But it was not foreseen then that the moss was full of large trees and roots, nor that the banks when made to their full breadth and depth would in a few days almost lean close together, nor that the bottom below the moss was rocky and full of great stones which cannot be raised without boring and blowing with powder. These are facts which the surveyor has now seen and which he acknowledges must have raised the expense greatly beyond his estimate.

There is subjoined a note of the different depths of the loch by which it will appear impracticable to drain it entirely, nor does the surveyor think it advisable to attempt even making the channel deeper than the last level the workmen were carrying on when the depths of the loch were taken that will carry off from 4½ to 5 feet water which will drain the meadow and other wet places about the loch side and towards the east end.

The surveyor advised the work men to let in the loch as soon as they had carried on the bottom of the ditch with their last level to the mouth of the outlet and to let it run with all its force in order to clean out the channel which ought to be widened by digging down the banks and tumbling them into the current, which will carry every thing along provided there is no great stones or fast roots left to interrupt it in its course and in case of accidents it should be made clear and wide enough at the lowermost end first. When the loch has subsided it may be stemmed up and only let out for every other day, which will give it the more force to carry away the feal and other trumpery that is tumbled down from the banks.

In this manner the current of water will do more work in an hour than twenty men will do in a day for as is already observed there is only the banks to dig down and the water performs the rest by clearing and carrying everything before it. The surveyor shewed the workmen an example by getting the water let in when he was there and then causing tumble down the banks on each side which the water carried away with great force.

Note of the different depths or soundings on Loch-Garth taken the 22 July 1763 as follows, viz.

	Feet
1st. Depth towards the south end and opposite to the outlet of the Burn of Loan	37
2d. Depth further up the loch about 200 yards	45½
3d. Depth opposite to the point called Airdrioch	38
4th. Depth opposite to the mouth of the drain or new channel	38½
5th. Depth also opposite to the mouth of the drain and about a hundred yards from the land side	10¼
6th. Depth about 400 yards up the loch and near the middle	22
7th. Depth further up the loch about 400 yards	42¼
8th. Depth about three hundred yards further up and near to the south side	37½
9th. Depth further up and opposite to Tomnardill about the middle	50
10th. Depth further up about 500 yards	14
11th. Depth still further up or eastward about 300 yards	7¼
12th. Depth still further up about 200 yards	4½
13th. Different depths from three to 4 and five feet deep which lies towards the east end and is what was said to be formerly meadow ground, most of which will be drained by the new channel presently digging for conveying off the water.	

From the above notes it appears that draining Loch Garth would be an immense work, or even any considerable part of it unless towards the east end where the depths are in sundry places from three to five feet, but in most other parts and even near the sides the water grows very suddenly deep.

Account Peter May to Capt. Forbes for Surveying SRO. E787/31/1

Castle Dounie, 28 July 1763

To surveying, planning, and lining out settlements for soldiers[1] admitted to the bounty on the said Annexed

[1] In Mar. 1763 the Commissioners set aside £6,600 to settle soldiers and sailors disbanded at the end of the Seven Year's War. They set apart some of the farms, 'to allot to each of them a portion of ground not exceeding three acres which are to be

Estates of Lovat together with the baronies of Castle Leod and Coigach on the Cromarty Estate, from the 12th of May 1763 to the 12th of August thereafter at 13s. per day for himself and assistants, as allowed by the Honourable Board in the former surveys of these estates, viz. for 93 days	£60 9s.
To expense of carrying surveying instruments from Aberdeen to Inverness, and from that to the different parts of the Lovat and Cromarty Estates and returning them back to Aberdeen	15s.
To extraordinary expense by boat over water to the different places in Coigach that was almost inaccessible by land as per account	11s.
To plan paper for the clean plans, together with coarse paper for the rude draughts and field sketches	5s.
	£62

Earl of Findlater and Alexander Gordon of Auchintoul to Peter May
SRO. GD248/678/7

3 November 1763

We at present possess in common a moss adjoining to our respective lands of Redford, Elrick and Culvie which we are resolved to have divided according to our different rights and interests in it.[1]

With that in view we have agreed to get an exact survey of the extent and different depths of the moss, and as we are well convinced of your capacity and distinctness we must ask of you to make such a survey as soon as you are disengaged from the business presently upon your hand.

---

cultivated by the spade and which will be the means of giving comfortable subsistence to a number of brave men . . . and also of introducing upon your Majesty's estates a number of good workmen for carrying on the different improvements, whose example by raising the spirit of emulation among the present inhabitants may promote industry, which has hitherto been at the lowest ebb . . .' (SRO. E723/2, pp. 37-46).

[1] The common moss, amounting to 61 acres, 3 roods, 34 falls Scots, was situated $1\frac{1}{4}$ miles N.W. of Aberchirder village, Marnoch parish, Banffshire. It was divided by John Forbes, factor at Meldrum, and Peter May, joint report dated 23 Aug. 1769 (SRO. GD248/672/3). Notes on the plan by P. May, *see* pp. 64-66.

We shall direct proper persons to attend in order to assist you in taking the depths, etc., and when you have finished the work, we shall pay you for your trouble. And as we are desirous to have the division made soon, we hope you will make the survey before you leave this corner of the country.

Lord Deskford to James Grant, younger of Grant

SRO. GD248/346/5

Castle of Banff, 6 May 1764

You never write, but we are glad to hear sometimes from Mr Lorimer. . . . The Commissioners of Supply in Moray have given the legal authority to John Grant, your Chamberlain in Mulben, to call in the people of your estate in that part of Moray and to employ them in making the road from the Boat o' Brig towards Keith in so far as it is in that county. I was desirous, as it appeared agreeable to John Grant, that the road from the Boat of Fiddich to Keith should have come near to the House of Mulben, and from thence come on in the same tract with the road from the Boat o' Brig to Keith, but Carron came down to our last meeting at Banff, and insisted much that the tract marked out by Sir Archibald was the only good one between the Boat of Fiddich and Keith, and that Sir Archibald and Auchmadies were of the same mind, and that going from the Boat of Fiddich by the House of Mulben would be near two miles about. As this is the case, I believe we must first set about making the road from the Boat o' Brig in consequence of the power from the Commissioners of Supply in Moray and afterwards a cross road can be made from Mulben into the road from the Boat of Fiddich to Keith. I shall direct Peter May to look at it with John Grant, as he goes to Elchies, probably next week.

This day Mr Robinson, who calls himself architect and layer out of pleasure grounds, stopped here on his way to Castle Grant, where he tells me he is to make a plan for what we in this country call policy for you. I told him, I should not be fond of having a thing of that kind done for me except I was present myself, and that I conceived it would be necessary for him to return to Castle Grant to correct this plan according to your own taste when you come to the country. By any thing I have seen of this man's doing, I have formed a good enough opinion of his taste, but it is an hundred to one if he can hit yours except he had studied the ground along with you to enable him to form a notion of your inclinations. . . .

Peter May to Alexander Duff of Hatton SRO. GD248/507/3

Cullen House, 13 May 1764

My Lord Deskford perused the plans and estimates upon Friday afternoon and asked if anything was necessary to make the marches convenient and distinct between Woodtown and the other lands of Towie. I observed that the marches were at present abundantly distinct, but that Mr Munro and I had proposed to cut off a nook from Woodtown which lay next to Birkenhills but which you objected against on account of your policies that you intended to carry up the public road from Broadford along the present march and to have a strip of planting there to cover it; which his lordship approved of and said he thought the angle above the road might accommodate Birkenhills and that as you wanted it for policies it would be wrong to scrimp you. I see they would like to have the croft of Smallburn, and I wish you could part with it easily. Lord Deskford appears disposed to accommodate you, and I hope you will believe me sincere when I mention my own inclination to represent things fairly and in an amicable manner.

I am sorry to acquaint you that my Lord Findlater is so much indisposed at present that puts it out of his power to mind business. Mr Ross I suppose will write you by this post what occurs to him. I heard my Lord Deskford mention that upon my return from Moray he would take a ride over and look at it himself. I wish so long delay be not a hardship on you, as I imagine I cannot return in less than three weeks or a month hence. Forgive me to suggest to you my opinion with respect to the multures which is to cause make out a neat clean copy of all the rent payable to that mill which Thomastown and Smallburn is presently thirled to, and then it will be a very easy matter to adjust the proportion they ought to be charged with, which appears to me at present to turn in your favour as the great increase of rent raised on them will of consequence raise their value of multure. . . .

Communing between Hatton and Lord Deskford

SRO. GD248/507/3

12 June 1764

It's agreed that the march in the bog shall be according to the props set out by Mr May and that a ditch shall be made to mark the march at the joint expense of the two heritors.

Lord Deskford is willing that no part of Woodtown shall be taken off for the tenant of Birkenhills.

Hatton is willing to engage to have the present tenant quit Ordley at Whitsunday 1767, providing the tenant of Oldmiln quit his tack at that term.

The tack of Curriedown expires at Whitsunday 1765, so that the increased value of it in the estimate may balance the increased value on Woodtown and the bargain be made out on Mr May's estimate of the rents on both sides. Hatton, however, insists much that the rents on the farms are let at present should be the rule.

Hatton agrees that the value of the multures should be settled by the rule followed in the contract between Lord Findlater and Lord Fife.

Hatton agrees that the feu duty of Thomastown and Smallburn should be considered as the land rent and sold by the same rule, and that the balance shall be paid for at the rate of 25 years purchase.

Hatton agrees that for the present entry and superiority he should take two years rent of land.

As to the Croft of Smallburn, Hatton agrees to give that part of it described in Mr May's note if my Lord Findlater insist on it.

Hatton thinks that the Deed of Excambion should be written by Mr Garner and Mr Innes, the commissary, who will split the valuations and proportion of the minister's stipend.

The multures of the lands exchanged will enter into the calculation of the multures, and be disponed along with the lands and all servitudes for the farms exchanged, upon the mosses or muirs of the heritor who parts with them to be given up. Roads and boundings as formerly.

The whole bargain to take place as from Whitsunday last.

Hatton wants that Lord Findlater should give directions for taking the inventory of John Gammock's house off without delay.

It's agreed that the small spot of ground belonging to Mill of Seggat and adjoining to the Croft of Smallburn should be given off to Hatton and rated at the same proportion with the land of that croft, 8s. 8d. per acre. This half croft to go to Hatton's mill during Peter Morison's tack and the purchase of the multures to be calculated as taking place 23 years hence.

That what relates to the teinds shall be settled equitably.

Deposition by Peter May at the division of the commonty of the Muir of Farrochie, Fetteresso parish, Kincardineshire[1]

SRO. CS29 5/8/1766

Urie, 12 June 1764

Compeared Peter May, land surveyor, and represented that he had in consequence of the commissioner's appointment proceeded so far to measure and survey the commonty, but that he had not got the whole accomplished tho' he had made out a rough plan thereof; and as he was necessarily obliged to attend other particular business he could not have the whole finished for sometime so as to be ready to lay the same before the commissioners for their approbation; which being considered by the commissioners and that the time of executing the commission expired on the fourteenth instant within which time as it appeared the land surveyor could not be ripe with his plan. They therefore in the meantime appoint him, the said Peter May, and George Kemlo at Mill of Forrest instantly to perambulate, go over and consider the different qualities of the common muir in question and of the marsh or morass lying on the east end of the Loch of Farrochie and comprehended between the new intended straight march from William Melvill's house and the march of Redcloak as marked upon the rough plan presently shown to the commissioners by the surveyor, and to report their opinion thereof upon oath; as also appoints them to go over and inspect the marches westward over the hill and to report their opinion of the

[1] The commonty of the Muir of Farrochie, Fetteresso parish, Kincardineshire, consisting of 33 acres, lay between the east end of the Loch of Farrochie and the lands of Arduthie and Redcloak and the Mill of Forest. Commission was granted to Sir Alexander Ramsay Irvine of Balmain and David Scott of Nether Benholm. The commonty was divided in 1766.

ground upon each side thereof. But as it appears from the commission that the commissioners' power will be at an end before Mr May can finish and make out his plan, they therefore recommend to Urie, if he shall think proper, to procure a renewal of the commission so as they may be enabled to proceed to the further execution thereof and to finish their report.

13 June 1764

. . . They deponed it was their unanimous opinion that every acre of the said Broadmyre and other marsh places in the moor is equal to two of the foresaid morass or marsh in the end of the Loch of Farrochie and equal to three of the dry moor ground, and consequently that every acre of the said morass in the end of the Loch of Farrochie is equal to one and a half of the moor ground; and deponed that to the best of their judgement and knowledge the dry moor ground all over the common is much of one quality, except a small angle next to Farrochie which they thought a little better but not worth the while to take notice of as it was such a small spot; and they further deponed that they proceeded from the foresaid morass westward over the hill marches and viewed and inspected the ground there, and they depone that according to the best of their skill and judgement the lands upon each side of the marches may be straightened from point to point advantageously for both parties.

Minutes of Commissioners of Annexed Estates incorporating Minutes of Committee Meeting of 17 January 1765

SRO. E721/8, pp. 77–78

Edinburgh, 21 January 1765

17 January. The factor of Lovat . . . having reported that with the assistance of Peter May, land surveyor, he intends to divide the farms of a barony or two of the estate of Lovat so as that the leases of them may be made out next summer, but it will be necessary that he should have the plans of that estate formerly made by May.

The factor on Lovat to employ Mr May, land surveyor, to take a new plan of the barony of Beauly.

The Committee were of opinion: That the factor do call for Mr May's assistance where necesary to divide the farms, that Mr May do make a new survey and plan of the barony of Beauly, and that the Secretary do cause the plans of the said estate to be traced or marked in the office so far as to answer the factor's purpose.

Alexander Innes, Commissary of Aberdeen, to James Grant, younger of Grant SRO. GD248/346/2

Aberdeen, 31 January 1765

. . . The advertisement for Alexandria is sent to Sir Ludovick and this day I have had an interview with Mr May. The Forfeited Estates and some engagements in this country he tells me will take him up this year. He sets out for Captain Forbes of New as soon as anything can be done in the field, and if you are in the country will call on you in his way. His business there will take him up to about six weeks and on his return, should you think proper, purposes doing anything you shall desire for other six weeks, which will let him and you know better how to settle afterwards on terms, and for that time he entirely will refer to yourself what shall be paid. I imagine in the six weeks he will if properly supplied with persons for informing of the boundaries, etc., survey Delnabo, the ground about the Newtown, or a little more, and from the specimen you both can judge what after agreement to make.

It's my opinion he will answer your purpose very well. I have likewise had a communing with John Home, land surveyor. If you do not approve of Mr May, Mr Home by what I learn will serve full as reasonable, and will give a specimen likewise. He has not had so much experience as Mr May, but by what he has done for me seems to be exact and applies very close. Should you incline to make trial of him, it may be on the Mulben estate. He cannot engage to do much this summer, so that I believe it's best to let him alone till you see how Mr May pleases as the tacks of Mulben are not near expiring. . . .

Peter May to James Grant of Grant SRO. GD248/178/2

Aberdeen, 3 February 1765

I should be ashamed at this distance of time to acknowledge the receipt of a letter from you in April last, had not the import of that letter been to signify your being pleased with an apology. I had formerly wrote you about a survey of your estate, and that you had something then in view of which kept me from answering your's in course. Mr Commissary Innes called upon me the other day and enquired how I was to be employed for the summer; I ingenuously told him that I was already under engagements for the spring and summer. He then mentioned his being at Castle Grant and that you had wanted something done about your estate. I told Mr Innes that I was obliged to go north as early as the weather would allow to do business in the fields, to divide the farms on the annexed estates of Lovat and Cromarty, that my friend Captain Forbes had said a couple of months would be sufficient to do it. If on my return from that country I could overtake anything for you in this time, I should steal six weeks or a couple of months from my other engagements and be extremely glad to have it in my power to serve you. In that time I could give you such a specimen as would let you know both the utility of it and whether it would be necessary to go on with a survey of your whole estate, and the expense of such a trial shall be made entirely to your satisfaction. If you are at Castle Grant I shall use the freedom to wait on you on my way north.

Sir Archibald Grant of Monymusk to James Grant, younger of Grant SRO. GD248/49/3

Monymusk, 15 April 1765

. . . Having lately received a letter from one Mr James Robertson, a land surveyor in Northumberland, who, with a letter from a correspondent of mine in that country, assures me he can be certified by gentlemen of note for whom he hath performed to be duly qualified, and offering to perform upon large projects much cheaper than our Scots surveyors demand, I thought it would be agreeable to you to be informed of it in case you continue resolved to have a survey of your estate and be not engaged to another. . . .

Peter May to Robert Barclay, the Secretary of the Commissioners of Annexed Estates SRO. E787/12/1

Inverness, 8 August 1765

I have been employed this summer by Captain Forbes, the factor on the Annexed Estates of Lovat and Cromarty, dividing the run-ridged lands in his collection.[1] In the course of which I observed some considerable inclosures made and carrying on with a view to plant the barren moor, and which has given rise to the inclosed proposals. If you think they deserve being laid before the Board I intreat you will do it. I have been in use for sometime in carrying on plantations in the same manner I have here represented it to the Board. If they want a character of me I have reason to believe that the factor will give it to their satisfaction, for I am well acquaint with him, and had wont to be better known at the Board and with the Secretary when I made out the first surveys of these estates. I wish it were agreeable to the Honourable Board to advise me soon if they approve of my proposals; if they do not, I must look out for a mercat for my trees and in the meantime will be in suspense until they are pleased to advise me. Any orders may be directed to Peter May, surveyor of land, at Aberdeen, or under cover to the factor, who will forward it to me. . . .

Proposals by Peter May to the Commissioners of Annexed Estates
SRO. E787/12/1(2)

Read in Edinburgh, 14 August 1765

The said Peter May was employed sometime ago by the Honourable Commissioners to survey and make out plans of the Annexed Estates of Lovat and Cromarty; he was also employed to measure and lay out settlements for the disbanded Soldiers and has been for some time this summer dividing the run-ridged lands on these Estates.

In the course of his business he has observed some considerable improvements begun with respect to enclosing and planting the barren moors. Last year there was an inclosure made out on the Lovat Estate and planted with firs consisting of 93 Scots acres, but by the accident of a very dry season coming soon on after planting these firs have succeeded but indifferently, which has made the said Peter May think of doing it in a way that will not be attended with the smallest risk to the Honourable Board, and at the same time the

[1] A discharged account by Capt. Forbes of New, at Beaufort, 6 Aug. 1765, is printed in A. H. Millar, *Forfeited Estates Papers*, Scottish History Society, Edinburgh, 1909, pp. 71-72.

plantations carried on with dispatch, and upon the most reasonable terms.

The said Peter May has a large nursery of firs and other trees at Aberdeen, and humbly thinks that he can afford to sell and plant them as reasonable as anybody; with that view he proposes, viz. To plant any quantity of ground, not less than one hundred acres, with Scots firs of the proper age and size, three feet distant plant from plant, at twenty shillings sterling the acre, in which is included the price of the plants, the carriage of them from Aberdeen to Inverness, and also the expense of planting. Or the said Peter May agrees to deliver them growing trees at the period of three years after planting at twenty five shillings sterling per acre provided the fences be made and kept in such repair as to defend sheep or other cattle, or a herd appointed to care for and prevent them. That the said Peter May undertakes to plant from eight hundred thousand to a million in the year according as there are inclosures ready to receive them, and as there is a large inclosure making out just now on the Lovat Estate consisting of 237 Scots acres and will be finished and ready to plant this autumn, he is content and agrees to begin with it then and to plant the above quantity the autumn and spring following.

As there are many spots of good ground in the hollows and on the banks of these moors, fit for better trees than firs, if the Honourable Board would approve of mixing some other sorts among them, such as ash and birch plants, with acorn and beechmast seed to be put in the deepest and richest soil, the said Peter May would very ingenuously lay before them what additional expense that would make in the said plantation.

If the Honourable Board approves of the first proposal of planting them at twenty shillings the acre, in that case it is expected that they will order the price of the plants to be paid upon their delivery, and the remainder when they are planted. But if they are done according to the last proposal of twenty-five shillings the acre, the said Peter May in that case hopes that they will allow him one third of the price when the plantation is begun, another third when they are planted, and the last third when they are delivered over at the period of three years after planting, the sufficiency of the plantation to be attested by two men mutually chosen.

The said Peter May has had it in view to make his proposals in the most equitable manner, and as many of the Honourable Board are judges and know from experience the expense of planting, he is persuaded they will agree that they are so, but in order to put it beyond doubt he has subjoined the net expense of planting an acre:

It will require 7,000 Firs to plant an acre at three feet distance plant from plant, viz. for 7,000 Firs at 1s. 10d. the thousand including the expense of carriage from Aberdeen to Inverness over Land, 70 miles	12s. 10d.
To Planting 7,000 Trees at 8d. the thousand, allowing each man to plant a thousand per day, and for every six labourers a gardener to work along with and to take the charge of them at 1s. per day, viz. for planting an acre	5s. 0d.
	17s. 10d.
To travelling charges for the undertaker in going to and from the country to direct the planting	[*blank*]

The Committee were of opinion, That the same should lie on the table to be considered by the Commissioners.

Captain John Forbes of New, Factor on the Annexed Estates of Lovat and Cromarty, to the Commissioners of Annexed Estates

SRO. E769/79/74

Beaufort, 25 November 1765

In Summer last the disbanded soldiers settled upon the estate were employed inclosing a barren muir of great extent in order to be planted with firs or such other barren timber as could be got. This inclosure was not finished when the men were dismissed to their harvest work and therefore I was obliged to employ them to complete it, otherwise all that was done would have been lost. I understand Peter May, surveyor of land, gave in proposals in July last for planting that inclosure, which I never saw, but he told me that he demanded 20 shillings an acre as the price of the plants and planting them, including carriage and all expenses, and that he would uphold and leave them complete and in a thriving way 3 or 5 years after they were planted. I think these are the terms he mentioned to me, which are high, but I can not get it done by anybody in this country so cheap for they take 2 shillings for each thousand firs besides the expense of planting. I was unwilling to lose the season and therefore agreed with Mr May to send 200,000 firs here with a proper person to oversee and direct the planting, and I am to pay him the ordinary price for the firs and all other expenses, or to hold by the proposals which he laid before the Honourable Board in case they shall please to approve of the same. I think the last is preferable because it insures a thriving plantation, which will much beautify the country, and turn out at last a great advantage to the Estate, and be a supply of wood and firing, which it will very much want in a few years. I beg, therefore, sir, that you will be pleased to let me know the determination of the Board upon this point.

I advised you formerly that Mr May had made a great progress in dividing the runrig'd lands, and that the tenants as far as he had gone did all agree to the divisions made by a writing of approbation under their hands, but I find now that many of them are dis-satisfied and want a new division; but I can venture to assure you that there is no reason for it because the surveyor went over it 2 or 3 different times, was at all possible pains, and took the assistance of the most judicious men in the country; besides they were told before signing, that if they were not content they might lay their objections before the Board. I am told that some of them are now preparing a complaint, but if any of them are gratified, the surveyor must be called here again and all that he has done will go for nothing. I am humbly of opinion that there should be a peremptory order for all of them to stand by the divisions which they had approved of under their hand and to leave a ridge or half a ridge on each side of the ritted lines of division unlaboured this year so as dykes or ditches may be carried on next summer for inclosing their different farms which will be work for the poor soldiers, who will in all probability be then reduced to great straits by the high price of victual: and this will be the beginning of a very effectual improvement which will soon make a great change upon the face of the country.

If this plan is agreeable to the Honourable Board it will be necessary to acquaint me as soon as possible that things may be concerted timeously, because where ditches are to be made the soldiers can do them very well, but where stone dykes or facing ditches with stone is necessary I would propose to agree with the tenants to lead the stones, each for his own farm, as grass or provender can not easily be had in another manner. . . .

Journal kept by James Grant, clerk to James Grant of Grant
SRO. GD248/1542/fo. 25r

Castle Grant, 30 November 1765

Orders left by Mr Grant: . . . A correspondence to be begin with the gardeners of Brahan Castle, Athol and Taymouth for plants, and also with Messrs Young and May. . . .

Account of the expenses laid out in the country by Robert Barclay of Ury Esquire in the process of division of commonty at his instance against the Governor and Company of Undertakers for raising Thames Water in York Building SRO. CS29, 5/8/1766

6 December 1765

	£	s.	d
To Peter May, surveyor of land, for surveying and measuring the commonty with the line of marches lying between the lands of Ury and that part of the estate of Marischal belonging to the York Building Company, in which he was employed 10 days from Wednesday the 27th June to 6th July thereafter, both inclusive, at 10s. per day	5	0	0
To ditto as paid by him to guides and assistants for said time, having four men attending at 8d. per day	1	6	8
To ditto for valuing the land cut off on each side by the excambion and placing the new line of marches in consequence of the commissioners' instructions upon the ground which employed five days	2	10	0
To paid the valuators and others, assistants at setting said marches		17	6
To paid Mr May for protracting and drawing out an ornamented plan of said common and line of marches with the proper observations necessary to explain and make it intelligible to the commissioners	2	2	
To paid for canvas and pasting it on the plan		7	4
To paid for a white iron box and lock and key for ditto		2	4
To paid the clerk to the commission for trouble in writing the report, etc., per receipt	2	2	
To the messenger for executing the summons against the pursuers' and defenders' tenants having interest in the subject to be divided		15	0
To the messengers' dues for executing the diligence against a number of witnesses to compear before the commissioners, witnesses expenses and other expenses at taking the proof		15	0
Summa	£15	17	10

But in regard it's agreed betwixt the parties that Mr Barclay is to have right to keep the plan for his own use and behoof, therefore it is also agreed that the following articles shall be deduced

		£ s. d.
To Mr May for protracting and drawing out the plan, etc.	£2 2 0	
To canvas and pasting	7 4	
To box, key and lock	2 4	
	£2 11s. 8d.	2 11 8
	Balance due	£13 6 2

Minutes of Commissioners of Annexed Estates

SRO. E721/9, pp. 20–21

Edinburgh, 9 December 1765

A letter from the factor on Lovat and Cromarty of 25 November being Read . . . the Board were of opinion, That the terms proposed by Peter May for planting the inclosures at the rate of 20s. per acre are too high. But authorised the factor to make a bargain with Peter May for planting the inclosure at the rate of 17 Shillings for each Scots acre as the price of the plants and planting them, including carriage and all expenses, the said Peter May obliging himself to uphold the plants and leave them complete and in a thriving way at the end of 5 years after they were planted.

The Board approved of the division of the runrig lands, and of the factor's proposal for leaving a rig or half a rig on each side of the ritted lines of division unlaboured this year so as dykes or ditches may be carried on.

Peter May to the Earl of Findlater SRO. E787/12/2

Aberdeen, 30 December 1765

Your Lordship's knowledge and long experience in carrying on extensive plantations makes me take the liberty to lay before you a project I have in view of carrying on some plantations on the Annexed Estates, of which the inclosed is a copy of my proposals sent Captain Forbes, and which he transmitted to the Board some time ago, but as far as I know the factor has no advice whether they approve of it or not. I have sent some hundred thousands to the Annexed Estate of Lovat this autumn, and a couple of gardeners to direct and help to plant them. I am to send more in the spring. If the Board approves of the undertaking, this I am planting just now is to be a part of the bargain, and if they should not, Captain Forbes pays me for my plants the common price, and also the gardeners I send to plant them. Were the undertaking approven of by the Board, in that event I would be very willing to extend it to any other of the Estates. I hear there are considerable plantations carrying on at the Perth Estate. Would it be proper for me to write a letter to Barcaldine, the factor, and communicate my plan to him: If your Lordship would take the trouble to advise me whether ye think my proposals fair and equitable, your Lordship's opinion would either encourage or hinder me from making any further application. One thing I can observe with much truth, that those they have already planted on the Lovat Estate have exceeded the Terms I have proposed, beside the ill success. I am busy just now bringing up my plans. If the weather will allow, I must leave the town and go to measure some contraverted Land between the Duke of Gordon and Cocklarachy. There has been two surveys made of it already, but it seems they do not please. After I have done there I am obliged to go to Buchan to the Cairnbulg Estate and some other things in that corner, but nothing shall hinder your plans from being completed before Whitsunday. It is with much respect that I take the liberty to wish my Lady Findlater, your Lordship and Lord Deskford many happy years. . . .

Peter May to Robert Barclay, Secretary to Commissioners of Annexed Estates SRO. E787/12/3

Aberdeen, 13 January 1766

I had a copy of the orders from the Board sent me by the factor on the Annexed Estates of Lovat and Cromarty last post, in answer to my proposals for carrying on some plantations on these estates, wherein they are pleased to allow me only 17s. per acre for planting, including the price of trees, carriage of them from Aberdeen to Inverness, with the expense of planting and to uphold them for five years. In the proposals already laid before them I subjoined a note of the net expense of planting an acre, which amounted to 17s. 10d. sterling and it is submitted whether it was not a fair state. I hope I will be forgiven to say what many of the Honourable Board know from experience, that it is a good plantation if two thirds hold and grow at first planting, therefore one third of 17s. 10d. is to be added for repairs, viz. 5s. 11$\frac{4}{12}$d. in all £1 13s. 9$\frac{4}{12}$d. for planting and upholding an acre. The profits arising from the undertaking was not at all the temptation. I did not mean to gain on that score. A mercat for my trees was the great point with me and it is still with that view I beg leave again to propose to the Honourable Board to plant and uphold the Scots acre three years at the rate of twenty shillings sterling the acre providing the fences are kept in sufficient repair at the Board's expense. Or to plant and uphold both trees and fences for five years at the rate of twenty-five shillings the acre, which is the lowest terms I am able to undertake it for. It is unnecessary to suggest that the whole plantations would be lost if the fences are not properly attended to, and in the present case they will be the more liable to breaches as they are only made of earth. I hope that the Board will find my proposals reasonable,[1] and will be pleased to give their instructions how soon they find it convenient as I propose to begin planting early in the spring. Any orders addressed to Peter May, surveyor at Aberdeen, or under the factor's cover will be forwarded to me.

Minutes of Commissioners of Annexed Estates

SRO. E721/9, p. 61

Edinburgh, 31 January 1766

Two letters from Peter May, land surveyor, with regard to planting upon the Estates of Lovat and Cromarty and proposing to plant and uphold both trees and fences for five years at the rate of 25 shillings per acre, with a letter from the factor upon the same subject being read, *Recommended:* To Lord Kames to consider the proposals of Peter May, land surveyor, and to report his opinion to the Board, who are disposed to agree to Peter May's proposals upon condition of his upholding the plants for five years, but are of opinion that all the trees should be planted with the spade and not with the dibble.

[1] Revised proposals were sent by Peter May to Lord Deskford on 20 Dec. 1765 (SRO. E787/12/1(2)) but do not differ significantly from the original proposals of 14 Aug. 1765, *see* pp. 47–49.

Peter May to Lord Kames, read to the Annexed Estates Commissioners, 3 March 1766 SRO. E787/12/3

Aberdeen, 4 February 1766

I have just now the honour of your Lordship's of the 27th ulto., the receipt of which I would have acknowledged sooner, but was from home at a survey of contraverted marches between the Duke of Gordon and one of his feuars. I acknowledge in the most respectful manner my obligations for your Lordship's friendly advice, altho' you do not approve of my proposals. Allow me to say that I had it in view to lay them before the Board in the most equal manner, otherwise I would not have taken the liberty to entreat your interest, nor would I expect it in any other way. Your Lordship has been pleased to mention as an experiment, that the Duke of Gordon has got a hundred acres inclosed, planted and upheld five years, for a £100 sterling; with great submission give me leave to inform you what I know as to that. Some years ago in the Duke's absence the Duchess and Colonel Mores agreed with one —— Smith to inclose and plant the hills above Gordon Castle, to the extent of a thousand acres at 20s. the acre, the plants to stand at 5 foot distance, and in that agreement the undertaker was not obliged to uphold either the fences or plants. In carrying on his work the fences were made insufficient and he was turned off; that this is the truth your lordship can be sufficiently informed. I need not observe that a thousand acres lying together can be much easier inclosed in proportion than a smaller quantity, and that the plants standing at five feet distance require only 2,190 plants to the acre, whereas at three feet distance the way I proposed, it requires 6,084; and it is well known from experience that the net calculation will not hold out, for in carrying on plantations many are lost, and sometimes two are put into the same hole, and with the greatest attention it is not in our power to correct these things. Your advice of raising plants in some convenient spots near where they are to be planted would no doubt save the expense of carriage, but allow me to say that I think it would not turn out to account unless the plantation consisted of some hundred acres; as there would be a necessity for having a gardener there on purpose to preserve them from birds, and to keep them clean from weeds, neither of which could be entrusted to the country people.

Were the plantations to carry on lying in the neighbourhood, I could make my terms lower, but as all parts of the Annexed Estates lie at a distance, the carrying on business there must be attended with a considerable additional expense, and loss of time, in travelling to and from the country to direct it: nor is it in our power to get gardeners to go there on the same terms they accept of at home. This very autumn, I sent at the factor's desire a couple of gardeners to plant the firs that went north to the Lovat Estate, but could not hire them under a shilling each per day and their travelling charges. I have considered with attention and candidly compared the profits with the risk which attends the undertaking, and I mean to perform my engagements like an honest man, for which I shall find caution to the Board if required, on the following terms, viz. That the Board will be pleased to employ me for carrying on their plantations on all the Annexed Estates, with that view I agree to plant such of the inclosures as are already finished at twenty shillings the Scotch acre, and the plants to be at three foot distance and maintained good for five years. Or to plant five thousand to the Scotch acre at seventeen shillings the acre and to uphold them for the same time, but in neither of these ways can I have a concern with keeping up the fences. Or I shall agree to inclose, plant, and maintain both trees and fences five years, the inclosures not less than fifty acres and upwards to a hundred, at the rate of thirty shillings the acre; and for all inclosures of a hundred acres and upwards to five hundred at twenty-five shillings the acre; and all above five hundred at the rate of twenty shillings the acre. That your lordship may know whether my estimate of inclosing be reasonable, allow me to inform you that last summer the soldiers were on stented work at the Lovat and Cromarty Estates, and as I was in the country the factor committed the direction of them to me. Those on the Lovat Estate were stented to two ells per day, two foot whereof was lined up with stones, and the rest made up with a ditch and feal dyke to the height of five foot. But on the Cromarty Estate they made only one ell and half per day, on account that they had quarry and gravel to cut through. This account the factor will confirm. Fifty acres of ground if lying square will require 2,160 ells to inclose it, which even at 3½d. per ell, the price it cost on the Lovat Estate (viz. each man 7d. a day, for which he wrought 2 ells) will amount to £31 10s. But if fifty acres lie oblong, nooked, or out of a square position, one third more ells may be added to the circumference at least, which adds considerably to the expense for the article of inclosing. If you think any part of it worth communicating to the Board I shall be extremely happy. . . .

Minutes of Commissioners of Annexed Estates

SRO. E721/9, pp. 105-6

Edinburgh, 3 March 1766

A letter from Peter May, land surveyor and nurseryman at Aberdeen, being read, in relation to planting and inclosing muirs on the Annexed Estates at a certain rate per acre, and Lord Kames having informed the Board that he had in the meantime directed May to go on with the planting of a moor upon the Estate of Lovat according to his own proposals, the Board approved of the orders given by Lord Kames to Peter May.

Minutes of Commissioners of Annexed Estates

SRO. E721/9, p. 148

Edinburgh, 24 March 1766

A letter from George Cumming at Brand [Brahan] being read, proposing to plant the moors upon the Estates of Lovat and Cromarty with fir plants for fifteen shillings per acre, *Recommended:* To the Inspector to enquire particularly as to the number of plants he will put in one acre, whether he means English or Scots measure, and also whether he will undertake to inclose the grounds at so much per acre and keep the same up for five years at a certain rate in the same manner as he proposes to keep the planting; and if the Inspector finds his terms moderate upon the whole that he do conclude a bargain with him accordingly.

Peter May to James Grant, younger of Grant

SRO. GD248/226/1

Aberdeen, 30 March 1766

Your favours of the 12 current came to Aberdeen in my absence. Mrs May tells me she wrote you and made some apology for my being in the country.[1] Had the weather been such as admitted of business I would have advised you before now, but we have had such a fall of snow here as almost interupted any correspondence of whatever kind. Mr Grant spoke to me about firs, but did it in such a way as I understood it intended to do me a favour rather than any real want of them on his part, and I was confirmed in my conjecture by the report of Thomas Smith who said that he himself was recommended to go to Monymusk by Mr Grant. Whatever may be in that I am extremely glad to have it in my power to serve Mr Grant in anything, and agreeable to your letter have ready for you 200 thousand and upwards; from 60 to 100 thousand of these are three years old and the rest only two. I had none of my own three-year-olds, nor are they ever to be got here or in the country, except when it happens that they lie on hand over a year unsold, as there are seldom any demand for them after two years growth. Immediately on receipt of this it will be necessary to advise me in course, where you want them sent and they shall be forwarded directly, but I must tell you that none of our carters here will go off the highway – I mean through the Highlands, so that I suppose Keith, Fochabers or Mulben will be the place they can be delivered at. Either of these they shall be carried to on the first notice which I beg may be in course, as my business in the country obliges me to leave the town soon. I need not tell you that the plants are good and will be carefully packed.

Peter May to James Grant, younger of Grant SRO. GD248/226/1

Aberdeen, 13 April 1766

I wrote you the 30th ulto. advising of my having kept for you 200 thousand firs and upwards, and wanted to be informed where I should send them agreeable to your former letter. I am much surprised at not hearing from you, particularly as the season is now so far advanced. I have a letter from Thomas Smith, gardener at Brodie, who plants also for Mr Grant, with a commission for a 100 thousand firs to be sent north to Keith immediately to John Christy's house there, which I have promised to have at that place on Thursday or Friday next at farthest being the 16th or 17th current. He

[1] Note from Euphemia May 24 Mar. 1766 (SRO. GD248/226/1).

says they are for Miss Grant. Along with these I am to send the remaining 100 thousand more or less as they turn out in the numbering for Mr Grant according to your former advice, and therefore it will be necessary to have horses at Keith on Sunday at farthest to receive them. I wish they may be careful to preserve them from the wind and drought by putting them in sacks or some proper covering to prevent their being exposed. I am certain the plants are extremely good and shall not be taken up until they are just ready to set out. They could have been with you already had you advised me in course.

PS. I have wrote Thomas Smith advising for Miss Grant of the 100,000 to be at Keith and with them the remaining part of your commission all on Thursday or Friday.

Peter May to James Grant, clerk at Castle Grant

SRO. GD248/226/1

Aberdeen, 15 April 1766

The enclosed letter was intended to have been sent by the post to Forres, but on reflection I thought it better to cause send it by express from Keith and for that purpose I have wrote to the postmaster there to hire one to be sent away immediately upon the arrival of the firs, which will be there on Thursday night precisely containing as in the note subjoined at the end of this. I have also wrote to John Christy, the man who keeps the public house there, to cause lay them by in some cool house until your horses receive them. I beg they may get particular orders to take sacks or sheets to preserve them from the sun and drought. I suppose they will speak for themselves, only the quantity of three-year-olds did not number so well as I expected in my last. If the season of planting would allow I believe I could procure you another hundred thousand of very fine two-year-olds. Had you any commission to execute here that I could be entrusted with you might freely commend me any time – Aberdeen is famous for stockings and stocking breeches. Pray if you want any such thing let me know of it.

PS. On reflection that the chamberlain of Mulben lay in the way and might order horses from his quarter to carry them from Keith to

Castle Grant, I have wrote and desired Mr Taylor's express to call on Mr Grant at Mulben in his way to whom I have also wrote in a very pressing manner, that if he did not choose to cause carry them he would forward express directly, have also mentioned sacks and packets and the number of horses that may be necessary.

Dorso: Three-year-old firs 30 bundles containing one thousand each bundle

Two-year-old do. 78½ do.

Peter May to James Grant, clerk at Castle Grant

SRO. GD248/226/1

Aberdeen, 28 April 1766

Your favours of the 10th current I duly received but it came too late with respect to the firs; they were sent away a day or two before, and as you had been extremely pressing in a former letter to have three hundred thousand sent you, I thought it was only answering a part of your commission to send you two and odds. I hope they came safe and fresh to Castle Grant, and I have reason to believe that upon comparison with those you had from Monymusk, the difference will be easily known. It was not in my power to provide you in more three-year-olds than the 60,000; they are seldom to be met with and are as seldom enquired for. It will be obliging to write me a line acknowledging the receipt of them which according to my account is three-year olds 60,000 and two-year-olds 217 for which the carrier brought a receipt from John Christy, the house they were left at in Keith. The expense of carriage from Aberdeen to Keith was one cart and one load on horseback. The cart a shilling a mile, the horse 3d. viz. for both 1s. 3d. and for 30 miles at 1s. 3d. per mile is £1 17s. 6d. Our carters and hirers in this place are extravagantly dear at all times of the year, but in the seedtime they are extremely ill to be got, and remarkably unreasonable in their demands which we are obliged to put up with, or want them altogether. We have excellent stockings and stocking breeches made here, which I know are scarce in your corner; did you want anything of that kind? Mrs May would take care to get them done for you in the best manner and upon the most reasonable terms.

Peter May to Henry Barclay SRO. E787/12/4

Aberdeen, 25 June 1766

I had your favours last post advising that it was the desire of the Commissioners for the Annexed Estates to write my terms about the plantations I am presently carrying on at the Lovat Estate and the progress I had made. In February last I had the honour to correspond with my Lord Kames about carrying on plantations on all the Annexed Estates, and I then made proposals to that purpose, which it seems were not approven of by the Honourable Board further than that his Lordship gave orders to proceed to plant such inclosures on the Lovat Estate about which we had communed, and this I understood to be agreeable to the first terms laid before the Board which was at the rate of twenty-five shillings the acre and upholding them for five years. But as my Lord Kames directed only 5,000 plants to the acre, instead of 7,000 which I at first proposed, on account of that abatement I am content to accept of twenty shillings the acre with the risk of upholding them for 5 years, only I must beg leave to observe that the maintaining and keeping up the fences is not included in these terms. If I am obliged to keep them in repair, which his Lordship insisted on, then I hope the Board will be pleased to allow me £4 sterling a year in consideration that they are earthen fences and will be ready to tumble down. As I mean no profits from this part but on the contrary would gladly be excused from it, therefore if the Commissioners should think my demands high whatever Captain Forbes the factor judges sufficient or can get it undertaken for by any proper person in the country, such an allowance shall satisfy me and I shall become bound for the performance of it. In autumn last I planted 264,000 at three feet distance plant from plant, being in terms of my last proposals, and in the spring 360,000 at five foot distance according to the instructions given by Lord Kames, in all 624,000. I could have planted more but there were some parts of the inclosures not then complete.

Had the Honourable Board been pleased to approve of my proposals with respect to carrying on plantations on all the Annexed Estates, in that case I would have gone over them all with much attention and marked out in concert with the factors such moors and hills as were a proper subject for planting and that could be spared without much prejudice to the tenantry. From a perambulation of this kind, together with rough draughts of such plantations as were judged proper to carry on, I could with more certainty have laid my proposals before the Board, particularly with respect to inclosing, than it was possible for me to do otherwise as the undertaking to inclose without seeing the ground must be attended with much uncertainty. It is also worth observing that had these inclosures been extensive the expense of carrying on the plantations would have come under the proposal already made, as my plan would have been to raise nurseries in the country and by that means freed me from the carriage which at present is the great article of expense upon me.

I saw an advertisement from the Board some time ago about gardeners to settle on the Annexed Estates. I intended to have taken notice of it but was then in the country making out a survey of contraverted marches and now I am afraid it is too late, therefore shall beg leave only to mention that we have at Aberdeen the best gardeners for raising kitchen stuffs of any in Scotland, I mean such as does not require to be tenderly brought up. Some of them know a little about raising nurseries also, and they are accustomed to hard labour. I am persuaded they would be useful on the Annexed Estates. Were any such wanted I would endeavour to procure them if I once knew the Commissioners' pleasure.

I saw my Lord Findlater on his way north, who said he believed that the Board had it in view to value the farms on the Annexed Estates in order to make out an adequate rental for them, and that he had thought of me for that purpose. For some years bygone I have along with my surveys made out rentals of gentlemen's estates. My plan is short and execute with accuracy after this manner, viz., as soon as the measures are taken and the rude draught protracted I repair to the fields and consider with attention the lying of the grounds and the convenience of the farmer. I remove the horrid practice of possessing their lands in runridge and when a farm lies in scattered fields and at a distance from the farmer I cut off the wings and outskirts and join them to some other to whom they lie more contiguous, or turn them into crofts if the land be such as will answer: in a word I do all I can to make the possessions commodious for the several possessors. After the buildings are settled I then examine the quality of the soil by digging holes in the several fields and according to their goodness I set down their value and what they are worth of yearly rent per acre. Along with the quality of the ground I have always under consideration both the situation of the place and the means of improvement. Lime, marle, or a command of water on an estate will add much to the value of the land, and so will a ready mercat for sale, particularly if the crops are vendible without long carriage, which is the case with land near a town. When I have valued and marked down on my rude draught every field and the rate per acre it is estimate at, I then make out a book wherein are engrossed the measures of each farm or croft classed according to their different denominations of infield, outfield, etc., and from the different rates a rental is made out of each possession and of the whole estate. I was laid to this practice by my Lord Findlater and have found it the most useful application of my business, as almost every estate may be improven in the rent if the lands are properly divided and valued with knowledge and discretion. If it were acceptable to the Board I should send you a specimen of the method I proceed by.

Minutes of Commissioners of Annexed Estates incorporating Minutes of Committee 30 June 1766 SRO. E721/9, p. 169

Edinburgh, 21 July 1766

A letter from Peter May, land surveyor, in relation to the plantations presently carrying on by him on the estate of Lovat and the progress he had made, and also in relation to settling kitchen gardeners on the Annexed Estates being read, The Committee were of opinion, That a calculation should be made out showing the extent of the ground planted by Peter May from the number of plants and the distance between them; That a copy of the resolution of the Board with regard to kitchen gardeners should be sent to the said Peter May; And that it should be remitted to the factor on Lovat and Cromarty to report whether the inclosures upon these estates were all completed.

State of the conjoined process, Anderson *v*. Forbes

SRO. CS245/680, pp. 28–29

2 August 1766

. . . Peter May, surveyor of land, appointed as commissioner in the division of commonty of Forest of Bunzeach,[1] or in case of refusal or non-attendence, John Home, surveyor of land.[2]

Notes referring to a plan of the moss adjoining to the lands of Elrick, Redford and Culvie[3] SRO. GD248/672/3

Culvie, 23 August 1766

Peter May, surveyor of land at Aberdeen, had a letter from the Earl of Findlater, Mr Gordon of Achintoul and Mr Ogilvie of Culvie dated 3 November 1763 directing him to make out a survey and plan of that moss adjoining to their respective lands of Redford, Elrick and Culvie, and that as soon as he could the said Peter May, being necessarily engaged for the most part at the Annexed Estates in the summer time, could not attend until now; when in consequence of the said letter he repaired to the moss in question, having previously advised the parties or their doers of his intention to begin the survey which he did on Monday the 18th of August 1766, and had for his guides Mr Ogilvie of Culvie, Mr Munro, factor to the Earl of Findlater, and William Cow, tacksman of Elrick, who went along and pointed out the moss and pasture ground used in common by the above lands of Elrick, Culvie and Redford. A sketch of which is herewith delivered containing the said moss and pasture grounds as the same is used in common by the tenants of the respective lands.

[1] The commonty of the Forest of Bunzeach, whose considerable extent is not known, lay on the northern slopes of the Grampians to the south of the River Don (NJ3607). A summons in a conjoined process of declarator of property and marches and division of commonty was raised in 31 Jan. 1766 by Capt. John Forbes of New against Charles Anderson of Candacraig. Commission was granted to Peter May, or in case of his refusal, John Home. Peter May made out a plan which was submitted to the Court of Session on 11 Mar. 1767 who ordered it to be engraved (original missing and no example of the engraving has been discovered). A new summons was raised in 1805 by John Forbes of New against Alexander Leith of Freefield and Alexander Anderson of Candacraig (Forbes v. Leith and Anderson, SRO. CS232 F/10/7). The process was withdrawn in Dec. 1806 and the legal situation appears to be unchanged in 1855.

[2] Another report: 'John Home to be appointed if Peter May does not act.' Macgregor papers, SRO. GD50/60, pp. 43–44.

[3] *See* p. 39, n. 1.

In making out the perambulation along with the guides it was observed that William Cow had a different opinion from Mr Ogilvie or Mr Munro in respect to the boundings of the common pasture next his own farm of Elrick. He alleges that the pasture ground lying north from his cornfields and between them and the moss, all the way eastward from the peat road leading past John Taylor's house, is the property of Elrick and not a common. But the other guides don't admit of that: they say it is a common and that they have exercised the same acts of possession there in common with Elrick that they have done on any of the other common moors or pasture. William Cow's account of the common pasture lying west from his cornfields, and opposite to George Chapman and Jean Chalmer's houses, went beyond the account of the other parties, but the difference here was very trifling being only the space between the lines A,A, and B,B, in which William Cow asserts a property and the others a common.

Captain John Gordon of Park has a farm called Thorax lying on the northwest corner of the plan and contiguous to the moss. The dotted line on the sketch at that side was pointed out to the surveyor to be the march and boundary of Thorax, but it has now run down the ends of the ridges close to the moss as represented on the draft, and upon the surveyor's advising Captain Gordon of such an alleged encroachment, he had for answer that he was just going from home and could not take time to enquire into it then, but that he never doubted of Thorax having a right in that moss.

Mr Innes, the minister of Marnoch, gets his peats presently from this moss and it seems that he and his predecessors have been in use of doing so for a considerable time back. The heritors of the parish are said to be liable for the payment of ten pounds Scots yearly as the rent of his moss but which, it seems, has neither been exacted nor paid.

There are alleged encroachments on all sides with respect to the common pasture and they are allowed to be partly true. The ends of the cornfields have been in some places ploughed out, in other parts ridges are taken in from the sides next to the common. But these encroachments could not be pointed out distinctly to the surveyor, nor was he very anxious about the discovery, it being his humble opinion, which he suggests with much submission, that the improvements might continue and stand entire with each party as they are at present, and this he thinks the more reasonable as it is allowed that there have been encroachments on all sides, and that these encroachments are upon the whole pretty equal.

When the marches are cleared up and the several rights to the moss in question ascertained, it occurs to the surveyor that the proper way to make a fair and equal division would be to run the lines nearly south and north (leaning a little to the S.E. and N.W.) whereby each party would get a proportion of the good and bad moss. The moss towards the south side is for the most part soft and boggy, and in some places much wore out particularly towards the southeast nook. On the west and north sides the moss is generally good, and will wear longer in proportion to the quantity as there appears to be more wet and drench towards these sides than the other parts of the moss, which are for the most part remarkably dry and little appearance of growth in them.

The moss towards the east side is in general the ebbest [thinnest] as appears from the several depths taken. On that account and in laying by a just proportion of moss there, the party who gets it will have more surface of moss and more of the interjected pieces of pasture than those whose shares fall where the moss is deeper. The parties concerned will best judge whether this is a consideration worth attending to. The surveyor humbly thinks it is not, as the quality on that side will require some allowance of quantity.

It will no doubt be attended to in the division of the common pasture to lay by the several proportions or shares to the respective cornlands to which they lie most adjacent and contiguous.

There is herewith delivered a sketch containing the whole moss and commons laid down locally, and in their full extent, as they were pointed out to the surveyor by his guides, together with the situation of the adjacent cornfields belonging to the respective lands of Elrick, Redford and Culvie as far as was thought necessary to comprehend in the survey. The depths of the moss were regularly and accurately taken by boring down with iron woombles, and the local places of all these depths are delineated on the plan and marked in feet and inches according as they turned out, from which the solid content of the moss is cast up in cubical feet.

Peter May to Lord Findlater SRO. GD248/346/5

Aberdeen, 29 September 1766

Your Lordship's of the 21st was sent me to Buchan which I left early this morning and am just got to Aberdeen. I am much obliged to your Lordship for recommending me to Mr Grant. There is nobody I would serve with more pleasure or greater attention, but I am afraid it will be late to begin with him after I have done at New and your town of Rothes settled. These are engagements which your Lordship knows of and I am uncertain but the contraverted marches between Sir James Innes and Leuchars still waits me. If that is the case I must certainly take that immediately after Rothes. Last post I had a letter from Captain Forbes and appointing me to meet him at Strathdon on the 4th. I am determined to keep that appointment, and shall make much despatch to finish his things and get to you, which I hope will be by the middle of October, but I shall advise your Lordship as soon as I can calculate my time. Mr Forbes will write you his opinion about David Aitken and I shall put him in mind to do it soon. Lord Adam Gordon was last week jaunting about among the Buchan gentlemen. I fell in with his Lordship at Captain Duff's on Thursday to dinner – the Captain makes an excellent landlord. Since I left Cullen I have put Mr Aberdeen's matters in order, and had much satisfaction in being assisting to him. He is a young gentleman of great discretion, and attentive to his country affairs beyond what might be expected from his time of life. I have also taken a survey and made out a rude draught of the contraverted moss marches between Pitfour and the heritors of Crimond, and some days before I left the country had begun to a survey of the lands of Broadland for Mr [Robert] Stevens, which I have left two of my young people to complete.[1]

Lord Findlater to James Grant of Grant SRO. GD248/672/4

Cullen House, 2 October 1766

. . . I enclose you the answer I received from Mr May [see above]. I know Sir James Innes and Leuchars are expecting him in the end of

[1] May's apprentices, Alexander Taylor and George Brown.

October, so except the weather be very fine, that will be too late for beginning to survey; but I think being in the neighbourhood, he should go to Castle Grant, make his bargain, and see what he is to do next year, as it is possible you may not be in the country, when the season for survey begins . . . I am extremely glad that the arbiters have made so much progress in your marches with the Duke of Gordon [see below]. As the Duke and you must have a meeting before it is ended, I hope it will procure us the pleasure of seeing you here. . . .

Duke of Gordon to Alexander Thomson of Banchory, advocate in Aberdeen SRO. GD44/15/8/7

Gordon Castle, 30 September 1766

I send you herewith my claims of marches with Mr Grant [of Grant]. It will be proper for me to have copies of the proof already adduced and of the interdict pronounced, both which I shall expect without loss of time – I mean the whole proof, Mr Grant's as well as my own. I shall also expect you will confer with Mr Innes[1] and give your directions to the planner as soon as convenient. In the meantime, as many of the old witnesses are infirm, I shall expect you'll transmit the commission for examining them without delay.

Alexander Thomson, advocate in Aberdeen, to the Duke of Gordon SRO. GD44/15/8/7

Aberdeen, 2 October 1766

I was honoured with your Grace's letter of the 30th ultimo along with the claims of Marches betwixt your Grace and Mr Grant. In obedience to your commands have set hands to work to make out copies of the proofs already adduced. The same is very long and will require some time. How soon the copies are done the same shall be transmitted to your Grace. Meantime a copy of the interdict is here

[1] John Innes of Muiryfold arbitrated in the settlement of the lengthy marches between James Grant of Grant and the Duke of Gordon (SRO. GD44/52/37). Innes was described by the Earl of Aboyne as 'a Man of established Character and Integrity and Knowledge in Country Affairs, and who, it is believed, determined more questions of controverted property and servitude than any other private Gentleman in Scotland'.

inclosed. I have been several times with Mr [John] Innes [of Muiryfold] conferring about this affair. We are to make out directions for the planners as soon as possible and have made out two copies of a commission for examining witnesses; one copy is inclosed for your Grace, the other is sent to Mr Grant [of Grant]. As the weather is very favourable perhaps it may be expedient to examine witnesses sometime this month on the marches betwixt Fochabers and Auchash, and if any examination can be gone about in the high country before winter it may be proper to do it. Mr Innes has spoke to Peter May, land measurer,[1] who inclines to plan by himself, but he doubts if he can do it in the high country before the winter's season come on.

Report, Archibald Menzies, General Inspector to the Board of Annexed Estates
SRO. E729/8, pp. 143-4

Undated [October 1766]

There are two considerable plantations made upon the Lovat estate, one by May,[2] the other by Cumming at Brand. Those planted by May do not appear to be thriving, altho' planted at a much greater expense than Cumming's, which are in very fine order.

May brought all his plants eighty miles distant, Cumming about three. However, May promises after this to do better if the Board will allow him a piece of ground to raise the nursery on the spot. The Board will judge how far this is necessary as long as Cumming is able to serve them.

Peter May to his apprentice, Alexander Taylor
SRO. GD248/350/5

Aberdeen, 3 November 1766

I came to Aberdeen Saturday night late with the persuasion of finding you before me and was much disappointed when it turned out otherwise as I had little else to do at Aberdeen but to give you

[1] The words 'land measurer' inserted in place of 'the planner', which have been deleted. Possibly Commissary Alexander Innes, not John Innes, is referred to.
[2] An account dated 31 Oct. 1766 by Peter May to Captain John Forbes of New for these plantations is printed in A. H. Millar, *Forfeited Estates Papers*, Scottish History Society, Edinburgh, 1909, p. 68.

instructions how to be employed until my return. Had I known that the mensuration of [Alexander Milne of] Crimonmogate's lands would have employed you so long I certainly would not have dispensed with you, but he only mentioned a survey of two or three farms to me which was the reason I agreed to it so readily. But to look forward I shall now expect you into town as soon as you can, although I cannot be here to see you, being obliged to set out early tomorrow morning for Rothes and I am uncertain when I shall return.

I believe I already wrote you that the plans of Grandhome, Cairnbulg and Craigelly were much spoiled in copying over particularly the print which you will find so very bad on Mr [James] Shand's plan of Craigellie that I am afraid we had better copy it over new than be able to mend it in such a way as to make it anything neat. The only direction I can give you as to that is to try a farm or so many fields and if the print will mend in such a way as you think will please me I would have you proceed to mend the whole, but if you don't think it would do tolerably neat you may let it alone till I either come home or advise you how to proceed. I think Grandhome may yet be mended so as to make it indifferently neat. Cairnbulg is almost as bad as Craigellie which gives me more concern as it is a plan that must go to Edinburgh. You must therefore be at more than ordinary pains about it as it is a performance that I am very anxious to have well executed. I only wish it may be in your power to correct it in such a way as it will pass. The explanation and every other part of the writeabout, the scale, etc., must be cut off and wrote anew. George [Brown] has attempted to write them down, but you will see his performances are wretched and therefore must be entirely cut off. I am not certain but I may have occasion for William in the country. If I do I will write Mrs May thereanent. In the meantime let him be employed drawing ridges and shading round the fields and I shall expect that William will for his own intent as well as mine be attentive and exact. Both you and he will see what additional trouble the careless way they have execute them last summer occasions us, besides throwing away a great deal of time and expense. There is a rude draught of the moss of Crimond which was made out last harvest. I want two copies of it, one for Mr Ferguson and another for Crimond and Logie, but I would have both of them contracted to a scale of 8 [Scots chains] in the inch which I suppose you can do very easily as it is only making as many squares in the clean plan of half inches as there are in the rude draught of whole inches. The way to set about it is to divide the rude draught with all the accuracy you can into squares or whole inches, and to divide these into half inches and then to number the squares on the rude draught with ink from one end to the other alongways and across; and then divide the clean plan into as many half inch squares as there are whole inch squares on the rude draught and to subdivide these half inch squares into quarters to be numbered the same way as the whole and half inch squares are on the rude draught. A specimen of what is intended is subjoined. There is likewise a rude draught of the survey I have made lately of Strathdon to copy over. I would have it also reduced to a scale of eight [Scots chains] in the inch after the same manner you do the moss of Crimond. But in the Strathdon plan it won't be convenient to write the same names on the clean plan that are upon the rude draught because they must be marked with alphabetical letters only and refer to the depositions of the witnesses.

This letter will be delivered you by Mrs May and I desire that in a day or two after you come home you will write me fully what progress you have made in the country and upon trying to mend the plans whether you think it would do in such a way as will please me which I know you can judge sufficiently of. Sandy May has behaved in every other particular as he has done with printing on the plans since Mrs May and I left Aberdeen. He has given no sort of application either to his writing or figuring. Mrs May has often prevailed on me again and again to make another trial, and he like a silly boy has promised to mend; but I see that all my endeavours goes for nothing and I repent it heartily that I have been at so much pains with him; and I am now as much difficulted what to do with him as ever as nothing can be trusted to unless I were hanging over his head constantly myself. Mrs May has asked it for the last time that I will make another trial and would fain make me believe that you will be at more than ordinary pains with him. I have no doubt but every means will be used on your side tho' I suspect your success much; in order to make it effectual as I can and give you authority, and desire that it may be peremptorily execute, that upon his either being careless or refusing to do with the greatest attention what you desire him, you carry him down to Mrs May directly and cause him write down his own trespass and let that be forwarded to me and I shall give the proper instructions how to dispose of him. I shall expect you'll attend to what I have here wrote you in every particular. I am your sincere friend and affectionate master.

Proposals for survey of estate of James Grant of Grant by Peter May, land surveyor SRO. GD248/449/3

April 1767

The surveyor has just now had a communing with Mr Forbes, who said it was recommended by Mr Grant that some notes should be marked down about carrying on the said survey in the most useful manner for the improvement of the estate, which the surveyor has here subjoined with much submission.

If a general survey and mensuration of the estate is wanted, in that case it would shorten the work to begin at a side and carry on the lands on both sides of the river at the same time. When davochs or farms are picked out here and there it protracts time much, and in the event of a general survey being taken afterwards, these partial surveys save but little labour.

As the cornlands are the most valuable part of the estate the greatest attention is necessary to them, and therefore the contents and measures of the several cornfields must be accurately surveyed agreeable to their present boundings, and their names and measures marked down accordingly, with the marches of the different farms and the hills and pasture ground that lie contiguous thereto, so far as may appear useful or necessary.

The courses of the burns and rivulets must be accurately surveyed to their sources (if such fall within the lines of survey), with proper remarks where they can be diverted from their channels for watering ground, etc., which in highland estates may be turned out to much account as there is generally a command of water.

In making out surveys of the low country estates, it has been the surveyor's practice for several years bygone, to value the ground and make out estimate rentals of what they are worth yearly; and that this may be done with the more judgement, as soon as the measures are taken and the rude draught protracted, the surveyor repairs to the ground and attentively examines the quality and situation of the soil, and rates it at so much per acre, and in this he has always in view that the landlord should have an adequate value for his lands and the tacksman live with industry, and this he has found the most useful application of the business.

After the lands are valued, he then proposes alterations in the boundings of the farms where they appear necessary. When lands lie discontiguous and at a distance from the farm house he generally cuts off the outskirts and joins them to some others with which they lie more contiguous, or turns them into crofts when the quality of the lands will bear it, and it will be necessary to have particular regard to give the several farms on this estate the most convenient access to the hill.

The situation of the country is particularly attended to by the surveyor, and the means of improvement that it affords. Lands near a mercat where crops are vendible without much carriage is of advantage particularly to a farmer. Again where lime, marl, or even a command of water can be had that must add very considerably to the intrinsic value of the lands, and are such means of improvement as the surveyor has much dependence on.

The above preceeding notes are just marked down as they occurred, without any order or method. If Mr Grant wants more particular information it can be given afterwards.

The surveyor has a couple of lads who are bred to the business[1] and can measure land by themselves who he means to employ at the survey and for whom he is accountable.[2] He has other two who serve as assistants at leading the chain, setting poles etc. For the first two, half-a-crown is to be charged for each per day, and the other two one shilling each, in all seven shillings; and the surveyor is to charge for himself eight shillings per day, in all fifteen shillings for himself and four lads.

If Mr Grant approves of these proposals, it will be necessary to give the surveyor a general order on all the tenants to show him their marches and the names of the fields and such other information

[1] George Brown and Alexander Taylor, *see* accounts pp. xxx-xxxvi.

[2] Up to this point the document is in the hand of James Grant, younger of Grant. What follows is probably added by a clerk at the dictation of Grant.

as shall be found necessary. Some hands to carry on the chain will also be wanted at Mr Grant's expense.

Journal of James Grant, clerk at Castle Grant

SRO. GD248/1542, fo. 27v.

Castle Grant, 25 April 1767

. . . Mr May came to Castle Grant and his men too. . . .[1]

Instructions to Peter May for a survey of the estates of James Grant, younger of Grant

SRO. GD248/371/7

Undated

A general survey of the estate is wanted with the quality of the soil, the method of improvement and inclosing proper, the clauses Mr May would have put into the tacks to enforce cultivation, the value as near as he can ascertain, the most commodious place for the farm-house and the cottars, the proper access to the hill; and that wherever marches of the tack are not so convenient Mr May should ascertain and fix new ones, and always as to every farm mark the boundaries distinctly so as to prevent all future dispute; and as to the hill as far as possible he should name what particular lands have a right to such and such pasture, the extent of the pasture, and how far he would limit the use of the pasture to the size of the farm or leave it open, which I believe will be the best way as no man will keep more cattle than he has a farm to maintain; likewise whether he does not think it proper to enforce winter herding, water improvement and lime, and to prohibit gall cattle, by which I mean taking in cattle from other countries to feed during the summer *in the hill*, as this must be attended with inequality and injustice. I specify the hill, because in their inland inclosures it is very profitable and meritorious. These and everything else which can possibly occur to Mr May as to conveying a distinct knowledge of the estate and the proper method of agriculture in its full extent. Likewise what land is fit for lint, the proper season to attend to the sale of

[1] George Taylor with either William Taylor or Sandy May.

sheep, and whether any parts are fit for hops, hemp etc. I should imagine many for hops. Mr May should likewise consider in his valuation of the tacks that the inland ground is by no means the only valuable part of a highland estate; on the contrary they place a much greater confidence as to paying their rents on their pasture than their land. I only mean by this that in valuing a tack Mr May is to have in view its pasture as well as corn land.

He will likewise give a note of what hill improvements he finds hurtful and what not, and wherever he finds an uncultivated place which lies properly and should be cultivated to mark it for an improver, cottar, or what he thinks proper.[1]

Likewise his ideas as to the manner he would have the houses on each farm, and what extent of melioration he would have given for building of stone dykes or other improvements on the place, and laying down ground in good heart with grass-seeds, as one of the most useful improvements in this country, and planting gardens with useful timber, if it be not proper to be a clause in the tacks?

James Urquhart of Byth, to Peter May

SRO. GD248/251/1/30/1

Byth, 7 July 1767

In answer to your letter of 21 June, I have spoke with a man has been in use of drawing water on land these many years past, and as I have often employed him, I am sure he understands it, and works with his own hand. If Mr Grant inclines, he will come to him at a shilling per day and his diet, but not under, nor does he choose to engage for a certain term, till he sees how he agrees with the country and people. As to this I think you are in no difficulty, the operation is so plain and easy that any person, though of the smallest capacity, will be as much master of it in four weeks as the undertaker himself or any other person can be. If these terms are agreeable to Mr Grant let me know, and I shall send him over about the beginning of August, or perhaps sooner, but that will depend on his having ended any job he has presently on hand. . . .

[1] Vouchers to various local men assisting for 7d. or 8d. per day, from 9 May to 8 June 1767 (SRO. GD248/448/1).

Peter May to James Grant of Grant SRO. GD248/371/7

Beaufort, 10 July 1767

I had the honour of your commands about straightening the river of Shewglie[1] delivered me by Mr Grant the tacksman. On Friday last I repaired to that country for executing them. I wish my capacity were equal to my inclination, I should then be extremely happy in doing my duty as I ought. With pleasure I take the liberty to assure you that my best endeavours shall always be ready in any manner you are pleased to entrust me with.

Enclosed is a sketch of that part of the river intended to be straightened whereon is delineated the present natural course with its different windings and also the new channel as laid down on the ground, to which is subjoined for your perusal some notes and instructions with respect to the manner it should be carried on, but in that I suspect you will meet with some difficulty. Upon my going to the country I sent for [the Laird of] Corrimony whose lands march with yours on the other side of the river, and communicated to him what I was to be about, and that it was by your advice I had come there; to which he made answer that the present course of the river did not prejudice him in the least at the places where we intended to straighten it, and that giving it a new channel might prejudice and hurt his lands; but that he would not interrupt any project that might contribute for your interest provided you engaged and became bound to preserve the banks on his side as well as your own, or be liable for any damages that might happen afterwards on account of the new channel, and to this purpose he desired I might write you. This modest demand almost frightened me to proceed, tho' I believe he had the law on his side for it. I suppose straightening a river is different from straightening a march; you can force the latter but the former can only be done by mutual consent of the co-terminous heritors; at the same time I was made believe by [the tenant of] Shewglie that he would not stand in the way if you insisted to have it done.

Upon looking further down the river we observed much greater

[1] The locus here is Glen Urquhart and the valley of the River Enrick which enters the west side of Loch Ness at Urquhart Bay. In the Glen is Loch Meiklie into which the 'river of Shewglie drains'.

encroachments made by the water than those complained of by [the tenant of] Shewglie particularly on the farms of Clunebeg, Borlummore and Borlumbeg. These encroachments ought to be attended to immediately at least as soon as they can be overtaken; for there the damage is very considerable, and the tacksmen have neither ability nor temptation to preserve them as their leases expire in two or three years hence. But this is not the case with [the tenant of] Shewglie. He has a lease for forty years at least, and does not want liability to preserve his own grounds. To prevent flooding the lands as well as preserving the banks are objects that deserve attention both from the proprietor and tacksman for whatever hurts the one must of consequence affect the other. But where the damage is greatest there I think the relief ought to be most immediate especially when we have it in view to recoup the profits of such repairs at a new set which comes on very soon. In this view things appeared to me at the time of the survey, which I thought it my duty to lay before you. I beg your forgiveness if I have done it with too much keenness.

After the business of the river was finished I took a ride over the country along with Mr Willox of Lochletter, and was made extremely happy with so delightful a prospect as the whole country there affords. The situation pointed out to me for your own shieling is exquisitely beautiful. The flat below is interspersed with an inimitable variety of cornfields, meadows and woods. The opening on Loch Ness is truly grand and beautiful and the naked rocks towering up to the sky has such a grandeur and wildness that no art can equal.

Next day I went along with Mr Willox and looked at the lime quarries, and gave it as my opinion that the limer should change the situation of both his quarry and kiln. At present they stand disjoined and at considerable distance from any of the cornfields, which I could see no temptation for except its being near the moss. The roads to it are so bad that almost makes it inaccessible to the greatest part of the Strath. As there are certain appearances of limestone close to the cornfields and towards the bottom of the Strath, I recommended to your factor to cause the limer make a proper trial for a quarry as low down as he could find one. This in my opinion would be of great consequence in the article of consumpt as it would be near and accessible to all the neighbourhood. I think the limer in Urquhart very capable of his business, but Mr Willox says he is drunken and not to be depended on; for that reason I advised to send some of the most sagacious labourers to learn with him in case of accidents. I think his advice might be useful in Strathspey; his method of burning is preferable to the limer you employ there at present. Mr Willox pointed out some spots which he said you intended for planting and meant to enclose immediately. I used the freedom to give him my advice as to the method of making there fences which he said he would attend to.

I am just now with your friend [Forbes of] New who desires me to present his most respectful compliments to you and the family at Castle Grant and to advise you of the inclination to give all the assistance in his power to open a communication betwixt the Aird and Urquhart, for which purpose he has recommended it to me to consider of a proper tract for a road which he wants to carry on in concert with you. I think it by much the easiest way from Inverness, besides the mutual advantage the country would reap from having a good road and a free communication with one another. I beg your forgiveness for the length of my letter.

Alexander Dirom of Muiresk, Sheriff-substitute of Banff, to Peter May
SRO. GD248/251/1/29

Banff, 11 July 1767

I have the favour of yours of the 30th June, and if any advice I am capable of giving can be of any use towards the improvement of Mr Grant's Estate, or any other part of the country, I shall be very happy.

First, as to the expense of quarrying the limestone, as you say the quarry is free both of rubbish and water, and the stone very good, I should think the boll might be quarried for about three farthings, even though it be a 4th part larger than our boll. Our quarry is very hard and requires often to be broken with powder, and the quarriers we employ quarry the stones at 4d. per ton, which yields about 10 of our bolls; but as many of your quarriers in Strathspey will be to learn, I should not think it unreasonable to give them a penny the boll at first, and make them a present of a little powder now and then for their encouragement. As to the expense of burning I can form no judgment unless I knew how far they have to carry the stones and whether or not you mean that they should slack or harp as well as break and burn. In general the worse the peats are, the smaller the stones must be broke. Yet bad peats may in some degree be mended by giving the kiln additional air. The smaller the kiln is, the expense of burning must be the greater, for with peats a large kiln will burn almost as soon as a small one, and the larger the body of heat is, the more thoroughly will the stones be calcined.

In burning lime with peats, the kiln must have a great deal of air, in burning with coal very little. Therefore your kiln should be placed if possible in such a situation that it may have plenty of air and at the same time that there may be a proper space upon a level with the top of it for laying down the stones and the firing. In fixing upon the situation of the kiln too, care must be taken to have sufficient space for a lime house to which the door or chief vent of the kiln should open so that the kiln forms one of the gavels of your limehouse, and to this limehouse water also must be brought for slacking, otherwise the expense of carrying water for slacking, even if it be but 10 yards, will be great.

I imagine a kiln 16 feet high, 16 feet wide within at the top and gradually brought in to 8 feet at the bottom would be a very proper size, but this will frighten your strylla [?] man, who will be prejudiced in favour of his own country kilns that burn from 10 to 16 bolls only. This kiln I imagine with peats may throw towards 300 bolls and with coal would throw above 600. In building your kiln, whatever the dimensions be at the top, let it be founded of the same dimensions at the bottom, or otherwise it will tumble at the first burning, as I have experienced myself. To make this more explicit, if your kiln is to be 16 feet wide at the top, found that dimensions at the bottom, with the walls three feet thick and carry them up straight to the top in that way, only the outside of the wall may batter about 4 inches to the top. When that is done let the intake within from the bottom to the top be built by way of lining, and then this lining supports the weight of the loading of the kiln without much connexion with the walls. The walls will probably rent [expand] when the kiln is burning; but if they are well built they will come close again as the kiln cools. The kiln must have 4 vents. It is needless to say anything about a kiln that draws and burns at same time, because that can only be done where the firing is coal. When the country people come to use the lime care should be taken to cause them lay it upon ground that is of a dry nature and not liable to be spouty in winter, and then they never can fail of success, and a small discouragement at first would have a very bad effect. This is all that occurs to me just now in answer to yours, but if you desire any other information that I can give you, you have only to drop me a line from time to time and I shall answer you as distinctly as I can . . . Pray would you not find wood for burning the lime which is better than peats.

Peter May to James Urquhart of Byth SRO. GD248/251/1/30/2

31 July 1767

Your favours of the 7th came regularly to hand, and would have been answered in course, but that I could not advise you properly until I had an opportunity to wait on Mr Grant and lay your letter before him, which was done only yesterday. He desires me to thank you for the trouble you have taken to procure a man for him who understands watering land. He approves of the terms you mention, viz. a shilling a day and his diet, and as you observe that a short time will be sufficient to instruct other people, it will therefore be the less necessary to engage him for any considerable time, until we see what progress the other labourers make that are employed with him. If he could be here by the middle or latter end of August, it would answer very well, as I must be out of the country until about that time, and I should like to point out the places we mean to begin with myself. . . .

Peter May to Alexander Taylor SRO. GD248/350/5

Beaufort, 5 August 1767

I wrote you long ago under cover to Mr [William] Forbes and I have a letter from him advising of the receipt of it; by that you will see I had not then heard from you, but since have got two, the first only a few days ago and that of the 28th this very post. My letters had been forwarded to Stratherrick and returned from that to Inverness which was the reason of their being so long delayed. In my last I advised you of the accounts I had of your progress, since that I have got no more information about it, altho' I have heard several times from Aberdeen. At this distance it is impossible for me to give you particular instructions as to your procedure, and therefore I must leave you to the rules already laid down; you know what they are and I hope will attend to them, and have everything accurately and fairly marked. Diligence is all I desire and that is your own interest as well as mine, your character depends on it and I have no doubt you will take care to have it established, and be particularly attentive in my absence. It will not be in my power to be with you for a couple of weeks hence; many unforeseen accidents happen in the way. Several disputes about marches must be surveyed and settled before I can get away and I am not certain but I must go to Coigach, a highland part of the Cromarty estate where there have been so many alterations made of late among the tenantry which has turned them almost mutinous; many petitions and complaints are daily received from that corner of the world, and I am particularly instructed to examine into them. Mr Menzies, the Inspector-general, who should have been here some months ago has not yet cast up, but we now expect him every day.

You see by my present situation it is impossible to fix my time exactly when I can be with you and therefore I hope you will proceed according to the general plan already laid down. I think I had fixed that you were not to proceed further west than the kirktown and cornlands about Duthil, but I cannot pretend to point out the precise line; you must consider and fix on that yourself and be sure to endeavour to have the last line as near as you can the boundary of some of the farms. I do not mean your leading line to be the boundary but in the course of your filling up afterwards take in at least all the cornlands of these farms which are included in the survey and that lie next to the line you leave off at.

If you are gone to the hills and pasture before I return be sure to have proper guides to direct as to the marches and boundaries of the estate. Be particular in marking down the coterminous lands and to whom they belong as well as the marches and, as far as you can, the names of the grazings, farms or hills, etc. I think you should apply to Mr Forbes to go along with you for a day when you are to be on the outside marches and to have some old people, and George

[Brown] and you to go along together according to these guides. I mean that you both take a day or more to perambulate the marches before you begin to the mensuration, but I would fain hope to be with you before that time. If you have any difficulty for people to lead the chain you must represent it to Mr Forbes. It is Mr Grant's interest to have the business forwarded and I am persuaded Mr Forbes will attend to that.

I cannot imagine what induces you to believe that I think your behaviour surly unless it proceeds from consciousness in yourself that it is so. If that is the case I am glad you are sensible of it. I hope you will make the proper application and amendment for the future. Remember that some devotion with a sweet obliging temper and a disposition to please is particularly necessary in your present situation. It is of the utmost consequence to yourself and will always secure my esteem and affection for you, and at the same time that it will make you agreeable in every neighbourhood you fall into.

PS. I hope George and you have taken a wet hour to put the measures of Crebston in order. I want it much. Write me once every week what you have been doing and the progress you have made.

Peter May to James Grant of Grant SRO. GD248/371/7

Beaufort, 23 August 1767

The constant rains we had in Stratherrick made my survey of that country extremely disagreeable and more tedious than I imagined when I left Castle Grant. I luckily fell in with Mr Willox at Glenmoriston on Wednesday last, and we set out together next day for Urquhart along the loch side and through the wood of Ruskich where your people are employed making the roads, which we examined so far as they had gone and also the remainder of the tract they intended to carry it by, some parts whereof we took the liberty to correct with a view to make the ascent as easy as possible. If they had not been so far gone, I believe I should have brought the tract lower down towards the east end, and by that means made it much easier, but the present tract may do well enough for horseback tho' I think it will be steep in some places for a wheel-carriage. In many places drainers will be wanted across it; the method of making them I pointed out to the workmen but I wish they may attend to it.

Next day I went along with Mr Willox and examined where the waters had made encroachments or were likely to do most mischief, which is towards the east end of the Strath. We looked out the possessors of these farms who were most hurt by them, and pointed out where bulwarks were necessary, and where in some places new channels ought to be cut. But no expense to be brought on, except that of an overseer for conducting the country people who are all obliged to give so many days labour, but that labour is so ill and backwardly executed that it turns out to very little purpose unless some proper person be appointed to conduct and keep them close to the work. After settling so far the business of the waters, we then looked at the farms Mr Willox presently lives at, and marked out an enclosure for him in such a way as to fall in with the rest of the farm when it should at any time be enclosed. As the whole farm is presently out of lease I recommended it to the factor to make the best of it he could until the other lands were open, which I believe is in a couple of years hence, and to take care that the present possessors did not waste the farm in the meantime. I gave the same advice with regard to a croft which is also open, but as it lies close to other cornfields and betwixt them and the hill I was not able to judge, but it might turn out better either to enlarge the croft or annex it with those other lands to which it lay most contiguous.

I am excessively disappointed with the limer's elopement; he was very knowing in making lime. I wish the people who were employed with him may be qualified for carrying on the business. Mr Willox says they inform him that they can. I had formerly recommended it to Mr Willox to be concerned in it himself and to get some of the country people to engage with him. I am glad that Lochletter and he has that in view; I think them exceedingly good men for the purpose. With a view that a fair and equal bargain might be made, I proposed that they should quarry, break and burn one or more kilnfuls of stones and make an exact account of the expense thereof including peats and every part of the manufacture, and of the quantity of lime produced from each kiln or kilnfuls, and this report to be sent to you to be considered of. Could a bargain be made so as to leave you a penny a boll in lieu of quarry rent and peats? I think it might do at that rate. 6,000 bolls manufactured yearly would produce £25 Stg. of rent to the proprietor.

I pointed out several fields to Lochletter which appeared to be an excellent subject and under the command of water. Lochletter has promised to follow my advice and I hope he will find his account by it. I think he has spirit to do something. Shewglie enquired very anxiously how his banks were not fortified. I told him that I believed you had no objection, but that Corrimony stood in the way and that you did not choose to bring matters to extremities with any neighbour. Our proposals with respect to your farm of Curr is over all the country and magnified in every corner. I should be extremely glad to know if anything is done with it. I am persuaded it is worth the rent we put on it and had I any advice to give it would be not to let it under.

I regret much that it will not be in my power to wait on you in less than a fortnight. A dispute of marches has fallen out betwixt Fairburn and the annexed estate of Lovat. The Sheriff, C[aptain] Forbes, Fairburn and some other gentlemen have appointed to be on the grounds Wednesday next where I am obliged to attend and make out a sketch of it. I shall make all the dispatch I can to be soon at Castle Grant, while I hope there will be no more interruption.

Account the Hon. James Grant of Grant to Peter May for surveying
SRO. GD248/539/1

Castle Grant, 11 December 1767

TO surveying and measuring part of the estate of Grant from Monday 27th of April to Wednesday the 10th of June thereafter inclusive makes 45 days for the said Peter May and a servant for writing or leading the chain, etc., viz. for Mr May 8s. per day and for his servant 1s., in all 9s.	£20	5	0
TO the said Peter May and his servant from the 3rd of July to the 8th inclusive, taking a survey and making a plan for a new channel to the Water of Shewglie in Urquhart, and marking out some inclosures and giving directions for repairing and mending up the broken down banks of said water as per advice from Mr Grant; 6 days at 9s. per day	£2	14	0
TO the said Peter May and a servant from the 25th of July giving directions for carrying on the survey at Castle Grant, dividing and valuing the lands of Curr, and making out conditions and minutes for tacks; 12 days at 9s.	£5	8	0

	£	s.	d.
TO the said Peter May and a servant who assists to write and take out the measures from the 9th of November to the 12th of December thereafter, at dividing, valuing and putting in order such farms as were out of tack, and setting and making out minutes for these tacks, viz. for 33 days at 9s. per day	£14	17	0
TO Alex. Taylor and George Brown, surveyors, who survey and measure by themselves from the 27th April to the 7th Dec. thereafter is 224 days from which deduct 12 days absence of one of them, viz. for George Brown; there remains 212 days at 5s. per day for both	£53	0	0
TO 3 days travelling from Aberdeen to Strathspey and as many returning home, in all 6 days for the surveyor and his assistants at 14s. per day	£4	4	0
TO a carriage horse for instruments and other necessaries from Aberdeen to Castle Grant being 50 miles at 3d. per mile and the same expense returning home	£1	5	0
TO monies paid out on account of Alex. Forbes when going along with the other surveyors		9	2
	£102	2	2
BY cash from William Forbes as per George Brown and Alex. Taylor's receipts for	£4	7	7
	£97	14s.	7d.

Altho' the balance be £97 14s. 7d. Sterling yet there is only to be be charged £90 net for which a note is accepted by Mr Grant payable against Whitsunday next, which, when paid is in full of this account and the same as discharged by Peter May.

1768—1778

FACTOR TO THE EARL OF FINDLATER

Peter May to James Grant of Grant SRO. GD248/345/5

Aberdeen, 23 December 1767

. . . The person I had in view for you was no other than myself, happy had it been for me if I had been a little more explicit. I am now obliged to own with much regret that it is out of my power. My Lord Findlater has for some years bygone been making me offers to settle with him and my business at Cullen last time was to that purpose.[1] I got it put off then, but I have a letter from his Lordship last post which I suspect must nail me down. The only joy I have is that my charge is to be his Moray estate and my settlement is to be at Elgin, but I need not say his Moray estate, for his Lordship insists on my dividing and valuing his other lands as they fall out of lease and that I shall give up entirely the business of surveying land as I do at present.

I have reserved time to help you forward and I am persuaded he will not scruple that when it does not interfere with his interest, which I must take care to avoid. As my residence must be in Elgin I can steal a day to go to Strathspey and be happy in doing everything in my power to promote your interest. I think I can engage a young lad for you to survey and measure your estate by the year, which will bring it much cheaper than if carried on otherwise. Let me know if you would approve of that. I can say now without being thought selfish that you will go wrong without having a survey, and that it is groping in the dark if you take another way to settle your farms.

I came from Banff to Hatton Lodge to breakfast and have the pleasure to inform you that Lady Ann was very well, and happy to hear my history. Her Ladyship mentioned writing you next post and to invite you for a month to Hatton Lodge. I promised to put in my mite and if my riding about your estate in Aberdeen there can be any inducement along with you I shall be extremely pleased.

[1] For a summary of this correspondence, see Grant, *op. cit.*, Appendix.

There is plenty of hay and corns, of good old peats, and old meal, and I am assured by Lady Ann that the cellars are equally well stored. Hatton Lodge would be a proper retreat for a month or six weeks. I was obliged to stay and walk about all the policies which indeed are vastly neat and clean.

What have you done with those farms that were not settled before I left you? Give me leave to put you in mind that there was a part of the Lethendy, Scurguie of Currachullie, two parts of Achrosk, Achafearns and the improvements on each side of the high road north from Belleward. I beg they may be put in order, and for God sake meet with the people yourself and do not trust it to others. I left notes that will help you to know the values of them. Give me leave to beg that you won't vary particularly with the Achnafearns. I can assure you the demand is very reasonable, and they will give it tho' they will stickle with you at present. Don't give them any further allowance for improving; you are much improved on already in that way; their improvements are naught.

Mrs May and I have been enquiring about some proper person for learning your people to spin and knit stockings. It is not easy to find a young girl that can be trusted or has direction enough to manage properly. We have in mind a weaver who is a very good one and his wife can spin and knit well and can wash and dress and sew a little. Mrs May knows them both and says they are such as can be recommended with safety. Would not that do better than a young girl? You want weavers, but they want something certain for the first year while they see how business turned out. If you approve of our choice I shall cause them to send you their terms. . . .

Peter May to James Ross, factor at Cullen House SRO. GD248/983/2

Aberdeen, 31 January 1768

I wrote you last post and have this day your favours, advising that my Lord Findlater thought it necessary that you should have a letter from me narrating all the terms of my agreement. I thought I had written fully on that head already, and believed everything had been settled, except about receiving the farms which I likewise agreed to do, and to that purpose I wrote both my Lord and you. As that has not been satisfactory, I am at a loss what to say further, except in obedience to his Lordship's instructions I mention again: That I engage to do everything relating to the business of a factor in my own collection, which I understand to comprehend all my Lord's land in Moray and on Speyside, and to forward as much as I can the good management of the farms, with the improvement of the moors and the proper regulation of the mosses. And if there are planting policies, or building, going on for my Lord's account within my collection, I am content and agree to give general directions about them. I further agree to divide and value, or to assist in dividing and valuing, the other parts of my Lord's estate as often as that will be found necessary. I am content to give up the business of measuring and planning ground entirely, but I would incline to retain all the spare time that is not necessarily employed in my Lord's business, to be at my own disposal, either for the management of a farm or to assist my friends, but neither of which shall in the least interfere with his Lordship's interest.

I believe it is unnecessary to mention the salary. You know that was already agreed to be £50 Stg. with a free house in Elgin, and the assistance of the tenants to lead my fire, and travelling charges when I am employed dividing or valuing the other parts of my Lord's estate. I think the business I am proposing to engage in should not engross all my time, otherwise it would not answer my intention, which was to get a little respite and in this view my Lord spoke of it himself and pointed it out as a proper retreat. At the same time I lay my account with having always a good deal to do, which I shall endeavour to go through with as much application and dispatch as possible.

I think the subject of this letter is agreeable to my former proposals but if it be necessary to put it in another form so as to please my Lord Findlater, I beg you will make out a scroll to this purpose which I shall copy over.

Alexander Taylor, surveyor, to James Grant, younger of Grant

SRO. GD248/371/7

Aberdeen, 5 February 1768

At Mr May's desire, I have taken the liberty to lay before you the result of a communing with him, about engaging to measure and plan your estates, according as they lie in different corners, or in any manner you are pleased to direct them, at £20 a year with bed, board, and washing in the family, and that for the space of three years after Whitsunday next, if the measuring and planning your lands shall require that time, with the addition of £5 of more wages for the third year, but which addition shall be on the footing, and depend entirely on, my diligence and good behaviour.

I need not mention that when I am out on the survey my travelling charges and entertainment are to be paid, and that I am also to be allowed the necessary guides and assistants. Surveying and drawing instruments with plan paper, etc., will also be wanted.

I have been bred with Mr May and served under him last summer in Strathspey (which makes me know from experience that the survey of an estate in a Highland country is a more laborious and extensive work than one in a corn country) and to him I refer you as to any information concerning my capacity and character. I proposed some perquisites to Mr May on account of the fatigue and extraordinary wear of shoes among the heath, but he thought it better to refer anything of that kind until you had an opportunity to see how I deserved it. Any return for me can be sent under Mr May's cover. . . .

Report by John Forbes, factor on Lovat with respect to the plan for augmenting the rents SRO. E769/114 (1)

Read in Edinburgh, 7 March 1768

In obedience to the order of the Committee I have looked over and considered the plan made out and presented by Peter May for augmenting the rents of the estate of Lovat, which is a most accurate, distinct, and laborious performance, and I am humbly of opinion, that it will be of great service in settling with the tenants upon the present occasion as well as in future times.

I can't pretend to say that I have had leisure enough to go through the scheme with such accuracy and precision as is necessary to form a proper judgement with respect to the additional rent proposed on all the different farms, but according to the general view which I have taken the whole appears to be equal and reasonable. I have particularly considered with attention a few of the best farms, viz.

Englishtoun, Inchberry, Groam, Easter and Wester Lovat, Castledonie, Bruich, and Tomich, and I think the additional rent proposed to be laid upon these farms is adequate, though perhaps not so much as might be exacted by a private proprietor, which I understand the surveyor had in view, and I suppose is agreeable to the intentions of the Board for, if the tenants were to be squeezed, and the rents raised as high as those of the neighbouring heritors, instead of promoting loyalty and affection to His Majesty's Government, which is one of the designs of the Annexing Act, it would diffuse a spirit of discontent and murmuring among all the tenantry.

In order to execute this plan of augmentation and settle everything properly, it will surely be necessary to authorise the Inspector General to treat with the tenants. But it is also in vain to imagine that the same form or plan of a lease will answer the whole, as on every barony there may happen to occur great difference in the soil and situation of the farms, as well as in the ability and circumstances of the tenants who possess them.

The substantial farmers may be tied down by leases to inclose and improve in a particular manner, and the smaller tenants to have an order of the Board for 7 or 9 years lease with a promise of prorogation to such as discover a spirit of industry and application. But in my humble apprehension, it will be very improper to overload the one or the other with many different articles or conditions which there is perhaps little probability of their being able to execute.

The tenants will certainly incline to have all the victual converted, but in my humble opinion it will be more equal to convert only the one half, at 10s. per boll, and to oblige them to pay the other half in kind, for otherwise the rent of the estate would be little increased when victual sells high; besides it may be very necessary to have some victual rent to supply manufacturers, or other people employed in carrying on improvements, upon the estates.

[The report was endorsed by Archibald Menzies, Inspector General]

I have considered the above report of Captain Forbes and am clearly of the same opinion with him having examined the articles specified above. It will be necessary Captain Forbes have authority finally to conclude bargains with the tenants, and I shall give him any assistance I can, and am hopeful it may be so ordered that we shall have it in our power to lay before the Board next summer a plan for letting leases and concluding bargains with all the tenants mentioned in Mr May's report.

Minutes of Commissioners of Annexed Estates

SRO. E721/18, pp. 15-16

Edinburgh, 7 March 1768

The Board having re-considered the petition of Lieutenant John McKenzie, possessor of the house and Mains of Castle Leod, praying for a lease of the same, together with a paper signed by the Countess of Cromarty[1] declaring that she has no objection to the granting a Lease during her lifetime of the said house and Mains to any person the Commissioners shall judge proper, *Delayed* the consideration of the above petition until Peter May, land surveyor, shall report the valuation of the different farms on the Estate of Cromarty. . . . *Ordered:* That Mr May do make out a sketch or plan of the proposed village at Beauly and of the village at Ullapool.[2] That no Lease of the farm of Tomich or of the lands adjacent to the said intended villages be granted – and that a skilful brick-maker be sent to Beauly when the plan comes to be put in execution. *Resolved:* That the bog of Tomich presently under Allars, etc., and all the other natural woods on the estate of Lovat be inclosed. *Remitted:* To the General Inspector and Captain Forbes to consider the present rental of the estate of Lovat and the estimate given in by Mr May and report their opinion of the estimate to the Board. *Ordered:* That Mr May do make out his account for the survey and plans of the estate of Lovat and lay the same before the Board.

Minutes of Commissioners of Annexed Estates

SRO. E721/18, pp. 17-18

Edinburgh, 10 March 1768

A report by the factor on Lovat upon the plan made out by Peter

[1] Isabel, daughter of Sir William Gordon of Invergordon, who married George, 3rd Earl of Cromarty. His support for the Jacobite cause led to a sentence of death for treason which was remitted on the forfeiture of his estates. He died on 28 Sept. 1766, and his wife on 23 Apr. 1769.

[2] He had already made a plan for the proposed village in the summer of 1756, *see* p. 12.

May, land surveyor, for putting an adequate rent or valuation upon the different farms on the estate of Lovat, being read,

The Committee were of opinion that it should be submitted to the Board to consider how far it might be proper that the one half of the rents of the low country or corn farms of the Annexed Estates should be paid in grain and that the whole rents of the highland or grass farms should be paid in money; and at what conversion from the estimate the grain should be taken,

The committee were also of opinion that it should be recommended to the General Inspector and Captain Forbes to treat with the tenants upon the said estate in order to concert a proper plan for letting leases for the space of 19 years of such farms as have been valued by Mr May but not under the rents specified in the valuation, and that the Inspector and factor should be ordered to go north immediately and treat with the tenants and report to the Board in June next how far they shall have then proceeded.

A plan by the said Peter May with regard to some particular clauses which he is humbly of opinion ought to be inserted in the intended leases in which he has left some blanks to be filled up by the direction of the Commissioners, being read,

The Committee were of opinion that Mr May should fill up these blanks, and that the said plan should be laid before the Board on Monday next for their consideration.

The Committee in looking over the said valuation having observed that the highland parts of the estate of Lovat are not included, they were of opinion, that Mr May should go on to fill up the same from the rough drafts in his possession and that he should thereafter proceed to make out plans of each particular farm for the use of the factor, but not in so nice a manner as the one now laid before the Board.

The Committee were of opinion that it should be recommended to Mr Oliphant and Mr Clerk to examine the articles of Mr May's account and to report their opinion thereupon to the Board.[1]

[1] An account by Peter May for £80 10s. 10d. for surveying 68,990 acres of the estate of Lovat was discharged on 4 Nov. 1767, *see* A. H. Millar *Forfeited Estates Papers*, Scottish History Society, Edinburgh, 1909, pp. 71–72.

Minutes ot Commissioners of Annexed Estates

SRO. E721/24, p. 14

Edinburgh, 10 March 1768

The Committee consisting of the Earl of Findlater, Mr Clerk and Mr Oliphant, having met by appointment of last Board were of opinion that Mr May should be directed to assist the Inspector General and the factor in making out a new plan of the intended feus in the village of Crieff and settling the division of the grounds there, and to have the same ready to be laid before the Board in June next.

Minutes of Commissioners of Annexed Estates

SRO. E721/18, pp. 19-21

Edinburgh, 14 March 1768

A precept, payable to Peter May, land surveyor, for £113 2s. being the amount of his account for making estimates and plans of the different farms on the estate of Lovat, and Mr Clerk and Mr Oliphant having reported that the articles in said account were moderately stated, the said precept was read, and signed by a quorum of the Commissioners. . . .

A petition of John Fraser of Dalchapple in the barony of Stratherrick being read, setting forth that there is a loch called the Loch of Knockie upwards of a mile in length partly surrounded by the estate of Lovat and partly by the property of the petitioner, that this loch appears in most places not very deep and the bottom rich and muddy, that by a declivity at the end it may very easily be drained, the expense whereof the petitioner is of opinion will not exceed £20, the proportion whereof belonging to the estate of Lovat he hopes the Honourable Board will give orders to their factor to pay. And Mr May, land surveyor, having reported that he had viewed the said loch and is of opinion the draining thereof will prove beneficial to the estate of Lovat and that he thinks £20 will be sufficient for that purpose, that the ground of the Estate of Lovat will surround about two thirds of the loch and that of the petitioner about one third, *Ordered:* That a copy of the above petition and report be transmitted to the factor and that he do contribute two-thirds of the

£20 proposed for draining the said loch on behalf of the Board in case he sees no material objection. . . .

A report by the General Inspector and the factor on Lovat being read, setting forth that it is necessary they should have a copy of Mr May's estimate and observations on the several farms of said estate for settling with the tenants, *Ordered:* That a copy thereof be accordingly made out for the above purpose, and that the Secretary do employ such additional hands to assist the clerks in making out the same as he shall judge necessary for the quick dispatch thereof.

Peter May to Alexander Taylor SRO. GD248/350/5

Belmont Castle, 27 March 1768

Some posts ago I had a letter from Mrs May advising that Mr Grant agreed to our proposals, at which I am extremely well pleased. I can assure you he is a man who has few equals and I hope you will find that satisfaction in serving him which your diligence and integrity will deserve. I believe I shall have some share in advising him about the distribution of his lands, and I shall be extremely ready at all times to give you any assistance in my power. It will give me pleasure that your operations be conducted according to our uniform practice of carrying on your business with the greatest accuracy.

Our plans and observations about the Annexed Estates got much commendation from the Board. I shall want plans of the several farms drawn out in single sheets, but you need be at little more pains than in our ordinary rude draughts; as they are only to be given to the factor, they will need the less decoration. You will advert that they are to be made out to the same scale with the rude drafts, and when one, two or more farms can be put upon the same sheet, be sure to let it be done; some lines of the contiguous farms will always be described to shew how they lie, and it will be necessary to leave room on every sheet for their contents and measures, in the same way we did with the plans of Rothes, and also room for our observations, and therefore altho' there should be put one farm upon a sheet, when it is large, never crowd them so full so as not to leave space enough for their measures and observations.

The best way for copying them over will be to square the rude drafts in the same way Thomas Milne did his; but in order to do it with the greater accuracy, it would be right to subdivide your squares into half inches, at least where the fields are small. You may square and make out the sheet maps from the plans of Kilmorack and Kiltarlity already made out, and not from the rude draughts, as the measures will correspond with those wrote out in the books sent up to the Board. The course of the ridges and the pasture ground must be sketched in very quickly, for there is no occasion for ornament. The designations of them may be delayed until I come home. The names of the several fields may be wrote down with a kind of print characters, either upright or lying aslant as will make the greatest dispatch, but I must recommend it to be carried on with more than ordinary application, and desire that you will set about them immediately on receipt of this, as they must all be ready by the middle of April.

I am quite uncertain as yet when I can be with you as I am but yet on my way to the Lord Privy Seal's,[1] whose estates in the South Country I have to put in order in the same manner we did Rosehaugh, but I shall push on as fast as I can. I think you need not take the largest plan paper for making out these sheet maps. Sandy tells me that Mr Angus has a large kind of paper which he bought at 1½d. the sheet. I would have you get a couple of quires of it, and make out your plans of that size. You need not comprehend or take in much of the hill pasture on the sheet maps; the general plans will be sufficient to shew that.

PS. Communicate the contents of this letter to George, to whom I have also wrote and directed him to do the same to you.

Since writing the above, I had a short line from you, advising of the progress you had made since my departure, of which I can form but little judgement, further than to believe that you have given the application I expect. Attend to what I have here wrote you. Adieu.

[1] James Stuart Mackenzie's seat at Belmont Castle, Meigle parish, Perthshire.

Alexander Taylor to Peter May[1] SRO, GD248/350/5

Aberdeen, 9 April 1768

I had your favours under Mrs May's cover dated the 27th March, directing us to make out sheet maps of the plans of Kilmorack and Kiltarlity and to begin them directly upon receipt of your letter, but as I was just in the middle of one of the sheets of Strathspey Mrs May thought it better to finish that as long as it was in hand; therefore I only began to the plan of Kiltarlity Monday last, and have done 5 sheets, which I think will be about the one-half of it. The rest I expect will be done by Saturday next. We commonly or at an average finish a sheet each day. Mr Angus's paper you spoke of was got and draws very well, but as it is of a small size there will be needed the more sheets of it. We are giving every sheet a scale and compass as we are going along, but the designation and contents are reserved till you return. We are also putting as much of the corn lands upon every sheet as it will contain leaving room for the contents and observations according to your orders. If you do not expect to be home on or before Saturday next you will please advise us in your next whether Kirkhill is to be done next or not.

Thomas Milne left us on Tuesday last just as the sheets of Strathspey were finished. It is spread over upon four and a half sheets but as there are some of them with a good deal of empty room we thought advisable not to join them together till you should see them and examine them, in case you should think it proper to fill up the empty places afterwards or annexe more sheets to it. There would be the less danger for breaking singly than if they had all been joined together.

There is nothing induces me so much to think myself happy at going to serve Mr Grant as having it in my power to get advice and directions from you (and that without ridicule), which I certainly must often stand in need of, and which I think is but the least of my duty to obey when you are so good to give me to understand that you will take that trouble. I believe Mr Grant's theodolite is not in good order. If you think proper, I shall write Mr Forbes to be helped mend it here.

[1] This is apparently a draft letter and is unsigned. It is on the back of part of a letter from Peter May to Alexander Taylor of 3 Nov. 1766.

Peter May to James Grant, younger of Grant

SRO. GD248/250

Aberdeen, 9 May 1768

I came north only a few days ago and had the pleasure to hear that Mrs Grant and you had been at Aberdeen at the election. Tho' my wife has not had the honour of Mrs Grant's acquaintance, yet she would have waited of her and thanked her for the respect I always met with at Castle Grant, but you were left the town before she knew of your being at all in it.

My being so long from home this spring has put it out of my power to attend to some of your nursery commissions with that care I would have otherwise done, for which I beg your forgiveness. The nursery I had of Scots firs were not near so numerous as I imagined which made me fall short in some of my engagements, but all these deficiences shall be fully made up next autumn.

Alex. Taylor who I had engaged for your surveyor has been bad of a fever for a couple of weeks and still continues. Doctor Livingston attends him and says that his recovery will be slow and tedious so that I cannot say when he will be able to set out for Strathspey.

Margaret Mackenzie will soon be ready and Mrs May will take care to give her the best advice she can and write along with her mentioning the way she should proceed to teach the children, which she thinks should be to continue sometime at one place until her scholars are become acquainted with the method.

On my way north I was recommended to my Lord Kinnoull by my Lord Findlater. I stayed some days at Dupplin [Castle] and was made happy in the good company of a great man. His Lordship was remarkably entertaining and we travelled sometimes through church and state and now and then made an excursion even the length of Strathspey, which he promises to visit next summer and I have undertaken to be his travelling governor. He is extremely anxious about you and your country affairs and was much pleased at the accounts I gave him of it. Everybody about Dupplin is discreet, wears a cheerful countenance and imitates their noble and indulgent master.

My next stage was Belmont Castle, the country seat of Lord Privy Seal, where I made a pretty long sederunt. His Lordship and

Mr Menzies applied to my Lord Findlater that I should survey his estates in Perth and Angus, and I was nailed down to make it out on my way north. I was at pains to do it as well as I could and was lucky enough to get his Lordship's approbation. He has a very fine estate but not at all well managed. He has two Prime Ministers who draw different ways and, to be revenged of one another, they sacrifice the landlord's interest.

If I did not pretend to be busy all the year over I should say I were more than ordinary so at present. I have sundry things to wind up at Aberdeen and I must soon move to a more northern latitude. I think of making an excursion to Elgin about the end of this week to give directions about the mosses of Birnie and some other things that must be put in order. I believe I shall be there for some days, and if you are at Moy will be extremely happy to wait of you and the good family there. Mrs May says there was a box of candles sent by a salmon smack to Findhorn directed to Baillie Grant's care. She hopes they come safe to hand. The candlemaker wants much to be advised about them. . . .

PS. I had almost forgot to inform you that I dined with Lord Kames at Aberdeen, who is very anxious about Strathspey. We had a long conversation about it and he has suggested some useful things. He recommends to push on industry slowly rather than rapidly; the success is more certain and the expense much less.

Peter May to James Grant, clerk at Castle Grant

SRO. GD248/524/1

Aberdeen, 15 June 1768

I had your favours some days ago wanting advice about the division of the yard of Achrosk. I wish I may be able to advise you right at this distance of time. I think the yard is divided into three equal parts, one of which was to be given to Colquhoun, but which of these parts I am not able to recollect. But there can be no great difficulty in settling that: I think Colquhoun reasonable and will take any third share that can be given him without inconvenience. At present I can think of no other way of settling it unless it was to make the division of the yard in proportion to his rent, but I certainly think that a third part of the yard was meant to be given Colquhoun. I shall be in Strathspey soon and if there should be a difficulty about that or anything else then I will be able to advise you much better when I am on the spot.

Peter May to James Ross, Cullen House SRO. GD248/978/5

Elgin, 11 July 1768

This will be delivered you by Robert Thomason who comes to treat about Dykeside. I have given him a rental of it containing Mr King's and his subtenants' rents. He makes objections to the victual oats being paid at 5 firlots to the boll, which I told him my Lord insisted for. If he does not agree about Dykeside he wants to have a tack on Glassgreen, otherwise he says he will look out for another place. I am told that his circumstances are good and I wish he may make such an offer for Dykeside as can be accepted of. I think he likes it better that Glassgreen, and I have been at pains to point it out as a very good corn farm, which in my opinion it really is. I have neither the rude draught nor the measures of Newmiln's lands so that I cannot make out an estimate rent, but from some notes that I had made when I was here last (a copy whereof is subjoined) I think the rent high. Instead of loads of peat you will advert that leets of peats is a much better way of paying them. Some fallowing and sown down ground with grass seeds will be necessary covenants in the tack.

Saturday last I went through the mosses and Hills of Birnie which fatigued me abundantly. My Lord Findlater's own tenants have obeyed and kept to the moss-grieve's instructions,[1] but the Pittendreich tenantry have not. They go on in the old way to cast where they please and they say that they were ordered to cast peats and turf in the manner they have wont to do. I have written to Mr Russell, their factor, a copy whereof is here enclosed which I hope will have some good effect. He is a sensible man and I am persuaded will not countenance their doing anything to abuse the mosses or hills. When I get his answer I shall communicate it.

[1] A minor estate official appointed to regulate the cutting of mosses for peat.

Tomorrow I propose taking a survey of the Hills of Rothes. I know that will be the business of some days. If the weather continues dry I shall keep pretty close to it until it be finished.

Since writing the above the inclosed petition from the tenants of Bishopmill was brought me. They say they applied to Mr Grant formerly and gave him a petition to be forwarded to the same purpose. If my Lord thought it right to accommodate them with some moss it would be of some consequence to the poor bodies. Even allowing them to pull some loads of heather would accommodate them much in the harvest time, but I have given no latitude until I get His Lordship's instructions. I beg to hear how Lord Deskford holds out. I hope he is now a good deal mended.

Rent of Dykeside as possessed by Mr King and his subtenants, viz.

Money rent £124 13s. 4d. Scots, in sterling	£10	7	9¼
Victual 54¼ bolls at 10s.	£27	2	6
4 reapers in harvest and 4 spades in the moss, 6d. each		4	0
Custom wedder[1]		4	0
6 custom hens and 4 reik hens		3	4
4 loads of peat at 4d. each load		1	4
	£38	2s.	11¼d.

	ac:r:fall				
Dykeside contains of better land	30:2:29	at 13s. 4d. per acre	£20	9	0
Do. of worse land	26:1:36	8s.	£10	11	10
Do. of new land	18:3:32	4s. 6d.	£4	5	2
Do. of pasture ground	22:0:13	1s. 8d.	£1	16	10
			£37	2s.	10d.

NB. The above estimates made out from J. Burges's character of the lands and not from my own inspection. The present rent of Dykeside brings the arable and pasture together to very near 8s. per acre overhead.

[1] A male sheep.

Peter May to James Russell, factor for the barony of Pittendreich[1]

SRO. GD248/978/5

Elgin, 11 July 1768

The concern I have with my Lord Findlater's country affairs in Moray I hope will be an apology for the subject of this letter. I came to Elgin a few days ago and was told by my Lord Findlater's moss-grieve that the tenantry of the barony of Pittendreich under your collection were casting at the mosses and moors of Birnie in an abusive manner, and would not take the moss-grieve's direction, alleging that they were ordered to cast where they had a mind and in any manner they pleased. I am not ready to believe every report and in order to judge the better of what was said I went to these mosses and muirs on Saturday last, when I was soon convinced that my information was too well founded. They go over the mosses and break them up in holes and pits here and there, and change their places every day they cast by which both the bank and lair is much abused and more of the moss wasted than they carry away for peat.

The casting of such large quantities of turf on the hills and pasture is attended with great inconveniences. I need not inform you that it destroys the pasture, and that the remains of these cast places seldom gathers a sward, but blows with the wind and hurts all the neighbouring grounds about them, which is precisely the case with the hills I am pointing out. Whatever right the barony may have for fuel on the mosses of Birnie, I am persuaded you will readily agree does not infer an injudicious method of wasting both the hills and mosses in the manner they are presently going on. I have hired a moss-grieve to my Lord Findlater to whom I have given instructions and pointed out the several mosses where they are to cast. That the bank and lair is to be carried on regularly and none of the mosses abused. That everybody shall get a sufficient quantity for their own firing only, and none of the mosses to be holed or pitted, but carried on in a breast. But the moss-grieve's attendance to my Lord Findlater's tenants will answer little purpose if yours are allowed to hole the mosses and cast up the hills and muirs as they please. I beg you will give the proper directions to prevent further complaints

[1] Belonging to Colonel John Stewart for whom James Russell acted as factor. James Russell resided at Earlsmill and was chamberlain to the Earl of Moray.

which shall never be made by me but where I cannot possibly avoid it. . . .

James Russell to Peter May SRO. GD248/978/5

Earlsmill, 15 July 1768

I am just now with your favour of the 11th inst. respecting the Birnie affair. For answer I've been always taught to believe that the tenants of Pittendreich have an unquestionable right to cast as many peats and turfs in the mosses and moors of Birnie as is necessary for their own firing, and I never heard of any complaint against them on this head till now. But if any of them have been so indiscreet of late as to use this right in an abusive or injudicious manner, I promise you they had no orders for so doing from their master or me, and as a proof of this I shall not only rebuke them smartly for what's past, but most readily join with you in such means as shall be thought necessary to prevent the like abuses in time to come, for I know nobody has better reason to attend to this matter than the proprietor of Pittendreich, as in the event of a division of the mosses and moors I apprehend a pretty large share of them would fall to his part.

Peter May to James Ross, Cullen House SRO. GD248/978/5

Elgin, 15 July 1768

I had your favour last night by express covering the rude draft with the measures of Bishopmill, and the contents of Linkwood; a sketch of the march between Birnie and Coxton; a sketch of Hugh Todd's farm; my Lord's memorandum and the letters of Doctor Brodie and Mr Burnet. The letters were delivered last night and the sketch of Mr Todd's farm shall be sent him today. The tenants of Bishopmill shall be acquainted with my Lord Findlater's answer to their petition about fire.

Tuesday last I perambulated the hills betwixt Rothes and Coxton and had some guides with me particularly George Davidson in Shainbuckie, Archd. Simpson in the Netherglen, John Thomson in Auchinroath with some others who pointed out many places of different names which are not marked in the first survey. As some of these places lie at a distance and close by the cornlands of my Lord Fife's Teindlands, a perambulation of them will not do. To obey the instructions contained in my Lord Findlater's memorandum will require a very particular mensuration. I am directed 'to describe and distinguish the nature, qualities and extent of the different parts' which cannot be done with accuracy but by a new survey of the whole hills in controversy. In case it should make a noise that I am measuring about my Lord Fife's Teindlands, I should like to have some advice. Lord Fife was already provoked with my first survey, a second may irritate his lordship more. I have no sort of difficulty in executing the survey except to avoid making the difference grow wider by giving my Lord Fife a new handle for complaint which he may trump up from extending the survey on his lands. You know this is a kind of business which cannot be done privately as I must have guides and assistants to carry on the survey.

Peter May to James Ross, Cullen House SRO. GD248/978/5

Elgin, 15 July 1768

I wrote just immediately by your express. The tenants of Glassgreen took the alarm at Robert Thomason's coming to Cullen and applied [to] me to write along with them. I went over Glassgreen yesterday and the rude draught in my hand and valued the whole farm which according to my notes is worth £34 Stg. That part of Muiry Tack [Muirton] is not convenient for Glassgreen; it lies at a distance from them and is runridged with other people. James Smith who is Robert Thomason's neighbour is against having the town divided and I believe has prevailed upon [Robert Anderson of] Linkwood to write that this town is already in proper divisions, but that is by no means the case for in some fields they are run-ridged. The march burn with Little Glassgreen will be much the better of being straightened whereby some lands will probably be taken from Meikle Glassgreen. It will be right to have these things in view. There is a worn-out moss on the bounds of Glassgreen, which is capable of improving. The tenants might be taken bound to drain it according to direction and to cover the mossy parts with sand. Alexr. Skene's possession is also cheap rentalled. The piece of new ground for which the enclosed petition is given is more convenient for him than anybody else. This offer is made according to my advice and I truly think it higher than a poor man would give to set down upon it. John and James Anderson made an offer for it to Mr Grant which is here transmitted to you also. Skene should be obliged to improve half an acre of his new ground yearly. James Burges can point out to you where it lies, as he was with me when the offer was made. Alex. Skene's other part wants draining [and] some engagements to that purpose should be made with him.

When I left Elgin I gave the moss-grieve orders to cause cast for me three hundred loads of peats and to tell the tenants that I would pay them for casting and leading in the same manner that Mr Duff paid to Lord Fife's tenants. They it seems were not pleased with such a bargain and with difficulty the moss-grieve has got about a hundred loads cast and which, by the by, are lying in a gutter and in a worse state than the day they were cast. I have no precedent how to behave. I thought putting them on the footing with Lord Fife's people was the safest way for both the tenants and me, but as that will not do I am at a loss how to proceed and beg to get advice. Mr Duff got six score of loads yearly; Lesmurdie three score and Mr Rose's mother the like quantity for which they pay a penny for casting and winning each load and meat and drink to the people when leading them to Elgin. Mrs May paid half a crown yesterday for four loads that were not worth a shilling altogether. I hope my Lord Findlater will give such orders as he thinks necessary about getting peats, which at any date will be ill to be had in this wet season.

Dorso: After closing my letter Alexr. Rhind gardener at Tyockside came in and goes along with the rest for Cullen. I am not able to give you the proper information about his croft but from the first survey I made of the lands along with James Burges I thought it dear. Enclosing is the best improvement that could be made on this place and as there are no stones it should be done with a hedge. The march on that side next the Stonecrosshill to be straightened. An acre of it at least to be turned into a garden to be surrounded with a hedge and the trees or bushes standing in the garden to remain and pertain to Lord Findlater at the issue of his lease.

Peter May to James Ross, Cullen House SRO. GD248/978/5

Elgin, 18 July 1768

I had yours on Saturday by the tenants of Glassgreen. I am well pleased I misunderstood my Lord Findlater's meaning about the Hills of Rothes. Your explanation of it will make it much easier, and you may acquaint my Lord that I will execute it as well as I can and for that purpose I set out tomorrow morning.

I am just come from a perambulation of the mosses and moors of Birnie, where I discovered some abuses by my Lord Findlater's tenants which the moss-grieve said he could not help. I sent immediately for the offenders and stayed on the spot until they came when I set them to work to put their banks and lair in order, and threatened to send their names to the sheriff for refusing to obey the moss-grieve. They have promised to behave better afterwards and I hope will do so.

I had Hugh Todd in Myreside with me who pointed out a piece of new ground where he wants to set down a servant for herding his sheep and casting his fire according to a proposal presented to my Lord when he was in Elgin. John McPherson in Bodingair wants the same place and so does Sueton Anderson who lives upon a part of it. The ground they want lies adjoining the march of Rothes on the Birnie side and along the east side of the Burn of Bardon, but as I have no survey of the hills and moors on the east side of that burn, cannot say what will be the extent, and therefore I told them I would not transmit their offers until I had got the contents. My Lord Findlater said he was to send James Burges to measure Coneloch and Gedloch. I wish that could be done soon; along with that it would be right to have the Hills of Birnie on the east side of the Burn of Bardon measured, and such improvements marked off on the ground as will set to the best account. I would then know how to treat with the offerers, but if that cannot be done conveniently I shall measure it myself and it must be done soon.

On my way from Birnie, I had made an appointment with Captain Donald to look at the farm of Dykeside. He wants to take it and has promised to call on me soon and give his terms. I pointed out the marches and the place seems to please him. I am told he has saved money and is an economical man. When I was at Dykeside the minister of Birnie called on me and said he had wrote you about repairing the kirk, and that he had for answer that I was to get orders about it. I went and looked at it and saw it in very bad repair. The minister gave me some notes of workmen about repairing it, but they are not distinct. I have promised to cause an estimate of the expense be made out in a better way. There was left in the house this day the enclosed note of the expense of the kirk and manse of New Spynie with the heritors' several proportions. As I was away from home, the man who left it (which I suppose was the tradesman) promised to call again in a day or two. But as I have neither instructions nor a shilling of money in my hands cannot give him a satisfactory answer. Shall I send workmen to inspect the Kirk of Birnie and get an estimate of the expense which I suppose will not exceed from £25 to £30 Stg.

As I cannot get authority for my peats or be put upon the same footing of my Lord Fife's factor, I have resolved to buy coals for this year rather than have the least interfering with the tenants.

Peter May to James Ross, Cullen House SRO. GD248/978/5

Elgin, 19 July 1768

James Milne at Mill of Boyndie has just now delivered me a packet containing the rude draught of Eastertown and a draft of Rashcrook, a draft of Dykeside and Castlehill, with a sketch of Tomshill and a letter to Captain Fraser which I sent to him. I kept James Milne and carried him over to Bishopmill and showed him the farms of that estate and of Linksfield with the Whinhill where the marl lies. James likes the marl but not the land. When I was there the tenants came prying for a few loads of peats. I really pity the poor bodies, they have not a clod nor can they get them to buy. A few cartloads would have served them all. I shall advise you as soon as I return from Rothes.

Peter May to James Ross, Cullen House SRO. GD248/978/5

Elgin, 29 July 1768

I was from home on Sunday when James Burges came here. I had gone to Rothes the Friday before and lodged at Burncrook when I was surveying the Hills of Rothes from which I only returned

Tuesday evening. I think I understand the situation of these hills perfectly and have got a pretty full information, but have not got it put in such order as to send you. I was yesterday at Birnie with James Burges and consulted with him what things are proper to be done there. I have got from Mr Grant £12 Stg. for which I have given receipt. I have not yet been able to wait on Provost Robertson to enquire about what he intends to do with the repairs of the kirk that fell due before Whitsunday. I suppose he will avoid it if he can. My Lord Fife was in the Hills of Rothes on Saturday last on his way from Balvenie to Innes [House]. There was nobody with him but Mr Rose.[1] They called on one of the tenants of Barluack and carried them along. His Lordship was expected in the hills on Monday and I kept on the hills that day on purpose to have fallen in with him, but he did not come. I fell in with Mr Archibald Duff at Burnworks and asked him to go to the hills and show me what they called their march, but he declined it and said he had no authority. But I think I have learnt what they claim. David Shioch in the Tiendlands has a brother called Robert who lives in Keith and knows something about the manner of pasturing and casting peats in these hills. I think you might send for him. I have some other people in view. Captain Donald has not yet given me in any proposal about Dykeside. Dr Brodie has not been in Elgin these eight days; he had been in the west country. Sir Ludovick and family is gone south. Yesternight Mr Ogilvie called on me and he with his friend Mr Grant breakfasted here this day. Mr Grant wants some lots of Burrowbrigs. I promised to shew him them all and he might give in his proposals. Mr Russell, Earlsmill, came to Elgin last night and appointed me to meet him today to look over Birnie, and as I am just setting out you will excuse me from further information.

Minutes of Commissioners of Annexed Estates

SRO. E721/24, pp. 40-41

Edinburgh, 1 August 1768

A report by Mr Keir, the factor, and William Keir and Peter May,

[1] William Rose (1740-1807) appointed factor for James, 2nd Earl Fife's estates in parishes of Banff, Alvah and Gamrie on 8 Dec. 1764. His correspondance with the Earl was published by A. and H. Taylor (eds), *Lord Fife and his factor*, London, 1952.

land surveyors, with respect to the proposed feuing out and extending the village of Crieff, being read as follows, viz.

That for the accommodation of the Inhabitants, feus should be laid off on each side of the highway leading from Crieff to Stirling consisting of 30 yards in front and 60 backwards from the street, amounting to 1 rood 10 falls, with a passage 12 feet wide betwixt every two feus for giving access to their several lots according as they shall be divided and laid out afterwards; that the present highway is only 24 feet broad, but in regard it will become the principal street it ought to be made at least 40 feet broad and that by keeping the front of the houses eight feet from the said highway on each side; that another street is projected leading in a direct line across the north east end of No. 37; and from that northwestward to No. 72, of 30 feet, the feus to be laid off on each side of this street 30 ells in front and 40 ells backwards, consisting of 33 falls each; but if in laying out the divisions on the ground there should be a fraction of a few ells then that should be divided equally among the different tenements. Another street is proposed of 30 feet wide leading across the Numbers 39, 48, 47, 46, and 45, and as this intended street crosses the highway upon a rising ground it would be some ornament if the street was enlarged 80 feet wide for the breadth of two feus so as to form a kind of square, but as this is merely for ornament it is submitted to the Board whether it is necessary or not. That as many of the inhabitants are but indifferently accommodated with gardens it would be proper to cut off a skirt from the end of No. 96 from the little park and croft to be divided into small gardens; it would be of consequence to the feuars or other possessors of Crieff to have their lands divided into small lots consisting of two or three acres, particularly these lands lying next the town, the other fields lying at a distance may be laid out in larger lots and it would add considerably to the value of them if they were inclosed. That it would be of great consequence to the feuars to have each an acre or two for growing a little straw to enable them to keep their cows through the winter, and the proper ground for this purpose would be the outfield of Milnabb, which consists of about 17 acres and lies very convenient for them, being just below the village, and the access to it may be made very easy and convenient by widening the lane leading from the corner of the intended feu marked in the plan

No. 27 and cutting off a corner of Mrs Thomson's inclosure marked No. 74 and 75. And as the villagers have not near cattle sufficient to stock the parks of Culcrieff but are obliged to take in horses and cattle from the tenants and neighbouring heritors, one of those parks might be given to John Caw in lieu of the ground taken from him for the feuars.

The Board approved of the proposals contained in the above report and direct the factor to take care that the cross line from No. 37 to No. 72 be first feued.

Peter May to James Ross, Cullen House SRO. GD248/978/5

Elgin, 3 August 1768

I wrote you the other day by Mr Ogilvie and mentioned my going out with Mr Russell to concert about the regulations of the mosses in Birnie, but he is tender and asthmatic and was not able to go through the hills and they were so wet that they would not ride. He gave orders to William Donaldson in Manbeen to go along with me and set by a moss for the accommodation of the Pittendreich tenantry and that they should be put under the same regulations with the Birnie people for the preservation of it, but he would not agree that their moss should be set apart by my Lord Findlater's orders, except in concert with somebody for Colonel Stewart [of Pittendreich]. As the season of casting for this year is now over, I declined taking any steps without advice as I was uncertain, but acting even incorrect might be a means of securing their right which I think my Lord said was doubtful. When I get any proper instructions I shall endeavour to execute them.

I think my information as to the marches betwixt Rothes and Coxton on the east side of the glen will put it beyond doubt that we have pastured considerably beyond the march pointed out by the Rothes people; I mean from the standing stone to the Wells of Moniemouies and to the Cairn of Findlay's Seat. On the other hand, they have pastured within it and cast peats but as far as I have been able to learn they have not casten peats in any of the mosses so long as to prescribe a right. I have one or two men yet to be informed about, and then I shall transmit their report to Cullen. James Smith's wife in Glassgreen acknowledges that she has seen the cattle of

Rothes pasturing to their cornlands in the Teindlands and were not interrupted if they kept out of the cornlands.

I was yesterday in Birnie along with James Burges pointing out such places in the moors as it was necessary measure. In the afternoon I had a communing with James Shaw in the Gedloch and with some of the tenants of the Netherglen about their marches with Lord Fife on the side next Findracey's lands, which according to their account is not at all favourable, and for some years bygone they have it seems kept Findracey's tenants much at bay. The landlord's own inattention made the tenants careless about their marches. I shall endeavour to get the best intelligence I can about that and also in the Cockmoor next to Rashcrook.

Captain Donald called on me the other day, and said he was to write you his proposals about Dykeside. I gave him an account of the measures and of the present rent. I understand he has been in terms with Colonel Monro about a farm in the Muirtown estate.

John Duncan goes to see his son and I suppose wants to treat about his tack. I am told he is not at all in a thriving way. I know he is drunken and inactive and the subject he has in view would need much application and a good stocking; but according to his account he considers it as already agreed on, in consequence of a proposal made my Lord sometime ago. Would it not be better to appoint tenants in Birnie who have not tacks to come to Cullen House, and I would come along with my notes ready and then their proposals would be the better judged of. They all want to run away one and one from a jealousy of one another. I have no rental of Blairnha' nor Findracey's lands. Blairnha' and Glenlatterach consists of 48 acres of arable lands exclusive of Glenchappell and the pasture ground is extensive, at least it lies near the hill. It is my opinion that it may be worth about 20 guineas and some leat peats exclusive of Glenchappell but I have not rated it particularly as I understood that he had a tack for some years, nor can I well say whether Glenchappell should be destroyed or not until I make a more accurate survey.

I had a letter some days ago from Mr Brodie enquiring if there was anybody at Cullen that could be engaged for making ploughs, large cartwheels, harrows and all implements of husbandry. He wants such a person to engage with him and would give him proper encouragement. I promised to give him an answer as soon as I heard from Cullen.

Peter May to James Ross, Cullen House SRO. GD248/978/5

Elgin, 5 August 1768

I had your favours last post. The bearer Robert Melven is a tenant in Linksfield and occupies a fourth part of that farm. He has been with me again and again importuning me to take his possession off his hand. He says if it is taken from him now that he will be able to pay his arrears and hypothec,[1] but if he is obliged to keep it longer that he will become a bankrupt. I have asked Mr Grant about him and his opinion tallies with the man's own information. I am told he was little better than a bankrupt when he came here. He brought me two people who were content to take his possession, but upon my desiring them to get somebody whom I knew to inform me of their circumstances I have heard nothing more about them, which makes be conclude that they have not been able to get themselves recommended. He has in a manner deserted his farm already and become a miller to Provost Robertson. Upon the present tenants getting a tack of Linksfield their lands were divided by Barlymen,[2] and laid pretty much together. This man complains that his part is the worst lot, but I cannot say whether it is, not from my own knowledge, and if I could I suppose it must stand as it is, as the tenants entered into a voluntary submission. I am at a loss to know what shall be done with him – my Lord will give his own directions. Wherever I am left at liberty my own plan would be never to force a tenant to stay with a farm longer than he found his account in the possession. When he becomes a bankrupt the land is but ill husbanded and loses daily in the possession of such a tenant, but I am sorry to say that all the tenants on both Bishopmill and Linksfield are almost bankrupt.

Mr Archd. Duff dined with me this day and we had a conversation about the marches betwixt Rothes and Coxton, and among other

[1] A legal security for rent or money due; the former right of a landlord to claim rent of his tenant in preference to other creditors.

[2] A local man appointed to arbitrate in local disputes and to value crops. He presided over the Birley Court which operated the Birley-by-laws. Spelt variously birlaman, birlawman, baileyman, boorlawman, burlawman, burleyman.

things about the extent of pasture. He says they can prove as clear as daylight that the cattle of the barony of Coxton pastured over all the Hills of Rothes on the eastside of the Glen and the cornlands of Dundorcas, Freefield and Colly, and that within this 20 years they were in the constant use of doing so without interruption. I have not been able to learn that from any of my information, nor do I believe it to be true whatever evidence they may get to support it. Mr Duff desired me to advise you that he had reason to believe that Lord Fife would be ready to submit all the differences whenever my Lord Findlater would agree to it.

James Burges has now done with the fieldwork of Birnie and I believe will get the bulk of his protraction brought up this week. As soon as that is done I shall have our intended settlements and marches laid off. Upon his coming here I asked him to stay with me, but he declined it, which made me imagine that my Lord had directed him to do it.

Peter May to James Ross, Cullen House SRO. GD248/978/5

Elgin, 10 August 1768

I had a note from you last post wanting four square yards of haircloth for a larder. There is no haircloth made here but for drying malt or corns, which I apprehend would not do for you. I sent for the man who makes it. He says you can get it much finer but that for so small a quantity it would not be worth his while to make graith[1] on purpose, but if it is desired I believe I can prevail on him as he looks for some aid from my Lord Findlater. Brodie the staymaker who put an application into your hands is the person who carries on the haircloth trade.

Mr Leslie Balnageith is in the mercat just now and begs his respectful compliments may be presented to my Lord Findlater. A friend of his has £100 Stg. to lend and would be very glad to have it in my Lord's hands; will ye advise about it? Mr Leslie waited of my Lord Fife lately and had a conference about the marches of Rothes. His Lordship's quarrel with me it seems has not subsided. He says

[1] The word graith in this context appears to mean 'special cloth'. Generally it covers all kinds of clothes, furniture, equipment, harness for horses, apparatus, tools, machinery, etc.

that the note about the interruption made by Blackhills is an anecdote that must be taken off. Mr Leslie says he considered the hills and mosses there to be the subject of division only betwixt him and the feuars and never thought of Lord Findlater becoming a party or having any interest in it. But I hope we will be able to convince his Lordship of its being otherwise and that the other lands of Rothes as well as the feuars have been in the constant practice of pasturing over these hills.

I had David Shioch in the Tiendlands with me this forenoon, but I could not learn much from him. I think him an honest man but he is terrified for giving offence. The information of the marches betwixt Coxton and Birnie are not very favourable as far as I have yet collected. I shall be at pains to glean all I can. Melvin in Linksfield has promised to find me caution for his arrears and hypothec; if that answers I suppose there will be no necessity for a disposition or instrument of possession but I believe it will be right to have one or either soon.

James Burges and I were in the hills yesterday laying off new settlements and will be for the rest of the week. I think to have my notes and report ready to send along with him about the marches and mosses. This is a busy day with me, and yet I cannot tell you how I am employed unless it be with the Birnie tenantry.

Peter May to James Ross, Cullen House SRO. GD248/978/5

Elgin, 14 August 1768

I wrote you Wednesday last by Mr Dee and the same afternoon had your favours by Charles Gordon covering the inventory of John McLean's houses, with a copy of Logie's interruption, and a letter to Mr Cuming which I forwarded in course. I was in Birnie every day last week except Wednesday and Friday, which were mercat days and I found it convenient to be at home. Most of the intended settlements are now laid off, and others divided in such a way as I think will be most convenient for the possessors. But there are yet several things to do that will employ some days before James Burges can get away. Since he began his protraction I have used the freedom to direct him to stay in our house so as to be under my inspection which he agreed to do with some difficulty.

Friday evening Mr William Grant called on me and complained of Mr Archibald Duff's having collected sundry tenants of Coxton on Thursday last and caused them to cast peats in the mosses of Auchinroath lying S.W. from Findlay's Seat. As I could not say anything until I heard Mr Duff I went along with Mr Grant and called on Mr Duff and we agreed to go to Baillie Leslie's and hear both sides. Mr Duff charged Mr Grant with his being the first aggressor and that what he had done was only with a view to make reprisals. About eight days ago it seems Mr Grant had directed his tenants of Auchinroath to cast peats in a moss at the head of the Burn of Auchinroath (about the place where it is marked on my plan that Lord Fife's tenants was interupted by Blackhills) which is a different moss from the place they usually cast in. Upon Mr Duff's hearing of this he went to the mosses on Thursday, last, and sundry tenants of Coxton with him, and caused them cast peats in the Moss of Auchinroath lying SW from Findlay's Seat, which is the moss of the tenants of Auchinroath presently cast in. Mr Duff alleged that Mr Grant had cast their peats in concert with me or by the advice from my Lord Findlater, to which I assured him that I knew nothing of it until that day and that I was certain my Lord Findlater did not know of it then, but that I considered what Mr Grant had done was nothing more than any of my Lord Findlater's tenants of Rothes had a title to do, as the place he had cast in was not only much within the boundaries of the estate, but precisely or very near the place where the late Blackhills had interrupted the tenants of Coxton about six years ago, of which interruption Mr Duff said he had never heard until then. I understand that Mr Duff and the tenants who were along with him perambulated the hills of Rothes down to the Burn of Sourden and he affirms that he can prove a promiscuous pasturage down to the cornlands of Speyside and a holing of fire[1] in the mosses south from Findlay's Seat by the Masons, tenants of the Teindlands, who I am told are gentlemen that can go a great length. But you know in a conjunct proof we can prove what we please. Mr Duff has assured me again and again that he wants above all things to have every dispute set in the most favourable light to the

[1] Fire = fuel, in this case peat. Fir, firr, or fire appears to be used synonymously although the SND states that fir is used mostly with special reference to fir wood, i.e. stumps dug out of peat-mosses for light or fuel.

parties concerned; but I believe he is rather keen and that my Lord Fife's tenants have been accustomed to overawe the tenants of the small conterminous heritors and to turn them in with their marches, of which I have got some instances since I came here, both in the Moss of Phewatt and also in a small patch of moss or rather a bog which lies on the east side of the Burn of Glassgreen and near the place where the marches of Linkwood, Coxton and New Miln terminate. You will see by your plan that this spot is marked within the boundings of Linkwood, but I am told that some of Lord Fife's tenants, who live next to it have been in use of casting there in common with Linkwood's and I find Linkwood acknowledges that himself. This summer and not long ago one of Lord Fife's tenants called James Shanks in Collbackhillock led some loads and destroyed others with his horses' feet, upon which the tenants of Little Glassgreen complained to me and I called on Mr Duff to see if they had any directions from him for doing so. But upon not finding Mr Duff at home I ordered the tenant of Glassgreen to lead home just as many of Shanks fire as he had done of his, but not to quarrel upon any account. There was no more of this until Sunday evening when Mr Duff told me that he had got a complaint from this same Mr Shanks upon our tenants of Glassgreen for leading away his fire from the Rotton Mossie, which it seems is the name of the bog I am pointing out, and I then told him that I had given orders for doing so with a view to make reprisals and that his tenant had been the first aggressor. Upon this we agreed to take a look at it next day which was yesterday at 10 o'clock. I kept the appointment and stayed until 11 but Mr Duff did not come up, and as I had made appointments in Birnie I could not wait any longer. This morning I sent for the tenant of Glassgreen who told me that Mr Duff did not come until three in the afternoon and that he said he would not give any directions until he met with me about the moss, but gave Shanks orders to cast close down to Alexander Skene's yard dyke where it seems the marches are not very clear. I called on Mr Duff this afternoon but was told he had gone abroad to dine with Mr Stuart his brother-in-law. Among other things I understood by Mr Duff's conversation last night that my Lord Fife had been at some pains to get him to accept of being his arbiter in case my Lord Findlater agreed to a submission, and that [Alexander Leslie of] Balnageith had been also mentioned. If a submission was to take place, which I am persuaded would be the best way of deciding it, I do not know where I could point out so good an arbiter for my Lord Findlater as Balnageith. He knows all the ground perfectly, and what has been the practice of pasturing and casting peats in the hills, and I have great reason to believe that he has my Lord Findlater's interest at heart – at least he has always expressed himself so to me. In the course of my inquiries I have found out some new names in the hills of Rothes which I intend to lay down on my draft tomorrow and to have it in view what would be an equal line of division in case it should be divided and ended by arbitration and for that purpose I set out early in the morning.

I have been endeavouring as much as I can to restrict the tenants in Birnie from selling peats, and to enforce it the more, I caused proclaim a second advertisement at the Kirk of Birnie and sent a copy of it to the ground officer at Pittendreich. But yet I see it will be attended with some difficulty, and I am persuaded there will be a necessity of making examples of the transgressors and there is just now a very good opportunity of doing it. I have an information and upon that a confession of their stealing or giving away fire under night to the people of Elgin and of their stealing and carrying it home to their own houses. What shall be done with the offenders? I wish there were a court held on the estate, I think it would strike more terror among them than the Sheriff Court here which is truly very trifling and they are much too well acquainted with it already. If I had more leisure I could inform you of the fire stealing with some very aggravating circumstances. I am tired writing and I dare not for my soul be absent from the Kirk here; Mr Rintoul[1] terrifies me and sends and enquires on Monday if I have been bad.

Peter May to James Ross, Cullen House SRO. GD248/978/5

Elgin, 19 August 1768

I had yours sent me yesterday by Mr Cuming. I hope this will answer it as James Burges brings with him the sketch of the Hills of

[1] David Rintoul (1714-78) minister of Church of Scotland, started in Dunfermline, then Kirkcaldy, transferring to Junior Charge at Elgin, 28 Sept. 1759, and became senior minister 5 Apr. 1774 (*Fasti Ecclesiae Scoticanae*, vol. 6, p. 391).

Rothes lying on the east side of the Glen, with particular places marked on according to the information I got from my guides. I purposely cut off from it the hills and pasture ground lying on the west side on account that Mr Duff made a handle of their being of such vast extent ever since he saw the plan of Rothes at Cullen. I have sent you also a pretty full information along with the plan containing all I could pick up relative to the marches with a memorandum of my own to which I refer you.

All the divisions are now made out in Birnie that can take place until the other tacks expire, and I am receiving offers from them according to the new divisions. I shall soon have the rates and estimates made out with such notes as occurs to me with respect to their tacks. I hope the new improvements will do well, if we could get some strangers transplanted to them. I wish I could say as much of the old farms.

I discovered by accident the other day that Hugh Todd in Myreside had been selling stones from the quarries from which he gets stones for his own dykes. Has he my Lord's allowance for it or should it be enquired into? If I am directed to make enquiry I wish my instructions were given as if the information had not come from me.

I had a letter from Mr Grant [of Grant] some time ago asking the favour to go to Westfield and settle with Doctor Walker about his farm. It should have been done sooner had not my Lord's affairs required my attention so much of late. A day or two will do it and I propose setting out there tomorrow as the Doctor is impatient to know what he is to do, and Mr Grant does not choose to finish with him until he gets my report. I shall expect to hear from you by Mr Grant who I understand by James Burges comes to Cullen tomorrow along with him.

PS. James Burges has made the rude draughts of his last surveys and can inform how he has been employed.

Peter May to James Grant of Grant SRO. GD248/346/5

Elgin, 21 August 1768

I wrote some posts ago begging your orders about some rubbish of small stones that lay on your garden wall next the street in Elgin to help to repair some of the avenues leading into the town. As there was no advice about it we have made a shift from other places.

I was last week at Westfield and looked at the Doctor's farm and perambulated the whole estate which I think a pretty cornfield, but as much neglected as to good husbandry as any other parts of Moray. I don't think there are plenty of moss, and yet from the freedom and manner the tenants are using it, one would be ready to conclude it inexhaustable. This is a practice that I think ought to be corrected as early as you can and I wish you would think of giving some instructions about it.

I heard the doctor's proposals: he wants an extensive farm – two or three other possessions added to his own for which he is content to give 14s. per acre for the arable lands and 10s. for the grass grounds of his own farm and two of the rest and £1 Stg. of additional rent on another. He showed me a kind of measures of his own farm, but whether that can be depended on or not the doctor does not pretend to say. The measures of the rest he says he knows nothing about. I cannot pretend to judge of the value of land without knowing the measures nor whether these farms the doctor wants would be convenient appendices to his own farm until I see first how they lie. I have no rental of any part of the lands, I must therefore beg you will cause transmit to me a rental of them as soon as you can. I could judge by it of the doctor's proposals as to his own farm, at least if the measures he counts on be right which I suppose they are or the doctor would not trust to them himself. Any regulations that occur to me as to the good management of your lands I shall mark down for your perusal but nothing can be done until you send me the rental and even then the new acquisitions the doctor wants cannot be easily ascertained until a survey of the grounds are made out that we may see their connection with one another.

Private memorandum from Peter May concerning the hills between Rothes and Coxton SRO. GD248/4395

August 1768

There is along with this a sketch of the hills and moors lying on the east side of the Glen of Rothes and between that and the barony of Coxton with the interjected mosses laid down as nearly in their local places and to their full extent as could be done without an actual survey of each particular place.

The towns and cornlands of Coxton are laid down from eye draughts. The Teindlands are about their proper place, but it is believed that the other towns lie at a greater distance from the hill than they are sketched out on the draught, which was only meant to show them as towns of Coxton lying next to the hill, but the towns of Rothes are all laid down in their local places, and at their proper distances according to the first survey. The appearance of the lands of Rothes, particularly the towns on Speyside lying farther from the hill than those of Coxton, may impress Lord Fife that they have a much greater proportion of hill than his lands of Coxton have, which is believed will turn out otherwise upon an actual survey.

The line claimed by the Earl of Findlater as the marches of property for the Lordship of Rothes, on the east side next Coxton, is laid down accurately according to the first survey and shaded green on the sketch. But the line for the barony of Coxton, according to the Earl of Fife and according to the best information that could be got, is only laid down from the known objects that were formerly surveyed, viz. from Findlay's Seat in a straight line to a cairn on the summit of Whities Hill and at the southend thereof above Barluack, and from this cairn along the ridge of the hills to the Sharping Stone. This line is also laid down on the draught and shaded yellow.

Between these two lines is the subject of controversy containing about 720 acres with the greatest part of the mosses and the most valuable part of the pasture. But there has been a promiscuous pasturing beyond these lines particularly by the Rothes side as appears by the information and it is believed that the Coxton people will also prove a promiscuous pasturing beyond what they call their line.

It will appear by the information that the cattle belonging to the feuars and tenants of Rothes have been, and still are, in the constant use of pasturing over these hills and moors as far as the old cornlands of the Teindlands, and northward from it on the face of the hills, looking down on the lands of Coxton, particularly about the Urnrigh and Sutherland Burns, and in the Park of Blackhills; and that their common pasture has been in the Firsaughs, the Chewgreen, the Greencove and about the Saughen Burn and often in the Rushiebawdes and the Cowshealling Burn. And that they have holed and taken fire from the mosses where there was any fire to be got, and in the constant use of doing so. All these acts of property are condescended on and can be proven by evidence of the very best character.

When Lord Fife was restricting his tenants from selling peats to Elgin and other parts of the low country, which happened about 10 or 12 years ago, the late Blackhills, as heritor of Barluack and Achinrothes of Rothes, did then order his tenants of Blackhills to come to the mosses at the head of the Burn of Auchinroath which lay within his boundings of property and to cast peats for selling; and upon hearing that the Masons, tenants of the Teindlands, had also gone there to cast peats, the said Blackhills went with his tenants in Barluack and ordered them to lead home to their houses of Barluack some loads of these peats which was accordingly done in presence of the said Blackhills.

That when the tenants of the low country came to pull heather in the Hills of Rothes lying on the east side of the glen, the late Blackhills gave orders to his tenants of Barluack to poind them when they came over to the fir saughs or about the Nibbed stone of Barluack, which he said was his marches of property for Barluack, and in consequence of that order, the tenants of Barluack did poind them when they found them pulling heather in the fir saughs or about the Nibbed stone, except they had leave from Blackhills which it seems Linkwood and some others had.

That 3 years ago Thomas Craig, tenant of Lhanbryde in the barony of Coxton, did cause a mason go to the Hills of Rothes and dress a stone for a milnstone lying within the marches of Barluack and well known by the name of the Nibbed stone. The said Blackhills gave orders that it should be broke, which was accordingly done and it lies yet in the same place.

On the other hand it is allowed that the cattle belonging to the tenants of Coxton lying next to the hills pastured over them and towards the Rothes side as far as the summit or top of Whities Hill, and now and then southward to the fir saughs, and their sheep might have gone further as well as the sheep of Rothes, for they lay in the hills and pastured in common for the summer season.

When the Teindland Moss was almost wore out which was about

16 or 18 years ago, then the moss of the Welleyes was begun to by the tenants of Coxton, and they have been casting there ever since. The moss at the end of the hard stack was broke up only about 7 or 8 years ago. The northwest end of the hard stack about 30 years ago. The Sheephillock Moss by the Frasers in Millbuies about 8 years ago. The information both as to pasture and casting in the several mosses was got chiefly from the tenants of Rothes.

About 7 or 8 years ago the tenants of the Netherglen of Rothes had built a sheep cot at or near the head of the Red Burn above their cornlands and had laboured a patch there. Lesmurdie was then factor to Lord Fife and caused tear down the cot and eat the corns that were sown. This is made a strong handle of by the other side, and it was from them that Mr May first heard of it, but finds it acknowledged by the tenants of the Netherglen. The place where the interruption was made is marked thus X on the plan. This year they have again sown corns and have not as yet been interrupted.

If the ground included between the lines claimed by Lord Findlater and the other by Lord Fife comprehended the whole subject in dispute, and that the division did not respect the valued rents on either side, then the division would be the more easily made. A straight line running from Curmulion alias the little Hunt Hill to the Sharping Stone above the Netherglen would be a good line for Rothes, although it would give more of the surface to Coxton, yet that would be made up by the pasture and moss which would fall to the Rothes side.

It is to be wished that the Earls themselves might confine their difference to the lines laid down on the sketch, and that would be much better done at Cullen than in this country. Lord Fife had the line he claims pointed out to him by Mr Rose when he was on the ground this summer. Mr Duff wants now to shift that line and have the whole hills from cornland to cornland turned into common and become the subject of a division.[1] Mr Duff had all the tenants of

[1] This contentious area, the commonty of Blackhills and Coxtown, consisting of 4,112 acres, lay to the south of Lhanbryde village rising to the high moorland at Brown Muir. Considerable controversy developed over the question whether Blackhills was a commonty or not. The Earl Fife, in 1803, claimed the lands as his exclusive property, but he was opposed by Lauchlan Cumming of Blackhills who

[*Footnote continued overleaf*

Coxton in Elgin a few days ago examining what they knew about the marches and other acts of possession. There is one David Shioch, an old man who has lived long on the Teindlands, but was not able to inform them distinctly of what they wanted, or thought necessary to prove and was on that account soon dismissed. Mr May on his way from Birnie, fell in with Shioch as he was going from Elgin, but could not pick up any materials from him. He was timid to say anything, but in the event of a proof it is believed his evidence will not hurt Lord Findlater. But there are two tenants called Masons who also dwell in the Teindlands and one Campbell, a tenant in Coleburn, who are said to be very liberal in their declarations. The Masons have always made a trade of selling peats, and Mr Duff says that he can prove by them, their having holed fire in the Mosses of Dundorcas and in the other mosses where they pleased without interruption.

Mr Dunbar of Thunderton and Mr George Duff, brother to Lord Fife, get their peats from the moss in dispute, and being authorised to do so by my Lord, or his factor, as an encroachment, and of such a kind as ought to be interrupted. Mr Dunbar got peats for some years before this in these mosses, but as he required a large quantity he was entirely prohibited, and did not get any peats from them until this or the last year. Mr George Duff has only got for two years also.

The house built by Lord Fife this summer and presently possessed by Andrew Taylor is set down in the fir saughs a considerable way beyond; that is southward of what the late Blackhills counted to be his marches of property for his lands of Barluack, and very near the line Lord Fife claims as his march running from Whities Hill to

contended it was commonty (SRO. CS 271/48113). To illustrate Cumming's case he produced a rough sketch of the controverted ground (SRO. RHP559). At the same time, however, all the parties involved in the dispute continued to make considerable encroachments on Blackhills, and the Earl Fife even went as far as building a cottage in a remote part of the muir in order to keep an eye on his opponents. Another plan of the commonty was made by George Brown in 1808, which showed all the intakes and improvements within its boundaries (SRO. RHP46, 858, and 1683). This plan was made for the process of division of commonty between James, 4th Earl Fife and Lauchlan Cumming of Blackhills. The commonty was finally divided around 1830. Immediately after division large tracts of it were tenanted and brought into cultivation, even though the western part of it was almost inaccessible to wheeled traffic (*New Statistical Account* xiii, p. 12).

Findlay's Seat. Taylor is appointed an interim kind of moss-grieve and brings information of everything that happens in the hill to Mr Duff.

Mr May is very seldom informed of anything about these hills but what he finds out from his own perambulations. The tenants of the glen don't consider themselves as connected with Lord Findlater nor has his Lordship any moss-grieve on that side. The place where Mr Duff put in the tenants of Coxton to cast peats in opposition to Mr Grant lies between Findlay's Seat and the town of Auchinroath and is marked on the plan *Moss where the tenants of Auchinroath cast their peats*. Mr Grant can inform fully as to this affair, and to him it is referred.

Peter May to James Ross, Cullen House SRO. GD248/978/5

Elgin, 6 September 1768

I had your favours sent me by Mr Grant covering the list of arrears. I went over yesterday and examined the tenants of Bishopmill, and shall make out a rental which shall be sent you in a post or two. I am busy making out estimates for the lands of Birnie and as soon as I can they shall be got ready, but you know very well that I have particular remarks to make on each farm, and that the distance betwixt Birnie and Elgin protracts a good deal of time. I hope I shall be able to satisfy you that with the Hills of Rothes and my other notes, there has not been much time lost since I came here. I have called on Mr [George] Duff and he has promised to acquaint me in a day or two what the tenants of Tomshill have paid into his mother. Mr Rintoul[1] is just now in the south country so that I cannot clear with him immediately.

I went over to Inverness yesterday and wrote a line to Andrew Keir (who happened not to be at home) desiring him to get for you half a peck of ripe pears, half a peck of good apples and some dozens of their best plums. But I was greatly disappointed when I opened the bag. Everyone almost bad of their kind, and no less charged than 8s. 4d. In order to make up for so bad a bargain I rummaged all the town this day myself and picked up some dozens of excellent pears and some plums which Mrs May wrapped up in

[1] David Rintoul, minister in Elgin, *see* p. 116, n. 1.

separate papers to preserve them in the carriage and has put them in a hamper of our own. . . .

I have seen Mr A[rthur] Duff sometimes of late. When seen we mention the marches, he cries out of my Lord Findlater's asking the feuars to join with him in a law suit against Lord Fife and says it is an open declaration of his going to law. I wish you could bring about some amicable agreement soon or at least settle the limits of your dispute within as narrow bounds as possible. If any concessions are made from the line running betwixt the Hunt Hill and the Sharping or Earl's Stone, it should be about the Sheephillock Moss rather than towards Findlay's Seat. Mr William Grant has been informing himself how long Shainbucky has been casting peats where he does at present and considers it as an encroachment upon Auchinroath.

Memorandum about Mr Grant of Grant's estate lying in the parishes of Forgue and Inverkeithny[1] by Peter May SRO GD248/672/6

Cullen House, 15 September 1768

These lands lie contiguous and connect together altho' in different counties. Forgue is in Aberdeenshire and Inverkeithny in Banff. The mercat for their victual is Banff and Portsoy from which they are distant nine miles from the former and eleven from the latter.

Inverkeithny is but tolerably accommodated with moss. The moss of Skibhill belongs to it in property, but is a good deal wore out. There is a servitude for ten spades casting yearly in the moss of Auchintoul. Each spade consists of 60 ells of lair and 12 ells of bank, and this tolerance is reckoned better than the property of the moss of Skeibhill. These mosses lie betwixt three and four miles distant, and

[1] This estate was put up for sale by the family of Grant for £15,000 by 17 Jan. 1769, but only £12,000 had been offered. A copy of the land tax for Aberdeenshire for 1771 (SRO. GD36/227) shows the estate to have been sold and broken down: Mr Allardyce had bought Boyndsmill; George Gerrard, Templeland; John Grant of Rothmaise, Gariochsford; Andrew Jamieson, Balgaveny; William Livingston, Glenmellan; Mr Munro, Sleepynook; Mr Wilson, Auchaber and Largue. The situation for Inverkeithny parish, Banffshire is not so clear, *see* Loretta R. Timperley (ed.) *A Directory of Landownership in Scotland c. 1770*, Scottish Record Society, Edinburgh, 1976, p. 70.

on the other side of the River Deveron. There are some other mosses on which they have a common right particularly in that called the Haremoss lying on the west boundary along the march with Hatton's lands of Balnoon. There are bogs and patches on other parts of the estate where they get some coarse peat and turf from the hills.

Forgue is better accommodated with peat and turf. It has a common right with Bognie's lands[1] in the Loch Moss lying south from Auchaber and on the march betwixt the lands of Forgue and Frendraught. It has also a right for peat and turf on the Bisset Hill belonging to Bognie and they have extensive hills and moors where they get turf, and in many places a kind of moss consisting of one peat deep only. The south side of the lands are well accommodated, Bogfouton has a considerable moss on itself, and Glenmellan and Balgaveny are also near and well served.

There are four meal milns belonging to these lands. The Milns of Ardfour and Tollo lie locally within the boundings of Inverkeithny. Miln of Gariochsford in the boundings of Forgue, and Boyndsmill lies disjoined half a mile distance from any part of the estate on the march betwixt Bognie and Hatton. These milns have of sucken,[2] viz. the Miln of Ardfour has the farm of Ardfour, Auchininna and Log Croft, which pay the 21st part of multure,[3] and Tollo has the Mains of Tollo, the Feith-hill, Crofts of Cottown and Newbigging with the Easter and Wester Haggs which pay the 33rd part of multure. Miln of Gariochsford has Glenmellen, Balgaveny, Gariochsford and Lenshie belonging to Mr Grant which pay the 33rd part, and the farm of Easiewalls belonging to Hatton which pays the 17th part. Boyndsmill has of thirlage[4] the two farms of Largue consisting of three ploughs belonging to Mr Grant. The four ploughs of Downies, Auchinhamper and Cromla belonging to Hatton, and four ploughs of Raich and Parkdargue belonging to Bognie; all these lands pay the 33rd part of multure. But there is a part of Mr Grant's lands thirled to milns not pertaining to the estate, viz. the towns of Auchaber and Templeland consisting of four ploughs are thirled to the place Miln of Bognie, and pay the 33rd part of multure

[1] Alexander Morrison of Bognie.
[2] A service of carrying corn.
[3] Payment for grinding at the lord's mill and the prohibition from grinding elsewhere.
[4] The compulsory services provided by the lord, especially milling.

except 8 bolls sowing of Templeland which pay the 13th part. Although Boyndsmill lies disjoined and is under lease for 20 years, yet in the event of the lands being purchased together, it would of all the rest be the most convenient purchase, not only that it will rise considerably in the rent, but will enable the proprietor to get an excambion[1] of these multures thirled to Bognie's and Hatton's mills.

Forgue and Inverkeithny together make a considerable estate. They extend from the River Deveron to the foot of the hill above Culsalmond which is computed to be 5 miles, and they will be about a mile and a half broad one part with another, which would make 4,800 acres. But the farms of Aucharnie belonging to Mr Duff [of Hatton] lie within these boundings and may contain from 4 to 500 acres. In such a large extent there must be great variety of soil. The arable lands particularly the infields and folds appear to be good soil. The faughs and high lands are middling. There is on many of the farms a command of water and the present tenants seem to know the value of it perfectly, for they lose very little. They are all obliged by their tacks to lay on some lime which can only be done in small quantities as they lie at the distance of 8 and 9 miles from it. But where it is used they have very fine corns. The farm houses are in excellent repair and the tenants have much the appearance of industry.

There is much extent of moor ground, some parts whereof may be improved with culture, and others with planting. Towards the south end of Forgue there is a good deal of improvable ground and with some attention several new settlements might be made. There are some small difficulties about the marches, but the difference is small and the subject very trifling.

There is an eye draught describing how the lands lie and of the marches with conterminous heritors, which will help to explain this memorandum.

In perambulating and looking over the ground a note of the sowing of the several farms were taken from the tenants but it was soon discovered that their account could not be depended on, and therefore a computation was made of the increase that would arise upon the leases being open which are as follows:

[1] An exchange of a piece of property for another (a Scots legal term).

Inverkeithny contains the following lands viz.: Increased rent

	£	s.	d.
Log Croft		13	4
2 Auchininna	20	0	0
2 Ardfours	20	10	0
Miln and miln croft of Ardfour	6	10	0
Miln of Tollo	4	0	0
Mains of Tollo if divided into two farms will raise	22	0	0
4 Cottartown crofts	2	10	0
2 Newbigging crofts	2	10	0
Easter Hagg	2	10	0
Wester Hagg	2	2	0
Feith-hill	4	0	0
	£87	5s.	4d.

Lands in the parish of Forgue, viz.:

	£	s.	d.
Largue into 2 farms at present but not well divided	16	0	0
Lenshie if divided into 2 farms	4	0	0
Balgaveny if divided into 2 farms	14	0	0
Gariochsford already in 4 crofts no rise can take place			
Miln of Gariochsford	3	0	0
Glenmellan	3	10	0
Sleepynook	4	0	0
Bogfouton to be in one farm or 4 crofts	12	12	0
Auchaber if properly divided	16	10	0
Templeland	3	0	0
Boyndsmill	9	10	0
Part of Lenshie lying next to the shares set to Hatton won't rise			
	86	2	0
Inverkeithny as above	87	5	4
	£173	7s.	4d.

The present rent of Inverkeithny after deducting the minister's stipend and feu duty as per rental of:

		£	s.	d.
Money rent	Scots	£1265	14	4
170 bolls 2 pints meal at £5 per boll		850	12	6
33 reek hens at £2 per dozen		5	10	0
110 bolls of lime, carriage 6d. each		33	0	0
45 hooks in harvest at 6d.		13	10	0
55 days work at do.		16	10	0
		£2184	16s.	10d.

		£	s.	d.	
Free rent of Forgue as per rental	Scots	£1542	9	4	
203 bolls 2 firlots $\frac{1}{6}$ pint meal at £5 per boll		1017	11	0	
4 stone butter at £4 per stone		16	0	0	
11 wedders at £3 each		33	0	0	
13 lambs at £1 each		13	0	0	
78 capons at £3 per dozen		19	10	0	
138 hens and 53 reek hens at £2 per dozen		31	16	8	
12 poultry at 18s. per dozen			18	0	
40¼ foot of peats at £1 per foot		40	5	0	
114 bolls of lime, carriage at 6d.		34	4	0	
	Scots	£2748	14	0	
	Inverkeithny as above	2184	16	10	
	Scots	£4933	10	10	
	which equals	£411	2	$6\frac{10}{12}$	Sterl.
	Increased rent according to estimate above	£173	7	4	
	Sterling	£584	9s.	$10\frac{10}{12}$d.	

But the additional rents cannot take place until the tacks expire which according to the rental are as follows:

	Years	Additional rent	£	s.	d.	
Inverkeithny:						
Mains of Tollo has 8 years of £22 Sterl. additional rent			£176	0	0	
4 Cottown of Tollo Crofts has	4 years of	£2 10s.	10	0	0	
Feith-hill	2	£4	8	0	0	
2 Crofts of Newbigging	2	£2 10s.	5	0	0	
Easter Hagg	4	£2 10s.	10	0	0	
Wester Hagg	4	£2 2s.	8	8	0	
Tollo Miln	1	£4	4	0	0	
2 Auchininna	6	£20	120	0	0	
2 Ardfours	8	£20 10s.	164	0	0	
Log Croft	4	13s. 4d.	2	13	4	
Miln of Ardfour	3	£6 10s.	19	10	0	
			£527	11s.	4d.	Sterl.
Forgue:						
Bogfouton	2 years of	£12 12s.	£25	4	0	
Glenmellan	10	£3 10s.	35	0	0	
Gariochsford:						
Miln of Gariochsford	16 years of	£3	48	0	0	
Balgaveny	9	£14	126	0	0	
Sleepynook	8	£4	32	0	0	
Templeland	10	£3	30	0	0	
Auchaber	5	£16	80	0	0	
Lenshie	6	£4	24	0	0	
Largue	11	£16	176	0	0	
Boyndsmill	20	£9 10s.	190	0	0	
			£766	4	0	
		Inverkeithny as above	£527	11	4	
Deduction on account of leases			£1293	15s.	4d.	

The surveyor had not time enough to inform himself fully about many particulars relative to these lands and therefore the preceding memorandum is but an imperfect one, but he is persuaded that the estimate rent is such as can be depended on, and that the value of the lands may still be increased, something above the estimate, if the leases were once out. By dividing the farms properly and making a few new settlements on the improveable moor ground it is believed that the rent may rise to £630 Sterling yearly over paying the whole cess.

Peter May to James Ross, Cullen House SRO. GD248/680/9

Elgin, 28 September 1768

I wrote you to Banff by Monday's post, since then I have been wandering about in different corners. Monday I took a survey of the damage done by Spey which indeed is very great. I have not yet had leisure to make out particular notes of those who have suffered most. I suppose you are pretty well informed by Mr Grant who says he wrote you fully about everything. There are some places where the river has been attempting to cut out new channels which would need to be guarded against before winter, but I cannot describe them in writing so as to be understood, until I have the plan before me and therefore I shall refer my remarks until I come to Cullen.

Brodie sent me his plan of Spynie Monday last and on Tuesday I took a second survey of the ground with the plan in my hands, which is a very inaccurate one. I tried some of the measures this day with the chain but did not find any of them right. One field marked by me on the plan No. 5 measures according to Mr Nicolson's scale 12 acres, and upon trying it on the ground it only turns out $9\frac{3}{4}$ acres. Another field marked by me No. 2 measures only $8\frac{1}{4}$ acres by Mr Nicolson's scale and from a remensuration it turns out to be 12 and some odds. You will see by the plan that none of his measures have been cast up until I set about it this day and marked down the measures of the several fields according as they were delineated by him, but none of them can be depended on. I wrote Mr Brodie to send my surveyor who he has employed measuring his estate to make a rude draught of it. We could have depended on his measures and made out our notes with more certainty but I suppose he does not choose it. I cannot see any convenience that Spynie will bring to my Lord's other lands except that it connects with it on two sides and that the marches in the moor ground are not very distinct betwixt it and Linksfield, but that is not of consequence. No doubt my Lord could accommodate it, and the tenants according to their own account would be glad to be his Lordship's tenants on the expectation of getting moss. A part of Spynie would add very properly to that part of Myreside possessed by Lawrence Sutherland and some little augmentation might be got by a division of that kind, tho' that could be but trifling. John Robb has a lease for 19 years from Whitsunday 1766 to him, his heirs and two subtenants, but according to his own account he will give it up upon being provided in any other tolerable farm. I suppose he thinks it dear. I have marked in my notes that it could be easily enclosed and no place is better for it than that large field which we saw next to Pitgaveny. I like the field much and yet I am loath to say that it should be purchased. We have so many bankrupt estates in that corner, at least bankrupt tenants, that I do not know what to make of them. Mr [James] Brander of Pitgaveny was at Brodie some days ago treating as they say about Spynie. I should think it much better appended to my Lord's other lands than to Pitgaveny. Yesterday I was told that Findrassie (who is still in town) was in terms with Pitgaveny about his lands of Findrassie, but I have contrary information this day by John Duncan who I sent for on purpose but did not let him know of it. Mr Peter Duff lives with Findrassie; he and Baillie Leslie are said to be his governors.

Mr William Grant called me out yesterday evening to look at two aughten[1] peats he means to sell. It was dark before we got half over them so that I cannot say whether they are a good or a bad bargain. They march with Mr Copland's lands in several places. If you are not in a hurry I shall inform myself better about them soon.

[1] Aughten, or auchten was a unit of measure associated with the davoch, i.e. one-eighth of a davoch, *see* I. H. Adams, *Agrarian Landscape Terms: a glossary for historical geography*, Special Publication No. 9, Institute of British Geographers 2nd Edition, 1977, p. 5.

Peter May to James Ross, Cullen House SRO. GD248/978/5

Elgin, 1 November 1768

I am just now returned from Rothes where I have been since Monday morning, employed in marking out a new tract for the road from the Boat of Fiddich to Rothes, and in concerting a plan for a bulwark to preserve the banks of the Mains, both which was done with the assistance of Mr Leslie and Gellovie. I have a memorandum about the bulwark, and therefore I shall refer saying anything about it at present. I told Gellovie and also all the tenants who have suffered by the late spate, that it was my Lord Findlater's desire to be informed of the quantity of corns they had saved as well as what they had lost. I find they are extremely shy to give an account of what is preserved and I suspect their own report will not be such as can be depended on. I believe this year they had in general a very great crop which is partly the reason why they are so unwilling to give an account of it. A declaration from barleymen[1] would not bring us to the truth as they behoved to guide themselves according to the tenants' information. Gellovie goes in a few days to Strathspey and says he cannot convene them until his return.

When I was at Rothes I enquired at Mr Leslie for a man who would settle in the hills and serve for a moss grieve. He mentioned Donald Melven, who lives in Blackhall, as one that would answer. Melven had got a letter of tack from Blackhills on the Fir saughs about the place where Lord Fife set down his man, and still wants a place. I appointed him to meet me this forenoon when I went to the hills with him and scrambled over them all from Findlay's Seat to the top of Whitieshill. You will remember my Lord pointed out the Hunt Hill as a proper place for settling a moss-grieve, but upon surveying it with some attention there is no such thing as making out a settlement there. The staple is either moss or a kind of turf that will not improve into cornland. The Fir saughs is the only place where a man can be set down and Melven is content to settle there, but I did not choose to come under treaty with him until I had further advice as it lies near to the lands of Barluack, but I told him I would acquaint my Lord Findlater of him.

[1] *See* p. 111, n. 2.

I am extremely obliged to my Lord for agreeing so easily to let me go to Belmont, even at the expense of putting off his own business for sometime, but I am vastly anxious that we had been able to have settled with the tenants of Birnie before I had gone away; many of the new improvers are impatient to know and I have assured them that they would be told as soon as the harvest was over. Could not they be appointed to be at Cullen on Monday, Tuesday or Wednesday and I would be there on my way south. If my Lord approved of this I beg you will write me that I may give them timeous notice. I am afraid I cannot get the proper information about your marches with Elgin before I set out. I have appointed ploughs to come in tomorrow and next day to plough a part of Dykeside and there is a necessity for my own attendance while they are employed there. I am to write to Mr Menzies by tomorrow's post that I must go to Aberdeen, but will take him up at Belmont any day he appoints after the 22nd. Have you got any answer from Mr Robertson about the remainder of victual we have on hand? I am persuaded we lose a firlot every week by the vermin.

Peter May to James Ross, Cullen House SRO. GD248/978/5

Elgin, 5 November 1768

I have just now yours of the 4th. If the Martinmas term is to be kept as usual there can be no difficulty in getting back in time. I am told they don't pay their Martinmas rents here until after Christmas, but if my Lord intends the term to be against the 22nd current going south just now would put it out of my power to return in time, nor can I concert measures with Mr Menzies until you advise me what is to be the Martinmas term here. My coming under engagements to Lord Privy Seal was by my Lord's advice and direction, but if his Lordship's affairs will not admit of time to finish these things just now I shall do in that as my Lord is pleased to direct. But I believe it will be of consequence for me to be at Aberdeen soon to put my affairs there in order. You know I have a large farm on hand and am expending very considerably upon it, and by the last accounts I have from Aberdeen it requires looking after. I have also my nurseries to dispose of and to see what state they are in, but my stay there shall be as short as I can.

Sir Ludovick Grant of Grant to James Grant, younger of Grant
SRO. GD248/49/4

Edinburgh, 14 December 1768

. . . I sincerely wish you could conclude a bargain [for the sale of Moy] with Lord Findlater. I cannot think but he will be much directed by Mr May's opinion. . . .

Factory the Earl of Findlater to Peter May[1] SRO. GD248/983/2

4 January 1769

I, James Earl of Findlater and Seafield, having trust and confidence in Peter May, surveyor of land, lately residing in Aberdeen now in Elgin, do by these presents nominate, constitute and appoint him my factor, to the effect under written, giving, granting and committing to him the said Peter May my full power, warrand and commission, for me and upon my account to uplift and receive the arrears given up by William Grant, late factor for me at Elgin, conform to a list or account thereof signed by me of this date as relative hereto; as also, to uplift and receive the whole rents, duties, farms, customs, casualties and feu duties due and payable to me by the several tenants, possessors and feuars of the whole lands, tenements and others belonging to me within the parishes of Elgin, Birnie, St Andrews and Spynie, of all which a rental is signed by me and the said Peter May as relative hereto, and that for the cropt and year Mdcc and sixty-eight, and in time coming until these presents shall be recalled; and if necessary to call, charge and pursue for the arrears, rents and others foresaid, decreets and sentences thereanent to obtain and cause execute; and upon payment to grant receipts and discharges which shall be valid to the receivers, with power also to warn and remove tenants of the foresaid lands, tenements and others, either in his own name or mine, and in general to do every other thing necessary for executing the premisses that

[1] This factory from May's patron, the 6th Earl of Findlater, was renewed after the Earl's death 3 Nov. 1770, by the 7th Earl on 6 Dec. 1770 (SRO. GD248/983/2). A new factory was issued on 11 Dec. 1773 by Theophilus Ogilvie, Collector of the Customs at Aberdeen, and John Ross, Professor of Oriental Languages, King's College, Aberdeen, commissioners for the 7th Earl (SRO. GD248/983/2). May renounced his commission on 20 July 1778.

I could do myself if personally present. All which I promise to hold firm and stable, the said Peter May always doing all reasonable diligence for recovering the arrears, rents, farms, and others foresaid, and being obliged to make just count, reckoning and payment to me, my heirs and successors of his whole intromissions therewith, He being to receive the gratification for his pains and trouble agreed upon, as expressed in the letters that passed betwixt us previous to his settling at Elgin, and I consent to the registration hereof in the Books of Council and Session, Sheriff Court Books of Elgin and Forres, or others competent, therein to remain for preservation and for that purpose I constitute [*blank*] my procurator.

In witness whereof of these presents (written upon this and the preceding page of stamped paper by David Manson my servant) are subscribed by me at Cullen House this fourth day of January in the year Mdcc and sixty-nine before witnesses James Ross, factor for me, and the said David Manson. (signed) Findlater and Seafield.

Peter May to James Ross, Cullen House SRO. GD248/978/5

Elgin, 10 January 1769

We arrived at Elgin on Friday about 5 o'clock. Saturday I got the officer and gave him instructions to call in the tenants to pay their rents this week. I appointed all Linkwood's tenants to come in on Tuesday, Newmiln's on Wednesday, Findrassie's on Thursday with Tomshill and the Over and Nether Bogg's, Friday Myreside and Linksfield and Bishopmill, and Saturday the town of Elgin, so that you see all this week will be employed at my collection. It is now almost ten o'clock at night and I have been receiving and hanging on waiting since nine this morning and I have not yet got above £47 Stg. I find Linkwood's tenants have all been a year behind, and that the rents for crop 1767 have been mostly collected from them very lately, as appears by Linkwood's discharges. I have told them all that my instructions were peremptory and that such as did not pay up their rents might depend on being prosecuted directly. I have called on Mr Burnet who tells me that some of the tenants have paid up their rents, but that David Taylor the gardener who rents the Tails is still in arrears, that he has a decreet against him. I wish we could get him out; he is a bankrupt and you know a gardener has not an hypothec[1] as the most of his crop is generally sold off before the term of payment falls due. If he does not find caution I am determined to turn him out, unless I am otherwise directed.

The bearer hereof, William Mitchell, is one of our tenants in the Stonecrosshill, at least his mother is and he lives with her. I have some thoughts of employing him as a ground officer but I have not yet been able to determine what will be allowed them. I mean that my officer here should have under his charge all my Lord's lands in Moray except Speyside. I wish you would mention this to my Lord and give me some instructions about their allowance. Tho' the yearly rent is but small yet you will have in view that they have a circle of three or four score miles to go through. I suppose the bulk of the salary is to be thrown on the tenants, whether that should be drawn from them in money or in corns, it is generally in corn they receive in this neighbourhood. As soon as my term is over I shall attend to the instructions given in the memorandum. I beg leave to trouble you as you go past to look in upon John Forsyth and put him in mind of my plough. Mr Stuart says he promised him one against Martinmas but he has neither seen nor heard of it yet. As soon as my plough is ready I would willingly have my horses brought north. Would my Lord lend a box cart for a month or six weeks until I get one made, a small one would serve and we could bring home the plough in it. If a cart is got I must cause J. Mellis get breaking cart horses. I am almost half blind and must conclude.

PS. I have got Alexander Garden's information with respect to the marks betwixt Elgin and Linkwood which is not favourable for Linkwood.

Peter May to James Ross, Cullen House SRO. GD248/978/5

Elgin, 17 January 1769

I had your favours by Mr Cranshaw, and though almost half blind with sore eyes set out with him yesterday morning in our perambulation over my Lord Findlater's lands. We began at the Stonecrosshill and Blacklands and afterwards viewed Linkwood, Boggs and Little Glassgreen. On our way to Birnie we surveyed

[1] *See* p. 111, n. 1.

Rashcrook and proceeded to the Gedloch and Conloch and from that to the new improvements of Birnie – Bardenside, Middleton and Rhynagairn and Glenlatterach with Blairnha'. When we were at Glenlatterach the day was very stormy, which prevented our making as particular a survey of it as we did of the rest. Shougle Redloan fell in the way on our return home as did Craighead, Tomshill, Castlehill and Dykeside, Shankhouse, Meikle Glassgreen and Muirytack. Today we surveyed the lands lying on the other side of [river] Lossie, comprehending Bishopmill, Myreside and Linksfield. I carried Mr Cranshaw also over Spynie with a view to give my Lord his opinion about it. I pointed out Linkwood, Dykeside or Bishopmill as the properest places for my Lord to appropriate a farm for Lord Deskford. Mr Cranshaw thinks that Dykeside, Castlehill, Tomshill and Monkhouse would be the best place for his Lordship, and that these farms all together would make a good sheep farm, and to be brought on with turnips, but I need not repeat what he could inform my Lord more perfectly himself. He does not seem to think much of our Cuttlehill treasure, I mean the marl on Bishopmill, nor of the appearance of a quarry there, but he seems to like the lands on the north side of Lossie much better than Birnie, especially Hugh Todd's farm of Myreside.

I have enquired very particularly about Crombie's subjects which according to the best information I could get are as follows – two crofts lying on the south side of the burgh, one whereof near Admiral Gordon's on the west side of the Moss Wynd, the other almost opposite to Provost Brodie's house. These crofts would set for 20s. or a guinea each, but are presently in P. Brodie's possession. A waird[1] also in the Provost's hands and about three fourths of an acre of it a morass, but may be sanded and improved equal to the rest at no great expense, the present rent not worth above 30s., two eighteenths set to William Mason, James Fraser and William Key, hirers, the free rents whereof is [*blank*] bolls of barley and 8s. 4d. of money each after paying public burdens. Provost Brodie's house and yard is also a part of the subjects; the house is in bad repair; on the first floor there are three rooms and the same above with garrets. There are some other houses in the close but are almost in ruins; the

[1] An enclosure, possibly a part of The Wards, fields lying to the south of the town extending to the Burn of Tyock.

yard stretches to the fields and is just the breadth of the close. The Provost has a kind of back entry for his own accommodation. The house and yard would be worth about £8 or eight guineas rent, the Provost pays only four, but in case my Lord meant the house for his own accommodation when he came to the country, in that event I suspect it would need to be like the Highlandman's gun. You can easily make up rental from what I have said but no great value can be had on the house which is in bad order at present. The Provost and Mr King both want to buy up the subjects, Newmiln has been picking up all the claims he could get. There is one Alex. Geddes alias Strong who lives in Fochabers and is a creditor by adjudication for a debt of 40 years standing, which Mr Burnet informs me will now be accumulated to between 2 and 3 thousand marks. He was offered £10 for this debt by Mr King. His papers are in Mr William Taylor's hands at Edinburgh who is his agent. Mr Burnet is Geddes's doer here and if any information was wanted Mr Burnet could get it more particularly. I have paid your interest for the £300 at 4s. per cent. The other accounts are to copy over being closed among others done for my Lord since you were here, which has prevented its being cleared, but it shall be done in a day or two and your discharge transmitted. I have collected about £300 Stg. which shall also be conveyed your way soon. I want much to be informed of the public burdens affecting my collection here. The clergy have been making demands on me, I wish you would send me a note of them so they lie in the several parishes. I have a blacksmith in view for James Laing's crofts. Would my Lord question any allowance of coal[1] from the Mosses of Birnie? I have a very good character of him and would be glad he were accommodated. I never doubted but you would have given me a loan of a cart to bring home my ploughs, I suppose you thought I would have converted the cart in to plans of bottles, but I assure you I had no such thing in view. Upon second thoughts I have resolved not to deal in grass seeds, as I have scarce any ground on my poor farm that they can be sown down and am not yet acquainted enough in the country. I thought it proper to advise you of this as my Lord said that Mr Innes was to bring down grass seeds.

[1] Fuel, i.e. peat.

Earl of Findlater to Peter May SRO. GD248/978/5

Cullen House, 15 February 1769

This goes by your man Mellis, whom I think very well of, and should be glad if he was settled in a farm in your country. Mr Ross informs me that you still continue to wish rather to have Linkwood's farm and the milns at the rent at which he sold them, subject to be taken back by Lord Deskford or me when we think proper, and reserving a power likewise to plant the knowes and barren spots; and that you think in that case you could set the farm of Dykeside for about £38. I am desirous you should be a farmer in Moray, but in the situation that is most agreeable to you, and therefore I am ready to agree to the above proposals.

I think it is right that your accounts preceding Whitsunday last should be finished immediately; as soon as they are ready I would have you send them to Mr Ross who will correspond constantly with me.

Peter May to the Earl of Findlater SRO. GD248/978/5

Elgin, 17 February 1769

I had the honour of your Lordship's by John Mellis. I own I did not like the farm of Dykeside, but your lordship's pleasure was sufficient to make me accept it. I am now extremely glad of the change you propose for me, it will induce me to farm in a very different way and with a good deal more spirit. I think I can now put Dykeside in such a way as to set it for £38 Stg. I consider myself engaged for it and my Lord Findlater may depend on my best endeavours in that or any other of his affairs entrusted to my care.

I am very well pleased to accept the milns and farm of Linkwood at the rent given up by Linkwood and am sensible of the obligations I lie under to you for putting them in my way. Your Lordship or my Lord Deskford may have them at any time you please, and in the meantime may plant such knowes or other unimprovable ground as you think proper. I consider it my duty to observe that any plan most approved of by your Lordship for the management of that farm shall be followed by me, and I have the vanity to imagine that its being in my possession will not put it in a worse state for

Lord Deskford when he shall think it necessary to have it. I would incline to have a gardener there whose business would be chiefly to raise nurseries if your lordship approved of it.

My accounts preceding Whitsunday last shall be soon ready and be forwarded to Mr Ross. I hope they will be easily settled to your Lordship's satisfaction.

I came from Cullen the other day with Mr Grant who said there was only £12,000 Stg offered for his estates of Forgue and Inverkeithny; that he was resolved to sell them at £15,000 if that price was offered. Your Lordship knows that they are advertised at Edinburgh. If they are bought for that sum I'll venture to assure the purchaser of 4 per cent for the money as soon as the tacks are out and that over paying public burdens and factor's salary. Your Lordship knows I have much affection for Mr Grant, but I would not take it upon me to recommend them to you if I were not certain of their being a good bargain. There is a necessity of their being sold and it is very likely they may go considerably under the £15,000.

I have been much pressed by Mr Grant to take the charge of his lands of Westfield[1] to make the survey and to put it into the best order I can, but have refused accepting a factory without your lordship's advice and approbation, which Mr Grant said he would apply for. Westfield is to be sold as soon as it can be got in order and so is Moy. I understand Moy is presently under treaty with Sir Alexander Grant.

Since writing the former part of my letter I have been along with Linkwood over his farm, and according to the best computation I think I can lay down 30 acres with grass seeds this season. There is an island comprehended between the branches of the miln water leading to the miln which is covered with heath and would make a fine patch of wood. Firs or birch would be the proper species; should I set about doing anything there this spring, or refer it until a general plan was agreed on? I have settled with Linkwood for the ground under nursery and what more ground they may want for this crop as they must be planted out at greater distances.

[1] These lands were situated 3½ miles N.W. of Elgin, but they had been disposed of by 1773, for in a valuation roll of that year they are recorded in the possession of Sir William Dunbar of Durn (L. R. Timperley (ed.) *A Directory of Landownership in Scotland c. 1770*, Scottish Record Society, Edinburgh, 1976, p. 238).

I have not been able to get an account from all the tenants of the quantity of victual they can pay this crop but shall have it against Sunday and will forward it by express to Mr Ross.

Peter May to James Ross, Cullen House SRO. GD248/978/5

Elgin, undated

I send you herewith my accompts for surveying, planning etc., be so good as to look over them and the memorandum before you send them south.

Yesterday I let by roup part of the lands of Linksfield and Bishopmill vacated by Arch. James; those fields of Linksfield that did not go at what I thought their value I caused roup and retained them in our own hands. I hope to get them set for grass. In the evening I met with Mr Burnet and Mr Petry, late vintner, who I prevailed upon to accept a conjunct bill for David Taylor's arrears, and Arch. Duff pays a part of them so that I think that point will get settled without any loss. I have given Mr Burnet a list of tenants to be warned out; should not I include David Taylor? I think you said it was not legal to remove him at Martinmas except he had been warned out at the Whitsunday before; pray advise me as to that. One of my eyes distresses me much. Linkwood I find will give me a good deal of additional trouble, I am there generally in the morning before I get anybody up.

Charles Russell to Peter May SRO. GD248/978/5

Elgin, 15 March 1769

I have looked over the farm of Dykeside along with you this day and considered it deliberately, and the expense it would cost before I could bring it into order. If my Lord Findlater will agree to give me a lease for 19 years after Whitsunday next I am content to pay his Lordship yearly for the first 5 years £30 Stg and for the remainder of the lease £35 Stg yearly. If I am preferred on these terms I shall endeavour to manage it in such a manner as shall be agreeable to his Lordship, as I would incline to lay down the ground with grass as soon as it were in condition for it, and to summer fallow and raise turnips. It will therefore be necessary for the neighbourhood to winter herd as well as me, and I shall expect that both my Lord and you will give me the necessary assistance for that purpose. Any reparation of office houses that were necessary for my accommodation, I suppose my Lord would help a little for that, and put the windows of the dwelling house in proper order. It will be obliging if you transmit my proposals to my Lord Findlater and let me know his answer as soon as convenient.

Peter May to James Ross, Cullen House SRO. GD248/978/5

Elgin, 19 March 1769

Last post brought me your favours. Mr Burnet thinks David Taylor's former agreement is taken away by the decreet of removal we have against him, and that if we mean to remove him at Mattinmass next he must be warned out immediately; I shall talk to Mr Burnet again about it and inform him of your opinion.

Charles Russell called on me Wednesday last and I went along with him to the farm of Dykeside and pointed out the marches of the possession, and of those parts I had set off. When we came home he made the inclosed offer which I am persuaded my Lord will not accept of. I told him that I had informed my Lord that I could set it for £38 Stg but as we expected something better from him than ordinary, was uncertain but he might be preferred if he made his offer £36 yearly from the beginning of the lease. As I have nothing to write my Lord at present will ye be so good as to transmit Mr Russell's offer, which I promised should be done.

Friday last I got the rent of Stankhouse paid me by Alex. Russell in Whitetree of Pluscardin, a farm of Lord Fife's, son to the late possessor and brother to the present ones; he made me an offer of 64 bolls for Dykeside and the present rent of Stankhouse, with £9 of additional rent, and that to commence with the first crop he lays down. In order to know what this offer comes to, it is necessary to have in view that there is 10 years of the tack of Stankhouse yet to run which this man says he can enjoy as he has paid the rent of it for his brothers ever since his father's death. This offer accounting the victual at 10s. only the boll is equal to £38 for Dykeside and £6 of addition when the tack is out. But the present possessors are such worthless fellows that they are ruining both the farm and houses. I believe I have told you formerly that I thought Dykeside and Stankhouse together would make an excellent farm as Stankhouse was well watered and a proper subject for grass, and Dykeside for corns. I told him I thought his offer was not equal to the value of the land and he promised to call on me on Friday next. Before that time I shall have more particular information of his circumstances. If he would give us ten guineas of addition and to commence as above I do think it would be a tempting offer. I was over Dykeside yesterday with another tenant of Lord Fife's, from the Mill of the Bauds, and am to have a meeting with him tomorrow morning. I am told the circumstances are well enough. He says he would not want the dwelling house, but only the kitchen to live in. I would fain have a better tenant for Dykeside. If it does not set to our wish I had rather keep it another year in my own possession and shall pay his lordship £38 for it though I own I would rather choose to have it set, and if we were not very nice of a tenant that could be done soon.

I was over Birnie yesterday and had a meeting with the most of the tenantry there. I find it difficult to get them to come to terms without a promise to continue them for some time. I was at pains to persuade them that there was no danger of their being removed as long as they were industrious and diligent, but even that did not satisfy. Some kind of agreement with them for a certain number of years would in my humble opinion tempt them to have done something in the way of improvement. I have kept them in suspense and said I could not enter into writing with them until my Lord came to the country. I wish you would advise his lordship of this, if any treaty is entered into I should like to know the form.

In your last but one you say 10s. 6d. is to be the ready money price of bere, but you do not say if that is to be the price of oats also; be so good as advise me, for I can't finish nor take bills from the tenants until I know the price. In my opinion it is as high as we can get for either, unless the prices rest above what they are at present. . . .

Peter May to James Ross, Cullen House SRO. GD248/978/5

Elgin, 2 April 1769

I had your favours of the 29th on Friday morning when I returned from Rothes. If the division of the moss would have been put off eight days it would have been answered extremely well to have taken it in my way to Aberdeen. At present I have twenty things to do. I will employ this week to finish planting out the nurseries among the tenants' yards. And I have quarriers employed at the Cuttlehill in search of lime quarries; add to this my own oatseed and garden jam-making out at Linkwood and you will allow that I have but little spare time, but as I suppose your appointment with respect to the division of the moss is now fixed upon and no concern of mine shall interfere with that. I shall be glad to know some days before, that I may leave the proper orders with my people.

I have been at pains, along with Balnageith and Gellovie to get the damages on Speyside put in a fair light, and yet as to their sufferings respecting the crop, we must use discretion for I find their accounts cannot be depended on. I have not been able as yet to arrange my notes in the proper order, but shall endeavour to have that done before I come to Cullen.

I forget if I wrote you that I had an offer for the farm of Dykeside by one George Stronach a farmer in the lands of Manbeen. I am told he has substance enough for it and he offers £23 Stg and 30 bolls victual, the one half bere and the other oats; the oats at 5 firlots to the boll; this is equal to £38 Stg accounting the victual at 10s. the boll and is the best offer we have had that I know of, but then if my Lord wants a gentleman this man would not do. He qualifies his offer to be binding on him only for 10 days and has been at me once and again wanting to know if he was to be preferred, which I have just put off expecting my Lord's own directions, but if that shall not come soon I am afraid we will lose him as he wants a place against Whitsunday. Dykeside is quite out-laboured, and must be thrown down with grass seeds if it is not set to a tenant. I wish the last took place as it would relieve my hand, if it does not it must be sown down with grass seeds this season. The house will suffer if it lies without a tenant. I had an express yesterday from Findhorn advising of a large cask of hawthorn berries come in there on board a brig, Peter Gray master, for my Lord. I have given orders to one James Ross in Findhorn to take them out of the ship and pay the freight, etc., and advise me if an Elgin cart will be able to carry them here. What shall be done with them? I suppose they must be sent to Cullen, except my Lord has intended their being sown here, which I suppose he has not or I would have heard of it. I have advice from London of five sacks of grass seeds being put on board the *Diligence*, George McGilligan of Banff; how shall I get them brought here? If your hawthorn berries are to be sent to Cullen and that a cart can carry them, it would be a good opportunity to bring north my seeds. You will be so good as contrive how to get them brought from Banff to Cullen. If it cannot be done otherwise a cart must be hired on purpose to bring them, I have wrote Dr Saunders to take charge of them; I hope he will do it, they are marked PM/Elgin; at any rate I think I may get a retour from Cullen. I must beg your assistance with my grass seed and pray continue how to get them to Cullen, I shall serve you as much in my turn. Last autumn Lord Findlater gave orders to keep for him 10,000 spruce trees, which was accordingly done. I think the collector was wrote to the purpose when I was at Aberdeen. I am now clearing the ground of all my nurseries and I believe that is the bulk I have now on hand. I wish you would give directions to some of the Banff carriers to call for them. John Coutts will take them up and pack them carefully, I shall send you an order for him to do so if you think it necessary. You have not wrote me if you have the estimates of the kirk of Birnie; I beg you will look for them.

PS. John McGillivrie, butcher of Elgin, wants to be advised if your fat cattle be all disposed of at Cullen or Craig.

Captain Alexander Donald to Peter May SRO. GD248/978/5

Elgin, 6 April 1769

I called at your house this forenoon, but found that you had taken your departure for the country before I came. You may signify to Lord Findlater or Mr Ross the first time you write to Cullen that I am a man of honour and am still willing to be as good as my word with respect to the farm of Dykeside. You may further add that I think Lord Findlater is under some sort of an honourable obligation if his Lordship or factor does not keep possession of it, to give me the first offer of it at the rate he formerly proposed to set it to me at, if twenty others should interfere. As for the pendicle of the possession which you have already subset, that will make no manner of odds, provided I am entitled to remove the tenants if I find them not agreeable.

Peter May to James Ross, Cullen House SRO. GD248/978/5

Elgin, 9 April 1769

I have received your favour covering the estimates for the kirk of Birnie, which I have delayed engaging with until my Lord returns. I wish with all my heart he would direct Mr Marr to give the estimates or approve of these already given in. It is time now to have it set about and nothing interrupts it but want of final orders. I had a letter from Cluny recommending James Riach at Fochabers to be the undertaker, I suppose Cluny will be caution for him if he is approved of by my Lord. The minister is impatient to have it begun too and I have promised to set about it without delay.

I send you inclosed a letter from Captain Donald about Dykeside; I told him I had higher offers for it and that I had said to my Lord I could set it at £38 Stg, but he thought his offer should be presented as he had already been in terms about it. George Stronach in the lands of Pittendreich is still unprovided for, his offer is the best and I have a good character of him from Mr Leslie and Mr Donaldson his neighbour; he has a couple of sons with him and we have one of his sons a tenant in Redloan. If a country plain man is acceptable I think Stronach might do, but if a better sort of tenant is wanted he is not the proper person. I send you also William Russell's offer at the Mill of the Bauds and I already sent you a copy of Charles Russell's at Deskford, which is all I have got for Dykeside. I should be content it were set, for I find it adds not a little to my attendance. Just now I have day labourers employed at Dykeside carrying on my oatseed with as much dispatch as I can, and I have labourers employed at Shankwood making out a garden, dressing the nurseries and planting out the biggest among the tenants' yards. I have quarries at the Cuttlehill of Bishopmill making trial for limestone in which we have not yet succeeded in finding a solid rock, but we have got a good deal of limestone lying in loose stones betwixt the stratums of clay and marl, and find it burns in the fire and falls

…ks bygone I have been an active grieve and … of my time betwixt Linkwood, Dykeside and …. I knew a farm would require much more attention …ould bestow on it in my present situation.

I am to send for the hawthorn berries on Monday but I must here choose for them as the tenants' carts nor their horses would not be able to draw them. Many of the tenants have been seeking lintseed, it seems they were in use of getting so much from my Lord at prime cost. Is that to be continued this year? I wish it had, it would be an inducement to cause the bodies sow flax. I have got tenants to all our new settlements except two and have given two or three lines of write. But I cannot get them to be easy without a tack. When my Lord comes to the country or has leisure I hope he will think it necessary to give them a lease.

Arch. Simpson who took possession of Kells Leys Whitsunday last was committed to gaol in this town for stealing a silver watch and is presently out on bail. I have seen the precognition which was taken before one of the magistrates of Elgin, the theft being committed in the town. The watch belonged to one David Brebner in Dandaleith, who was drinking with Simpson and Simpson asked a sight of the watch, and went out a little and on his return refused his having got the watch, but upon searching it was found he'd it in the back part of his breeches towards his garter. Is that a cause to turn him out of his possession? If he is a thief he has chosen a proper place for having fresh mutton. I believe I could set his improvement if it is necessary to have him turned out which I think it is. A thief in such a situation is a dangerous neighbour.

Is Captain McGilligan yet arrived at Banff? I wish I could get my grass seeds that are on board of him brought the length of Cullen. The expense of carriage adds not a little to the high price of the seeds.

Peter May to James Ross, Cullen House SRO. GD248/978/5

Elgin, 10 April 1769

I wrote you with John McGillivery yesterday. This comes by George Stronach who wants to know my Lord's first resolution about Dykeside, which I advised him to. I already wrote you what I know about his character and circumstances, both which are favourable, but you are not to imagine him equal to Boyne's tenant. The farm of Dykeside is in very bad order at present. I will sow about 36 bolls there this season and I am persuaded I will not reap double my seed in many of the fields; it is quite out-laboured and extended. The tenant is a little suspicious of its ruining him in the beginning and would fain have a little care for the first five years, though I believe he will stand to his offer without any abatement rather than want it. Enclosing here for a tenant is entirely out of the question; draining some parts of the low ground would be of use. There are more offices than would accommodate George Stronach or any other ordinary tenant and I suppose he will not take under inventory more houses than is useful for him. The other houses can be sold for the least account. The slate house might be reserved as I suppose they would not choose to live in it, but this my Lord will judge of himself. Captain Donald looks for an answer.

I have a note from Mr Grant pressing me for two or three days to give him some assistance in setting one or two farms in Strathspey. My own affairs make it inconvenient for me, but that I would get over to serve Mr Grant, providing your moss or any other pressing affair be out of the question.

PS. If Mr Charles could spare us 40 or 50 cauliflowers it would be extremely obliging; the bearer would bring them along.

dorso: 11 April. Wrote him to conclude a bargain with G. Stronach in terms of his signed offer, reserving the slated house and such offices as he has not use for, with a power to build others if necessary.

Peter May to James Ross, Cullen House SRO. GD248/978/5

Elgin, 13 April 1769

I had your favours along with Geo. Stronach who has appointed tomorrow to meet with me about Dykeside. I shall endeavour to finish with him as well as I can. I have this moment yours by the express and shall stop selling any more victual. I find they have not delivered as much into the granary as I had reason to expect from their first account. The oats was in general so bad that I could not receive several of their farms. The tenants of Tomshill pay in their farms to Mr Duff, they are always in arrears and what they don't pay we must pay otherwise. We have only in the granary just now 197 bolls 1 firlot bere and 23 bolls, 3 firlots and 2 pecks of oats. Linkwood is to pay 2 chalders bere and 20 bolls of oats, which he says shall be ready to put on board the same ship with the rest. I have a letter from Mr Robertson advising me of their having a ship in Lossiemouth to take it away immediately but according to his account he has expected a larger quantity. I have appointed all the deficient tenants to come in tomorrow and give me an exact list of what they can pay and then I shall make out a state and send it to you.

I wish I had got instructions about the kirk of Birnie but I shall manage as well as I can, and if I finish with James Riach it shall be on the best terms and his finding Cluny caution.

I suppose Simpson's affair will soon be forgot, the magistrates here are not very attentive and I imagine we will hear no more of it.[1]

Mr Williams has been here these two days and has engrossed the most of my time travelling over my Lord's estates in this neighbourhood. He thinks well of the Cuttlehill, which I have people employed at, but as he is to be at Cullen in a day or two I refer you to his own account.

Peter May to James Ross, Cullen House SRO. GD248/978/5

Elgin, 14 April 1769

This comes by Mr Williams to whose account I refer you about our lime quarry at the Cuttlehill with the clay, marl, etc. I am no conjurer in these things but Mr Williams persuades me that it is a thing of consequence. I had a letter from [John Innes of] Edingight who went along with me to the Cuttlehill; he thinks it of value, but not so high as Mr Williams. If it is to be prosecuted I believe it would be necessary to have some hands who understand more about quarrying. I am much difficulted here, they cannot be had and such as we get are extremely bad. I give them all the attention I can but that is not sufficient.

I have finished with George Stronach about Dykeside and made

[1] He stole a silver watch, *see* p. 146.

out a minute with him for 19 years to my Lord's satisfaction and have bound him to such covenants as thought most useful and could get him to agree to, indeed I had much ado to get him to agree to any improvements. Fallowing and sowing grass seeds are so rare in this neighbourhood that they are frighted at it. I have reserved the slate house and a stable or liberty to build one.

Upon looking over the victual book I find there is only 213 bolls of bere and 24 bolls of oats of this crop put into the granary and I have made enquiry the most of the tenants, and from their account there will not be above three chalders more to receive. Most of the arrears I have bills for, payable at Whitsunday at 10s. 6d. the boll and some few to Martinmas at 11s. There will be some of them in arrears. One tenant who has not paid a shilling of his money rent or farm has just now given up his possession – Jonean James, smith in Rashrock, so that the crop to lay down will have the bulk of two rents on it. These arrears to their late master are now striking to them. I wish I may get Smith's possession set as it is now so close on the term, I shall try to do the best I can. I have sent you Mr Sampson's commission.

Decreet arbitral for division of runrig lands of Kinloss between Colonel Hector Munro of Novar and Alexander Brodie of Lethen

SRO. GD247/67/20/18[1]

Kinloss, 19 April 1769

. . . Captain John Forbes of New and Charles Robertson of Kindeace arbiters mutually named and chosen by the said parties . . . not only to divide their several lands lying runrig as they shall think right but also to excamb and exchange such parts of their respective lands and divide such part of their commonties as they shall think needful so that both parties submitters may have their lands contiguous and convenient . . . [there follows a description of the various holdings] . . . this day lined and poled by Messrs Peter May and Charles Ross,[2] land surveyors.

[1] *Also* SRO. RS29/8/206v.

[2] Charles Ross, land surveyor and nurseryman, from Greenlaw near Paisley, Renfrewshire. He had a long career surveying mainly in his home county, but he made several professional excursions to the north.

Peter May to James Ross, Cullen House SRO. GD248/978/5

Elgin, 23 April 1769

I had your favours of the 17th. I am glad my Lord approves of Dykeside being set. James Smith is an entire bankrupt, and I must take it off his hand or lose by continuing him in the possession. James Asher, his neighbour, is much in the same situation, their arrears to New Miln will, I am afraid, soon dish them up. I have advertised Smith's part at the neighbouring kirks.

I wrote you sometime ago about the 10,000 spruce firs which came to Elgin Saturday last by mistake. The carrier says he got them from my man Couts at Aberdeen with orders to carry them to Cullen, but he did not come that way. The smallest of them should be transplanted in a nursery. They come by this express.

I would have been ready to have set out for Aberdeen some days ago but had advice from Messrs Robertson and Co. that there was a ship at Lossiemouth to receive our farms, but it seems they have given orders to carry away the old victual and not this years. I look for a letter by the Monday post and if I am not interrupted by then I think I can be ready to set out by the middle of the week. I shall bring my accounts about surveying of which you have a double already. If the divisions of Bogbain would have been delayed until my return it would have been more convenient for me, but if it must be otherwise I shall take them in my way.

I imagine I cannot be ready to set out for Belmont before the middle of June; if that would answer for Lord Privy Seal it would occasion least interruption to our business here. Eight days sooner or later would make no difference with me.

The hawthorn berries and your plaster hair come to Cullen Friday next along with Mr Harris the carrier. I have from Dr Saunders of my grass seeds being come to Banff and put under Mr Cranshaw's care. If they could be brought to Cullen against Friday next, the carrier would bring them forward here. I beg you will try what can be done for me.

The quarriers are going on at the Cuttlehill but they have not got any solid rock only stone mixed with layings of clay and scarce any stone above three foot deep but I think the clay a very great mean of improvement and I believe the limestone is worth the bulk of the expense especially for these sandy fields.

John Adam to Lord Findlater SRO. GD248/982/1

Edinburgh, 26 April 1769

. . . Your lordship lays me under great obligations by offering to spare Mr May to take a look of Woodstone and New Thornton.[1] I had the mortification to find these lands not only under lease, but most of them under long ones, so that no great improvement can be expected from them for sometime. I was indeed informed that some of the farms were rather set too high, and would scarce stand at the present rent. It would therefore be of great use to have Mr May's judgement how far that is really the case; and if they must be let down, what would be a proper rent to let them at, so as not to oppress the tenant, but to have what they agree for well paid. I do not perceive that any of them are tied down to a method of improvement which I believe would be very necessary, in case any of the leases were to be renewed, and in that Mr May's assistance would be of the greatest use. In all this, however, your Lordship will perceive there can be no immediate hurry, but at any time when he has occasion to be in that part of the country however, or is passing my Lord Privy Seal's, or any other part of that neighbourhood. I should be extremely happy if he could allot as much time as to consider these things. For this purpose, if your Lordship give me leave, I shall write to him. . . .

Peter May to James Ross, Cullen House SRO. GD248/978/5

Elgin, 28 April 1769

This comes by John McKerran who brings you 24 stone weight of plaster hair, which I believe is four stone more than you wanted, but the man I got it from had no more on hand and he would not sell less than the whole together. It is extremely ill to be had, many people are wanting it just now. The hawthorn berries also comes along.

[1] In St Cyrus parish and Marykirk parish, Kincardineshire.

Upon my writing Cluny about his being caution for James Riach his undertaking to repair the kirk of Birnie I had the enclosed from his son whereby you will see his father declines accepting to be his caution. I have since employed Peter Grant who lives at Sheriffmill to make out an estimate. Mr Grant is a man of some circumstance, and will easily find caution. He was employed for putting up the mill at Rothes. Enclosed I send you his estimates both for repairing the roof and also for putting on a new one. It is my opinion that the new one would be the most economical plan, but I beg to have directions that I may proceed to one or either. The minister is quite impatient and threatens to have recourse to the presbytery. If you have any particular form of a contract with the undertaker I wish you would send me one. The minister thinks that taking down the choir (which is on the end of the kirk and only communicates with it by a large arched door) and making a loft to supply for it would answer better. I have caused the undertaker make two estimates, one of them supposing the choir kept up and the other it taken down, which makes some difference in the estimates. It is also my own opinion that the choir might be wanted both in point of neatness and convenience, but when I consider the parish of Birnie as daily increasing in numbers I am doubtful but it would be more prudent to keep it up. Pray will you direct me in these things.

I am quite tired in attending the delivery of my lime and God knows when I shall have done for all the fishers have given up working. Going into a ship with unslaked limestone and working among it is going into hell. I know no other comparison strong enough for so horrid a work, but I must persevere. Be so good as give orders that McKerran get my grass seed and that he gets orders to be careful of them.

Peter May to James Ross, Cullen House SRO. GD248/978/5

Elgin, 30 April 1769

I had your favours covering my Lord's which I laid before the gentlemen and to which they seemed to pay a good deal of respect. The road to Lossiemouth is to be the first operation this summer; but I am told by the clerk that there is not funds to make a bridge. I am appointed to direct the proper tract and to get in estimates for the bridge to be laid before a committee. I gave in a memorandum about that part of the road leading from Elgin to Rothes and have got an order for employing the tenants of Birnic, Linkwood and a part of Coxton to help to repair it. I pointed out that a bridge would be necessary at the Wakemill of Linkwood and got an order for £5, but they qualified the order until there should be money in the clerk's hands. Mr George Duff was present who seems to be but little acquaint with the geography or the situation of the country. Brodie did not attend, Mr Grant wrote an apology that his attendance on Knockando's burying had put it out of his power to be present at the meeting. He sent them a form of an address to His Majesty, which was espied over with little variation and to be forwarded to Col. Grant, the county member. None of the Grants were present at the meeting, which was but a very thin one. Altyre, Burdsyards, Logie and Provost Brodie and son were the acting part, but they are all in parties.

I am loathe to lose my plough which is presently engaged in the first fur of a fallow field and have therefore hired a horse on purpose to bring the cart my Lord has been so obliging as to lend. McKerran left one of the bags of rye grass behind him; give me leave to beg you will cause give it to the boy and order some of the servants to help him to fasten it on his cart, if a cart saddle could be spared along with the cart to help us forward.

I have taken up the most part of last week with my lime which I hope to get clear tomorrow; it has been a terrible piece of business, but little can be done here without lime, and I propose to have ten acres under fallow to be laid down with wheat this autumn, which I mean to lime at the rate of 100 bolls to the acre at 4 firlots to each boll. Mr Stronach and the Old Mill Company were here on Friday last directing where their flour mill was to be built; they applied to me for lime but I begged to be excused.

I am much puzzled about going to Aberdeen. All my grass seeds are yet to sow. The reparations of the kirk of Birnie must be begun immediately and the season of casting peats is just coming on. On the other hand I am under promise to give the Collector some days and P[rovost] Duncan a plan; you saw a letter to that purpose from a friend who I cannot break with. Last post I had a letter from Mr Alison advising that Lord Privy Seal was to be in the country about the 20 May and that he supposed I would be wanted soon after. I have wrote to Aberdeen to be excused until I am in my way south to Belmont and if I can be at liberty from my engagements there I mean to delay it. If not I can only be there for a few days as the term must hurry me back. Send me the estimates for Birnie and your directions; put up the plea and send it by the bearer.

James Stewart Mackenzie, Lord Privy Seal, to James Ogilvy, 6th Earl of Findlater SRO. GD248/3408/6

Hill Street, 13 May 1769

I take the very first opportunity of acknowledging the honor of your letter of the 4th inst. inclosing one from Mr [Peter] May concerning the time of his coming to Belmont. I should be extremely sorry to pu your Lordship to any inconvenience upon my account and notwithstanding the value I very justly set on his skilfull assistance I would far rather be deprived of it than subject you to any disappointment or disadvantage, or himself to any difficulties. If therefore he can be with me at Belmont Castle about the 16 June as he mentions in his letter and that without the bad consequences I have mentioned, it will answer my purpose perfectly well; or should your Lordship's or his own affairs detain him some days longer than the 16th June, I should wish him rather to postpone his coming to me than to neglect them. May I therefore beg your Lordship to communicate to him what I have here said on this subject.

Peter May to James Ross, Cullen House SRO. GD248/978/5

Elgin, 19 May 1769

I wrote you a line from Keith and sent by James Burges notes referring to the enclosing and draining the Bogbains and Burnside.

Mr Robertson of Portsoy and his partner Mr Milne called on me this day in their way from the west country. They very readily agreed to let me have barley of my Lord Findlater's bere and from the growth of his own farm. If I could get it carried to Speyside it would do me a particular favour; the odds betwixt that and Portsoy are not great, but in case there should be difficulty to find it that length the next to that would be to send it in bags to Portsoy, the bags to be put on board a sloop which Mr Robertson intends sending to Lossie beginning of next week – a chalder or 20 bolls would do. The sacks should be carefully returned, but still if it could be sent to Speyside it would answer better. We have very good barley in the country but by its being partly barley and partly Scots bere the size is unequal and that occasions a waste in striking it down for the largest must be reduced to the same size with the smallest.

Friday next is the term day and upon that day our mills must be appreciate. I am at a loss where to get proper people for birliemen. There are flour millers at Forres and Kilravóck; shall I apply to them, or will you send the General's miller? You know, I, as tacksman of the mill, become a party and would be glad to get instructions and I beg you will forward them in course.

I have this day repeated applications by the tenants of Bishopmill to be allowed some peats, if that could be done easily it would accommodate them greatly and the few loads they would want can hurt the mosses almost nothing. Before the mosses of Birnie were shut up they got peats to buy, now they have no fire at all; Mr William Burnet, my Lord's man of business wishes to know if my Lord would oblige him with 20 cartloads from Birnie.

Lord Findlater to Alex. Duffus and James Chalmers

NLS. MS.3258, f. 1

Cullen House, 25 May 1769

I desire that you would go to Elgin and taking such other assistance along with you as Mr May shall direct, that you make out a distinct state of all the mills at Linkwood, as well the houses as the machinery, and that you put such a value upon each of them as you shall think they are worth. Mr May will be along with you and see that your inventory and state be rightly made up. You will write just two copies of the state and inventory which is to be signed by you and any persons Mr May sends along with you, and Mr May is to sign a note on the foot of one of the copies obliging himself to be accountable for the contents. After I have signed the other copy it will be sent to Mr May.

Peter May to James Ross, Cullen House SRO. GD248/978/5

Elgin, 28 May 1769

I had your note along with Mr Duffus with a line from the company about the 20 bolls of bere I wanted from them. They were in a mistake as to its being Moray bere. It was only on account of its being entirely barley and that Mr Wilson recommended it as the very best he had seen that induced me to ask it; I have wrote them to that purpose and put them in mind of what passed at Elgin.

I enclose you the inventories of the mills, with the victual house and the house Linkwood servants lived in and his own chamber on the end of it. The other offices were comprised. Mr Duffus said he had not skill of country houses nor did I think it necessary to appreciate them. They are fitter for the dunghill than offices and I have referred them until my Lord have an opportunity of being in the country to give his own instructions about them. There is a necessity for putting them in repair, the walls as well as the roofs are ruinous.

I have wrote my Lord Privy Seal the enclosed letter and left it open for my Lord Findlater's perusal. It is impossible for me to fix my time of being there with more precision than I have done. I have many things to do at Aberdeen, I proposed setting out there the beginning of this week, which must now be postponed for some days. I shall wait of Mr Robertson and give him all the information I can as to the lying of the grounds, names of places, marks, etc.

I have paid Mr Duffus and J. Chalmers' bill at B[aillie] Leslies. Fraser did not come from Castle Grant but I had a mill carpenter from Forres who assisted at the mills. The machinery of the flour mill is extremely trifling, and the house a hampered hole. I shall have the pleasure to see you soon in my way south.

Division of the runrigs of Blairton[1] SRO. CS29 2/3/1770

Hopeshill, 10 June 1769

Compeared Peter May, land measurer, who was appointed to attend this day and place in order he might be present to witness

[1] Belhelvie parish, Aberdeenshire. A summons of division of runrig and common property lands of Blairton was raised by John Duncan of Mosstown, provost of

the division of the different lots of the foresaid lands. And he being solemnly sworn depones that George Brown, one of his surveyors, at the deponent's desire and by the appointment of the commissioner made an actual survey of the whole lands under division, and protracted a rude draught thereof, distinguishing and expressing the different measures of the several fields by their different qualities of infield, outfield and pasture according as they were pointed out to him by the possessors. And also for the satisfaction of the inspectors extended the measures of the several farms and crofts classed under their different denominations, Depones that the said George Brown is a qualified measurer and is and has been constantly employed as such by the deponent and other persons for several years past; Depones that after the said survey and rude draught was finished he the deponent came to the ground, along with John Lumsden one of the appreciators, and viewed the lands under division and pointed out where he apprehended the lines of division would run, and also made a memorandum in writing in what manner, according to the deponent's opinion, the appreciators should proceed most properly; Depones that he has this day surveyed some of the fields and finds the measures accurate and exact conform to the survey made by the said George Brown, and the Deponent makes no doubt but that the rest of the survey is equally just; And further depones that he shall in presence of the commissioner and inspector perambulate and measure the different lines of marches made out by them, to distinguish and divide the lots of the foresaid lands and shall thereafter make out and delineate the same upon a new plan, and this he declares to be truth as he shall answer to God.

[The process continued at Aberdeen on 16 June 1769]

Compeared the said Peter May and produced a plan of the lands of Blairton made out by him in terms of the order of last meeting, And he being solemnly sworn depones that he has faithfully and honestly execute the said plan and has therein pointed out and

---

Aberdeen, and John Lickly, minister of Old Meldrum, against Mrs Margaret Gordon and others in 1768. Although this process was essentially about the division of 592 statute acres of runrig lands, it included the commonty of Muir of Drum and Red Moss. It was found that the latter could not be divided so it remained common to all proprietors.

distinguished the lines of division between the different lots, conform to the report of the inspectors, which plan is marked and signed by the deponent and by the commissioner and clerk of this date and this truth as he shall answer to God.

Thereafter the commissioner having compared the foresaid plan with the report of the inspectors before engrossed and found them to correspond and agree together, he approves of the said plan and appoints the same to be reported herewith.

Account for surveying the runrigs of Blairton

TO surveying the lands of Blairton consisting of 469 Scots acres and making out a plan thereof according to the division of it into three lots as also the contents and measures engrossed in a book classed according to their different denomination of infields, outfields, etc. The whole at £1 Stg the hundred acre, viz. for 469 acres.	£4 13s. 4d.
TO attendance on the appreciators giving them assistance about the lines of division and remeasuring their lines when marked out on the ground, two days with an assistant at 10s. per day for both.	£1
	£5 13s. 4d.

Aberdeen 17 June 1769. Received payment of the above account from the hands of Mr John Clerk, and the same is discharged by Peter May.

Lord Findlater to Sir Alexander Grant of Dalvey

SRO. GD248/681/4

Cullen House, 1 July 1769

Upon my return from Troup and Banff I found here this day your letter of the 28 June, and immediately have directed a rough copy to be made of the survey Mr May made of the Corry and of the grounds in the neighbourhood of it. I hope it will be done before the post goes, though somewhat in a hurry. My intention in desiring to make that survey was only to know the fact, how the ground lay and Mr May assured me it was done with accuracy and attention, which I have no sort of reason to doubt of as it was done with no other view than what is mentioned above. The person who copies the survey was along with him at the measuring of it. Mr May himself is now in the south and I cannot tell when he will be north. I think the more fully people are prepared before coming to a meeting of this kind, the better. I cannot say that I am as yet, but I think in forming our ideas of it the valued rent of the different proprietors having right would be in view, and after considering that, along with the extent of the ground in the Corry, it would be desirable that everybody had a part appropriated to him in proportion to his valued rent, and in the situation most convenient for his property. My Lord Fife's property contiguous to the Corry is only Kellas, but it is asserted that Pluscarden has had immemorial pasturing on it. Pluscarden and Old Miln are valued together and that valuation can be easily divided by us when we meet together upon seeing the rentals. I am glad that you undertake to answer fully on this matter with Knockando and Elchies. There was formerly a line of marches drawn there by the late Lord Fife[1] and Sir Robert Gordon, which I suppose you and the other gentlemen in your neighbourhood are no strangers to; but in meeting with an intention to agree we must not take umbrage at what may have been wrong done formerly and as far as possible refrain from starting claims or making objections that may indispose any of the parties concerned from coming to a reasonable settlement, which, with your experience and coolness to guide us, I flatter myself will be done at this meeting. If it is not done then I see no prospect of it's ever being done.

If I have omitted any that are in the use of pasturing there or inserted any that are not, I shall be obliged to you if you will let me know.

dorso: Copies of three letters of this date to Lord Fife, John Grant at Easter Elchies and Leslie of Balnageith on the subject of the quarry.[2]

James Stuart Mackenzie to the Earl of Findlater

SRO. GD248/3408/6

Belmont Castle, 2 July 1769

I give you the trouble of this in consequence of the contents of your letter to Mr May which he has communicated to me, wherein I see your Lordship would incline that he should be with you before the 18th inst. Now, my Lord, as I apprehend we shall not be able to

[1] William Duff, 1st Earl Fife, died 30 Sept. 1763 at Rothiemay.

[2] Not reproduced here, *see* SRO. GD248/681/4.

put the finishing hand to our matters here before that period, I greatly wish that you could contrive to dispense with his attendance on you for a week or ten days longer than the 18th in order to get our bottoms entirely wound up before his departure from hence; for if that be not done effectually, the infallible consequence to me, situated as I am here, will be this, that all will be, in a manner, to begin again, and the whole time and trouble hitherto employed will be thrown away. This being the state of the case I dare say your Lordship will acquiesce in the delay above mentioned of a few days, unless Mr May's being with you by the 18th should be indispensably and absolutely necessary. . . .

Account between James Stuart Mackenzie and Robert Menzies, W.S.
SRO. RH9/18/44/236

July 1769

To Peter May, land surveyor, for valuing your Lordship's estates in Angus and Perthshire, per Archibald Menzies's bill on the account, £79 0s. 0d.

James Stuart Mackenzie to the Earl of Findlater
SRO. GD248/3408/6

Belmont Castle, 16 August 1769

I had yesterday the honour of your letter of the 11th inst. and return you a thousand thanks for the suggestions contained in it of one or two persons who you think may answer my purpose. The sort of man I want is one perfectly skilled in country affairs, upon whose integrity, ability, and the exact execution of my orders in my absence, I may with confidence rely. I need not add that he must be a competent master of his pen. Your Lordship, who is almost constantly on the spot and superintending your own affairs, can with facility correct at once any error or impropriety in the conduct of your agents or servants, should there be any; but my case is widely different. I am here perhaps three or four months in a couple of years, almost a stranger to the country and to the ways of doing here from never having, I may say, resided in it during the whole course of my life; in my situation therefore it is of much greater importance to have a person thoroughly fit for his duty than it is to any other man whatever residing on his estate with long experience and knowledge of the country about him. Of the two persons your Lordship has done me the favour to suggest to me, I think Walker's character seems to come nearest to my point of view, and I will have some enquiry made about him, tho' I must be very cautious in fixing on the person, as so much will depend on setting out right at first. By what I learn in this country, I observe there is hardly such a thing as what they call in England a land steward, regularly bred to that service; what is called a factor here seems to be only a sort of agent and receiver, which is a mighty small part indeed of an English land steward's business, who does not employ three days in the year in receiving rents, but his great and material business is attending to the proper laying out of farms, and instructing the tenants in the cultivation of their lands, directing the making and keeping in repair all fences and inclosures, valuing woods, timber, etc., directing the regular cutting of it, etc., etc. In these and many other works he is constantly on horseback going about the estate of which he has the management so as to see everything that is going forward among the tenants. By what I have heard, there are not half a dozen such land stewards in all Scotland. Your Lordship's own country affairs are, I am told, carried on in that proper manner, but those of mighty few other persons in Scotland are. Now, my dear Lord, I have endeavoured to explain to you what I am in quest of, and I should be much obliged to you if you could give me, or get me, a right man for my purpose. I should choose to have him on the footing of eating with me when I happen to be here, and as to his salary whatever you would think proper for me to give him I should acquiesce in. I ought to ask many pardons for taking the liberty to trouble you with a matter of this kind, which I should not have done had not your obliging letter led me into it. . . .

Peter May to ? James Grant, clerk at Castle Grant

SRO. GD248/979/2

Elgin, 19 September 1769

I appointed the tenants of Dundorcas, whose peat were partly destroyed at the moss at the head of the burn of Auchenroath by

Mr Grant, to come in here this day to give Mr Burnet their sanction for prosecuting Mr Grant; but upon my informing him that we only possessed that moss as to pasture, except this year I directed them to cast peats there, which he said was not a proper foundation for a criminal action. That though Mr Grant had more possession there than we, he might interrupt them from casting there or in any other moss in which they had not been in possession, and that the sheriff could not judge of right but of possession only. I suggested to Mr Burnet that as Mr Grant had never been in possession of that moss he had no right to disturb or molest my Lord Findlater's tenants, but as I have already mentioned he thinks the point of right does not come under the sheriff's cognisance and is of opinion that it is better to let that alone until we get advice.

Since writing the above Mr Burnet and I waited of Whitely the sheriff and requested of him to give a court for calling the action against Mr Grant, but he says it is contrary to the rules he has laid down, and would not consent to a court for calling a new cause on account of the court being formerly adjourned until November; but he offered to give an interdict in the meantime upon a petition for that purpose, but Mr Burnet was of opinion that it was not proper that Mr Grant should know our strength until we were ready to bring proof and the action in form. As we can do nothing at present he expects to hear from you with respect to the Dundorcas people and your instructions thereanent.

Since I left Cullen I have been attending my shearers. I find that the more necessary as I have a great many hired hooks every day. I am anxious to get my harvest cut down in this good weather, and would fain hope to get through the bulk of it in a fortnight hence. My engagements with my Lord to value the lands of Deskford makes it necessary to put my own affairs in order so as to spare time to his Lordship's. I have not been able to get my information filled up since I left Cullen. The harvest is on hand every day, and I am loathe to ask people to come here and I must own I have little spare time to go abroad, but that shall be soon supplied and I hope in time. I wish the sheriff had consented to have given us a court for the action against Mr Grant. I suspect he does not care to engage with it, he is timid of himself and his clerk I believe is imperfect. I am told the feuars are all in concert; how far this may be depended on I will not venture to say, but I shall try what I can pick up and you may depend on every information I can give you. When am I to expect the sketch? I want it to lay before Mr Burnet in order to explain the mosses to him and their local situation.

Memorandum respecting the wood on the Mains of Elchies by Messrs Grant and May SRO. GD248/982/3

28 October 1769

Mr Grant the factor walked through the woods at Elchies along with Mr May and it is their joint opinion that the trees growing upon the water banks should be cut down as the weight of the tops assists the stream to carry them away but this only refers to such trees as are within reach of ordinary spates.

That the birch woods in general don't appear to be thriving, but rather growing worse daily; it is therefore their opinion that they should be sold at least such part of them one year and such another part a second year, so as to have the bulk cut down in 3 years, leaving some standards to seed the ground again.

The allers in the Aller ward are too thick in many places and would require to be thinned and so would the belts along the river side. The hawthorn hedge along that enclosure called the Well Park lying on the left hand of the avenue to the house is overgrown and become thin at the root and should in our opinion be cut down within half a foot of the ground so as the young shoots may get up and make a close thick hedge.

As many people want timber for houses and utensils this would be a proper time to dispose of them among the country tenants.

Dorso: Cullen House, 19 December 1769. All that is mentioned in the within memorandum may be done; and Peter Charles is to be sent up for that purpose in the end of January or beginning of February with directions likewise to cut down some straight allers for making flake heads; Mr Hall and Mr Cranshaw will inform me as to the quantity and orders will be given about it.

Peter May to James Ross, factor to the Duke of Gordon

SRO. GD44/43/14

Cullen House, 5 November 1769

I have wrote George Brown to wait of you on his way to Aberdeen which I believe will be in a few days. It is very likely that he will take my advice before he determine himself entirely. His connection with me makes me bleak to commend him, but I believe I can venture to assure you that he is honest, diligent and tractable, and can measure land with as much accuracy and dispatch as anybody. He draws and lays down his plans well enough, but in that part some of my other lads have excelled him. He writes well enough, but has not that correctness in spelling though he improves in that particular daily. I can recommend his skill in farming and gardening more than his brother surveyors. But I forget myself and say too much.

You know that I am a flour miller and tacksman of my Lord Findlater's mills of Linkwood, which I am afraid I shall have cause to repent. My Lord Fife has lately built a flour mill at the old mills of Elgin, to which you know the whole town and liberties are thirled. The decreet pronounced lately in his Lordship's favours prohibits anybody to lodge wheat or other grain in the town of Elgin that is to be used for the inhabitants, except it be grinded at his mills to which it is subjected to pay multure and thirlage. This is particularly hard on me, for I cannot buy wheat in the country and lodge in a granary in Elgin without paying multure to Lord Fife's mills, and I have no granary any other way. The other day I was advising with Whitely the sheriff about it, who told me that he would put me in the way of being accommodated. He mentioned the Duke's having an empty house in that part of the town called the College which is without the liberties of the town, and that he was persuaded the use of it might be had. I have not the honour of being known to His Grace, nor do I know how to apply for it except you can venture to do it for me. The windows and some parts of the floors are very insufficient, but I would help them myself with boards. There is a garden about the house which is waste at present. If His Grace was to cause throw it down with grass seeds it would yield a rent. If any advice in my power were acceptable I would be extremely ready to give it. Any rent for a few months accommodation with the house I would frankly agree to and if I could get the use of it soon it would add to my accommodation much, as this is the time of buying in wheat for the year. I believe I shall be a couple of weeks at Cullen valuing the lands of Deskford, etc. I will wait of you in my way to Elgin, but if you have leisure will be glad to hear from you before that time. Any time when I am not immediately engaged in my Lord Findlater's affairs, any assistance I could give you valuing land I would be extremely ready upon the smallest notice, and I have the vanity to think it might be useful.

George Brown, Land Surveyor, to James Ross, Factor to the Duke of Gordon SRO. GD44/49/22

Aberdeen, 15 November 1769

I waited of Mr May in my way to Aberdeen and communicated to him your proposals. He leaves me at liberty to judge for my self, and is rather for my engaging with the Duke than otherwise. But my present inclination is more disposed to prosecute my business in the way I am in than to engage by the year. I was recommended by Mr May to Brodie, and Brodie recommended me to some of the neighbouring gentlemen, so that I have found plenty of business even in my first outset. I find I am now under engagements for eight or nine months at least, and I have reason to believe that more will cast up in time, and this turns out greatly more advantageous than any engagement I can get by the year. But if his Grace shall not be accommodated soon with a surveyor by the year, I would be extremely glad to have the honour of serving him, and its very like upon having a trial, that I may come under engagements for some time afterwards. Give me leave to assure you that being under your directions would be a very great inducement, and I think I can promise that I would do every thing in my power either in the way of my business or otherwise to deserve your countenance.

Peter May to James Ross, factor to the Duke of Gordon

SRO. GD44/49/22

Cullen House, 16 November 1769

I had your favours by George Brown who came here just as

indetermined as he left Gordon Castle and went forward to advise with his friends at Aberdeen. I am very sincere when I tell you that my advice was to accept of the Duke's terms and to put himself entirely under your direction, and I have no doubt but he would have given satisfaction, and found his account from being in the Duke's service. He has promised to write me from Aberdeen which shall be immediately communicated to you. I learned from J. Burges that George had a suspicion of William Anderson;[1] it seems he had heard at Fochabers that Mr Anderson meddled with Mr [John] Baxter[2] and was the cause of Roumieu's[3] leaving the Castle. I am persuaded this is without foundation, and had George mentioned it to me I would have pointed out the ridiculousness of it.

I am still wandering thro the fields, which turns out a disagreeable business in this bad weather. I find the rents of Deskford will double in many places, and I believe will rise two thirds on the whole. I think of getting to Elgin on Friday morning or Thursday evening to take a look of my own affairs, when I will have the pleasure to wait of you.[4]

Peter May to William Grant SRO. GD248/979/2

Elgin, 22 December 1769

Baillie Simpson of this place comes to Cullen tomorrow to get a tack on two lots of the moor of Linkwood. I shall send a sketch of the moor along with him and the terms of our agreement. I wish

[1] Land surveyor in service of Duke of Gordon, *see* I. H. Adams, *Descriptive List of Plans in the Scottish Record Office*, H.M.S.O., Edinburgh, vol. 2, 1970, pp. vii–xvi.

[2] Architect from Edinburgh who designed the large extensions to Gordon Castle in the early 1770s and who, in May 1776, laid out the new town of Fochabers.

[3] Abraham Roumieu, architect, son of John Roumieu of London, refiner, was a member of a Huguenot family. He was apprenticed to Isaac Ware (1748) and then to Thomas Reynolds (1753). No building designed by him is known, but in 1766–7 he was in the service of the 4th Duke of Gordon for whom he made unexecuted designs for Gordon Castle (SRO. RHP2389–91).

[4] About this time May was expected to return to Belmont, for James Stuart Mackenzie wrote to the Earl of Findlater from Hill Street, London, on 23 Nov., 'I have been wishing to hear of Peter May's arrival at Belmont. Archy Menzies writes me that he is waiting his summons with impatience'. He had not arrived by 12 Dec. for, 'I fear Peter May will hardly get to Belmont before the gentleman he was to meet there will be obliged to repair to Edinburgh'. (SRO. GD248/3408/6). In fact he was still in Elgin on 24 Dec. (SRO. GD248/979/2).

any instructions respecting Mr Grant's process could be sent by him, for I am extremely anxious to have it finished and at present the whole lies open. I suspect I must take another review of the hills and get the Red Myre pointed with some other informations that I am not yet clear about.[1] I have got an offer from Alex. Taylor, late in Consack, for the farm of Kellockhead which I think a good one. The present tenant likewise spoke to me about it but I am persuaded Taylor who has 4 or 5 sons will make a much better tenant. Kellockhead is a farm lying above Dandaleith in Gallovie's collection. I shall send you the offer tomorrow and if it pleases the man may be trysted to Cullen when I come there which must be soon.

Minutes of Commissioners of Annexed Estates

SRO. E721/18, p. 67

Edinburgh, 12 February 1770

. . . Captain Forbes having given in to the office a book of plans of certain farms on the said estate of Lovat, being 30 in number, drawn by Peter May, land surveyor, and having reported that Mr May's charge for the same amounts to £30, *Ordered:* That the factor do pay the same and take Mr May's discharge therefore, and that he employ Mr May to make out plans in the same manner of the farms in the barony of Stratherrick and in Glenstrathfarrar. *Remitted:* To Mr Menzies, General Inspector, and the said Captain Forbes to examine the rental of the barony of Stratherrick given in by Mr May and report their opinion thereupon to the Board.[2]

Peter May to George Brown NLS. MS. 3258, f. 4

Bellmont Castle, 20 April 1770

I wrote you several posts ago and also wrote [Robert Barclay of] Ury at the same time about engaging with a survey of his estate. I hope you have waited of him as I directed, and that you have ad-

[1] The grazings and mosses referred to in this account lay on the flanks of the 1,000-ft summit of Brown Muir which was the southern limits of the commonty of Coxton and Blackhills. *See* p. 121, n. 1.

[2] The General Inspector reported back on 26 Feb. 1770 that the factor's representation was true and the proposed abatements of rent be allowed. The Commissioners agreed.

justed the terms of your agreement. I think of being north in about eight days hence and must be some days at Achortes. I want to have a survey of the parks as they are now laid out there, and of the other possessions as they are presently occupied by the tenants. I wish you would find leisure to do that for me before I come to the country. I want nothing but a rude draught of the lands according to their present situation, but I would have everything marked locally and the quality of the ground, particularly the pasture, taken notice of. I suppose a couple of days would do. You may stay in Jeallies or in Bourtrees as you think proper. Your expense shall be paid by me and when I get an estate you shall be further employed and paid for your labour. At any rate I must have it measured before I leave the country. In case you be employed with Mr Barclay make my best compliments to him and in my name ask it as a favour to me, and I am persuaded he will not refuse you leisure. There will be a good deal of work to do here this summer, which I can bring your way very easily. I can make nothing of Jock. I am so ill pleased with him that I have determined in the most express terms not to carry him past Aberdeen.

Peter May to George Brown NLS. MS. 3258, f. 5

Chapel of Seggat, 14 July 1770

I have wrote Mr Adam and sent your letter inclosed in mine, with advice that he may write you to Aberdeen. I have promised on your accuracy and attention, and I would wish that you answer my character and his expectation. Mr Adam is a polite well bred man and has much knowledge and discernment. I must recommend all the care imaginable in taking his survey, for the smallest error would soon be discovered and your notes as well as your protraction must be kept neat and clean, for he is a drawer himself and has finer hands than anybody. In a word George you must consider Mr Adam as a superior man and your being able to complete his things with approbation will be a matter of some consequence to you; and therefore I must repeat again that you be extremely accurate in every part of the mensuration. If you want advice you know I am always ready to give you my assistance in any thing, and therefore do not be backward in asking it.

I hope you have got my turnip and cabbage seeds. You know the season of sowing the cabbage plants is now at hand and therefore I beg they may not be forgot. My father will help to procure them for me. It will be the end of next week before I can get home. I go to Culsh to my brother. . . . Now George I shall be extremely glad to hear of your going to Mr Adam and of your deserving approbation; you know I have your welfare much at heart, but all your friends together cannot push you forward without your own merit. Everything depends on yourself.

Account of expense given out by Peter May when inspecting and valuing lands for His Grace the Duke of Gordon

SRO. GD44/51/377

24 September 1770. Went to Gordon Castle along with Mr Barclay of Ury, and remained there until the 27th. The business at this time was concerting with Ury and Mr Ross about a proper farm for the Duke, when the Badfours was pitched on. Paid for my servant and horses at Edward Smith's,	£0	8s.	7d.
October 2nd. Set out early for Gordon Castle and remained there until the 5th employed inspecting and valuing the Farms of Badfours and Clochins along with Mr Tod, paid to Edward Smith for servant and horses,	£0	12s.	6d.
13th March 1771. Set out to Fochabers on Wednesday morning the 13th and remained there until Saturday night the 16th employed dividing the lands of Clochens and other improvements, and perambulating the intended marches betwixt the Duke and Lord Fife along with Mr Ross, paid at Fochabers,		11s.	7d.
April 18th. Set out to Gordon Castle and continued there from Thursday the 18th to Saturday evening the 20th employed in dividing and laying out a farm for his Grace at Badfours, paid at Edward Smith's,		6s.	4d.
November 5th. Set out on Tuesday morning for Huntly along with Mr Ross to inspect and value the lands of Carvichen, and continued there until Sunday the 10th, paid at Edward Smith's and crossing the Spey in coming and going,		3s.	7d.
Expense of horse hire at the above operations.			
4 days in the first article for two horses at 2s. per day		8s.	od.
4 do. in the second article at do.		8s.	od.
4 do. in the third article at do.		8s.	od.
3 do. in the fourth article at do.		6s.	od.
6 do. in the fifth article at do.		12s.	od.
	£2	2s.	od.
Carried Forward	£4	4s.	7d.

Brought Forward	£4 4s. 7d.
21 days to the surveyor	5 5s. 0d.
To the plan of Newtongarry with book of reference	10 10s. 0d.
	£19 19s. 7d

[The above is taken from the Vouchers of Accounts. The following entry appears in the Account Book of James Ross, cashier to the Duke of Gordon]

To Peter May, land surveyor, for a plan of Newtongarry made by him in Sir Alexander Gordon's time[1] but kept until paid for, now delivered to your Grace, and for his trouble and expense attending several times at Gordon Castle and Huntly assisting to lay off the farms of Badfour and Clochan and the lands of Carvichen, per account, £19 19s. 7d.[2]

Scheme proposed for setting the farm at Cullen

SRO. GD248/982/3

Cullen House, 15 November 1770

The two parks at Upstrath contains 40 acres. One of those parks is sown down with the finest grass seeds and was not deemed to be sowed up for many years. The other have been in grass for one year. Both park is fenced round by a sunk fence faced up with stone and planted with thorn upon a border in the inside; these two parks should be kept for hay and cut for his Lordship's account.

The Cow Park contains [*blank*]. This park have been in grass for seven years and well fenced about with hedge and dyke; this park may be set for grazing.

The Old Sheep Park containing [*blank*]. This park is well fenced with dyke and hedge, it have been in grass for six years and may be set for grazing.

The Pond Park contains [*blank*]. This park have been one year in grass; it is now laid up in to the planting on every side and can be eat by nothing but by sheep and cannot be set for grazing.

The Well Park contain [*blank*]. This park have been three years in grass; it is not very well fenced but with a little it might be made fit for setting for grazing.

[1] This plan was made in 1761 (RHP2222) and the book of reference was dated Apr. 1762 (CR8/168).

[2] SRO. GD44/52/32, p. 216.

Bindhill Park contains 25 acres. This park was only ploughed up last year and has been in fallow; one quarter of this park is well improved and drained, dunged and now in turnips; the rest of this park was desired to be well dunged in the spring and either sowed down with barley and grasses or with turnips; this park is very badly fenced and cannot be set out for some years as it is all open on most every side.

Aughingall Park contains [*blank*]. This park have been in grass for seven years or more; it is well fenced and may be set for grazing. Craghead Park contains [*blank*]. This park have been in grass only two years; the dykes round is all good and may be set for grazing.

Lord Deskford's Park contains [*blank*]. This park have been long in grass; the dykes round the whole is all good and may be set for grazing.

Longshanks Park contains [*blank*]. This park have been long in grass; the dykes round the whole park is good and may be set for grazing.

The Mill Bray contains [*blank*]. This piece of ground part of it is in cabbage the other part in turnips, etc. If the dyke alongst the head were made good it is very convenient for keeping two horses or two cows.

The Millhaugh contains [*blank*]. This piece of ground my Lord Findlater was determined to drain and improve; it will keep two horses or three cows but was mostly the goose pasture.

Notes respecting the improvements at Greenhill

SRO. GD248/982/3

Cullen, 5 December 1770

These improvements are little more than well begun. In case they are to be kept going, that is, carried on in the easiest manner, a plan of the annual expense may be made out. There is one already sketched out by Mr May for improving 20 acres yearly, which will cost according to his estimate about £76 14s. Sterling.

But if it is thought more advisable to give up the working part at the Greenhill, it will then remain to enquire what shall be done to keep the improvements already made in such a state as that they will not suffer in the mean time, and how they may be disposed of to the best account; and with this view the following notes are subjoined.

The 40 acre field lying to the south of the house to be laid down with grass seeds. The lower part of this 40 acres being the one half has got a kind of fallow, and ten acres thereof is already limed; the other ten acres must be limed before seed time, which will require 1,000 bolls to lime it thoroughly, that 20 acres to be laid with grass seeds along with a crop of oats. The lesser part being the other half of the said 40 acres was pared and burnt last summer, but it is not in that state which is proper for grass seeds; at least the soil is not broke nor well enough prepared, except with the view to take the benefit of the burnt ashes, and to add thereto 1,000 bolls of powdered lime to be harrowed in with the seed crop. The ashes and lime together would greatly meliorate the soil and help forward the grass seeds, and if this application of the lime be well conducted there is reason to expect a tolerable crop of grass. *Note:* the seed oats for the Greenhill should be barley oats, which ripen early, and they should be spoke for soon. They may be got in Bogmuchals or that neighbourhood.

Those two parks inclosed, limed and laid down with grass seeds as projected above will set in grass at 8s. the acre £16.

The other part of the Greenhill that has never been cultivated should be inclosed and divided into parks agreeable to the first plan of inclosures. Could the outfences be made with stones it would have been greatly better than earthen fences, but this cannot be got done except the ground had been wrought at the same time to have got the stones; earthen therefore seem to be the only choice, and that can be done at 3d. per ell according to the pattern of the fences already made and which appear to be well done.

The whole fence necessary to complete the plan of division already agreed on will amount to about 6,648 ells, which at the above estimate of 3d. per ell is £83 2s.

These inclosures will set to the tenants in the neighbourhood and may be worth 4s. per acre, viz. for 371 acres at 4s. £74 4s.

The 40-acre field from the other side at £16

£90 4s.

There are some peats set down at the lime kiln in Deskford which were put there with an intention to burn lime. As far as they will go for that purpose seems the best way to dispose of them. If any coal could be spared from Cullen they would be likewise necessity as there will be 2,000 bolls of lime wanted at the Greenhill against next seed time.

In case there should be any difficulty in completing the necessary operations respecting farming against Whitsunday next, the assistance of the tenants can be called in, either to plough, harrow or to lead lime, coal, etc., and this right to be had particularly in view. Inclosing the Greenhill should be set about immediately. The increase of rent will depend greatly upon inclosing for without inclosing it will not yield 2s. the acre.

In carrying on the inclosing it must be attended to – 1st, To complete the inclosures already begun; 2nd, To finish one inclosure before beginning another; and 3rd, To inclose the best of the ground first.

When the work is given up at Whitsunday, in case some person does not offer as a tenant for the houses and some of the inclosures, the house may be inhabited by one or more labourers, to whom the inspection of the planting and fences is committed, who may be charged with such rent for the house and yard as shall be judged reasonable, it being always understood that any person or persons who may take the house and some of the inclosures are not to be allowed to break up any part of the ground already held.

The dung about the farmstead to be applied to the ground proposed to be laid down with grass seeds, and such places thereof as seem to want it most.

6 December 1770. My Lord Findlater approved of carrying on the operations at the Greenhill and it may be carried into execution.

Notes made out in consequence of a perambulation and inspection of farm of Cullen by James Wilson in Ardoch, Alex. Wilson, and Peter May, factors for the Earl of Findlater SRO. GD248/982/3

Cullen House, 5 December 1770

In case housekeeping is given up at Cullen it is their unanimous opinion that all the parks lying to the west of the bridge should be kept in grass which they think is the cheapest and most advantageous way to use them and at the same time will be attended with the least risk or inconvenience.

That they should be grazed with cattle taken in from the neighbourhood, viz., oxen at 10s. piece for the summer grass, that is from the first of June to the first of October, or until the harvest shall be so far advanced as to afford the owners of the cattle keeping their cattle at home, provided they are not kept on any account after the 20 October, the owners paying for every day the cattle remain after the 1st October, by the same rule by which they pay for the summer grass.

As some of the inclosures yield but poor grass, particularly the Craighead and Binhill Parks it is their opinion that they should be grazed with young cattle of year-olds and two-year-olds and that they should pay 5s. for each.

That the glen lying next to the Shirralds should be grazed with horses at 20s. each for the summer grass, but horses may continue until the first of November.

There are two inclosures called the parks of Upstrath which have been lately improved at a considerable expense. One of these parks have carried only one crop of hay and the other laid down with grass last season. From the culture these two fields have got, some fine crops of hay may be expected and it is their opinion that they should be kept in that way for some years. Cropping these parks with hay will also protect the hedges as there will be no danger from cattle. In case the hay foggage[1] is eat, there should always be a herd attending the cattle to prevent their cropping the hedges.

NB. The Earl is of opinion that the foggage should not be eat but allowed to rot on the ground; unless in the case of a scarcity of fodder for the grazing cattle, or unless Mr Wilson thinks there is danger to the next crop from the rankness of the foggage.

The parks lying to the west of the bridge consisting of nine inclosures containing 129 acres, but the Upperhaughead and Binhill Parks are considered only fit for young cattle amounting to 38.1 acres, 90.3 remains to graze with oxen which will maintain at 10s.

[1] Food which cattle can pick up for themselves in fields during the winter months.

each	£75
38.1 to graze with young cattle will maintain 50 stirks at 5s. each	£12 10s.
Glen lying south from the parks will maintain 8 horses at 20s. each	£8
40 Upstrath Parks may produce 200 stone of hay at a medium from the one, worth 4d. the stone 8,000	£133 6s. 8d.
	£228 16s. 8d.
63 In the parks of Hillocks which will maintain 100 oxen at 10s. each	£50
	£278 16s. 8d.

The parks to the west of the bridge have for the most part sufficient fences, but any stops or insufficient parts should be repaired in the spring and in the summer time the herd who looks after the cattle can mend up any accidental stops. The restoration of the fences is recommended to the particular care and constant attention of the factor.

If the park of Hillocks presently under tillage is laid down next crop with grass seeds, in that case it should be cropt in hay for the two subsequent crops at least, which will be the most advantageous way to treat them.

The Binhill Park is presently in tillage and has already got two ploughings. It would have required a summer fallow to have put it in proper order. There is a large dunghill collected for it, and if there had been time to have given it at least a couple of more ploughings and laid it down with turnips, and next year with grass seeds, it would have mended the swaird very much; or if there is a necessity to have it laid down this spring then it can be dunged and laid down with oats and grass seeds. The best kind of grasses would be white clover plantain and a little rye grass. The proportions may be 10lbs of white clover, 6 lbs of plantain, with 2 bushels of hay seed to the acre.

To be laid down this year in the manner proposed.

There is one of the parks of Hillocks likewise presently in tillage and will be soon ploughed over. This is only the second crop after being several years in grass, and to appearance the soil is not yet in proper order for grass seeds, but according to the general plan of having them all in grass it can be tolerably prepared against spring to be laid down with barley and grass seeds. If this last plan is approved of, it will require two more ploughings than the one they are presently working at.

To be laid down this spring as proposed.

The Binhill Parks and the upper park of Hillock can be wrought in the manner here proposed with the same servants and bestial they have at present, viz., one ploughing over to the Binhill Park and twice over to the park of Hillocks, and as soon as the Greenhill is in condition to work, 4 or 6 of the draught horses can be grazed to help forward the improvements there.

The disposal of the hay to be disposed of must be left to the judgement of Mr Wilson, but it is my Lord's pleasure that after the crops 1772 and 1773 of the Upstrath Parks are to be kept for his own use and likewise the crop of the park of Hillocks of 1773, so that there may be a good stock of hay on hand.

Notes about the disposal of the fat cattle and sheep on the farm of Cullen SRO. GD248/982/3

7 December 1770

There are 10 small fat oxen and 3 cows that are likewise fat, which should be sold off as soon as possible for they will suffer by being kept on hand. In case the townspeople of Cullen want any they may be served and information should be given them to that purpose. Butchers should likewise be wrote to about them.

There is a large parcel of sheep on hand and most of them fat. They should also be sold off immediately; keeping them over winter would hurt the pasture greatly. George Gray at Forfar is a dealer in sheep and cattle and an acquaintance of Mr Wilson's; Mr Wilson will write to him about the sheep and fat cattle; There will be from 100 to 120 sheep.

There are nine milk cows including two Lancashire cows. These cows will not sell until spring, no doubt by they will all have calves except the two Lancashire cows who have young calves just now.

There are likewise three young quoys[1] that will probably be with calve, none of them will sell just now. But in open weather they will shift for their subsistence as there is good foggage in the parks. A Lancashire bull may also run out in the parks among the quoys; neither of them will need straw but in stormy weather.

There are 3 cow calves of last summer and two late ones of the Lancashire breed, a bull and cow calf; none of these will sell until next spring at soonest.

Six old oxen are put in the stall to feed with turnips, but will not be ready soon as most of them are in a lean condition just now.

10 small oxen with a small cow intended to be sold to butcher as soon as possible worth at a medium £3 each	£33	
2 cows, a black and a dun worth	9	9s.
	£42	9s.

There is no ascertaining the value of the sheep with any degree of certainty; the family is daily using them. The best way to prepare them for sale is to draught them by in scores or half scores, taking care to class the best and fattest together, and when that is done to put particular marks on the several lots and a value on each lot. There is from 100 to 120 sheep.

All the draught horses and plough cattle that are presently on hand will be necessary for completing the work until the seed time is over, and then a roup should be made of all the bestial and of all the utensils if any are intended to be sold.

What is pointed out in the memorandum may be done. [initialed] F. and S. [Findlater and Seafield].

Peter May to James Ross, Gordon Castle SRO. GD44/43/20

Elgin, 9 January 1771

I wrote you lately that I had secured five bolls of potatoes for the family. If the hurry of business give you leisure to talk to George Brown, he waits of you for that purpose. He has been with me for some days. Mr Clerk at Aberdeen, who is extremely friendly to

[1] A heifer.

him, insisted on his coming to Brodie to get payment or a bill. When he came to me I foretold him that he would get neither, but contrary to my expectation Brodie was extremely kind and gave him a bill payable at Martinmas next. George says he can engage with you for three or four months and begin as early in the spring as the weather will allow. He assures me that he makes 7s. 6d. a day and that he finds plenty of business. I have advised him to accept of 7s. for himself and a shilling for a lad that works with him in full of everything, but Sundays be excluded. I know this demand is considerably higher than you pay Mr Taylor by the year, but then it is to be understood that the time George is to be employed is the season that most work can be done.[1] I need not use arguments with you, I know you will tell him at once whether his terms are acceptable. I think he will please, and I am more confirmed in my opinion from the character he has from his employers, particularly our friend Urie.

Peter May to James Grant of Grant, Castle Grant

SRO. GD248/524/1

Elgin, 12 March 1771

I have just now your favours by George Taylor with whom I have sent the contracted plans of Strathspey, and the rude draughts of Moy and Westfield. That of Moy was surveyed by me the autumn I made the survey of the River Findhorn. I never put it into an account as it was not complete. The clean plans of Strathspey are not quite finished. The policies of Castle Grant were not taken into the general survey, as that part was not thought so immediately useful according to the plan then in view, which was to get through the survey of such parts of the estate as were soonest out of lease. If these plans can be of use, which I am persuaded they will, I shall be extremely glad. Had I continued earlier on the survey of the whole estate, they would have answered very well, but in case they should not turn out of such consequence from partial surveys I have likewise avoided charging them into an account hitherto, at least until I see whether they are approved or not.

[1] For the accounts of surveying the Gordon Castle estates, *see* I. H. Adams, *Descriptive List of Plans in the Scottish Record Office*, H.M.S.O., Edinburgh, 1970, vol. 2, p. xv.

Forgive me to mention that I have a note of yours for a £104 10s. Sterling, which was payable in April or May last. The capital is £100 at 4½ per cent. The trifling sums that I have I find no difficulty to loan out at 5 per cent. But I would not wish to deal with you as I would with mercantile people. If you incline to pay 4½ per cent annually or 5 per cent every other year I shall be extremely well satisfied, and in either of these ways you may have your choice. . . .

Peter May to George Brown NLS. MS. 3258, f. 7

Linkwood, 17 March 1771

I was at Gordon Castle last week, Mr Ross wishes that you set out to Badenoch as soon as you can. The weather now is set in favourable and they are very desirous to have a survey finished as early in the summer as it can be got thereon.[1] I therefore think you should lose no time in coming forward; I am very desirous to push you forward as much as I can. Last post brought me a letter from London from [Alexander Garden of] Troup who is just now there, wanting me to make a survey of the estate of Ballbegny adjoining to Sir Alexander Ramsay's estate in the Mearns. My answer was that I could not do it myself, but recommending you as my friend and who was bred with myself – at the same time advised Troup of your present engagement with the Duke of Gordon, but that you would be open and ready to do it in the Goe harvest.[2] I know Troup will have respect to my recommendation. As soon as I have his answer I shall advise you of it. If you are distinct and accurate I can easily find out business for you, but without distinctness it's impossible to get a character. Your great want is that of writing and spelling distinctly, if you were half as sensible of that as I am you would be at infinite pains to improve yourself.

[1] Brown started to survey the Gordon Castle estates about the end of April. He was held up in the first two weeks of June, 'We have been drowned with rain . . . which has hurt their corns very much . . . in many places the seed carried off'. (Letter by George Brown dated 15 June, SRO. GD44/27/10).

[2] The latter end of the summer; the time from the end of harvest till the beginning of winter.

Peter May's son, Alexander, to George Brown

NLS. MS. 3258, f. 9

Elgin, 3 April 1771

I have at last prevailed upon myself to write you a few lines in order to break through the long silence that has been between us in both sides. But I hope for the future we will be better correspondents and which in my humble opinion is the best way to make amends for own past faults.

Allow me to trouble you with a small journal of my work for fourteen days past. I set out from Linkwood this day fortnight for Buckie, an estate belonging to Mr Cosmo Gordon of Cluny.[1] The weather was very stormy, however Mr May and I measured and set two small farms. I kept the [*blank*] with his assistance. On the Saturday after I went to Cullen with Mr May, had very little to do there but continued till Wednesday night. On Thursday morning Mr May went home to Elgin and I began the survey of two farms. I have measured, protracted, cast up the measures and wrote out the contents without the least assistance. They consist of about 130 acres. I can assure you I have improved more in measuring these two farms than ever I did in my life before and I think with a month's practice I would become pretty well acquainted with the field work.

I wish you would enquire at Mr May if he would allow me to go for that time along with you to Badenoch. I should be well pleased if Mr May would dispense with me to serve you for a year for very moderate wages, but more of this at meeting.

Enquiries to the Earl of Kinnoull[2] and the rest of the principal managers, from Peter Charles, gardener SRO. GD248/680/6

24 June 1771

1. I want to know if that part of the nursery is to be trenched in October that is lying undone because there is a great many oaks	1. Such ground in addition to the nursery as is proper should be trenched for the purposes mentioned in this note; and for

[1] Peter May took on his factorship receiving a salary of £42 per annum.

[2] The Earl was acting as Commissioner for the absent 7th Earl of Findlater.

and beeches to be planted out next year that has been two years in the seed bed; and there will be occasion to plant out a great many thorns this autumn from the seed bed.

the meliorating the same, a dunghill composed of clay, some street dung, and lime in proper proportions should be prepared near the nursery, which after being properly mixed, should be turned three times at least this season.

2. And if the dyke round the Cloon Hill is to go on this winter as mentioned in my orders to be done.

2. Obey your instructions.

3. And if there is rowan berries to be gathered in their season and likewise hawberries.

3. To be gathered by boys for so much a peck.

4. The gardener wants that the poindlers may be ordered to work to him when called for as they cannot engage themselves to any harvest, as other labourers that have nothing to depend on from Lord Findlater must do.

4. Mr Wilson and William Robertson will talk with the pundlers about working at my Lord Findlater's work.

5. The gardener wants that the doors in the melon ground and on the bridges may be made sufficient that none may have occasion to go there, but his Lordship's principal servants and those whom they may be pleased to take along with them, as some of them uses the freedom to pull flowers and flowering shrubs and destroy the dressed borders with their feet and makes no enquiry at any person where they may enter in.

5. Set the doors and locks in proper places, and nobody but the principal servants, and people authorised by Mr Robertson or Mr Alex. Wilson must go into the gardens and policies.

6. Wants if it is with submission of your Lordship or any other, begs that we may have the stable dung with some of the street dung to mix amongst it for the New Nursery as it is poor ground, no plants takes with it for the first year. I refer myself to Mr May whether or not he thinks it proper that the dung be mixed with some lime and the surface of the drain together as we will have a good many drains there.	6. Answered under article 1st.

Endorsed: Lord Kinnoull, in company with Mr May, has examined carefully the ground from the Pigeon House round the bowling green and nine pin alley, and also the bank from the pigeon house to the southmost extremity of the glen, and has marked the trees which are to be cut down, and has also pointed out to the gardener the trees that should be removed, and the openings that should be filled up when the planting season comes. He has also pointed out to the gardener the ground which he may trench in addition to the nursery, and directed a drain to be made.

Peter May to James Ross, Gordon Castle SRO. GD44/43/23

Linkwood, 5 July 1771

I got your note and the measures of Lesmoir which are now almost copied over by Sandy[1] and I hope will please. I could have wished to have subjoined notes to the several farms in the way I used to do with my Lord Findlater's, but the truth is that the lying of the ground is now so much out of my head that I cannot attempt it with accuracy, and without that I think it better not to attempt observations at all. Where the boundaries of the farms appear interjected on the plan, you will be able to judge of that yourself and can point out what alterations appear necessary. If a ride over the ground

[1] Peter May's son, Alexander.

could be of the smallest consequence you may command that when you please.

Is there no advice of your ship's arrival about the meal? I find Cluny will have a remainder on hand over the 300 bolls you sold for him. What are the prices just now? I am wrote from Edinburgh that the prices there are on the rise, but to what extent I don't know.

I breakfast this day in Baillie Leslie's with your friend Miss Paton on her way to Ross in company with Hatton and Mrs Duff. Your friend Miss Paton regretted not seeing you as she passed.

I am busy just now sowing my turnips and think myself lucky in a good season. For two days past I have been confined to the house with a sore throat.

Peter May to James Ross, Gordon Castle SRO. GD44/43/23

Linkwood, 4 August 1771

Our friends from Old Aberdeen are still with us, they like Linkwood where we have made a shift to accommodate them. They talk of setting out for Aberdeen in the end of the week, but that I believe is not yet fixed. I cannot go from home while they are with us, if I did I am not sure but the parson[1] might take the pet. I had notice from William Clerk that a ship was come about your meal but not a word of the quantity he had delivered. Can you do me a favour to advise of the quantity they have put on board? I need not say anything about the surplus 50 bolls. I know if you had room for it what was already mentioned to that purpose would be effectual. I had ordered William Clerk to try to sell it out among the country people but he writes that tho' he offered it at several parish kirks at £9 Martinmas 9 stone, nobody had come for any. In case you do not know the precise quantity received of the Buckie meal I have ordered the bearer forward to William Clerk, because if the 50 bolls is yet on hand I have some view of getting it off here, but in that event it must be put on board at Lossiemouth and I want to see if the Buckie tenants will carry it there, if they could ford at Garmouth the distance would not be much, at least in comparison with many inland farms.

[1] Peter May's father-in-law.

Will it be impertinent or at least over curious to enquire if the settlement at Huntly be yet determined and in whose favours? If you continue to think that the district on this side of Spey could be entrusted under my management, I should be very well pleased to take the charge, along with my Lord Findlater's consent.

Minute and procedure of Peter May and Alexander Milne, factors to the Earl of Findlater and Seafield concerning the Burn of Drum[1]
SRO. GD248/981/8

Drum, 31 August 1771

Peter May and Alexander Milne, factors to the Earl of Findlater and Seafield, having met in consequence of an order from His Lordship's Commissioners proceeding on a petition given to them by Mr Thurburn, tacksman of Drum, craving that a part of the haugh grounds of the lands of Ardemanoch possessed by John and James McWilliam might be added to the possession of Drum in order that he might get the Burn of Drum straightened and the inclosing of Drum completed. They called for the saids John and James McWilliam and perambulated the ground along with them and Mr Thurburn, and the saids John and James McWilliam agreed to yield that part of their possession which Mr Thurburn wanted for straightening the Burn of Drum for an equivalent of land to be given by him to them out of the lands of the Mile of Wood, and referred to Mr May and Mr Milne to set apart for them such part of the lands of Mile of Wood adjoining to their possession of Ardemanoch as they should judge an equivalent for that part of their possession which Mr Thurburn wanted from them for the purpose before mentioned, being about two acres or thereby. And Mr May and Mr Milne having considered the ground yielded by the saids James and John McWilliam to Mr Thurburn proceeded to the lands of Mile of Wood and set apart as much thereof along the east side of the lands of Ardemanoch as they judged a proper equivalent for the lands or ground yielded by the saids John and James McWilliam to Mr Thurburn, quantity and quality considered, and Mr May and Mr Milne did also in consequence of the powers committed to them by the

[1] The lands in question lay 1 mile to the east of Keith.

said order set up several props betwixt the possession of Ardemanoch and that part thereof yielded by the possessors to Mr Thurburn and also betwixt the possession of Mile of Wood and that part thereof set apart by them to the saids John and James McWilliams. And they are of opinion that they have acted entirely conform to their instructions and that the lines of march proposed by them this day should take place accordingly in time coming. (signed) Alex. Milne, Peter May.

Thereafter the above minute and procedure being read over to Mr Thurburn and John and James McWilliam, they declared that they were satisfied therewith and in testimony of their approbation subscribe these presents, the place, day of the month and year of God first before written.

John Ross, one of the Commissioners for Lord Findlater, to Peter May SRO. GD248/346/7

Dupplin House,[1] 4 January 1772

My Lord Kinnoull is of opinion that my Lord Findlater must support the present town council of Elgin in the law suit that is carrying on for reducing their late election, and has by this post written on that subject to Mr Grant. His Lordship has directed that £20 should be distributed among the poor in Elgin in this winter in my Lord Findlater's name, and desires that Mr Robertson and you may consult with the present magistrates, and such other friends as is thought proper, as to the best manner of distributing it. My Lord thinks that indulgence should be allowed to the inhabitants with regard to peats as far as is consistent with Lord Findlater's interest, and that all prudent measures should be taken for rendering my Lord and Mr Grant popular in the burgh. You may let me know how meal is selling, and whether there is any appearance of scarcity of it about Elgin this winter. As you live on the spot my Lord Findlater's friends will rely much on your prudence and discretion in promoting my Lord's interest, and suggesting to them what occurs to you from time to time for that purpose. As my Lord Findlater and Mr Grant are now heartily embarked in support of the present council, I

[1] Seat of Earl of Kinnoull.

doubt not but they will readily co-operate with them in restoring peace to their borough and preventing as far as possible such contests for the future.

Peter May to James Ross, Gordon Castle SRO. GD44/43/26

Elgin, 12 January 1772

If it were not a pretention to business I think you and I would almost wear out of all acquaintance.

Some posts ago brought me a letter from [Cosmo Gordon of] Cluny, who among other things expresses some anxiety to have the fishing posts altered that were set last autumn. I have delayed writing him until I could say that they were corrected, agreeable to the manner Mr Gordon [of Cluny] and you had conceded before he went south. I wish to know what day you would have leisure for that purpose, that I might wait on you. I think of being in Fochabers on Wednesday and would take that day or the Thursday following to put them right. I beg you will write me if either of these days be convenient for you, as that would determine my motions.

Peter May to James Grant of Grant, Castle Grant

SRO. GD248/346/7

Elgin, 14 January 1772

I beg leave in the most respectful manner to wish all at Castle Grant many happy years. May every return of that season add to the prosperity of your family and friends.

Last post brought me a letter from Mr John Ross, then at Dupplin House, the contents whereof gave me great satisfaction; as I am persuaded it will be acceptable to you I have subjoined a copy of it. Although I did not doubt but my Lord Findlater and you would mutually support one another, yet as I had no manner of instructions how to act in the late emergencies, either from my Lord Findlater or his Commissioners, I was under the more restraint how to conduct myself. I am happy to see that I can now act with more freedom, but I believe that in supporting our friends some reserve as well as discretion and respect is necessary. I mean the less noise the better.

I have always considered Provost Brodie as a superior man, and I do really believe he is attached to my Lord Findlater and you, but the present discords has almost made him peevish, and I understand it is with some difficulty he is prevailed upon to attend their counsels. I am glad of the good hopes every body has of the last election. Were that once confirmed, I think it should be suggested to the present magistrates to fill up their council with friends that have some character and that can be depended on; without some amendment of this part of the police it will always be attended with expense and even uncertainty, but I believe this attempt will require to be gone about prudently, lest it should raise a jealousy.

I have wrote Mr Robertson at Cullen acquainting him of Mr Ross's letter and asking him over here. I expect him as soon as he can. The result of our deliberations shall be communicated to you.

Peter May to James Grant of Grant, Castle Grant

SRO. GD248/346/7

Elgin, 14 January 1772

The clean plans made out from that part of Strathspey I had made a survey of were searched for in all corners here but without success; some time ago they were discovered by accident wrapped up in an old draught of the Annexed Estates. I shall cause them be put up in a timber box and get them forward to Forres. I think they are neatly done.

I have just now a £100 sterling that I could lend out. I wish to have it in your hands before anybody. Will it be accepted? The hundred pound you have already is payable at Whitsunday. If this is accepted it might be joined in the same note with the other when renewed at Whitsunday next. Is it necessary to mention 5 per cent payable once in two years? Provost Brodie says his interests are paid in that way.

Peter May to George Brown NLS. MS. 3258, f. 11

Elgin, 9 February 1772

Upon receiving your letter along with Mr James Clerk's I wrote to Mr Brodie and made an apology for your application in the manner you did to which I had a very polite answer, advising me at the same time that he expected a demand from you which would be answered as soon as presented. Upon the receipt of your draft from Mr Clerk I sent Sandy with it to Mr Brodie, who paid the money very readily, and it lies here waiting an opportunity of getting it forwarded to Mr Clerk. I hope you will lay this sum by as a nest-egg to which you are to add something annually. It is of consequence for everybody to manage their affairs with economy. It is particularly so to you whose living depends entirely upon your application to business. Remember the phrase that 'it is good making hay while the sun shines'. You have many opportunities in your present situation, and therefore you ought to make the proper use of them. I can assure you that your esteem and respect will in some measure depend upon your circumstances. A man in poverty or want, tho' otherwise very deserving, does not meet with that respect which those who are opulent although their parts are not superior. One thing I would caution and that is to avoid being expensive about trifles. Many people can gain money, but very few have the address to make the proper use of it. By what I have said I would not have you to apprehend that I mean to enforce your being a miser. I only mean to recommend economy and that too in a very decent manner, and the earlier that this is implanted it takes root the better.

I need not put you in mind of the survey and mensuration of the estate of Cluny; you know I spoke it to be done in March or April next at the farthest, and I must insist upon its being peremptorily kept to. I believe no clean plan will be required which will make the survey much the shorter. Remember me in the most affectionate manner to my father in which Mrs May joins very cordially; assure the venerable old man how happy we would have been to have had him with us. I am sure it would have been much more comfortable in this cold weather than he can be in his present situation. Tell him I will write him in a post or two, with compliments to your mother.

Provost Thomas Stephen and others v. Provost John Duff and others, Elgin Election, 1771. SRO. CS236/5/15/1

[20 April 1772, Edinburgh]

Mr Peter May, factor to Lord Findlater, aged 40 years and upwards, married. . . . Who being interrogated for the complainers whether previous to last Michaelmas election[1] he had any meetings or conversations with Provost Brodie or any of the other counsellors in the borough of Elgin in his interest, Mr Lauchlan Grant, Mr Duff the Town Clerk, or any others employed as agents for that party, or with any gentlemen or others known to support their interest in the Town Council, and if he had such meetings, what passed at them. Depones that the deponent before last Michaelmas election supp'd once or twice in Baillie Leslie's with the Brodie party and with Mr Lauchlan Grant; Provost Duff and his brother were present as the deponent thinks. Depones that during the time the deponent was in the company in Leslie's the conversation chiefly turned upon what measures were proper to be taken for their own preservation. That the deponent left the company in a short time after supper and went to his own farm about half a mile distance in the country, and the deponent while he remained in the company heard no particulars relating to their political operations. That the gentlemen in Leslie's complained to the deponent for his not staying all night with them. Depones that the deponent had no conversation with any of the said gentlemen other than what passed in the public company except

[1] The Elgin burgh council election of Michaelmas 1771 was disputed. The Earl of Findlater had taken up residence abroad in somewhat scandalous circumstances, and the Duke of Gordon and James Grant of Grant (allied with the Brodie family) were struggling for control of the burgh, for Elgin held the balance of power in the Parliamentary election of an M.P. for the group of burghs. Adam Watson and Joseph Wilson, two of the town councillors, were fairly substantially in debt and had letters of caption for debt issued against them which were in the hands of the Gordon faction, who had also kidnapped Alexander Cook, one of the other councillors. Lauchlan Grant, an Edinburgh writer, was sent to Elgin with gold to pay the debts of Watson and Wilson in case any attempt was made to arrest them, and a number of Strathspey gentlemen went to ensure no further kidnapping attempts were made by the Gordon party. The Gordon party (Provost Stephen, etc.) did not appear at the election, but later brought an action for reduction on the grounds that they had been intimidated from voting by the Highlanders and that the payment of the debts of Watson and Wilson was bribery under the Election Acts. The process which ensued has the evidence of a very large number of witnesses, and there was much of what contemporaries would have termed 'hard swearing', as both sides tried to explain away their shadier moves. William Robertson, Cashier and principal Factor for the Earl of Findlater, deponed that he had taken no sides in the matter, but had suggested that Peter May be included in one of the lists of proposed Councillors. This was not, at this time, done. In the 1772 elections, again disputed, Peter May was included as one of the baillies by the party ultimately declared duly elected. He was objected to in the second election on the ground of non-residence, but showed that he had paid stent until 1771 when he was removed from the stent-roll.

with Mr Lauchlan Grant with whom the deponent had some private conversations. Depones that said conversation did not relate any way to the manner of conducting the election but was composed of what the deponent told Mr Grant as to his not choosing to intermeddle in the elections at Elgin. [(*Deleted*) That Mr Grant said that the deponent was too shy and read to the deponent a paragraph of a letter from Mr Grant of Grant in which it was said that Mr Grant of Grant look'd upon it as the d(uty)] That Mr Lauchlan Grant upon this read to the deponent a paragraph of a letter from Mr Grant of Grant in which it was said that the deponent need not be so shy. Depones that the deponent's reason for being averse to concern himself in these elections was because he had no orders from Lord Findlater or his Commissioners. Depones that the deponent knows nothing of money being furnished to Mr Lauchlan Grant or any other person on account of last Michaelmass elections. Depones that a day or two before the election Mr Brodie, younger, came to the deponent and got from him forty guineas in gold for which Mr Brodie gave the deponent banknotes. And Mr Brodie told the deponent his reason for doing so was that in case they should have to pay any debts it would prevent all objections if the payment was offered in gold, and the deponent understood at this time it was intended for the payment of such debts due by the counsellors on which diligence was ready to be executed against them, but does not remember whether Mr Brodie told him so or not, tho' its probable he might have done so, and upon reflection believes he did so. Depones that the deponent in Leslie's after breakfast on the Monday and before going into the election and about ten o'clock, as he thinks, heard the counsellors talking of diligence being against some of them, and that they had money ready to pay the debts for which the diligence was out, and the deponent's hearing this was owing to William Dunbar, writer, having come into the room, and told that he had been at Baillie Forsyth's, and complained that he had been used indiscreetly because he had offered payment of a debt due by Leslie upon which Forsyth had diligence. Depones that at this time were present Mr Lauchlan Grant, Mr Brodie, younger, Baillie Duff, Baillie Simpson, Mr William Robertson, a preceding witness, Dean of Guild Robertson and some others whom the deponent does not recollect. Neither does he remember whether Leslie, Watson and

Wilson were there or not. Depones that the deponent heard after the election that such debts had been paid as diligence had been raised upon, and that Mr Brodie, younger, Lauchlan Grant and Peter Duff had paid such debts, but from what fund they did so the deponent cannot tell. Depones that the deponent never heard that any debts were paid upon which diligence had not been raised. Depones that the deponent supp'd only twice with the gentlemen before mentioned in Baillie Leslie's on which occasions he came there on purpose to sup with them, as he did likewise to breakfast with them on the Monday of the election as before. That the deponent after he heard the paragraph in Mr Grant's letter read, thought it his duty to join and unite with the Brodie party, but the deponent even after this took no active hand or concern in their operations, and on the day of the election walked up and down the street the forenoon of the election. And being interrogate depones that he did not lend a shilling to Mr Lauchlan Grant or any of the Brodie party on this occasion nor did they ask it. And being interrogate, Depones that the deponent has heard that application was made to Mr Thomas Lockhart, member for that District of Boroughs, immediately after his being elected by Provost Brodies friends, that he should provide for Wilson, and that Mr Lockhart had returned for answer that he would apply and get him a Tides waiter place. And being interrogate if the deponent knows or has heard that Convener Wilson immediately before last Michaelmass election threatened to desert the Brodie party unless they renewed their application to Mr Lockhart, accordingly depones negative. And being interrogated for the respondents, depones that, when the deponent was in Leslie's on the Monday as before, he saw there Mr Grant of Kinchurdy, Glenmore and Auchterblair, Inverowrie, Tullochgorum, and James Grant, clerk to Mr Grant of Grant, and Mr Lauchlan Grant, and Mr John Grant, writer in Edinburgh. And he saw Humphrey Grant and Mr Duncan Grant of Forres there previous to the Monday. Depones that he saw the counsellors go to the counsel house on the Monday, and the Sheriff go along with them, and read the mob act either upon or at the foot of the counsel house stair. That the mob pelted the counsellors on their way with mud and dirt, and depones that the streets from Leslie's to the Tolboooth were lined with a row of the townspeople on each side. Depones that the deponent heard that the Sheriff Depute was sent for by the Brodie party to quell the mob and to protect them in going to the counsel house. Depones that the deponent saw Mr Ross from Gordon Castle and Mr Peter Gordon at Avochie at Elgin, and he understood that their reason for being there was in order to give their advice and assistance to Provost Stephen and his party. Depones that the deponent saw Provost Stephen walking upon the street near the cross on the Monday forenoon and going towards Baillie Laing's. Depones that the deponent heard the mob on the Monday and the Tuesday regretting that Watson and Jamieson had got safe to the counsel house and expressing their vengeance against these men. Depones that the deponent knows Provost Stephen and his party did not go up to the election, and the deponent heard after the election a day or two, that the reason why they did not go was, that they had not a majority. Depones that the deponent neither saw, nor does it consist with his knowledge, that any of the gentlemen from Strathspey in Leslie's, either did disturb, or had any intention of disturbing, Provost Stephen or his party or any of the inhabitants in Elgin; on the contrary he is convinced they had no such intention. And depones that he did not see them on the street either the Monday or the Tuesday, though they might have been there without his knowledge. Depones that when the gentlemen counsellors in Leslie's talk'd of their own preservation as before, they told the deponent their fears were occasioned by their apprehensions of being carried away, and particularly Baillie Leslie who slept in a low room; and that this was the reason of their quarrelling the deponent for not staying with them all night. Depones that the deponent as well as all the rest of the town of Elgin has heard of one Cook being carried away, and that this happened some days previous to the election. Depones that the deponent came to Fochabers in his way from Keith market having business there with Mr Charles Gordon. That the deponent as he could not get a bed in Mr Gordon's, Mr Gordon's house being full, he went to Edward Smith's the public house to get a bed. That Smith told the deponent he could not give him one as he had Colonel Morrice in his house, and as he believed some of the Elgin people and Smith afterwards told the deponent that it was Alexander Cook, the man that was said to be carried off. That the deponent was afterwards offered a bed by

Smith, but the deponent went to another house. Depones that the deponent did not see Cook when at Fochabers, but Cook since told the deponent in Elgin that he saw the deponent from a window in Smith's house as he was mounting his horse. Depones that the deponent thinks Smith told him at this time that one Captain Leith was in his house at the same time. Depones that the deponent left Fochabers on the Thursday morning after Keith market about nine o'clock, and preceding the Michaelmas election in Elgin. . . .

Peter May to George Brown NLS. MS. 3258, f. 12

Linkwood, 3 May 1772

I was told by your brother at Aberdeen that you was to be home the next day, and that you had determined to be at Cluny, beginning last week, that is by the 27th April. I have a letter by Mrs May (who I left in Aberdeen) advising that you are not yet left Buchan. I own I am much disappointed. I need not remind you of your engagements 9 months ago, engagements that I depended upon and assured Mr Cosmo Gordon that his estate was to be surveyed April last. This you know was likewise our treaty at Aberdeen when I was on my way to Edinburgh. Had you told Mr Fraser of your engagements with me, I am sure he is too good a man to have kept you at the peril of disappointing another. . . .

I have engaged to be at Cluny on my way to Aberdeen by the 11th. I am very much vexed that I cannot have the benefit of the survey, especially as Mr Gordon is on his way to the country and depends on having everything made out. I am astonished how you can trifle with me in an affair that does not concern myself.

Peter May to James Ross, Gordon Castle SRO. GD44/43/39

Elgin, 3 February 1773

You have herewith transmitted the rude draught with the contents and estimated rent of Gladhill and Mathie Mill. I have made out some notes on each of these farms which will help you a little.

What are you to do with the present tenants? A fourth part of Gladhill is just now open and should be let for crop 1773. It fell vacant by the death of Alexander Piper. William Newlands who lives in the neighbourhood would take it and enter to the possession of the land immediately. His offer is also sent you. John Innes, a tenant of my Lord Fife's has been in possession for last crop of the half of Gladhill that was occupied by the late Mrs Anderson. He wanted the whole possession for one of his brothers, and made an offer which is also sent you. An obligation was taken from all the tenants to pay the same rent for crop 1773, that it should be set for afterwards.

The vacant part should be set soon as there is now no time to lose. If you want any assistance in my power you may depend on its being ready upon the least notice. I believe John Innes would be a good tenant for the whole of Gladhill if you think proper to prefer him. If you can give me any advice about the mode of a tack for fishing it will be very obliging.

You have no doubt heard that our worthy citizens of Elgin were attempting to mob some people who they apprehended had meal to dispose of, but they were easily quelled. It seems our moral is very ill supplied just now, and indeed it cannot well be otherwise, for we have many forestallers[1] that distress the poor people to a great degree.

Peter May to James Ross, Gordon Castle SRO. GD44/43/39

Elgin, 14 February 1773

Last post brought me your favours covering the rude draught of Gladhill and Mathie Mill, and leaving me to execute the instructions received from Mr Charles Gordon respecting the management of these lands. Mr Charles Gordon did not give me any instructions in writing about these lands. The only concert was that the tenants should pay for crop 177[–] in the same manner they should be let for afterwards and this the possessors agreed to in writing. The last correspondence with Mr Gordon on that matter, was advising to give up the draught to you or any of the Duke's doers who should call first, so that at present I have no instructions how to act, nor will I interfere without advice from you or Mr Gordon; and I rather wish to avoid any more application to Mr Gordon on that subject, for in some late times on that score it has been rather unpleasant.

[1] One who interferes with normal trading by buying up produce before it reaches the market with the object of running up and controlling the price.

The lands of Mathie Mill in my apprehension are of a superior quality to those of Gladhill, at least that was my idea, and the only reason I rated them higher. I already wrote you that a fourth part of Gladhill was vacant for the ensuing crop; something should be done with it immediately otherwise it will be wasted for next crop.

Peter May to James Ross, Gordon Castle SRO. GD44/43/39

Elgin, 17 February 1773

Yesterday's post gave me the pleasure of yours. I am very ready to do everything I can to accommodate either Mr Charles Gordon or you respecting the management of Gladhill and Mathie Mill, and it shall be gone about agreeable to your advice.

As I have no rental of Starwood, or Corny tack, may I beg the favour of you to supply me with one, if such a thing is by you. My information about Cluny's matters are got only piece and piece. It is only of late that I knew of these places belonging to him.

Report concerning the state of the policies at Cullen House, and of the hedges about the inclosures of White House, the Upstrath and Binnhill Parks, by Peter May SRO. GD248/680/6

30 November 1773

The following report would have been comparatively more distinct had a state been made out of their condition they were in at the gardener's entry, that is at Martinmas 1770, for Mr Charles does now aver that they are in better order just now than they were then. But the Commissioners were acquainted with the keeping of the policies formerly, and along with this report, if they will take the trouble to view the ground, that matter will be easily cleared up.

The gravel walk leading from the principal gate to the house has got a dressing and harrowing, which it seems was the way it was usually kept. The verge of grass on each side have been lately cut and the edges trimmed, but in some places not very neat. The shrubbery betwixt the gravel walk and the kitchen garden has been digged over, and the plants thinned where they were too much crowded. This remark with respect to digging and thinning the shrubbery along the side of the gravel walk, will also apply to the shrubbery on each side of the forecourt, and to all the other patches that are kept in tillage, but it must be acknowledged that the digged ground among the shrubbery is rough and ill dressed, and has the appearance of being done in a hurry. This remark was made to Mr Charles in going along, but he said it was the better be roughly turned up before winter.

The paths and alleys leading through the policies on both sides of the burn have been lately dressed up and were in better order at the survey, than since the commencement of Mr Charles undertaking. Some incorrectness appeared on the cutting of the margins of the verge of grass along the sides of the alleys, which was pointed out to Mr Charles and which he promised to mend.

The grass plots among the policy have not been kept neat, which has hurt the sward and made it coarse. But the fore and back courts with the grass along the sides of the principal approach to the house, have been kept better of late than formerly, and they appear to be in a pretty good order just now. The bowling green is rough and ill-swarded, and the nine-pin alley with the skittle ground in disrepair, but the gardener says, that the latter two cannot be dressed up before spring.

The little mount on the west side of the burn and above the Chinese bridge, is now planted into a kind of shrubbery, but it is grown wild and run over with grass. It was recommended to the gardener to get it digged and cleaned in order to forward the growth of the shrubs, but he said the digging would be attended with much difficulty, as it was little else but a cairn of stones. Yet if it should be a little laborious, it ought to be done, for at present it is foul with grass and weeds, and has the appearance of a grave rather than a mount.

The nursery ground under Mr Charles's management is now almost full. It is in general in tolerable order but not neat. The operation there appears to be carried out in a hurry, or by inexperienced hands who work it clumsily. There is a want of neatness in the little paths, and in the division of the plots. But it would be unfair not to observe that the nursery ground has been more expensive and more laborious to keep in order than was at first imagined. Many of the trees in the nursery are fit for planting out. The hawthorn plants in the seminary are by much too thick. They should be transplanted, the biggest plants might be given to the farmers who are under engagements to enclose their farms. Thorns are in much demand.

The hedges about the White House inclosures and the Upstrath and Binnhill Parks are in good order, so far as respects the dressing and keeping clean, but there are sundry places of these inclosures where the plants appear stinted and not thriving. Those about the Parks of White House suffer from a want of attention in preserving them from cattle, but more from the quality of the soil, for where the ground is good, the plants push away in spite of all opposition. Therefore where the plants are stinted, the borders should be enriched with some proper manure. The Binnhill Park will require more attention, particularly the northmost fence of that inclosure, for there the plants are little more than alive. The ground appears to be bad in most places of that fence, and the plants stand so high on the bank that they suffer with a dry season. If the hedges are not helped forward with some application of manure, they will be long in making a fence. A composition of lime, dung and earth should be prepared for them.

The hedges about the Upstrath Parks are in general doing well. Yet even there some places would require mending. This was also hinted to the gardener, and as the horses were just there employed laying on dung on the poor places of the fields adjoining to the hedge, the application of some of it was recommended. In examining the dressing of the Upstrath hedges, some parts appeared to have been much better done than others. This was occasioned by having them cleaned with different hands and done by the piece. Mr Charles promised to have the worst places mended.

Peter May to James Ross, Gordon Castle SRO. GD44/43/52

Elgin, 3 March 1774

I had a joint letter from you, Messrs Smyth and Rose, as managers for the Duke of Gordon, with the Earls of Moray and Fife, dated Garmouth the 25th May last, advising that some of the march poles bounding the tugnet fishing on the River Spey were thrown down; at the same you were pleased to recommend that these march poles should be replaced by me at the sight of Mr Stuart of Tannochie, Mr Shand in Garmouth, and Edward Norman. In obedience to this letter, I went to Garmouth on the 19th July last, having previously advised the gentlemen to attend that day, and at their sight did replace the march poles, by affixing new ones, at the local places where the old poles had stood. The expenses whereof including my own trouble, labourers, etc., is enclosed.

I apprehend the sum of the account which will be divided into three equal divisions, one third thereof amounts to £1 1s. 9d. sterling.

Peter May to James Ross, Gordon Castle SRO. GD44/43/53

Linkwood, 19 April 1774

I was told some days ago that your clerk Mr Logie wanted a boy to write for him. If that is the case, give me leave to recommend the bearer John Cormie, a young lad from Elgin of whom I have a very good character; he was recommended to me for the school of Birnie, which is on the point of being vacant, but the encouragement there is so small for a young man, that I think if he could get into a place where he could be more employed in writing and figuring it would be a better prospect. His mother is a widow and cannot support his education. I beg you will forgive the liberty I have taken, and if you think the inclosed to Mr [John] Logie[1] will be of use the boy will deliver it.

I wrote you and sent a receipt for the money you had advanced Lady Anne Gordon[2] on my account, in consequence of Mr Charles Gordon's draft. If the draft has not come by this post you may send it by bearer.

[There is a considerable gap in the documentary record from this point until the spring of 1778. Peter May spent May and June of

[1] John Logie, later factor to Duke of Gordon, born 1744, was from 9 June 1772 clerk to James Ross, secretary to the Duke of Gordon. In Crop 1782 he succeeded John Menzies as factor for the Duke of Gordon on Duffus, Dipple and barony of Garmouth.

[2] Anne Gordon (1748-1816), dau. George, 3rd Duke of Gordon. In 1782 she married Alexander Chalmers, minister of the parish of Cairnie.

1776 surveying his new charge at Bute and returned to Linkwood, near Elgin by the summer of 1777. The following twelve months were spent winding up his affairs both there and at Aberdeen. Just at the point of departure his father died and it was not till late July 1778 that he finally arrived to settle in Bute.]

1778—1794

FACTOR TO THE EARL OF BUTE

Memorandum from Peter May's letters in November and December 1776 [in unknown hand] SRO. RH9/1/84/13

He says he has at present from Lord Findlater as follows:

A house, etc., value	£25 per annum
A farm whereby he clears net	25
Of salary	50
	£100
From Cosmo Gordon [of Cluny]	42
	£142
	or 150

Note

Lord Bute agrees to give him his lodging and coal at

Mount Stuart, value supposed	25 per annum
He is also to have sheriff substitute	30
As collector of the cess[1] in Bute	20
And his salary to be	125
	£200

£55 per annum more than his predecessors.

James Stewart Mackenzie to Archibald Menzies of Culdares, one of the Earl of Bute's commissioners SRO. RH9/1/84/13

Luton Park, 30 January 1777

I have your letter of the 21st inst. inclosing two of Peter May's to you. I also by the same post a letter from Rossie,[2] with one he likewise had received from P. May. As they all relate to the same subject,

[1] A land tax; the collector had the responsibility for gathering it in the county.

[2] Robert Oliphant of Rossie, a commissioner appointed by the Earl of Bute for management of his affairs in Scotland.

I shall answer them all here and you will communicate this to Rossie.

I observe from P. May's letter that the two principal points he has in view are, that on his settling at Bute, he shall be allowed *between salary* and other acknowledged emoluments £200 Stg per annum; and that when the general mode of improvement there shall either be carried into actual execution, or, at least the plan thereof fully established, and his young friend[1] (whom he wishes to carry with him to Bute) sufficiently instructed by him to pursue the same with ability, and that his (the young man's) conduct shall be such as Lord Bute, or his commissioners shall be entirely approve of, that then in the event of Peter May's wishing to retire from business, he may hope that his young friend may succeed him as factor on the estate of Bute, on the same terms that he (P. May) expects now to hold that office. This, I think, is the whole substance of what is material in P. May's letters.

With respect, therefore, to the first point, his demand of salary and other emoluments to the amount of £200 sterling per annum is fully and freely granted without hesitation.

As to the second point; tho' we have much too good an opinion of his qualifications to consent with the same facility to his retreat from business, as to the former point (the amount of his annual income) yet on the supposition of all things being so circumstanced as I have just now mentioned; should Peter May then wish to retire from business, there is not a doubt but that his young friend would be appointed to his (P. May's) wishes.

I think I have now fully answered all that is material in P. May's letters. As to his not going to settle in Bute until Whitsunday 1778, I could have wished much had he been there sooner, but we must do the best we can to supply that defect.[2]

Earl of Findlater and Seafield to John Ross, commissioner at Cullen
SRO. GD248/800/4

Brussels, 14th April 1777

. . . I don't think Peter May's departure will be my material loss and I can't blame him for wanting a better place when offered him;

[1] Peter May's son, Alexander.
[2] The existing factor Mr Edington continued until May took over.

he could only be looked upon as attached to my service for monetary views, not from motives of a more exalted nature. From what you say of Mr Brown I think he would be a satisfactory person to succeed him, but I would not have you trust to Ury's report of him, as I have learnt from past and present experience how little these pretty animals called country gentlemen are to be trusted to. . . .

James Stuart Mackenzie to Lord Bute BUTE

Belmont Castle, 18 July 1777

Since my last from hence, Mr May has been here some days with me. Rossie also came with him and Commissioner Menzies would have been here at the same time, but Peter May had made out before he came here a very full state of his and your Commissioners' transactions when they were at Bute in May and June last, which we went through here; and I then made him make out an abstract of it, which I shall enclose to you in this letter; the *full* notes and observations I shall send you in two or three days, when I expect Rossie here again to frank them, as they are too bulky for Parliamentary franking. I am happy to be able to tell you that I now have every reason to think that your affairs in this country are put in the way I wished them to be. I more and more approve of Mr May's method of going to work. He has great temper in treating with the many absurd heads he has to deal with. He shows great judgment in forming his plans of future improvements. He is most active and assiduous in whatever he undertakes, and it is surprising to see what an insight he has already acquired, not only into the land in Bute, but likewise into the turn and genius of the people there; to this I may add that he has a liberal way of thinking, and your having so readily acquiesced in the terms he was desirous of obtaining on settling at Bute, he feels very strongly as an additional motive to make him exert every faculty he has to serve you, and in *that* he will be aided and constantly encouraged by your two Commissioners whom he is acquainted with already very intimately, and has a great opinion of their skill and abilities in all matters wherein they will have to do with him. On their part, again, from their thorough knowledge of his abilities in every respect, they have a confidence in him and can depend on his execution in the best manner, of all orders they give him. To this I may add a circumstance which from my experience of the former management of your affairs, has considerable weight with me; and that is, that neither your Commissioners nor your factor (when he goes to reside there) has any Bute connections, predilections, or aversions, to induce them to sacrifice your real interest on those accounts. I have strongly impressed upon your Commissioners and on Mr May's minds, what you wished me to do, viz. that whatever future improvements were planned, they should constantly keep in view, that you were to be at no expense further than might be absolutely necessary, either for keeping up the present rents, or, for an immediate return of any extraordinary expenditure. There must unavoidably be several houses built, for (particularly on the 1,700 acres) they are mostly in absolute ruins; but I have desired (and I have not a doubt of its being done, *now* that P. May will have the conducting of it) that nothing but the mere farm houses in use in the island may be built, for it is scandalous the expense you have been put to in the article of farm houses heretofore; but, if I live, that shall not be the case again upon any account whatever. I am out of all temper when I think on the subject of you being absolutely robbed in that article.

As you mention being out of humour (and indeed with reason) with Macmillan's strange lightheaded conduct, I have been thinking how to arrange matters, so as without entirely taking your business out of his hands, we may have as little as possible to do with him, and the method I believe I shall adopt, if you like it, is this; P. May and I have settled it together that he is to collect the rents twice in the year; as soon as he has made his collection, he is to remit the money to Macmillan at Edinburgh writing at the same time to the Commissioners that he has made such a remittance. They again will order the sum, whatever it be, to be immediately remitted to Coutts and Co. on your account, and I have desired Rossie (if this method be adopted) always to drop you a single line to give you notice that such a remittance is made. By this means Macmillan will not have it in his power to detain your money a single day. Then with respect to the accounts (which is the other grievance I complain of with Macmillan) I propose that Peter May shall send or bring in to Edinburgh his accounts and vouchers at some stated time annually between Lammas and Martinmas (that is, 1 August and 11 November) to be there cleared by Macmillan, but at the sight of your Commissioners, assisted by Mr David Ross, Comptroller of the Post Office at Edinburgh, whom I formerly mentioned to you, to whom you might allow £10 per annum or perhaps less, for auditing Peter May's and Macmillan's accounts at *one* and the *same time* every year, in presence of your Commissioners, who will then finally settle all your accounts in a regular proper method, at a fixed time *every year*. . . .

I wished to tell you as much as I could about the situation of your affairs, which I think have *now* the fairest prospect of going on well, and to your mind, though things of this kind must take time, more expecially as we have a great deal of leeway to work up. I omitted to mention to you that after conversing with Rossie and Peter May here, I found my going to Bute at this time before Mr May is settled there would be quite unnecessary, otherwise I should have gone there the end of this month. . . .

Peter May to James Stuart Mackenzie BUTE, letter book, 1754–88

Elgin, 13 August 1777

I have the honour to transmit your Lordship a copy of the abstract containing the measures and estimated rents of the several farms on the Island of Bute, conform to my survey and valuation made of that island summer 1776. But I must yet acknowledge what I have mentioned formerly to your Lordship with regret, that I cannot recommend the estimations with that confidence I would have done, had the plans and measures been tolerable, but they were extremely inaccurate, and left me often to guide myself by computation and the comprising books.

Your Lordship will observe that there are considerable abatements made in the abstract on such farms as appeared over-rented, as well as an increase on others, but I have the satisfaction to acquaint you that sundry of these farms were let by me this summer and with very little deduction of rent. This leads me to imagine that upon the whole I shall be able to bring the increased rent to £500 sterling over and above the abatements.

I am persuaded your Lordship will not suspect my inclination to promote the interest of the island which is soon to become the subject of my management under my Lord Bute's Commissioners, but I acknowledge in the most ingenuous manner that I am more apprehensive of exceeding the real and adequate value of the lands, than being under that standard. I am aware of the dangerous consequences that always attend over-renting lands. A bankrupt estate occasioned by injudicious management is the most dismal situation both for the landlord and the tenantry. But altho' I take the liberty to express my sentiments to your Lordship without reserve, yet I hope to conduct myself as that there will be no reason for applying my suspicions to any part of the land under consideration.

I am to make out another duplicate of the abstract and shall transmit it soon to the Commissioners, that it may enable them to commune with any offerers for farms, if such shall be made them in my absence, and if on any emergency it shall appear necessary for me to repair again to Bute before Whitsunday next, I shall in that event be ready at command. I correspond with Messrs. Thorburn, Edington, and Blain, and I hope by that means to keep matters pretty much in order. I have only to beg your Lordship's advice and instructions when you have leisure.

Robert Oliphant to Peter May BUTE

Edinburgh, 29 April 1778

I received your letter with the account of the Kilmory estate, etc.

What I am going to write you now is of a different nature. By a letter I had from my Lord Bute of the 20th, he mentions that Lord Frederick Campbell had offered to raise a thousand men for the defence of the west coast, and that the King has accepted this offer. My Lord says that the calling out of the Fencible men is a step so necessary with a war hanging over us, and the troops already raised withdrawn, that his wishes are that a company of one hundred men should be raised in the County of Bute. Mr Kennedy, a gentleman in Ayreshire, is proposed to have the command of that company, and my Lord mentions Stewart Robertson as his Lieutenant. His Lordship says, however averse the people in Bute are to a military life, that this is merely to defend their own coast, and after learning their exercise it is proposed that they shall be stationed at Rothesay. I suppose a good many men may be got from Arran, as those who did not choose to go with the Duke of Hamilton may incline to be Fencible men as they are not to go out of the country. The sooner you send for Stewart Robertson the better, and try what he can do among the Arran people, a number of whom I am told are now skulking in the Island of Bute. As to the Bute people, I would have you to call a meeting with John Robertson at Rothesay, Mr Thorburn, and some of the most sensible of the farmers in the island, acquainting them of my Lord's very earnest wish that this hundred men should be immediately raised, and to get a list prepared with all possible haste of what Bute people will be ready to join the corps.

Mr Kennedy will be able to raise some men on his own estate in Ayrshire. I expect a good many will be got from Arran, and the remainder I would only propose to raise in Bute. I expect Mr Kennedy down from London this week, and he and I, in a few days thereafter, will proceed to Bute. I expect that immediately upon receipt of this letter, you will set about this business with all the prudence and activity that you are master of.

Mr MacMillan will be of use in forwarding this plan, and take in every other person with you that you think will be of service in getting it speedily executed. Mr Macleod, the Sheriff, will write a letter to Kames along with me. Take an early opportunity of waiting on him and mention this to him; at the same time present him my respectful compliments.

After an American privateer[1] has plundered the house of Lord Selkirk, I suppose the Bute people to a man would take up arms, rather than see the House of Mount Stuart attacked.

Appreciation of grass at Linkwood valued by James Mitchell, proofman in Elgin, at the mutual desire of Peter May, removing tenant, and George Brown, his successor NLS. MS. 3258, f. 13

[1] John Paul Jones (1747–92), was born at Kirkbean, Kirkcudbright. In 1775, after some years in the British merchant navy, he obtained a commission in the American continental navy. As captain of the sloop *Ranger* he made a series of daring raids in the Irish Sea including on 21 Apr. 1778 spiking the guns at Whitehaven. Later that day the ship anchored in Kirkcudbright Bay, and Jones with a party of men landed on St Mary's Isle intending to kidnap the Earl of Selkirk. In his absence the house was plundered, but Jones purchased the booty and returned it to Lady Selkirk.

Linkwood, 30 June 1778

	victuals						
Uncultivated ground in Barmuckety Park and in the north side of ditto	..	2	..				
Cultivated ground in said park	..	3	..	1	1	..	
Burnside from John Roy's upwards to the garden Park valued at				..	2	..	
James Alexander's Park, all in grass							
A piece of improved ground next to the march with Trews				2	1	..	
Greens commonly called Hadyade	1	2	..				
Smith's Croft in ditto arable land	..	2	..	2	..	..	
Ground lying in fallow				2	2	..	
Ground lying next to the march of Muirtown and west of the road leading from Linkwood to Elgin in grass				4	..	..	
Millar's Croft in grass valued at				..	1	2	
Broom Hillock with field surrounding it				4	2	..	
Calf Park next to the flour mill				1	2	2	
				19	..	..	bolls
Deduct from above arable lands under tillage crop 1778 being part of that improvement called the Greens of Linkwood in Peter May's possession and estimated at				4	..	..	
				15	..	..	bolls

I, James Mitchell, proofman in Elgin, did at the request of the said Peter May and George Brown, value the lands on the farm of Linkwood presently under grass, and which I have execute agreeable to the above state, and I further declare that in summer of 1769 I then valued the lands in grass delivered over by the late Robert Anderson, tacksman of the said farm to Peter May, his successor, who paid him for the summer grass, as well as the grass of the arable lands according to my valuation thereof. The above state amounting to fifteen bolls of victual after deducting four bolls for the Greens of Linkwood under corns as above. In witness whereof I have signed this attestation date and place foresaid before these witnesses, Mr George Morison, schoolmaster at Urquhart, and Alexander May, clerk to the said Peter May.

Endorsed: In consequence of the within valuation, I hereby acknowledge to have received from George Brown, my successor in the farm of Linkwood, the sum of £9 sterling, as the converted price of fifteen bolls bere agreed on betwixt us, and I further declare that I did in like manner pay the late Linkwood for the summer grass as well as the infield grass at my entry according to a state thereof herewith delivered. The above £9 being in lieu of grass victual and for which I have given my receipt.

Peter May to John Blain, sheriff clerk of Bute BUTE

Aberdeen, 11 July 1778

. . . My dispatch south has been interrupted by the death of a venerable old man my father, who died in the 103rd year of his age. My duty as well as my inclination made it necessary to care for him in his last illness, and which continued only about a fortnight, that is not above a fortnight confined to his bed; his burial place was at Aberdeen and his request was to be interred there, and this request was punctually obeyed. He died the 17th ultimo.

I am now on my way south, but as I have a large farm in the neighbourhood of Aberdeen, and have sundry things to settle there that I am anxious to get done before I leave the country, that will take me up some days.[1] My Lord Findlater's commissioners are likewise in Aberdeen and I have my factory accounts to deliver over, I mean the accounts for crop 1777 but that will be little more than the business of a forenoon. I hope to be able to set out from this place about the 18th, but it will be towards the 24th before I can propose to get forward to Bute for I have sundry things to transact at Edinburgh that will keep me there for some days. . . .

Endorsement on Factory, the Earl of Findlater to Peter May dated 4 January 1769 SRO. GD248/983/2

Aberdeen, 20 July 1778

I hereby acknowledge to have renounced and given up the within factory, and that at Whitsunday last by witness my hand. Peter May.

Robert Oliphant to Lord Bute BUTE

General Post Office Edinburgh, 19 August 1778

. . . I have recommended them [two men starting a cotton mill][2] to Mr May to show them every mark of attention. . . .

[1] His household goods and farm stock were advertised for roup in the *Aberdeen Journal*, 1 June 1778.

[2] *See* p. 210, n. 2.

Peter May to John Robertson BUTE, letter-book, 1754-88

Mount Stuart, 20 March 1779

I was at Rothesay yesterday and had the pleasure to wait of Mrs Robertson and your family there, who are all well. I heard part of your last letter read, containing your kind enquiries for your friends at Mount Stuart, which I listened to with grateful attention, at the same time that I blamed myself at being so late in my correspondence with you; and now when I begin to write I am uncertain but you may be left London before my letter arrive. However, that I may not be left entirely without an apology, I have resolved that this letter shall take its fate.

Give me leave then to congratulate you on the certain prospect of renewing the Bill for the Herring Bounty. I hope your endeavours will meet with the success they deserve, and that before this reach you, we shall be informed by the papers that the Bill passed without opposition. Altho' I am not in the least personally connected with the herring fishing, yet I consider myself as peculiarly interested in its success. I consider it as a capital object for the Island, an object from which the undertakers find advantage. The operative fishers likewise get money by their labour. The landlord must of consequence avail himself from both. Every branch of business, whether commerce, agriculture or manufacture, that is once established on a proper foundation, is not only of consequence to the adventurers, but the whole community derive benefit from it. Upon the whole, I hope the Noble Family who are so intimately concerned in the welfare of the Island, are satisfied of the importance of the herring fishing and that before this time, they have wrought out your deliverance.

Privateering just now engrosses the attention of many people in the mercantile way. I wish they may find their account in it. I suspect they will not upon the whole. It is not a favourable branch of mine in one particular for it interferes very much with every other part of industry. The high terms they give to sailors and even landmen, has drained our little kingdom exceedingly, and at this season of the year it is felt severely by all the farmers. Many of them cannot get servants to work their farms even in the seed time.

A privateer from Clyde called the *Portsmouth* has been in Rothesay

Bay for a couple of weeks and upwards, and almost gives any terms they ask, and makes no exceptions of either land-men or sailors. The farmers have been complaining to me again and again, but the complaint is such as I cannot remedy. An interference happened at Rothesay the other day betwixt an officer of the Fencibles and the privateer's men. Ensign Bruce was sent over from Greenock to attend the Commissioners in their several districts about recruiting for the Army agreeable to the late Act. Your brother, who has the care of the party at Greenock, had given Mr Bruce notice of one *Sterling*, a Bute man, a deserter from the Fencibles, who was then in the Island. Upon this information we were all on the lookout. At last Sterling was discovered to be in Rothesay, in Stuarts commonly called Straddy, engaging with the *Portsmouth* privateer. Mr Bruce and your nephew Jack Muir went about ten o'clock at night and laid hold of Sterling, but were soon deforced by the sailors supported by the riotous mob of idle women, who you know are exceedingly troublesome on every emergency of this kind. I have mentioned this at more length with a view to point out how little authority the Civil Magistrates have in Rothesay, an object which requires both attention and also a little dignity. Your son Archy was very active in detecting the deserter, for which he narrowly escaped being beaten.

The weather has been remarkably fine almost since you left us, and I am told the Spring and verdure is more forward just now in Bute than it usually is at the end of April; yet when I write this not one lippie[1] is yet sown in the Island, altho' the ground is abundantly dry. I pressed them to sow, but without effect. They all with one voice say the season is not advanced enough for them, and that if the month of May turned out cold their crop would suffer very much if sown so early. I am almost an infidel to these assertions, yet as I cannot from my own knowledge or experience confute them, I must suspend my judgement until I have an opportunity to try how far the information is real or imaginary.

I hope the project of the cotton manufacture will now go on briskly.[2] Mr Wheelhouse is arrived and very busy putting the mach-

[1] A small amount, i.e. a lippie = 1½ pints; 4 lippies = 1 peck.

[2] Sir John Sinclair in his *General Report* . . ., 1814, vol. 3, pp. 311–12 records, 'The first cotton spun by water in Scotland was at Rothesay in Bute, but it was only an experi-

inery in order. They are to begin a little in the flax miln until the larger plan take place. I hope it will succeed, and I wish with all my heart it may, as many people in the Island would be benefited by the employment it would circulate. Your manufacture of herring nets on the one hand, and the cotton manufacture on the other, should keep the young people of the Island in business and consequently make them useful to themselves and to the community – a very different line from which is observable among many of the young ones just now. I was lately along with the minister of Kingarth visiting the schools in his parish, one at Kerricroy, one at Ambrisbeg, and the parochial school at Kingarth. Each school was numerous; altogether they amounted to upwards of 150 boys and girls, who had much appearance of health and not a little degree of cleanliness. I saw nothing wanting but the early seeds of industry; many of them were at a period of life which was the most tractable to receive habits of diligence. These good purposes I hope too will be improven by the very useful branches of manufacture I have already mentioned.

I have in consequence of instructions from Mr Oliphant set off sundry feus for the herring buss masters, along with the East End of Baillie Bruce house and yard. Were I to guide myself by my own opinion, I should be desirous to accommodate all the industrious and useful people and to connect their interest with that of the Island. Houses and yards in property is a strong inducement to fix their residence at Rothesay. I am persuaded such small properties can never interfere with any political plan, for I would confine feuing to houses and yards only; but I forget that I am writing to my friend who is perfectly acquainted with the situation in Bute, and that all I have said, however it may entertain one, has nothing new to Mr Robertson.

I have not the honour to be known to my Lord Bute.[1] I had an opportunity to wait of my Lord Mount Stuart[2] the last time his

---

mental trial in a lint-mill. The first regularly at work was that at Penicuik near Edinburgh and those at Barrhead and Johnstone in Renfrewshire, Woodside in Lanarkshire, Persley in Aberdeenshire, and the very extensive works [New Lanark] of the late Mr Dale of Glasgow soon followed'.

[1] John, 3rd Earl of Bute.

[2] John, 4th Earl of Bute.

Lordship was at Edinburgh. I am well acquainted with Lord Privy Seal[1] and have often experienced his friendship. If you be with him after the receipt of this, I beg you will present my grateful respects to his Lordship.

James Stuart Mackenzie to John, 3rd Earl of Bute, his brother
BUTE, letter book, 1754-88

Belmont Castle, 12 July 1779

I have had [Robert Oliphant of] Rossie and Mr May here with me some days talking over and considering of your Bute affairs. Mr May had made out when he came here a memorial relating to several things at Bute to lay before Rossie, which memorial I have gone through and considered with them; and upon the margin I have given what I judged to be the properest directions on each article. I shall here inclose the whole to you, that you may confirm or reject what is ordered, but you will return to Rossie (directed to Robert Oliphant, Esq., Post Master of Scotland, Edinburgh) this memorial, as we have no copy of it. Peter May wanted to have made out a shorter state of matters, not to trouble you with so much writing, but I thought it better to send it you just as it is, as his remarks and propositions are very sensible, and what I have given my *fiat* to, I will be answerable for the propriety of, as I have myself the experience that the conducting things as here proposed is highly beneficial. There are some expenses proposed in the memorial which have not any relation to the improvement or management of the estate, but which are either absolutely necessary or very proper (in my opinion) to be approved of. I shall also here enclose a letter Rossie wrote me before he came hither on the subject of the new cotton manufactory, with a specimen of the cotton thread made already at Bute, which, in the opinion of the Glasgow people, is most excellent for various purposes of manufacture. In short I have every reason to hope that your Bute affairs will, in all branches, go on wonderfully well now. Peter May seems very well pleased with his situation there and I am no less so with the commencement of his

[1] James Stuart Mackenzie, the 3rd Earl of Bute's brother, for whom Peter May had done surveys from the 1750s.

management and his ideas of conducting things in future. I firmly believe that had you been fortunate enough to have him these twenty years ago, without being hampered by several sub-directors in the Island, you would have had this day a net rent from Bute of £5,000 per annum at least, if not £6,000 or £7,000. We reckon that within these 15 years past there has been about £18,000 of your money absolutely thrown away on wild schemes of one sort or another and abominable imposition and picking of your pocket.

Memorandum in the hand of Robert Oliphant SRO. RH9/1/84/4

October 1779

Mr May entered to the factory at Martinmas 1777 and accounted for that year's crop, but did not reside in the island till late in the following summer. Mr Edington continued till his arrival in receipt of the rents for which Mr May allowed him at the rate of his usual salary in his accounts from Marts. 1777 to Marts. 1778.

Mr Edington drew the emolument of sheriff substitute till Mr May's appointment to that office which was Marts. 1778; of course it fell to my Lord to make up this part of Mr May's £200 for the first year.

The collecting of the land tax for that year was in the same predicament, and that sum in future can only be rated to Mr May at £16, as John Blain draws the remaining £4.

With respect to the article of £25 charged in lieu of coal and lodging at Mount Stuart, as there had been formerly an establishment for a housekeeper, which Mrs May now very properly superintends, it is submitted whether my Lord Bute will remit this charge. Peter's own demand for coals to that part of the house that he inhabits will amount to a very small sum, and there is reason to believe that the expenses formerly charged at Mount Stuart will be very considerably lessened.

Mr May very modestly hinted that living at Mount Stuart was attended with an additional expense, from people often thrown upon him by bad weather and other accidents, of which Mr Oliphant had occasion to see some instances during his short stay there.

Memorandum, Peter May to Lord Findlater

NLS. MS. 3258, f. 14

1779

The only encouragement that can be given on a lease of nineteen years are as follows, viz.

If the inclosures are made by the tenants and at his own expense, he should be allowed therefore at the end of the nineteen years for the value of the dykes and inclosures made by him during the tack, and that to be ascertained by two men mutually chosen. The tenant should be bound to make one inclosure every year, or two years at most till the whole of the farm is inclosed. The proprietor should reserve full power in the lease to lay out the inclosures conform to some regular plan, and determine the size of the several inclosures, or ten to one but they will be done improperly. The proprietor to be bound to pay for no inclosures that the dykes thereof are not completed and fully fencible at the expiration of the lease. But these rules will not so well apply to the inclosing with thorn hedges; nor is there common tenants to be met with in this country that will easily engage to inclose with thorn hedges at their own expense, because without they are railed in with wood there is no immediate fence, tho' upon the whole, I think them by much the best, and particularly in Moray where no stones are to be got. Where the fields is stony and the inclosing with stones serves to clear the ground at the same time, to be sure stone dykes is the thing, or even along high roads or avenues they are better to be faced up with stone and hedge rows in the inside.

The inclosing with hedges should therefore be done by the proprietor and at his own expense. The tenant taken bound to keep the hedges from cattle and clean from weeds, and also to pay so many per cents for the money so expended on the inclosing, to be collected along with his rents as soon as the farm is inclosed.

Mr Barclay of Ury, who knows more of these matters than most people, incloses all at his own expense and takes only 5 per cent from his tenants during their lease. He says that any proprietor who gets that is very well paid. As he is sure of 20 per cent of advance rent at the end of nineteen years, he rather chooses to inclose himself in this way than bind his tenants and be obliged to pay them at the end of their lease, as he gets it done properly himself and the hedges railed, which they will not normally be by any common tenant. They must also be bound to agree to the laying out of the fields in the most proper manner tho' inclosed by the proprietor.

Ury reserves the power to cut drains on any part of the farm where he finds occasion and obliges the tenants to fill them with small stones and cover them up, which is no small improvement on a wet farm in the course of 19 years, and the casting of drains is but a small expense.

If the proprietor inclose with stone dykes then the tenant must be bound to uphold the same during the lease, and leave the same fencible at his removal.

Peter May to Robert Barclay of Ury NLS. MS. 3258, f. 15

26 January 1780

It gives me infinite pleasure to keep up an acquaintance with a gentleman so universally useful and so generous in friendship. I beg leave to assure you these sentiments are not that of flattery; they are perfectly sincere, resulting from long experience and gratitude both on myself and other connections, particularly on behalf of George Brown, for whom I have many obligations to acknowledge, of whom the present instance of friendship is not the least. For by a letter from Mr Brown of the 18th current he writes me of his being some days at Ury, and that you had generously offered to join in surety for a credit of £500 Sterling in the Bank of Aberdeen on his account; and in consequence thereof he transmits me a bond of cautionry to be signed by me advising to return it to you for the like purpose, thereafter to be forwarded to the cashier of the Aberdeen Bank. I flatter myself that George has not taken this step without consulting and obtaining your approbation. In full persuasion of this, I have signed the bond and herewith forwarded to you. I hope there will be no risk attending this mark of friendship, for I am confident Brown has good principles, and think he is industrious. I shall, therefore, only add on this subject, that notwithstanding of your confidence and mine we ought in prudence to enquire that his cash accounts be annually balanced. In my correspondence with George, I recommended economy and a great degree of accuracy; these are necessary ingredients in any time of life, but more particularly so to a young man whose funds require the greatest frugality. When you have occasion to write George, give me leave to beg you will improve on my doctrine. I have resigned in his favour the post office of Elgin, and have got a new commission for him. The profits of that office is worth from £25 to £30 a year, but an old fellow and a clerk run away with most of it just now.

Give me leave now to transfer my ideas to a more interesting subject than that of any individual, I mean the community at large; and here I must express my feelings for the situation of our country, and in particular for that of farmers who are in general the most useful part of the community. I need not enumerate to you the many disadvantages which attend their profession, especially at this present juncture; you know intimately and will feel in proportion to their distress. Bestial have not sold, at least to advantage; victual is low priced, and the country overstocked, that it is hardly vendible; oat meal is a drug and the wheat crop will do little more than indemnify the husbandman for his labour. On the other hand the expense of management is increased exceedingly of late, servants' wages, utensils, wearing apparal and almost every other commodity is doubled in value within a score of years or a little more. These disadvantages are more immediately felt by the farmers, but ultimately the loss terminates with the landlord; a strong proof of this is already too evident, by the rapid reduction of the price of land, as well as many estates daily exposed to sale. To what chapter of accidents is our unfavourable situation imputed: is it to account of the American War, or is it to the luxury and depravity of the times?[1] Whatever the cause of our misfortune, the effects are evident, but what signifies enquiring into the cause unless we could apply a proper remedy. I can preach upon industry and have not been altogether without practice of it, but that will not always avail, for although I can raise a good crop, yet I cannot create a market, and therefore I had better give over grumbling and leave the times to their fate. But now that I have resolved to fill up my paper, where am I to find a proper

[1] Probably the American War, for the *deficit* on Public Expenditure of Great Britain had reached £7,861,000 in 1779 and was to rise to even higher levels until 1786. *See* John Butt, the American War of Independence and the Scottish economy, *New Edinburgh Review*, Nos. 35 and 36, 1976, p. 57.

subject for your entertainment? The circle of our little kingdom is so narrow that it cannot afford amusement, and yet I wish to abide by it for the subsequent part of my letter. In the first place then indulge me to inform you that Bute consists of from 16 to 18 miles in length, and from 3 to 4 miles in breadth, or rather 3 at average. The produce of grain is chiefly oats and bere, and the arable lands are generally divided into infield and outfield. The infield, that is the croft land, is again subdivided into three ideal portions, one whereof is under oats, and the other under bere, and the last under grass. The rotation is bere, then oats and the third year in grass. The mode or course of cropping has not an unfavourable appearance at first, but when I tell you that the ground so let out in grass lies only one year, and that it is not sown down with grass seeds, but that it is entirely overrun with thistles and ragwort, the idea is entirely changed for the grass is not in general worth half-a-crown an acre. The produce of the infield as to grain is about a fourth return overhead, including oats and bere. The outfields is generally the largest part of the arable lands, altho' not the most valuable. Two successive crops of oats and sometimes three is taken from the outfields, but the returns would astonish you, for according to the best information I have been able to pick up they seldom exceed 2½ overhead – so poor a crop is not worth culture. The bere crop gets three ploughings, the oats only one for each crop. The farmers seldom begin to plough before the 1st February. Indeed betwixt harvest and February there is very little done in Bute as to husbandry, except daily threshing out the corns. The stocking of cattle consists of horses, cows and sheep. The horses have mended their size and quality within these few years. Lord Bute kept stallions for the use of the country which has improved on the brood very much. The cows are small and the brood of an indifferent quality – weight from 10 to 12 stone at 24 lb to the stone. When sold lean give from 40s. to 50s. or 55s., and when fed from £3 to £4 but the last is seldom arrived at. The sheep are mostly of the Linton breed. Until this year fat sheep generally sold at from 13s. to 15s. to the Greenock mercat. I had almost forgot to mention that horses bred in the island sell for £8 to £10 and upwards. The south side of the island is mostly a cornfield, and has cost Lord Bute an enormous expense inclosing and dividing the lands with ditch and hedge. But I must observe with regret that they have not been attended to and are now in wretched order. The northmost end is high land and less cultivated. One part of the island towards the southeast projects like a peninsula, and is let at £200 a year for a sheep park. It contains about 800 acres. We have a limestone quarry in the island, which is wrought for the tenants who are supplied with lime at 7d. per boll; and there is a command of shells in sundry places along the shore (they are called coral). A good deal of seaweed is also to be had from the shore. Upon the whole we are not wanting in the means of improvement, but we are greatly in arrear to industry. I am not without hope, however, to mend their mode as well as to improve their diligence a little. I have already been sketching down some notes to that purpose, on which I may in some future letter beg your criticism and advice.

James Stuart Mackenzie to John, 3rd Earl of Bute

BUTE, letter book, 1754–88

Mount Stuart, 25 July 1780

. . . I never saw a house that was inhabited so délabré and so cruelly neglected in every part as this poor house has been by the various odd occupiers it has had since you left it. Since Peter May came here, whose wife is a most genteel, decent and careful woman, I believe no sort of attention in keeping everything in the greatest order possible has been neglected, but unfortunately the mischief was done before they came, and all that can now be done is to keep things from growing worse. . . .

As to P. May's dwelling, I think by one means or other we shall manage that pretty well. There is a tenant at Kerrylamont farm who it is thought probable will not be able to continue there; if not, the house with some small additions will answer for P. May and his family, which upon many accounts would be the most advantageous situation you could wish for him. This matter (whether the tenant can or cannot remain there) depends pretty much on a decision now lying before the sheriff, which he will determine in October next. If the tenant remains where he is, a house may be built in a proper situation next Spring for P. May, which [Robert Oliphant of] Rossie is to look out for before we leave this, and in the meanwhile till such a house can be finished, we have a view to a place where he can be accommodated for some months. Such a house as will do for P. May will not cost more than some of the farm houses which were very unwisely erected some years ago on farms of only £50 per annum of rent.

James Stuart Mackenzie to John, 3rd Earl of Bute

BUTE, letter book, 1754-88

Mount Stuart, 27 July 1780

. . . As the principal floor, if anything at all be done about the house, must be entirely cleared of all such lumber, I have desired Mr May to clear all these things out, to sell or exchange or give away to poor people, or to burn all this rubbish as soon as possible. He tells me that as to the old iron, pewter and copper, he may be able to exchange them for things that are *now* absolutely wanted in the kitchen; that he will sell by auction several things that the people hereabouts will buy merely because they have been in Mount Stuart House. The rest he will dispose of as I have directed. . . . Mr May thinks plenty of water may be easily brought in to serve all purposes of the house.

Sunday 30 July

I had wrote the above intending sending it you last post but we found it absolutely impossible to get all plans and estimates made out in time altho' Mr May's son (who, by the bye, I like mightily, for I think him a treasure to you) copied fair Mr Paterson's drawings. . . . What is now proposed to be done will make this house five hundred per cent better than it ever was, in all respects, and that for about £1,800 (excluding of what Mr May estimates the freight and carriage of all materials). . . .

James Stuart Mackenzie to John, 3rd Earl of Bute

BUTE, letter book, 1754-88

Belmont Castle, 7 August 1780

. . . As to the rents of the Estate [of Bute], I think Peter May has arranged things so that he will be able to raise some of them even next year and more the year after. In short all seems to be going on well there. . . .

James Stuart Mackenzie to John, 3rd Earl of Bute

BUTE, letter book, 1754–88

Belmont Castle, 9 August 1780

. . . As to Peter May's habitation, you need be in no sort of uneasiness about it for I have arranged that affair in such a manner that if one or more methods do not answer, I can suggest others that would. You have really in him and his family an admirable little colony; besides himself, his wife, and his son, of whom I have formerly given you an account, he has a niece (a daughter of a younger brother of his) about 14 years of age who is excellent in her way.[1] Lady Betty[2] is vastly fond of her and thinks her a prodigious clever sensible girl, and she manages a small department that is allotted to her with uncommon ability. . . .

James Stuart Mackenzie to John, 3rd Earl of Bute

BUTE, letter book, 1754–88

Belmont Castle, 14 August 1780

. . . With respects to a constant supply of water for all the offices about the House, before I left Bute, Mr May and his son took the levels with great accuracy, and he was clear that water could be thrown at top of the House in great plenty and without much expense, and afterwards he, Mr Paterson and I had a full conversation on the subject the night before I left Mount Stuart. . . .

James Stuart Mackenzie to John, 3rd Earl of Bute

BUTE, letter book, 1754–88

Belmont Castle, 14 September 1780

I have your letters of the 6th inst. from Luton enclosing a very strange one indeed from the D. of Argyll to you. With respect to the Rothesay delegate, I wrote to Rossie last week on that subject, and he, in consequence of my letter, wrote to Peter May to have a

[1] Barbara May, the eighth child of James and Elizabeth May, Peter May's brother, was born around 1766 and was taken into Peter May's home and raised as their own daughter. In fact James May was the elder brother.

[2] James Stuart Mackenzie's wife who was also his cousin, Lady Elizabeth Campbell, 4th daughter of John, 2nd Duke of Argyll. They had no children.

proper delegate sent from Rothesay to the place of election, there to concur with the delegates from Inveraray and Campbeltown in the choice of the Member for that district.[1] Peter May will have received those directions before I got your letter so there will be ample time for settling that matter, as the Borough Elections will not come on till the 2nd of October. . . .

Peter May to George Brown NLS. MS. 3258, f. 17

Mount Stuart, 25 November 1780

I received with pleasure your letter of the 12th covering one from my old Mr Fashioner Deacon Hervie, from whom I have got many a scrape and bow. I regret you did not forward Hervie's letter earlier, for altho' Simpson has not yet left me, I have nevertheless been obliged to advance him from time to time almost the whole of his wages. I believe I shall be able to reserve a couple of notes or thereby for account of the Deacon, but as to the account of expense which constitutes a considerable part of the debt, that I cannot insist for, without having the proper vouchers, impressed in my hands. I mean first the bill itself, then the diligence raised thereon which constitute the expense. Simpson may (as I dare say he will) refuse to pay his bill without having it delivered, or even to pay any part of it to a second hand without having it noted on the back of his bill. Therefore if the Deacon wishes that I should serve him, he must accommodate me with the means of doing it. Simpson leaves me in a few days, but he is engaged in the neighbourhood with a gentleman of my acquaintance, and perhaps I may have influence to get the Deacon's debt cleared. I wish he had the principal in the meantime. Simpson has wrought well, but he has no turn for being a gardener. He loses all his garden things for want of attention, he has not behaved so well as I expected, but I know the reason of his leaving me was, that he could not get into the sort of tippling company which he liked. The place he goes to will suit him perfectly.

David Mortimer leaves me also. I find the expense of bringing servants from the north increases their wages amazingly, especially when they continue only for one year. Mortimer never had it so easy

[1] Peter May himself, as provost of Rothesay, was appointed as the delegate. J. S. Mackenzie reported this fact to the Earl on 25 September.

a life with any master as with me, for he has not put a flail above his head since he came to Bute, nor does he any one thing except cleaning his stable of four horses, and yoking them by ten o'clock and loosing before three. While I am on this head, I must ask your advice about a servant or rather a workman recommended to me by Erick Sutherland, commonly called *Laird of the Kime*. Mr Sutherland writes Sandy that there is a young man, a nephew of his, who was a tenant of Sir Alexander Dunbar's, but that his matters had gone wrong and that he was designed to push for bread, that he did not incline to remain in Moray and therefore recommending him to Sandy as a farm servant in Bute; but Mr Sutherland does not say whether he is married or not, nor does he tell me his name. I only suppose that he is married from his having a farm. In that event if he inclines to serve at Mount Stuart as a labourer or farm servant I will employ him at 7d. a day in winter and 8d. a day in summer, and he can get a house and a cow's grass for a moderate rent. I will allow his wages to take place from the day he sets out, and instead of 7d. a day while he is on his journey, I will allow him one shilling sterling, that is I agree to allow him ten shillings to help to bring him here. I will allow him the same encouragement to bring him here if he is a young man, but while I make these tempting offers, I wish to be advised of his qualifications, such as can he drive a double cart, can he plough with two horses. I suppose he can neither mow hay, nor hoe turnips, but altho' he could not, yet if he is tractable I could learn him. In the event of his being a young man, I would agree to give him £5 5s. sterling for the year, and his bed and diet. But if I could get a more capable servant, I should be better pleased to give him higher terms. The north country servants grumble much with our wet climate; this is the reason which has induced David to leave me. I must request the favour of you to cause John Roy go to Andrew Keir, who will inform you honestly about this same nephew. Give my compliments to Mr Keir, and tell him I will rely on what he says. If he has a good character, I will accept him. You can give him a route, which at this season of the year, I think should be by Huntly, and Cairn o' Mount, then Fettercairn, Brechin, Forfar, Perth, Auchterarder, Stirling, Glasgow and Greenock, where he should call for a merchant, Mr Thomas MacAlpin, grocer there who will direct him for Bute. If he choose to come the Highland road, by

Aviemore, Badenoch, Dalwhinnie, Dalnacardoch, Blair Atholl and Dunkeld, and from there to Perth, and then forward as in the other route.

My servant George Mitchell has left me at this last term, and I want a boy for to serve in his place. What has become of Robert Cumming, James Cumming's son at Bishopmiln. I thought Bob a fine boy, and if he is not engaged in business, I would take him and would promise to help him forward. Pray would you send for James and talk to him about Bob, but I must tell you that you pay no attention to my requests, at least in the way of procuring a servant for me, for I have wrote you several times since, yet not one word of an answer to my request as to these particulars. I shall, however, overlook what is past, but I will expect an answer to this in course.

Mrs May and I were happy to hear of Lord Findlater's generosity. I have no doubt but you will continue to deserve it, and I am extremely pleased that your situation turns out to be so comfortable. I should have regretted it exceedingly if it had been otherwise, as I had a hand in your engagement there.

About a fortnight ago I very unluckily sprained the same knee I had formerly hurt at Linkwood, and am just now confined to the house and have great dread of a long confinement as I can hardly put my foot to the ground just now.

Peter May to George Brown, Linkwood NLS. MS. 3258, f. 21

Edinburgh, 4 January 1781

Mrs May and I came here on Saturday last. I have been clearing my accounts, but am exceedingly disappointed in not having a state of my accounts with you, especially as to the hogshead of wine which you paid to Mr Shand, and which I have been obliged to omit out of this year's discharge for want of a voucher. I request to hear from you in course, with a state of our matters, that I may know how to balance my own accounts and which I do once a year in December, which I find extremely necessary.

I understand that Jenny MacGillivray has brought the fruit of her Bute amours to Moray. I have reason to believe at the same time that A. May and you have been corresponding on the subject of this unlucky amour.[1] I will not pretend to say that I ought, at least that I would have expected advice as soon as any other friend from Mr Brown, but this I leave yourself to judge of the propriety. I shall be here for eight days, and in that time I cannot doubt of hearing from you.

PS. I wrote you lately about Rob Cumming, son of James Cumming, who was miller at Linkwood, now at Bishopmiln, but to this I have no return. I see the necessity of finding out another channel of correspondence.

Copy Peter May's answers to the queries made by Lord Privy Seal, relative to the factory accounts of the estate of Bute for Crop 1779
SRO. RH9/1/84/18

March 1781

1. 'That the arrears on Bute increased at Martinmas last to no less than £64 2s. 3d., tho' at Martinmas 1779 there was so large a sum as £1,010 13s. 8d. of arrears and debts given up as desperate, and at Martinmas 1778 there was £61 1s. 4d. struck out in like manner as desperate.'

In answer to this, Peter May begs leave to observe in the first place, that those debts and arrears were of long standing, for no part of them were incurred during the present commissioner or factor's management. That the increase of £64 2s. 3d. will be accounted for partly from the tenants having formed an idea that they were only to pay per cents for the lime annually instead of prime cost. The latter, however, was exacted and where any arrear was due, it was thrown on the land rent rather than on the lime. Stewarthall always increases the list of arrears annually, his situation being such that he cannot pay even the public burdens on his estate until a part of his lands are sold. P. May observes with great submission that the arrear at the clearance of his last accounts Crop 1779 was only £451 8s. 11$\frac{9}{12}$d. which on a gross rent of almost £4,000 will not be thought an extraordinary arrear, especially as it will be recovered in his next accounts of Crop 1780. Peter May will use all his industry, yet he

[1] This marks the finding out about his son's affair with this girl and the consequent birth of a daughter.

cannot promise that they will not sometimes unavoidably increase. The downfall of the prices of cattle and sheep interfere very much with the payments of rents in Bute.

2. 'Another thing that wants explanation is the great abatement of rents amounting to £76 5s. 11d., viz. £21 for the Paddock Park, Nether Scoullag Park £8 15s., Little Towns £7 13s. 5d., besides £31 13s. allowed to Coupar in Kirrylamont and other small articles. Whence are these abatements of rents?'

In answer 1st. The Paddock Park having been formerly used for breeding horses had lying long in grass and was set for raising corns for two or three crops at almost double the rent it could afford to give for grass; but this, however, behoved to take place as soon as the land was exhausted from bearing corns and at present set for grass rent. 2nd. Nether Scoullag Park was in the same predicament with the paddock and was set at an extravagant rent. The tenant, however, finding that he could not afford to keep the possession, prayed to be relieved from his lease or to have an annual deduction of £10 15s. The commissioner being informed by P. May that the tenant was industrious and that the farm was too high rented, ordered an abatement of £8 15s. to be allowed him annually. Were the present lease of this park expired, it is suspected that a further reduction will yet be necessary, for it is a very poor subject and had been let without any idea to its adequate value. 3rd. The tenant of Little Towns had long complained of his rent being too high; at last he became bankrupt, and his effects were sold for the payment of his debts. No tenant could be got for the first year, it was therefore set in grass at the deduction of £7 13s. 5d. But it is now let to two tenants in lease, tho' at the loss of £3 of an annual abatement. 4th. The £31 13s. stated to Coupar was partly owing to a shortcoming on effects poinded from him and partly by a compromise with him in full of his claims of damages, particularly respecting houses and inclosures. The compromise was made in presence of Mr McLeod, the sheriff, of which he approved rather than go to law with a litigious tenant. Lost on the poinded corns £5 8s. and allowed him in full of his damages £26 5s.

3. 'The repairs and inclosing accounts run high; are there many more of them to be executed?'

The expense of inclosing last year amounted to £104 11s. 3d.

whereof £71 5s. was expended on Kirrylamont and £21 14s. 10d. for inclosing part of the woods; the other articles being of less consequence are not enumerated. That on Kirrylamont were carried on in terms of the lease grant to J. Coupar and that of the woods to prepare them for sale, which are now advertised to be sold by public roup at Rothesay the 22nd current [March]; but it is to be observed that the expense of enclosing the whole woods will be considerable, even with a ditch and paling, and that those tenants on whose farms the woods lie will likewise require an abatement of rent, at least during the first five years until the wood get up. The repairs on farm houses will very soon be reduced as most of the tenants have now entered into leases and by their leases are to be accountable for their houses.

4. 'Why there remains on hand 77 bolls victual, value £51 5s.'

Last year meal was very low priced: the factor offered it for sale to the buss-masters and other people and got most of it disposed at 13s. 4d. The meal reserved was partly to accommodate the masons, carpenters and work people employed at Mount Stuart and because there was no demand for it, but the remainder will be accounted for at 14s. 6d. in the next year's accounts, so that there is a profit on this article of 1s. 2d. per boll.

5. 'Send up a note of the debts now remaining due to Lord Bute since Coupar in Kerrylamont has paid up the £70 18s. 6d. his part of these debts.'

The debts now remaining due are, viz.

Mr Stewart of Kilwhinleck per decreet arbitral pronounced by Mr McLeod, the sheriff, is due	£118	4	11¾
Bryce Duncan, late tacksman of corn mill of Rothesay, is due per heritable bond and interest thereon to Martinmas 1780	£131	19	6½
The Earl of Glasgow for half the expense of building march dykes in Cumbrae	£44	17	0
The burgh of Rothesay are due per two bonds	£60	0	0
	£355	1	6¼

Additional Remarks

Lord Glasgow's doers have refused to pay arrear of £44 17s. stated against his Lordship as due for his proportion of the march dykes in Cumbrae; no written or even verbal agreement can be referred to against them. On examining Mr Edington, the late factor, how that affair had been transacted, he had only to say that Baron Mure gave orders to execute the inclosures and that the Mount Stuart gardener Mitchell and Lord Glasgow's gardener Hill were employed to line them out. P. May has been at pains to get this settled, but is now told by Lord Glasgow's doers that another heritor Baron Hill, as well as Lord Glasgow, must be applied to. Baron Hill it seems has lands in run-rig with Lord Glasgow's, and he is said to be bankrupt. Lord Glasgow's factor has agreed to pay for his constituent.

In the survey and estimate of the island of Bute made by Peter May in summer 1776, the increased rent according to that estimate (of which an abstract was delivered to the then commissioners) was £568 13s. $2\frac{8}{12}$d. But from this increase he abated the sum of £136 5s. 9d. on account of such farms as appeared over rented. These abatements have only taken place in part, and upon the whole the increase will rather be improved; but it must be acknowledged at the same time that farming just now in Bute is not an advantageous business. The farmers are much distressed for labourers, for almost every man that can go on board a vessel is employed either in the navy, privateering or merchant service, so that the island is destitute of servants.

P. May had almost forgot to answer viz.

'When are the increased rents to be added to the rental?'

Had he been at liberty, he would have prefixed rentals to his factory accounts, and on the margin of these rentals he would have marked down the variations and the reasons for them, with a short abstract subjoined. But according to his instructions, he was directed to the rental of 1777 and add to that rental the increase, or abate the decrease, which model he has followed for his accounts of 1778 and 1779. He proposed to make out a complete rental for Crop 1781, as by that time the lands will be arranged and let. But it may be done for Crop 1780 if the Lord Privy Seal approves of it.

Peter May to George Brown NLS. MS. 3258, f. 35

Mount Stuart, 8 April 1781

Last post brought me your favours of the 30th ult. I regret exceedingly the cause of your delay and wish with all my heart your unlucky fall may leave no dregs behind. I have to acknowledge also, the receipt of your note for the balance arising on your current account with me, viz. £152 of principal with twelve months interest, in all £159 12s. sterling payable the 21 December next at the bank office in Aberdeen, and with which I am perfectly pleased, and herewith return your former notes to me. I have only to add as to money matters, that altho' your note is payable at the Aberdeen term, yet let your own convenience direct that period entirely for my wishes shall be subservient to yours.

I would rather avoid the subject relative to Jenny MacGillivray; it is not only unpleasant but will in the end become expensive. Sandy is from home just now, otherwise he would have wrote, but as far as I can judge, the child should be taken from her and be given out to nurse. I thought it had been in that way already, for I think Sandy Young had wrote so, but by all means cause that be done. John Nicol, moss-grieve in Birnie, will I am persuaded take charge of her on moderate terms. I always found him obliging, but you should find no difficulty in finding quarters either in Birnie or Rothes; at any rate, I wish even the appearance of every connection to be dissolved betwixt her and Sandy. I therefore leave it to you to manage matters in the best way you can. While I am on this head, I must observe that I did not approve of the channel of Sandy's correspondence which he carried on with Sandy Young, who, to my knowledge along with Sandy Duff and others, were acquaintances and companions which did not improve his manners, nor his pocket; the last I felt pretty well before all scores were cleared when we set out for this country. However, I desire now to forget that and I hope Sandy has forgot it also for there is less temptation here.

I regret very much that I cannot have the pleasure to enjoy my friends in the north this summer, for altho' Mrs May and I had set our hearts upon it and had promised our connections a visit, yet I now see that will not be in our power. Lord Bute proposes being at Mount Stuart some time in July, and if so, I need not tell you how imprudent it would be for me to be from home. But supposing his Lordship's visit should not take place, which I suspect very much, yet his brother Lord Privy Seal will certainly be with us and I would be equally averse to be out of the way when he was here. The repairs here have been principally planned out by L.P.S. and he is extremely anxious to have them finished by the first of June, and is to be at Mount Stuart soon thereafter. Besides these great folks to attend, there is just now such a number of work people – masons, carpenters, brickmakers and day labourers – to look after which for some time must suspend every idea that I can form of getting north at least early in the summer. But while I give these reasons which I hope my friends will sustain, yet I am not without hopes of overtaking this same longed for jaunt before harvest, that is if we get clear of our great folks, but you will be advised in time. I often anticipate the pleasure of a journey to Elgin, for I am exceedingly attached to that hospitable place, and retain with the utmost respect the memory of my good neighbours there.

I am extremely pleased with your accounts of my favourite *Linkwood.* I shall never spend a few years more to my wish than I did there. I am interested in all its improvements and long exceedingly to have a walk along the clump of planting next to Barmuckity where I have spent some time with the utmost pleasure. Farming here is uphill work – servants cannot be had in the island. Sandy was engaging a farm servant the other day and offered him £8 with a free house and cow's grass, but he would not agree. I must again apply for a good farm servant from Banffshire or some way from the north. It would be a very great favour if you could help one to me.

I thought Lord Findlater had been going abroad, I am glad he is not. I hope his design of building a home at Elchies will amuse him at home. I esteem much and will not forget the respect he paid to us at Edinburgh.

Prices of victual very dull at present, but I am told there will be some demand from Ireland for meal very soon; when I can give you more certain intelligence you shall be advised.

Peter May to George Brown NLS. MS. 3258, f. 40

Mount Stuart, 4 August 1781

I have been long, very long in your debt in the way of correspondence. Your last letter advised that you was going to Aberdeen to divide the lands of Belhelvie into lots, and to assist Doctor Thom to let the lands of Kintore. I was induced to delay writing until you should return and I was also prevented by the arrival of Lord and

Lady Privy Seal here, but tho' I mention these things, yet I do not propose them as an apology, for I confess I have not a good one. I should rather say that Sandy's writing would in some measure atone for me. . . . [There follows a long section on his brother-in-law's matrimonial problems.][1]

I believe I have engaged myself to go north in this same month of August. I propose being at Belmont Castle by the 20th, to be there some days, and then beat my march forward to Aberdeen, where I must remain a week with my friends, and afterwards set out for Moray by way of Banff Castle. I am afraid a visit to you in the time of harvest will be rather improper, but I flatter myself that a visit with you will meet with a hearty welcome at any time, and as I forsee that next year the Noble Lord will certainly pay us a visit, I therefore embrace this time least afterwards it should not be in my power to make choice of another.

I find our friend Provost Duncan has some thoughts of purchasing some part of the Belhelvie lands; of this he has wrote me, but has not said that he has yet fixed on any lot, but wishes to have my opinion of them. I must therefore request you to give me your ideas of the worth of them, and if you have any copy of their measures to send it me addressed under the Provost's cover, to whom I have wrote this post and asked him to apply to you for information and to tell you what lot he has an eye upon, at least if he has any preference of choice. You must give me your opinion in confidence which I promise to make only the proper use of – nobody but our friend the Provost shall know of our concert.

That I may fill up my paper, let me tell you that my little crop has a very fine appearance, too good indeed, for a great part of it is already laid down, and as I have sown grass seeds among all my barley, and also among some oats, the grass will be utterly destroyed with the laid corns. However, I shall sow grass on the bare places in the spring, which is the next best to make up the damage it has got from the crop. I must tell you that I was some weeks ago at the mercate in Glasgow where I bought no less than five horses, two for Provost Duncan and three for myself. Two of the horses which

[1] Archibald Mitchell, Euphemia May's brother, who was a major in the East India Company. The breakdown of an unhappy marriage concerned Peter May in the following few weeks.

I bought for myself turned out a bad bargain, I wish my friend the Provost may do better. Our cows only five in number are remarkably good, and I have some fine young cattle. In particular a bull calf that I have some thoughts of advertising him for show. He is the brood of a fine Highland bull with one of our own cows, and is remarkably handsome. I begin tomorrow to hoe our turnips, which consists only of about 3½ acres, but they promise to be a good crop. I do not find stall feeding here turns out so advantageous as in the north, for the Highland cattle are so small and wild that don't come forward near so well as old oxen.

Sandy has come from his apprenticeship; he was for some weeks attending the Custom House at Port Glasgow in order to commence as comptroller at Rothesay. Babie continues to do very well and became a great favourite of Lady Betty Mackenzie. Her Ladyship made Babie a present of a silk gown. I need not tell you that Mrs May comes with me, and with Sandy and Babie, joins in best wishes to you, Mrs Brown and young folks.

Peter May to George Brown NLS. MS. 3258, f. 42

Old Aberdeen, 31 August 1781

I arrived at the Major's on Saturday night the 25th and have remained with him ever since. I go to Achortes today, and return in the evening. I have appointed my sister and other relations to meet me tomorrow in Aberdeen at Mrs Frenche's. On Saturday I go to Drumside and return from there on Tuesday morning. I go to Kingcausie that same day and return in the evening. Wednesday I go through all my friends here, and on Thursday I intend setting off for Banff. I propose dining with my brother at Idoch, and getting into Banff in the evening where I shall spend the next day with Lady Findlater, go to Cullen House in the afternoon, and sleep there that night and get away next day; but some of my dispatch, as here pointed out, may be a little deranged and therefore I shall take another day into the bargain and that will postpone my arrival at Linkwood to Sunday or Monday the 9th or 10th of August, when I shall have the pleasure to see my friends there.

Robert Johnston, who lived with me two years and who was a very fine young lad, left me the beginning of this month to go to

Strichen in consequence of a letter from Mr Fraser.[1] I find I must have another person to help Sandy to complete the survey of Bute, for the other business with which he is now connected, puts it out of his power to give the application necessary to finish the mensuration of the island. I am to call on your assistant Mr Innes, who I suppose can inform me if there be any sober young lad here that I could engage to assist Sandy in taking the measures and to make out the plans which I wish to be a masterpiece. I beg you will say nothing of my coming to see you as I mean to be entirely private and can only spend one or two days with you.

Peter May to George Brown NLS. MS. 3258, f. 44

Edinburgh, 22 September 1781

I left my favourite spot Linkwood and my favourite friends there with not a little regret – the very happy days I had spent in that neighbourhood returned to my mind with full force. Even the trees did not escape a sighing farewell. One consolation, however, took place, namely that a friend had succeeded, one in whose interest I was sensibly interested. But while I am on this subject, indulge me to mark down my own wishes in so far as they respect you and proceed from my attachment for your welfare. In the first place then, I am to observe that from every appearance of your crop and the produce of your farm in so far as I could discover, I think it must turn out disadvantageous, nay exceedingly unfavourable. A very great expense of management is unavoidable, but to which the produce is not nearly adequate. I would have you therefore to contract your expense into a narrower circle, and I would have you also to stock your farm only with such a number of bestial as it can maintain well and easily, for I cannot apprehend that you can derive profit from the necessity of sending away your black cattle and sheep to other grazings, except these grazings were lower rented than yours are. In the second place, I would recommend your culture for corns only on such parts of your farm as you have reason to expect a good crop from. I suspect your ground (except very little) to be unfit for oats after wheat; these crops are too scourging for

[1] Alexander Fraser of Strichen who owned about three-quarters of the parish of Strichen, or William Fraser of Park, factor to Lord Saltoun.

Linkwood. I therefore recommend ploughing less and dunging well what you plough.[1] By having less in tillage the expense would also be lessened. Land in grass and producing a poor crop is no doubt unprofitable, but poor land sown with corns is exceedingly more unprofitable. In the third place, I would wish you to compare profit and loss as to your crops on Linkwood. I am afraid this would not answer to your wish and yet it is extremely necessary; for if your farm must be fostered by the profits of your other businesses, the consequence is clear – that it is a bad bargain. However, I hope my suspicions may be magnified from the wretched appearance I saw every way in Moray. I must further remark, that your being engaged so often in business, which obliges you to be from home, militates against your being a successful farmer. You should remember the old saying that 'the master's eye makes the horse full'. Not that I am against your going abroad, but in that view I should wish you to have less to do as a farmer. The expense of servants too is a heavy article, and the managing of them still more disagreeable, but grass adds little to our expense. Therefore, I approve much of your plan of sowing down grass, but I must recommend you, that before you can expect good grass you must lay your land down in good heart, or dung it on the grass afterwards.

I must go further in my observations. I am to remark that in consequence of your acting for the Aberdeen Bank as their agent at

[1] This advice accords closely to that given by Alexander Wight when he visited Brown in 1780 which he recorded in his *Present State of Husbandry in Scotland*, Edinburgh, 1784, vol. iv, pp. 85-86: 'Linkwood, a farm near Elgin, belonging to the Earl of Findlater, consists of near 300 acres, and is possessed by Mr George Brown, upon a nineteen-years lease, rent £76 sterling. One hundred acres of this farm are fit for nothing but bearing trees. The other 200 are very capable of improvement. A very neat commodious dwelling-house was built for him by his landlord; to which Brown himself has added a complete set of offices. Tho' this is but the second year of his possession, yet I there found wheat, drilled beans, and pease of the Peebles kind, all in good order. Nor had he neglected to store his kitchen-garden with cabbages, carrots, etc. The stock of sheep on this farm is not despicable. It was Mr Brown's intention to improve his breed by rams of the finest kinds from England. I endeavoured to dissuade him from this, recommending the best sort of rams from Tweeddale. He listened. But a great bar against sheep, was his being bound in his lease to inclose with thorn-hedges. I cannot help, however, being of opinion, that this farm would be more improved with sheep than by inclosing. It is not well watered. The soil is dry, and fit for turnips to be eaten by sheep in hurdles during winter. The home breed of cattle is good here. Oxen ploughs are used. Two oxen are put to plough, and harnessed, without a driver. It is the Rotheram plough, or what is called the chain-plough, but without the chain'.

Elgin, you will be possessed of their notes, which will give you a command of cash, at least of notes which answers for cash. I flatter myself that you will keep your cash accounts as to your intromissions with that bank perfectly clear. I suppose that your accounts are balanced once a year, but I suppose also that there is a balance in your hands at your clearance and which is stated to your debt of next account: now if this balance shall be interfered with, to answer any other debt of yours, you need not be told that this is using freedom with money which is not your own. Shall I caution you also as to your neighbours, if from their knowledge that you are in cash they should apply to you, I hope you will only supply such as are perfectly good. In a word your conduct as to the bank transactions should not only be accurate but secure for the bank, and profitable to yourself.

I suspect this year's collection of rents will be attended with a good deal of trouble over most parts of Scotland, but in Moray it more particularly so; of this I am fully satisfied from the experience I had, and from the poor appearance of the crop. Will not that occasion you to pay exceeding great attention to recover all you can while the little crop they have is among their hands? The possessors of the Stonecrosshill, Blacklands, and other parts about Elgin, were always troublesome, but by dunning them and craving hard, little was lost. I need not tell you of the necessity of exerting yourself to make the rents in your collection as effectual as you can. Rothes will give you less trouble than your other concerns, for I considered it as a thriving estate.

The inclosed to James MacIntosh, be so good as deliver. I wish you to send for him and tell him your own opinion. I have not the least objection to delay his coming to me until Mr Brodie come up to Edinburgh in November; that would suit me very well as I must be there in December and could then carry him with me to Bute. The only danger I can apprehend is from Mr Brodie's having a view on him for a servant to himself. If that is the case he may insinuate in the boy unfavourable circumstances relative to his serving me, and yet I can hardly think our friend Brodie would do that, yet if you knew how he advised and acted by Mrs M[itchell][1] at Edinburgh you

[1] Wife of Major Archibald Mitchell, Euphemia May's brother. Archibald broke down under the strain of his wife's extravagance and May took over his interests.

would not be surprised if I laid more to his charge. He carried her to the first counsel here, and consulted them on the validity of her separation, and did not leave a stone unturned to avail her against the Major. But he was one of her *Gallants*. The advice she got at Edinburgh by Mr Brodie's means will oblige the Major to go up to London, which must be expensive and exceedingly troublesome. I must not omit to inform you that when I was at Belmont Castle on my way here, I fell in with Mr Ross of the Post Office, and in our conversation about Elgin, he told me of his being informed by way of complaint, that Mr Brodie was generally in the Post Office at Elgin as soon as the mail arrived, that he canvassed the letters and Mr Ross added that according to his information he made too detailed a search into people's correspondence. Mr Ross said he was to write you such a letter as would totally debar any future attempts of that sort, and which should certainly be attended to. You need not take any notice of this caveat from me as you will hear soon from Mr Ross to the same purpose, at least he assured me he would write you an ostensible letter, that is such a letter as you could show Squire Brodie.

Peter May to George Brown NLS. MS. 3258, f. 48

Mount Stuart, 6 October 1781

I received this post your letter of the 27th ulto. which gave all your friends here very sincere pleasure. My anxiety for your welfare very likely creates difficulties which a less attachment would not perceive. I am very glad, however, to have so favourable accounts from your own hand, and therefore have only to request that your plans may be steadfastly pursued, and in the most frugal manner. As to your little concern of money matters with me, that shall be regulated to your wish. When you find it convenient to discharge it let that be done; but consult your own convenience, not mine, for I am only ready to receive it when your funds can easily answer. I only wish to caution your attention to matters of more consequence, particularly in giving credits to the neighbourhood where you live, except to those in whom you have the most entire confidence of their responsibility.

You say Mr William Grant created a brulzie[1] in the worshipful council of Elgin, but that he was repulsed with the loss of three friends. I suppose you have been reading a newspaper wherein some engagement has occurred to you, where the rebels have been repulsed, and I imagine you consider William Grant to be, if not a rebel, an officious meddler, of which I am not ignorant from repeated experience; but pray Mr Treasurer what could you mean to engage with the troublesome business of collecting the perplexing funds of the town of Elgin? I find you have been anxious of the honour to be an office bearer, and of all others you have chosen the line that will require more attention than the whole other branches of the council taken together. Altho' I have no objections to your being a member of the council of Elgin, yet I cannot approve of your being treasurer. I would advise you to avoid every concern there that will give you trouble, and by being on the council you will have as much political influence as if you were a baillie. I was for some time a baillie in Elgin, and I could have been provost, but had I been to have remained longer in Elgin I should certainly have withdrawn my connection from the council altogether, except my Lord Findlater's commissioners had said that it would oblige his Lordship, and that they would indemnify my expense, which was very considerable and for which I never received a shilling. But altho' you say that William Grant and his friends were repulsed, yet you don't advise me who are the magistrates and the other members of the council. Pray do so in your next, and tell me of all your manoeuvres thereanent. I was informed at Edinburgh that Archie Duff was to be a candidate for provost, and that Baillie Jameson was pewtering for him with all his might, and that [Alex. Brodie of] Windyhills was in opposition.

It is now time to advise you that we arrived in our kingdom here on Thursday the 27th ulto. in perfect good health, and that we were received with open arms from Sandy and Babie, and I hope met with a hearty welcome from our other friends in the island. My little crop was all put into the corn yards and thatched some days before our arrival, and from its appearance I think it will turn out very well, but when I tell you that it is only the produce of 11 acres you will think I am very vain to talk of my crop or my farm either. My cattle

[1] A disturbance.

are all in fine order; I have half a score fat cows that would do honour to any table, even for the council of Elgin. Mrs May since her arrival here has been oppressed sending pears to our neighbours, which is all the fruit we have at Mount Stuart this season. I wish you could send me some of your gardeners', and in return I'll send you some pears to feed the rest. I suppose you understand what I mean as to your gardener's. Every improvement respecting the fields has been postponed at Mount Stuart on account of buildings and repairs, and which are not yet finished. I find masonry and farming interfere exceedingly with one another. All the corns are not got in in the island, and in general the crop is very good especially the bere which is remarkably so.

If James MacIntosh's son has any intention to serve me, of which I have already wrote you, I should be glad to know; be so good therefore as to talk to James and let him say if his son can meet me in Edinburgh towards the end of December next, or if he could come along with two servant maids that come from Aberdeen to serve Mrs May, and who will set out from Aberdeen by the first of November. They come by the Aberdeen waggon to Edinburgh and from there to Glasgow, and when at Glasgow they come in the fly to Greenock. But as I said formerly if he comes with Mr Brodie to Edinburgh I shall in that case find him before me. I only wish to know whether I am to depend upon him or not, and I beg you will write me in course what James MacIntosh says.

When I was at Aberdeen I spoke to Colin Innes about coming sometime to Bute to help A. May to complete the survey which his other business interferes with a good deal, but Colin said he could not come this autumn, but said he would in the spring. I wish in the meantime I could find some young lad that would hire by the year, and who understood a little of drawing, for I foresee the survey of the island will be a long work as Sandy cannot pay attention to it, and I am exceedingly anxious for various reasons to have it accomplished soon. I am told that your old man Mackay is about Peterhead and rather idle than otherwise; would he answer for my purpose if I were to make proposals to him? Tell me what you think as to this? There is one Coul at Cullen House who works in the gardens, and sometimes on the roads as overseer. I was told by Mr Morison that he could measure a little. I wish you would inform yourself at Mr John Wilson as to his capacity and character, and let me know the result of your enquiry, for one way or another I see I must get an assistant.

I am very glad that Mr Ross speaks favourably of the view we have for my brother. I wish he may succeed, but I am not pleased with his shabby way of living. When I go to see my brother, I am almost ashamed to find him and his family in such a pickle. Were he in needy circumstances, I would make the proper allowance for him, but both you and I know that his funds can afford a decent economy, without which he cannot look for respect. I regret that his disposition is so attracted to save a penny, that every other object must give way to it. I commend frugality as much as anybody and I wish to practice it, but I detest being a miser.

Robert Oliphant to ?Lord Privy Seal SRO. RH9/1/84/19

Post Office Edinburgh, 1 February 1782

I am favoured with your Lordship's letter of the 25th past, inclosing the Bute accounts, etc. and shall now endeavour to give you all the satisfaction I can with regard to your remarks.

1. As to the arrears, I formerly mentioned to your Lordship that an increase would naturally arise from the accounts being brought up so much sooner than ordinary, tho' that effect, barring accidents, should no longer exist. Without going into particulars I shall only mention one article of £60 18s. 10d. due by the cotton company that would not have appeared in the list but for Mr MacAlpine's being in London when the factor [Peter May] settled his accounts.

2. As to Coupar, the first article of £26 5s. was allowed him by a decree of the sheriff for the *loss* he sustained in *not* having houses agreeable to his bargain, which was owing to the interregnum of the two factors. And the last two articles were for the expense of fulfilling the engagement that Mr Menzies and I entered into with him.

3. The mistake in the tax for Mount Stuart was noticed at clearing the accounts. But as the voucher, tho' for a year was only for 17s. 10d., was passed and the factor was to have explained the matter when he returned home, but has not yet done it. The correspondence with the island has for a great while past been very irregular owing to the high winds.

4. As the number of horses kept, there were only two bought at my Lord's expense. One of them died in the service, but the factor bought another at his own expense, as the great work being nearly finished, he would afterwards have use of him. There were five more belonging to the factor employed in the works for which their maintenance *only* is charged to my Lord's account, but the works being now mostly over, that expense will cease of course.
5. As to the expense of the building and alterations on Mount Stuart House exceeding the estimate so much, the same may be accounted for by the prodigious rise in the price of materials, particularly wood, which is nearly doubled in price, and a considerable advance in freights, etc. The accounts which the factor presented for being cleared were chiefly for materials purchased by the order of Mr Paterson himself. Others were for freights, carriages, etc. And a very considerable part of the expense was money advanced *on receipt* to Mr Paterson's workmen, the accounts of which are not yet made up, but the whole of the money so advanced will be accounted for when the works are finally ended.
6. The expense of the garden, nurseries and policy appears certainly too high and I challenged it at the time of passing the accounts. In this expense, however, is included near £30 for grass seeds, cartwheels and smith and wright's accounts. The grass seeds could not have been charged to my Lord's account with any degree of propriety, but that the hay produced from them was all given to horses employed in his Lordship's works, over and above what was purchased, and the cartwheels are employed in the works in general.
7. Mrs Robertson's interest and Margaret Campbell's annuity, ought, according to the last model for the accounts, to have been stated under the head of pensions, and shall be observed in future.
8. The expense of the factor's coming to Edinburgh may now be avoided.

Lord Mount Stuart to Peter May

BUTE, letter book, agents in Scotland, vol. 1, pp. 1-5

Luton Park, 9 September 1783

You forgot before I left Mount Stuart to give me a list of several articles you told me in the course of our conversation were much wanted. I endeavoured when on board the cutter to recollect them and made Mr Alexander May note it down, such as, telescope, barometer, thermometer, machine for measuring rain-water; this I gave to my father, who says you shall certainly be supplied.

I have talked to him also on many subjects which required in my opinion immediate and decisive steps to be taken; the garden, you may be sure, was a principal point. I did not omit observing that without some skilful hand was authorised to thin the plantation, many a noble tree must infallibly become a victim. I adverted likewise to the bad declining state of the nursery, to the absolute occasion there was for some expense in preserving those woods planted by Baron Mure and others, to the advantage which might accrue from making considerable plantations in other parts, and hinted as far as I could that the present system of rigid economy might be as prejudicial to the true interests of the property in that part of the world as the former extravagant and injudicious management. I am confident my father is fully impressed with the truth of the whole, but without he was present himself it is not to be expected he will give any immediate order, and I cannot yet flatter you with hopes of his taking such a journey.

I beg to recall to your memory my views on the estate of Ascog, and hope you will not lose sight of an object which I should think by underhand means might be effected without paying an extravagant price.

I have talked over so often the castle-ditch and my abhorrence at the idea of feuing what formerly was a royal residence and so noble a feather in our cap that I need not now enlarge any more thereon, except to say that if it pleased God I live, I never shall be satisfied until I get the whole back, and I shall endeavour to impress my son with the same idea: in the meantime there is a part of those feus absolutely necessary for a serious scheme I have in view, I mean what is opposite the old gate-way. I request therefore you will privately endeavour to purchase back sufficient to make a wide, what I should wish a noble, approach to that old gate, that is to say, fifty feet wide at least, and down into the street so that a coach and six might turn: as this is a matter I wish to keep private you will be so good as let it remain locked up in your breast, indeed my whole letter I mean as confidential.

I enclose the list of pictures made out by Mr Alexander May, for my father and I having agreed to bring most of them to London. It is necessary he should have it in order to select those we want. I have opposite to each put a figure, thirty-three in all, and that there may be no mistake I have over and above drawn an additional line under each picture that is wanted: the list must be returned to me when you have done with it. It remains to explain in what manner they are to be sent, and we judge the best way will be by land, taking great care in the passage across that no sea-water gets at the boxes, which would effectually destroy the pictures. With regard to the boxes, there must be a small ridge or rise at the bottom of each to prevent anything but the *side* of the picture which is lowest from touching the wood. I think I explain the idea so as to be understood. The joinings of the wood on the outside must have pieces of coarse cloth glued all along, and then covered with pitch, care being taken that none gets into the inside, the same round the top when nailed on, and, after the pictures are placed in the box, little pieces of wood must be nailed all round in the *inside* to keep the pictures from moving or shaking. The pictures are to be sent without frames, and as many in a box as conveniently can without making it too bulky. At the same time no picture can be placed together but what is nearly of a size for it must be contrived that each picture rests upon the other's straining frame, or in other words, the wooden frame on which the canvas is nailed. They must be arranged accordingly, and where that cannot be effected you must make use of separate boxes, but when you come to place them altogether, I durst say you will find the sizes such that no picture need have one. I trust this description is very accurate, no mistake can be made. I must only recommend once more to guard against the passage by sea. The boxes must be directed to me to the care of Philip Deare, Esquire, Auditor of Imprests Office, London,[1] and you will appraise that gentleman of the time of their arrival, and where he is to send for them, which is meant in case I happen to be out of town.

[1] A department of the Admiralty which attended to the advances made to paymasters and other officials.

Philip Deare to Peter May

BUTE, letter book, agents in Scotland, vol. 1, pp. 5–6

Hill Street, London, 16 December 1783

I have the pleasure to acquaint you that the pictures arrived on Tuesday and I hope perfectly safe, though the cases are not yet opened.

Lord Mount Stuart, who is so much taken up with business that he is unable to write, has laid his commands on me to apprise you that it is probable there will be an immediate dissolution of Parliament. He therefore requests that you will *look* to the County of Bute, it being Lord Bute's turn to nominate, and to the Borough of Rothesay, and take care to keep all right. His Lordship requests you to sound the Borough of Ayr and see whether it is to be come at by any means, and what, and to let him know in the most expeditious manner possible, except by express. If it is to be obtained, pray secure it without waiting to consult him, resting in the most perfect assurance that you shall hear from his Lordship the moment the dissolution is determined on. The greatest caution and circumspection will be necessary, as the whole of this communication is made in the perfect confidence of your keeping it a profound secret. . . .

Lord Mount Stuart to Peter May

BUTE, letter book, agents in Scotland, vol. 1, pp. 6–9

Hill Street, London, 28 January 1784

I have received your several letters, which a variety of circumstances has hitherto prevented me from answering, though the contents were by no means a matter of indifference to me.

I am ignorant whether Lady Mount Stuart ever mentioned the receipt of the tin roller enclosing a plan of Mount Stuart: if she did not I must do it, and express at the same time a strong commendation of the neat manner in which it was executed: but I am well acquainted with Mr Alexander May's various talents in that way.

Mr Deare has already informed you of the safe arrival of the pictures. I have only therefore to add that I never saw anything better packed, and to wish that the intrinsic merit of each was equal to the attention you bestowed upon them; but I am not ignorant of the great exactness you observe in every particular committed to your care, even in the most trifling matter.

The extract you transmit of Mr Beveridge's answer relative to the estate of Ascog is very satisfactory. I say satisfactory because knowing it to be entailed I shall not be uneasy lest the heir should dispose of it to other persons, and I have no doubt but in good time and by *proper application* I shall succeed in my views concerning it.

In regard to the Castle of Rothesay I must once again lament the unwise system which ever thought of feuing so hallowed a piece of ground. I remember too well the house you speak of; it was the first object struck me: but it cannot be helped. I certainly shall persevere in my former intentions, and recommend it to you therefore to put as cheap as you can an entrance to the old gate. I shall afterwards consider how far it may be worth while to extend the idea of purchasing the whole.

I am glad to hear from you that notwithstanding the bad year of 1782[1] your accounts turn out so well, but beg you will not think of sending me a copy as it might not be well taken; but I wish you would let me know what I am indebted to you for several expenses of post horses, etc., I desired you to liquidate.

In respect to your answer to Mr Deare's letter concerning the Borough, I think the way you conducted yourself perfectly right. I should have wrote myself had any thing pressed, but now I have lost sight of the object.

Lord Bute having been good enough to leave to me the filling up of the vacant qualifications for the County, I did not hesitate to name my friends Sir William Cunynghame[2] and Mr Kennedy and also to recommend yourself, of whom I have the highest opinion and for whom I have a very great regard. I do not know whether on sending down the names it was told that the nomination was mine. You will be so good as to let me know whether there remains any other vacancy in order to its being immediately filled up. . . .

[1] This refers to the crop failure suffered nearly everywhere in Scotland and the dearth that followed.

[2] Sir William Augustus Cunynghame, 4th Bart. of Milncraig.

Lord Mount Stuart to Peter May

BUTE, letter book, agents in Scotland, vol. 1, pp. 9-10

Brighthelmstone,[1] 23 August 1784

I should certainly have long since answered your letters of the fourteenth of February and twenty-fifth of April if I could in any shape have contributed to forward the judicious hints they contain. I thank you for the communication of the papers enclosed in them, and you may be assured I will keep your counsel.

In regard to these *feus* which I requested you to endeavour to buy back, particularly the ground in front of the entrance of the castle, I must give up all thoughts of it if Mr Oliphant is to be made acquainted with the design, but I do not see why you might not act for yourself and wait (as you observe) a favourable opportunity two or three years hence of making a more frugal bargain.

I have not lost sight of the coal scheme, but don't think it prudent to move in that business until we know how far Ascog may be won over to part with that estate, as perhaps his land might interfere. Mr Beveridge informs me that you had lately written him word that a Mr Gordon, a native of Bute, had arrived from India with a considerable fortune, who proposed buying it, and desiring he would find out whether any sort of treaty was on foot. He tells me he has discovered in consequence that Gordon has actually offered four thousand guineas which has been refused, but as this leads him to think Ascog may listen to greater proposals he begs I will let him know how far I would choose to go, and states the rent at one hundred and fifty pounds. I direct him in answer on that supposition to bid thirty years' purchase, and I will not stand for a little more. I have not time to consult Lord Bute, but should the bargain be made, and he like to take it hereafter, I can always make it over. I advise Beveridge at the same time to go underhand to work in order that Mr Gordon may not be bidding against me.

Peter May to the Earl of Findlater SRO. GD248/952/3

Edinburgh, 13 December 1784

Having seen your Lordship's letter to Mr Oliphant recommending

[1] Brighton, Sussex.

Mr George Fenton to succeed Mr Grant as Stamp Master[1] at Elgin, and having also a letter from my friend Mr [George] Brown to the same purpose, I have the honour to inform your Lordship that every little exertion in my power has been employed to accomplish your wishes. I have applied to Lords Ankerville and Stonefield; the former had your Lordship's application by letter and says he will attend to your accommodation, and Lord Stonefield has marked down his name at my request. I have also waited of Baron Gordon to whom Mr Brown wrote, and the Baron signified to me he wishes to oblige your Lordship. These are the only acquaintances I have at the Board. I must, however, observe to your Lordship an objection which occurred to Mr Oliphant, namely that Mr Fenton had not been bred a manufacturer, and this requisite, it seems, the Trustees pay much respect to. I apprehend this may easily be obtained by Mr Brown's influence and for that purpose I have wrote him by this post so as no time may be lost.

I have been here for some days settling my accounts with Mr Oliphant, Lord Bute's commissioner. I shall leave town in a few days. In the meantime I beg leave to acknowledge my obligations to your Lordship for the very friendly manner you have treated George Brown. I shall be happy if he continues to deserve your Lordship's indulgence.

Peter May to the Earl of Findlater SRO. GD248/952/7

Mount Stuart, 26 February 1785

I received the honour of your Lordship's letter of the 11th approving in a flattering manner of the attention I had paid to your recommendation in favour of Mr George Fenton for the appointment of Stamp Master of Elgin of whose success your Lordship's letter gave me the first information. I beg leave to express the satisfaction I shall always feel when any exertion of mine meets with your applause. I cannot write your Lordship and omit to repeat my attachment which grows older with myself, but not the less sincere. I receive your Lordship's invitation to Cullen House

[1] A district supervisor for the Board of Trustees for Fisheries and Manufacturers whose duty was to inspect linen cloth and to stamp it if it reached requisite standards.

with that respect I ought, and I already anticipate the honour of paying my humble respects there next summer.

I am happy with the good opinion your Lordship is pleased to entertain of my friend George Brown. I wish he may continue to manage your affairs in such a manner as to merit that friendship and generosity he has already met with, of which I am not ignorant. I am persuaded of his attachment for your Lordship's interest, but I know from experience that his collection is of that sort as hardly to bring him credit. His brother John, who had the honour of paying his respects to your Lordship, I believe has some genius, but I suspect it is a little variable. I have accused him of inactivity, at least have pointed out the necessity to push forward by every assiduous and prudent method. I regret that my situation does not enable me to help him forward in the military line. I have, however, agreed to purchase a lieutenancy for him as soon as he pleases.[1]

Our situation along the West Coast in regard to a supply of victual has been favourable; Glasgow, Greenock, and the neighbourhood of the Clyde, have been supplied for the most part from Ireland, from which there has been large importations. Prices in Ireland, viz. meal from 9s. to 11s. the hundred-weight, that is something almost equal to our six stone. The retailing prices along the Clyde have been: meal 16s., oats 13s. 4d., bere 17s., but latterly they are on the decline.

As I have not the honour to write your Lordship often, I therefore presume to add a little to the length of this letter. I am then to communicate my plan in regard to myself which is to withdraw from Bute as soon as I can with the friendship of the family, and to leave a young friend to succeed me. I must not omit, however, to do justice to the place I now hold, which is both respectful and advantageous, and that I am fortunate to enjoy the confidence of Lord Bute and his friends. To their friendship I lay some claim, for I have not been idle nor inattentive to their interest since I came to the island. When I began my intromissions with Crop 1777 I got a rental of £3,500, with £1,700 of arrear. Upon clearing my first year's accounts £700 of the arrears was struck off by Lord Privy Seal as irrecoverable. The rental for Crop 1783 amounted to £4,300, and which I accounted for with no more than £119 of arrear. I

[1] He ultimately rose to become a colonel.

shall leave the tenantry in excellent order, and I hope without any arrear. I wish, however, to retire among my friends in the north, and, if I can, accomplish that in a year or two.

Lord Mount Stuart to Peter May

BUTE, letter book, agents in Scotland, vol. 1, p. 11

Hallingbury, 15 March 1785

I write this merely to acknowledge the receipt of your letter of the twelfth of January with the several papers enclosed, for as to the matter principally treated it can be of no use giving any opinion. I shall content myself with saying that I disapprove in the strongest manner the pernicious system of granting feus, which must ultimately ruin the estate.

In regard to Ascog I am persuaded from the conduct of the laird [John Stewart] that he is tied up in such a manner as not to have it in his power to part with the property. He therefore amuses himself with laughing at the folly of those who bid for it.

I wish with all my heart I could be of any service in relation to the removal of the Custom-house boat, but the part I have taken in politics absolutely precludes all possibility of success, were I weak enough to make the attempt.

I cannot conclude without repeating the assurances of the high opinion and regard I entertain for you; it will give me much pleasure should I be enabled in the course of the summer to pay you another visit in the island: but whether I do or not my best wishes will always attend you.

Lord Mount Stuart to Peter May

BUTE, letter book, agents in Scotland, vol. 1, pp. 12-14

Newcastle, 14 July 1786

William Casson,[1] the bearer of this letter, is a person I have fixed on to search for coal in Bute; he carries with him all the

[1] Mining engineer, the following year 1787, he was advising the Earl of Leven about the introduction of horses into Balgonie Colliery (Baron F. Duckham, *A history of the Scottish coal industry*, vol. 1, 1700-1815, David & Charles, Newton Abbot, 1970, p. 103).

necessary implements: any little job he may chance to want can easily be supplied in the island.

He is attended by an assistant and may perhaps call for another on the spot. You will be so good as to provide them with lodging and food in the house, and there will be no difficulty as to my coming, because they are not of that sort to object to eating with the servants, though Casson is much superior to the other, who is a common working man.

In order to promote secrecy as much as possible Casson does not know that he goes on my account. On the contrary he believes it is wholly a scheme of Mr Rayne's, my agent at this place, who has directed him to open his lips to no one; you must not therefore be surprised if even to you he gives evasive answers.

I beg you will endeavour to prevent the artful people of Rothesay from approaching. I shall be with you before great matters are effected, and in directing him to the several spots I wish those near Ascog should be reserved until I come.

I must also recommend to you neither to let him see any former reports on the subject, nor to give him hints that trials have already been made; let him search out his own way in the best manner he is able. The result in such case will be much more to be depended on.

Memorandum Lord Mount Stuart to Peter May

BUTE, letter book, agents in Scotland, vol. I, p. 14

Mount Stuart, 29 August 1786

To send word immediately when any bits of land are to be sold in the island.

To throw cold water as much as possible upon feus of every sort.

To endeavour to purchase underhand the feu possessed by Archibald Sharp adjoining to Mr Gordon's: and also the feu on the west side belonging to the heirs of Archibald Maconochie, late fiscal in Rothesay.

To resolve whether it will be worth while to buy the inn at the Largs, and to endeavour to find out for what sum a feu of three acres could be obtained from the laird of Brisbane on the shore.

The town of Rothesay must in future be continually watched. There is no harm in immediately canvassing all those councillors not yet spoken to, to support my nomination. Mr May will by this means be able to discover their sentiments and how far they are to be depended upon.

Lord Mount Stuart to Peter May

BUTE, letter book, agents in Scotland, vol. I, pp. 15-17

Hallingbury, 18 October 1786

Your several letters of the tenth, twenty-fourth, twenty-fifth of September, and third and fifth instant have been all received with their various enclosures, and I take the first opportunity of my return home to answer them.

In regard to the success of our attempts to find coal, I am not better pleased with what has been done than the inhabitants of Rothesay, and I shall undoubtedly make a further trial when the season proves more favourable, which I take to be in the month of May. Upon this account I am glad the rods are deposited at Mount Stuart, where I beg they may remain until persons authorised by me shall proceed in the business, for I do not choose to permit anyone else.

The spirited manner in which the Duke of Argyll has taken up the obnoxious clause of the last Fishery bill will tend more to remedy that evil than all the memorials upon earth. I enclose a copy of the Duke's answer to my letter to be communicated to the Council of Rothesay.

The decided majority you seem to have obtained at the late election will, I hope, make all matters easy; it still requires, however, a watchful eye, which I am certain you will not neglect; and as to what may be necessary to do further, it will be a sensible mortification to me if I am not able to make you another visit in the course of next year, and of course to give my advice in person.

After the strong recommendation you transmit of *John Coul*, I have not the smallest difficulty in immediately closing with the terms. I consent to his coming next Whitsuntide, to his returning the end of the year to fetch his wife, and to my paying those expenses. I likewise accede to the wages being forty pounds certain, and ten pounds more should our expectations be answered. A question, notwithstanding, occurs. Are those wages in lieu of all demands, such as food and lodging, though the latter I could accommodate?[1]

You will be glad to learn that my father in his answer to that part of my letter which respects the thinning of the trees makes use of the following words: 'I am persuaded you are right about the trees being too close. They certainly want thinning, and I desire you would give any orders you think necessary about it.' I, in consequence of this direction, request of you to use your own judgement, and to proceed as soon as you please, particularly recommending it to you to clear in such a manner as may admit a free circulation of air round the house.

I trust you will not forget the two feus I want to purchase; if you will transmit the names, particulars, and so forth, of the one belonging to the person resident in London, I will soon conclude that part.

The footman and two grooms who behaved so ill are all dispatched. I shall take care the next journey to bring you more civilised gentry.

Lord Mount Stuart to Peter May

BUTE, letter book agents in Scotland, vol. I, pp. 18–21

Hallingbury, 17 December 1786

. . . It is no small mortification to me to learn that Sharpe will not part with his feu: could you not employ some indifferent person to persuade him to change that resolution? I am in hopes Mr Duncan will not be so inexorable. There is another matter likewise of which I do not lose sight, the feu at the Largs. Mr Beveridge informed me that feus in that parish were a penny pie, one hundred pounds an acre. I cannot help thinking he must have made a mistake, because the price of freehold land at the very gates of London is not higher.

In thinning the trees you have perfectly well recollected the little value I comparatively set upon planes and limes. As to the mode of thinning I leave it entirely in your hands.

The post office scheme had better sleep for the present. I once thought of writing to Robinson and Muir desiring to be furnished with their reasons for objecting to the bag being left at the Largs. Unless the convenience of a water communication with Greenock

[1] The job in question was to take charge of a tree-nursery and woods on Bute's Glamorganshire estates. John Coul did not get the job because he made excessive demands (BUTE, letter 17 Dec. 1786).

surpasses the convenience of a regular receipt of letters I cannot find out the objection. When the city of Rothesay and I become better acquainted and of course better friends, my opinion may perhaps decide this and many other matters; we must hold our tongues relative to the money allotted, or rather not allotted, to improvement. My sentiments are not unknown to you.

Lord Mount Stuart to Peter May

BUTE, letter book, agents in Scotland, vol. 1, pp. 21-22

Hallingbury, 24 December 1786

Your letters of the seventeenth and nineteenth instant have been duly received. The order given to place the expenditure at Mount Stuart in the abstract to the account of me and my company I can only consider as an artful attempt to debar me the pleasure of going there. Pray let me know the amount, and whether in the arrangement you have observed the direction I suggested of separating the wages and other outgoings incident to the boring for coal. The contrary might be more prejudicial than you are perhaps aware. Whatever money was expended in that pursuit I desire to reimburse out of hand, and for that purpose I hope the charge will be immediately transmitted.

Mr Macleod's plan of buying the teind duties upon the land of Kames will never be accomplished with my consent; those who wish to lower the consequence of the family may countenance it, but otherwise your reasoning appears conclusive. The building, repairing, and so forth, joined to the wish of total independence, does not look like selling. Were we possessed of Kames's property the remainder might be overlooked. I confess myself a little disappointed.

It having always escaped me to take notice of the subscription to the Rothesay pier, I think it proper to say I have not lost sight of the intention.[1] I postpone deciding the quantum till my next visit, and, between ourselves, until the next election of councillors takes

[1] On 9 August 1779 a petition was placed before the Commissioners of the Annexed Estates requesting £600 and upwards for repairing the harbour at Rothesay. Lord Stonefield and Robert Oliphant of Rossie who found that of the total estimate of £1,449, some £525 would allow work to be undertaken. Lord Bute indicated he was willing to contribute £100, and thus the Commissioners fixed on £425 as their contribution (SRO. E728/33/4).

place, when I look to have Mackinlay and Bannatyne left out and two worthy farmers elected in their stead.

Be so good to make my best thanks acceptable to Mrs May for the cheeses.

The barometer and other articles in your list are preparing. I have also commissioned some prints for Captain Craufurd's new room at the Millport, and a travelling bureau.

Lord Mount Stuart to Peter May

BUTE, letter book, agents in Scotland, vol. I, pp. 23–24

Hallingbury, 10 January 1787

Owing to my father having remained longer than usual in the country I had no opportunity of seeing him until Saturday last, when I did not fail laying before him the memorial of the Baron of Ambrisbeg stating at the same time the peculiar hardship under which he laboured. Lord Bute has in consequence authorised me to acquaint you that he means to give orders for the reimbursement of Mr Macleod and for payment of the money remaining due to the minister of Kingarth. I am not able to say whether this instance of generosity and goodwill towards an old zealous adherent of the family is to be followed by any further indulgence, but it is a relief for which Mr Maconochie ought to feel himself greatly indebted, considering that the claim of the minister appears upon the very face of his own memorial to have been legally established. It is impossible for me to drop this subject without expressing my indignation at the conduct of Mr Thorburn when he knew that contrary to my usual practice I had received the memorial and had likewise undertaken to recommend it with all my might; surely that motive, did not humanity supply a better, might have induced him to wait the event before he proceeded to the extremity you mention, and which no doubt has covered the poor man with severe affliction. Had a similar conduct been observed by a simple parishioner what anathemas should we not hear from the pulpit.

Lord Mount Stuart to Peter May

BUTE, letter book, agents in Scotland, vol. 1, pp. 24-27

Hallingbury, 14 March 1787

Your letter of the twenty-fourth of February with its several enclosures has been duly received.

In order to follow the various matters as they there present themselves, I shall begin with the Baron of Ambrisbeg, and observe to you that you have done perfectly right in opposing any deduction from the money you were authorised by Lord Bute to pay for that old fellow, as he undoubtedly meant to bestow it as a free and charitable gift. The idea of withholding a part could only arise in the narrow minded breast of an attorney: should the plan, however, be stamped with higher authority I hope to receive immediate notice as I shall in that case make up the deficit from my own pocket. I say nothing of the teinds; that matter may be left to the discussion of a future day, and in good truth, Scotch terms are so new to me I am unable to reason on the matter.

[John] Stewart of Ascog's conduct both with respect to Gordon and Craufurd is quite incomprehensible. I shall devise other means of getting round him, as I think the purchase of that property of infinite consequence. Would to God there were likewise a possibility of obtaining Kames.

The price of feus at the Largs surpasses all my ideas of the value of land; but as you very properly remark, no bargain of that sort can be entered into until I am able to visit the spot.

A conversation which I have lately holden with Lord Bute has set me much at ease with regard to purchasing in Bute, for on mentioning the acre of land now upon sale, he expressed a determination never to lay out any more money, but said at the same time he was desirous I should, and hoped I might one day or another be fortunate enough to acquire the whole island. This circumstance removes all difficulties, and I authorise you in consequence to close immediately with Mr Campbell, whose letter I return for that purpose. The mystery with Sharp, also, ought to be no longer adhered to than prudence may justify, and I wish him much to be tempted with a large premium. It is a method I have already adopted through the channel of a friend with respect to Mr Duncan of Worcester, and I feel a strong inclination to open myself to Robertson on the subject of the Castle Ditch. You know in desiring to get back that ground I have no other view than to restore a part of the ancient grandeur: it would be a garden, a place of resort for the inhabitants, who possess at present no such resource. My idea is that Robertson would be so much flattered with the confidence he would set heartily to work to serve me. What do you say? The matter is simply in embryo. Shall we hatch it?

Knowing full well that were I to advise you to throw cold water on the proposal of letting some land to Mr Gordon a mandate would issue from greater powers, I have only to request that the lease may be as short as possible.

The motives for observing secrecy in regard to your corresponding with me exist as forcibly as ever. I therefore once more recommend the most rigid silence. Let that, as well as the variety of topics on which I have so freely opened myself, be absolutely and wholly committed to the custody of your own mind alone. Secrecy is the nerve of all business, and you are little aware how far I push it.

The first journey I make to Newcastle, and by the by you had better direct your next letter there, a viewer is to be dispatched for Bute in search of coal.

Lord Mount Stuart to Peter May

BUTE, letter book, agents in Scotland, vol. 1, pp. 28–29

Balford, 14 April 1787

Mr Duncan of Worcester has agreed to sell his bit of land, but cannot fix a price; he comes soon to London in his way to Bute, when he has promised to call upon a friend of mine and converse over the business. He says it is not only a bit of land, but some buildings and young trees, of the value of which he pretends to be wholly unacquainted. I therefore beg you without delay to examine into the state of the matter and make your report specifying what you think a fair price, and to what it might amount at the rate, supposing of Mr Campbell's purchase. These parcels of land are undoubtedly dear, but they must be had. I shall expect your answer at Newcastle as soon as possible.

The borers will soon set forward; they go upon a different footing from the last. They are entirely to shift for themselves, which will give you less trouble. Mr Rayne will write to you more fully concerning them; they carry fifty fathom of additional rods.

It is my earnest desire to have the consideration of both church and manse postponed as long as possible. Mr Bannatyne has written to me concerning the teinds, and I have likewise begged him to drop that matter until Mr Stuart comes of age. With respect to the feus, I shall defer coming to any determination until I have it in my power to be present on the spot.

Lord Mount Stuart to Peter May

BUTE, letter book, agents in Scotland, vol. 1, pp. 29-30

Newcastle, 8 May 1787

Mr Rawlins, the viewer, set out yesterday from Morpeth with his son. He only proposes to remain four or five days in the island, a time, he pretends, fully sufficient for examining the lay of metals and marking the spots proper for boring, the management of which he leaves to an able workman who will keep up a constant correspondence. Should any certain prospect of coal appear he will in such case return. It gives me regret to see him go without me, and I have still some faint hopes of being able to follow him in the course of next week and to stay two or three days, which is all I shall be able to spare, but pray do not depend too much upon the intention. In the expectation, however, of such a thing happening I have laid hold of what you mention concerning a bailiff to write myself to Mr [George] Brown at Elgin desiring him, if possible, to send the man immediately to Bute: if I am there so much the better, but, if not, it will afford you an opportunity to judge of his abilities.

Memorandum Lord Mount Stuart to Peter May

BUTE muniments, letter book, agents in Scotland, vol. 1, pp. 30-31

20 May 1787

To pay the annual subscription to the Highland society.

To write to the secretary of ditto: enquiring into whose hands the donation of fifty pounds is to be paid and whether at once, or by instalment, and to pay it accordingly.

Calculation for the gravel paths.

All expenses incurred by Lord Mount Stuart's direction of every sort to be charged to his separate account, for which Mr May will draw upon him.

To pick up any bits of land without waiting to give advice.

Ground for inn at the Largs – rather take a lease than a feu.

Correcting damp on stair cases and passage.

Painting library – Mr Alexander May understands in what manner and how to fit up the closet opposite to it.

Mr Alexander May has directions to enquire the price of eighteen Bath stoves, and what the old grates will sell for. NB. The stoves must be square with straight bars. What likewise will be the price of pokers, tongs, shovels, and fenders plain.

Mr May has full instructions relative to the price of land as the Largs – a long lease preferable to a feu.

Baron Ambrisbeg – to pay no more for him.

Mr Gordon had better content himself with holding his five acres from year to year until Lord Mount Stuart at least has a little more to say in the management of the property.

Lord Mount Stuart to Peter May

BUTE, letter book, agents in Scotland, vol. I, pp. 32–36

Hallingbury, 22 August 1787

I am sorry to find from your letter of this month's date which I have just received with the several enclosures that you still complain of giddiness. I am afraid you do not pay that attention to your health your friends have a right to exact: and were I on the spot I should endeavour to prevent your rising so early as well as the constant exposure to damps, what I recommend to Mrs May to enforce.

After the decided opinion you offer relative to the gardener sent upon trial by Mr Brown, you may easily imagine that I shall not choose to employ him. I must therefore trouble you to signify as much; in the meantime you did perfectly right in paying his expenses, and I beg you to advance what further sum may be necessary. Inefficiency would be ruin to my Welsh affairs. I require experience, resolution, and address.

Mr Brisbane's conduct surprises me greatly. If I did not expect a ready compliance, I at least looked to receive in common civility an answer to my letter. I confess myself a good deal disappointed, being in hopes of having a small stable and coach houses ready to receive me by the end of the year, and before any arrangement can now be made another twelvemonth must necessarily elapse. As the laird of Brisbane inclines to bear so hard upon us why should not Mr Alexander May, without seeming to be keen, look out for some convenient extended feu amongst those already granted: the inhabitants of the Largs, knowing where I mean to encamp, will never suspect the drift.

The word drift brings to my recollection the search for coal, what appears to go on heavily enough. You must not compare it with the trial of last year, because my presence made then, and would even now occasion, a difference. If we succeed in our endeavours we shall soon forget all untoward circumstances. Should we fail, the comfort remains that no pains or expense have been omitted.

As the term of Michaelmas approaches I take for granted you are already employed in securing a majority at the approaching election, which I look upon to be decisive as to the power over the borough. Whatever party now prevails will clearly maintain the pre-eminence, and upon that issue depends my conduct respecting the Rothesay pier.[1]

When I was at Edinburgh I purposely omitted ordering any grates, not being supplied with the dimensions. The measures, according to a scale you talk of preparing, will answer best of all; and, as you observe, whatever may be wanted, you can commission yourself in November; before that time, however, I will write again, unless you are able to procure from Carron a drawing of the *plainest* stove they make with the *sides and bars straight* as was before understood and settled at Mount Stuart. The prices might likewise be ascertained both of them and the appurtenances such as fenders and so forth.

Whenever any Rothesay vessels go to London I wish to be constantly informed, that I may have it in my power to send several articles now preparing, without they exact an exorbitant freight. After all would it not be cheaper to send the Carron stoves from

[1] *See* p. 251, n. 1.

London? I looked into the upholsterers' shops at Glasgow, but the workmanship was so inferior to what my London eye is accustomed I could not prevail with myself to purchase.

The herring fishery is a two-edged sword to which I dare not speak.

Where a man is called upon to pay money his observing silence is not extraordinary: but when a voluntary tender is made, too much attention cannot be shown. It would appear that my intended Highland donation from the silence of the writer is not worth accepting. I shall consequently be the less out of pocket, for I no longer mean to give it. I desire you will explain to Mr Bannatyne, at whose request I originally subscribed, my reason for so acting.

Mr Bannatyne [of Kames] is certainly right in endeavouring to settle his marches, and you have acted with equal prudence in directing my father's tenants to keep none. As far as I am concerned I have not the smallest objection to the matter being settled by arbitration: I should indeed wish first to see the proposed line of division. In allowing Kames permission to use the old gallery in Rothesay church I suppose you will have it well understood that his family claim is in no shape assented to by such concession, but this between ourselves.

You say you have enclosed the field for Mr Gordon; what is become of my acre, who is to rent it?

Lord Mount Stuart to Peter May

BUTE, letter book, agents in Scotland, vol. I, pp. 36–37

Hallingbury, 23 August 1787

Recollecting that perhaps Mr Bannatyne may have already pledged my subscription to the Highland society, instead of withdrawing it as I before desired, I beg you will explain to him the uncivil treatment I have experienced in your person, and act afterwards according to his advice.

Lord Mount Stuart to Peter May

BUTE, letter book, agents in Scotland, vol. I, pp. 37–38

Hallingbury, 11 September 1787

Having maturely considered the paper enclosed in your letter of the second instant as well as what you say upon the subject, I am of opinion that it is more advisable to trust to the adherence of your own friends than, by coaxing the enemy, to lay myself under obligations which I shall be called upon hereafter to acquit, and which, in their imagination, I shall never be able to accomplish satisfactorily. The choice of candidates I leave entirely with you.

I return the letter from the secretary of the Highland Society, as you may perhaps choose to peruse it.

The commission concerning the Carron grates shall be deferred until I hear from you again. In regard to the communication by sea, there were six ships from Rothesay last year in the Port of London looking out for freight.

Supposing that you may have occasion to draw upon me for your various disbursements, I beg you will either do it previous to the tenth of October or not until the middle of December, as I shall probably be absent during the intermediate space, having a scheme of that sort in contemplation.

Lord Mount Stuart to Peter May

BUTE, letter book, agents in Scotland, vol. 1, pp. 38-39

Hallingbury, 9 October 1787

Your letter of the second instant finds me just setting out upon the expedition I before announced, from whence I shall hardly return before the first week of December. The information it conveys afforded me infinite pleasure, as I suppose we may now fairly reckon ourselves in possession of a decided majority; and I beg you will return my warmest thanks to those friends who assisted in bringing it forward. The anonymous paper is too paltry a contrivance to deserve the smallest notice.

I require no memorandum to put me in mind of Lieutenant Muir, who may be assured that I shall not neglect to avail myself of any opportunity that falls in my way of rendering him service.

Lord Mount Stuart to Peter May

BUTE, letter book, agents in Scotland, vol. 1, pp. 40-43

Hill Street, London, 31 March 1788

Your letter of the second of February reached in due course, and found me employed in an attendance at Westminster-hall, which, while it lasted, afforded no leisure or inclination to follow up private business.

You will doubtless feel surprised at perceiving your account sent back. But discovering that the expenses incurred by the borers form a part I return it for the purpose of revision as every out-going relative to coal falls to Mr Rayne's department at Newcastle, to whom you will be so good as to apply. I likewise beg to be informed when you transmit a new statement where in London I can pay the Balance, it being preferable to liquidate the whole immediately rather than to wait, as you proposed, until my next visit.

In regard to a forest-gardener I remain just where I was, and with the same desire of engaging an able person. At the same time without such a person proves uncommonly honest and efficient I prefer my present situation.[1]

The season of my journey to Bute is rendered very uncertain on account of the trial; if I cannot make it out in the summer I will contrive to see you at Michaelmas. As to borough politics, I wish you much to confer with Mr Kennedy, being in good truth afraid of my letters being opened, and he is perfectly apprised of all my schemes. You may set your mind at ease concerning the reform, which seems to meet the countenance of no party. It has been reported that Mr Gordon bought a piece of land over your head at the advanced price of thirty guineas. I trust no lease will ever be granted to that gentleman.

I send as you desire Mrs May's note of linen wanted at Mount Stuart.

The idea of a Nursery-ground must lay over until we meet.

Pray find out —— Stewart, late a principal farmer on Bannatyne's estate, and tell him that in consequence of his application to me in 1786 I have prevailed with the Duke of Argyll to set down his son's name, Francis Stewart, on the list of applications for kirks belonging to his Grace, and recommended him strongly to his protection.

Your Barometer, etc., and Captain Craufurd's articles have been laying packed up for months – how shall they be forwarded?

[1] This position was at Cardiff Castle in Wales; for an abortive appointment two years earlier *see* pp. 249–250.

Lord Mount Stuart to Peter May

BUTE, letter book, agents in Scotland, vol. 1, pp. 44-47

Hill Street, London, 22 December 1788

Your letters of the fifteenth, twenty-ninth of November, and fourteenth instant, have all been received. The first announces your draft for six hundred and forty-eight pounds, thirteen shillings, long since accepted, and the intention of the Rothesay inhabitants to petition against the Michaelmas election of magistrates. The second contains particulars on the same subject, what the last still further explains. Having, however, opened myself very fully to Mr Beveridge, and vested him with the necessary powers to watch over the business, there remains nothing to observe. To the question whether measures should not be taken to lessen the accommodation of those who have publicly avowed their opposition, I reply, most undoubtedly; but I desire to be previously supplied with a general list of all who possess lands under the predicament of what you term accommodation, specifying who, and who have not, joined the malcontents, and suggesting the best means of retaliation. At the same time I call for a list of the enemy; I should like equally to be informed how, in case of future necessity, even our friends stand in point of such accommodation. A similar paper will be attended with infinite and lasting utility.

Unable to flatter you with the most distant prospect of an alteration of measures in the district where you preside, I know not how to answer it to myself in longer opposing your plan of retiring, of which intention I have not omitted to apprise Lord Bute. Still, prior to the absolute decision, for the sake of the individual, for the better government of the property, I feel extremely anxious that Mr Alexander May should make a tour in this country. Preparatory to the step, I have already consulted Commissioner Reid, who recommends a common application to the board for an absence of six weeks on private business, and that on passing Edinburgh he will concert with your son in what manner to prolong it to the full extent of our wishes. Being on the spot, you may as well call on Mr Reid and talk over the project in person. This preliminary settled, consult with your son touching the season as well as the mode; possibly the career may be profitably opened by remaining some time with Rayne at Newcastle. From thence he may traverse Norfolk, come to me in Essex, proceed to Wales, or to wherever the learned direct, for, professing entire ignorance, I am unable myself to offer an opinion. After all, the whole is merely thrown out by way of advice; act therefore I entreat as you please.

Lord Mount Stuart to Alexander May

BUTE, letter book, agents in Scotland, vol. 1, p. 47

Hill Street, London, 6 May 1789

A letter from Mr Peter May[1] in January last appeared to my conception so very averse to the scheme of your coming to England that I gave up all thoughts of the matter. I therefore received with surprise the account of your arrival at Newcastle. Had previous notice been sent me I should have prepared Rayne for your reception; however, wishing you well, I am very well pleased you are there, and desire you will follow your own inclinations in the prosecution of your journey throughout the kingdom, and according to my original intention I will reimburse the expenses.

Peter May to Isaac Grant, Brown's Square, Edinburgh

SRO. GD248/684/6

15 St Andrews Square, Edinburgh.[2] 12 November 1793

I apply to you as my friend, and as doer for Sir James Grant, requesting your advice relative the interest of money I have in Sir James's hands. I need not inform you that money is now in request at 5 per cent and that I have been advised to demand the legal interest. I am, however, from a personal regard to Sir James, very desirous to accommodate him. In this view I propose that the interest of the £1,000 due at this term (and for which a receipt is enclosed) shall only be at 4½ per cent conform to his bond. But that afterwards, I am to charge the interest at 5 per cent and to begin with the bond for a £1,000 due at Whitsunday next. Both these bonds only bear interest at 4½ per cent, but I suppose that can easily

[1] This is the last notice of a communication between Peter May and the family of Bute.

[2] The *Edinburgh Directories* show that Peter May lived at No. 15 St Andrew's Square from July 1793 to July 1794, from then to July 1795 at No. 4 St James's Square, S. side. From July 1795 to July 1796 Mrs May is shown to be living at No. 55 Princes Street.

be corrected without any new security. I will be exceedingly pleased if this proposition meet with Sir James Grant's and your approbation.

State of the settlement made by Mr May NLS. MS. 3258 f. 67a

18 December 1793

By settlement upon Mrs May dated the 3rd February 1790 he leaves her an annuity, payable twice in the year, of £120 yearly. £100 payable at his death, to be disposed of by her, by writing under her hand. One half the household furniture, silver plate, etc., or in her option £100 Sterling in lieu thereof.

The settlement is dated the 18th of December 1793, and registered 30th June 1795, of which the tenor follows:

I Peter May, late factor to the late Earl of Bute, being resolved to make the following settlement of my estate real and personal do hereby give, grant, and dispone to and in favours of John Duncan of Mosstown, Esq., my uncle-in-law, Mr James Beveridge, my friend, Mr William Beveridge, my nephew-in-law, James May, farmer at Idoch, my brother germane, George Brown, factor to the Earl of Findlater, at Elgin, my nephew, Alexander May, my near and dear relation, now factor to the now Earl of Bute, and such of them that shall survive me, and accept, as Trustees, for the uses and purposes after mentioned. Here is contained the disposition in favour of the said Trustees who are directed to settle in secure hands as much of the funds as will answer his wife's annuity and take security therefore in their own names. He then directs them to pay the following legacies, viz.

To the foresaid Alex. May and to his heirs the sum of £1,500 – £1,000 whereof I am bound to pay him by contract of marriage, which obligation is hereby declared to be discharged and satisfied by the sum now left him deducting any payments made since the date of the contract.

To the children of Alex. May, £500.

To Barbara May, my niece, daughter to the foresaid James May, and spouse to the said Wm. Beveridge, who has been brought up in my family, and who I consider as an adopted child £1,000 Sterling, £800 whereof I am bound to pay to her by contract of marriage, deducting therefrom any sums paid on that may be paid since that date.

To the said James May, my brother, and to his wife and longest liver of them in life rent and children in fee mentioning the sums to his son and daughters, Barbara being already provided for, £400.

To the children of the deceased Margaret May, my oldest sister and their heirs equally divided among them, £100.

To the children of the deceased Barbara May, my second sister, and their heirs £500 whereof to George Brown, her oldest son now alive £300, declaring that the sum of £200 already advanced him by me (and for which I have his bond) to be part thereof. Should, however, the whole or any part thereof be paid to me during my life time, then I appoint an equivalent sum to be paid him so as to make up £300.

To the said Barbara May's three daughters £100, whereof to Isobel £60 and Elizabeth and Margaret £20 each, and to John Brown, son to the said Barbara May, now Captain Lieutenant in the Royal Engineers £100. I have already advanced him £150 to purchase a lieutenancy and for which I have his bond, the contents whereof I hereby discharge, as freely and fully as if the same had been paid.

In addition to the said George Brown, I hereby leave to his youngest son Peter Brown, as being my name son £100.

To Elizabeth May, my third sister, in life rent and her children and their assignees in fee equally divided £100.

Sums payable at Mr May's death when his funds answer, £4,200.

He hereby declares that in case my funds, after paying my just debts and appropriating what will be necessary to answer the foresaid annuity and other sums to my wife, shall at my death issued the amount of the foresaid respective sums, that then the surpluses shall be divided betwixt the said Alexander May and the said Barbara May, my niece and their heirs – three-fourth parts to the said Alexander May and one-fourth part to the said Barbara May – and on the other hand if my funds shall fall short, then the shortcomings is to fall on the said James May and his children, on the children of the said Margaret May, on the children of the said Barbara May, and on the said Elizabeth May and her children, according to the sums left to them respectively, and that no part thereof shall fall upon the sums appointed to be paid to the said Alexander May and his children, nor upon Barbara May, spouse to the said William Beveridge.

And in regard to the capital, which is to be set apart by the Trustees for answering my wife's annuity, the said Trustees shall after death pay the same to the persons following, viz.

To the said Alex. May, his or their assignees, the sum of £500.

To the said Barbara May, my niece and heirs of her body over and above the other provisions I have made for her, £200.

To the said James May, and his wife and longest liver of them in life rent, his children in fee mentioning them, £400.

To the children of the deceased Margaret May equally £100.

To the children of the deceased Barbara May the sum of £600, whereof £400 to be paid her oldest son, George Brown, £100 to her youngest son Captain John Brown, £60 to the said Isobel Brown, and £40 to Elizabeth and Margaret equally.

To the said Elizabeth May in life rent and her children in fee £100.

To the foresaid John Duncan of Mosstown and his heirs, as a small mark of my regard £100.

To the Rev. Mr Wm. Mitchell of the Scots Church at Leyden, and his heirs, £100.

To Archibald Mitchell, Esq., late Major in the East India Company's service, and his heirs, £100.

To the widow of the deceased Thomas Mitchell, late shipmaster in London, and her heirs, £40.

The above three persons late named were brothers german to my wife, on whose account, as well as my own regard for them, this small mark of attention is paid.

To the foresaid James Beveridge and his heirs, in remembrance of my esteem for him, £60.

Sums payable upon Mrs May's death £2,300	£2,300
Ditto, at Mrs May's death when collected	£4,200
To which add the £100 at Mrs May's disposal	£100
	£6,600

Abstract of the funds belonging to Peter May by bonds, bills, or otherwise, made out with his own hand this 8th day of January 1794

NLS. MS. 3258, f. 67b

Dec. 18 1792. Bond of this date the Duke of Gordon for £1,000, with interest at 4½ per cent.	£1,000
July 5 1780. Bond of this date the Earl of Findlater and Seafield £1,300, at 4½ per cent.	£1,300
Jan. 31 1784. Another bond of this date by the said noble Earl for £800, with interest at 4½ per cent.	£800
Dec. 18 1788. A third bond of this date by the said noble Earl for £1,000 at 4½ per cent.	£1,000
Dec. 10 1784. Bond of this date Sir James Grant of Grant for £1,000, interest at 4½ per cent.	£1,000
May 14 1791. Another bond of this date due by Sir James.	£1,000
Bank of Aberdeen for one share estimated at	£400
May 16 1792. Bond William MacLeod Bannatyne of Kames, advocate, £500 interest thereof at 4½ per cent.	£500
Oct. 1 1791. Bond George Brown, factor to the Earl of Findlater, at Linkwood, £200, interest at 4½ per cent.	£200
June 7 1788. Bond John Johnston, shipmaster, heritable on his subjects in the burgh of Rothesay for £170 is yet due balance £58 10s. with interest of 5 per cent with a year's interest £2 18s. 6d.	£61 8s. 6d.

Appendices

1. CARTO-BIBLIOGRAPHY

Chronological list of maps and plans drawn by Peter May or prepared under his direction. The place-names are rendered as the original.

1751 Plan of the lands of Old Ferryhill divided into five lots (wanting).

1753 A survey of Gordonsburgh (plan wanting; list of inhabitants, RHP35982).

1754 (Sept.) Plan of part of the lands of Badentoul belonging to Col. James Abercromby of Glassaugh (RHP11773).

1755 (May) Plan of all and whole the towns, lands and barony of Elsick (wanting).

1755 (Aug.) Plan of part of the lands of Lovat lying in the parish of Kirkhill (wanting).

1755 (Aug.) Plan of the parish of Kiltarlity (wanting).

1756 (May) Plan of the Barony of Castle Leod (wanting). [A copy was made of this plan by John Ainslie, land surveyor in Edinburgh, in 1796 (Cromarty MSS).]

1756 (May) Plan of the Barony of New Tarbet (wanting).

1756 (June) A plan of the coast and other remarkable places between the rivers Dee and Don (RHP6308/2 – photocopy).

1756 (Aug.) A survey and design for a village at Ullapool (RHP 3400).

[1756] A survey of Little Gruinard (RHP3478).

[1756] A survey of Achtaskayle (RHP3401).

[1756] A plan of Island Martin (RHP3399 – a copy by another hand).

1756 Plan of the glebe of Kirkhill (wanting).

1756 A survey of the Creaves (SRO. E787/18/2).

1756 Survey of the Hill of Weaves and other barren ground contiguous, being part of the Barony of Castle Leod, drawn by

James Turnbull, 1762, from a survey by Peter May, 1756 (Cromarty MSS.).

1757 Plan of the lands in Glenstrathferrar (wanting).

1757 Plan of the Barony of Stratherrick (wanting).

1757 Plan of the parish of Kilmorack (wanting).

1757 Plan of the Barony of Lovat (wanting).

1757 A plan of that part of the Annexed Estate lying in the parish of Kilmorack and county of Inverness (RHP6586 – a later lithographed copy).

1757 Plan of the farms of Dalcattick, Easter and Wester Portclair (wanting).

[1757] Plan of the grounds lying in the south side of the Burn of Cappiloch in dispute between Sir Ludovick Grant of Grant and the Commissioners of the Fortified Estates (wanting).

1757 Plans of the Barony of Coigach (SRO. E746/189 – a volume of 25 plans copied by William Morrison in 1775).

1758 Plan of the Barony of Coigach (Cromarty MSS.).

1758 (May) A survey of the River Findhorn with the Fishing Places, etc. Engraved by Thomas Phinn (Session Paper in Signet Library, 145:3).

1760 (Oct.) A plan of the River Spey from low water mark to Ballhagarty's Gavin with the coast at high and low water surveyed October 1760 (wanting). [Reduced copies engraved by Thomas Phinn, Edinburgh, 1761 (RHP287, 3088)].

1761 Plan of the Barony of Findlater (RHP11840; a copy was made by Robert Johnston in 1795, RHP12887).

1761 Plan of the farms of Craigherbs and Buchraigy (RHP11843).

1761 A plan of the lands and Barony of Newtown Garrioch belonging heritably to the Honble. Sir Alexander Gordon of Lesmoir lying in the parish of Drumblet and Sheriffdom of Aberdeen (RHP2222, book of reference dated April 1762, CR8/168).

1762 (June) Plan of proposed outlet to be made from the Loch of Garth (wanting).

1762 Plan of lands and Barony of Muchalls (Silver of Netherley papers per Messrs Davidson and Garden, Aberdeen, NRA (Scot.) 0051).

1762 Plan of the estate of Muirtown (wanting).

1762 Plan of the lands of Cullen, as divided into regular fields or lots, together with the town and yards, etc., and farms of Seafield, Patten-Bringan and Tochienal (wanting; copy made by Robert Johnston in 1797 – RHP12874).

1763 Plan of the Hill of Nigg as divided 1763. Engraved by A. Bell (RHP680).

[*c.* 1763] Plan of the towns and lands of Sliach (wanting).

1764 (Jan.) Plan of the lands of Murtle (wanting).

1764 (June) A plan of the water-course leading to the miln of west Grange with the Sogers-Burn and such other contiguous fields and places as were thought necessary to be shewn in the survey (RHP32).

1764 (June) Plan of the commonty of the Muir of Farrochie (wanting).

1764 Plan of town and lands of Fordyce, as divided into regular lots, and of the farms of Bogtown (RHP11841).

1764 Plan of the town and lands about Keith according as they are now divided into regular lots (RHP11838).

1764 Plan of the lands of Myreside and Linksfield (RHP11823).

1764 Plan of the farm, gardens, policies and town of Cullen as they lie at present with the natural situation and lying of the ground (RHP12875).

1765 (Jan.) Plan of the Barony of Bewlie on annexed estate of Lovate (wanting).

1765 (Sept.) A plan of the River Findhorn from Sluy-pool, downward to the river's mouth, at low water, together with the coast and lands adjacent (RHP10; 19th-century copy, RHP 14655).

1765 (Autumn) plan of Moy and Westfield (wanting).

1766 (Aug.) A plan of the Moss adjoining to the Lands of Elrick, Redfoord and Culvie (wanting).

1766 (Sept.) A survey of lands of Broadland (wanting).

1766 (Sept.) A rude draught of the contraverted moss marches between Pitfour and the heritors of Crimond (wanting).

1766 (Sept.) Plan of Craigellie belonging to Mr James Shand of Craigellie (wanting).

1766 (Sept.) Plan of Grandhome (wanting).

1766 (Sept.) Plan of Cairnbulg (wanting).

1766 Plan of Strathdon (wanting).

1766 Plan of lands of Boyndie and Whitehills and farms of Craigherbs, Wairy-Lipp, Blackpotts and Over Dallachy (RHP 11842).

1766 Plan of Bruntown, Farskine, Findochty and Woodside (RHP 11839).

1766 A plan of the lands and Barony of Carveichen belonging heritably to George Hay, Esq., of Mountblairy made out from an accurate survey and mensuration taken Anno 1766 (RHP2235).

1766 Plan of that part of Greenhill of Deskford intended for improvements (RHP11844).

1766 Plan of the lands of Glencarve with the Hills and Pasture called the Bunzeach (Candacraig Mss; engraved copies ordered March 1767, wanting).

1767 (July) Plan for a new channel to the Water of Shewglie in Urquhart (wanting).

1767 Plan of the controverted marches of Glaschyle betwixt the lairds of Grant and Altyre (RHP9019).

1767 Plan of the east side of the Knock Hill and the moor ground adjoining thereto (RHP11849).

[*c.* 1767] Plan of the estate of Rosehaugh, belonging to James Stuart Mackenzie (wanting).

1768 (Apr.) Plan of Belmont Castle estates (wanting).

1768 (July) A sketch of Hugh Tod's farm (wanting).

1768 (July) A sketch of the march betwixt Birny and Coxton (wanting).

1768 (July) Rude draught with the measures of Bishopmiln (wanting).

1768 (Aug.) Sketch of the hills and moors lying on the East side of the Glen of Rothes and betwixt that and the Barony of Coxton with the interjected mosses laid down (wanting).

1768 (Sept.) Eye draught of the lands belonging to Mr Grant lying in the parishes of Forgue and Inverkeithny (wanting).

1768 Plan of the lands of Linkwood (RHP11821).

1769 (June) Plan of the lands of Blairton (wanting).

1769 (Dec.) Sketch of the moor of Linkwood (wanting).

1770 Plan of the lands of Cairntown, Broadley and Broadley Park (RHP8847).

1771 Plan of Coulnakyle, Rothiemoon, Culvoulen and Balnagowhan, showing proposed alteration to the course of the River Nethy (RHP8893).

n.d. A plan for the Morass [of Whitehouse Moss] (RHP118541).

n.d. A plan of the Hills of Boyndie and Braeface of Colleonard (RHP11850).

n.d. A general plan of the parks and gardens at Fintray House, the seat of the Hon. Sir Arthur Forbes of Craigievar (RHP 10788).

2. BIOGRAPHICAL INDEX

Adam, John (1721-92), eldest son of William Adam, architect, and brother of the famous Robert. John inherited his family's estate of Blair Adam in Kinross-shire in 1748 and developed a large Scottish practice with especially profitable works at Fort George and elsewhere in the Highlands. Financial speculation forced him to mortgage the Blair Adam estate in 1772 to avoid bankruptcy. His own business activities included the sale of stone from the Aberdeen quarries and a partnership in the Carron Iron Works. He was the architect who converted Lord Lovat's house in the High Street, Edinburgh, into an office for the Commissioners of the Annexed Estates (SRO. E727/3, E727/8/1).

Anderson, Robert, of Linkwood (?-1766), writer, commissary-clerk and sheriff-substitute of Moray, factor to James Brodie of Brodie. His lands of Linkwood were sold to the Earl of Findlater, Dec. 1767, and occupied by Peter May from 1768.

Anderson, William (?-1780), land surveyor who worked for the Duke of Gordon from 1749 to 1770; thenceforth he was on a pension from the Duke until his death in January 1780. *See* for details of life and portrait, I. H. Adams, *Descriptive List of Plans in the Scottish Record Office*, H.M.S.O., Edinburgh, vol. 2, pp. vii-viii.

Argyll, 3rd Duke of, *see* Campbell, Archibald.

Argyll, 5th Duke of, *see* Campbell, John.

Barclay, Robert, of Ury (1730-97). In 1760 he succeeded to the Ury estate of over 3,000 acres, all unimproved. He began his improvements by taking under his own management all the farms in the vicinity of the mansion house as their leases expired. Barclay had acquired his ideas on agriculture in Norfolk from where he brought English labourers to assist in carrying out his schemes and teaching his own tenants. *See* J. E. Handley, *Scottish Farming in the Eighteenth Century*, London, 1953, pp. 164-5.

Beveridge, James, writer in Edinburgh, close friend of Peter May.

Beveridge, William, Writer to the Signet, in Edinburgh, son of the above James, married to Barbara May, Peter May's niece and adopted daughter.

Bland, Humphrey (?1686-1763), governor of Fort William, 1743-52. Held major-general's command under the Duke of Cumberland in the Culloden campaign. On 17 November 1753 he was appointed commander-in-chief of forces in Scotland and, as such, was a commissioner of Annexed Estates.

Brown, George, land surveyor and factor, *see* Introduction, pp. xxxiii-xxxvi.

Brown, Peter, son of George Brown, *see* Introduction, p. xxxvi.

Burges, James, servant of Peter May, later became a land surveyor making estate plans in Banffshire. Emigrated to America in 1773.

Bute, John 3rd Earl of, *see* Stuart, John.

Bute, John 4th Earl and 1st Marquis of, *see* Stuart, John.

Campbell, Archibald, 3rd Duke of Argyll (1682-1761), one of the great eighteenth-century agricultural improvers when Inveraray became the focus of improvements of unprecedented splendour and expense. The new town of Inveraray was begun, the new castle built, and the surrounding policies developed as gardens, farms and woodlands. These works in some years absorbed almost the whole of the property rents of the Argyll lands. Such immense outlays were made possible by the Duke's considerable revenues from his lands, offices and prerogatives. These he augmented by expanding the domain lands in the neighbourhood of Inveraray and Rosneath, for the market, by selling farm produce and growing timber for sale to the new iron foundry on Lochfyneside.

Campbell, John, 5th Duke of Argyll (1723-1806). With the loss of political power with the accession of George III and the rise of Lord Bute, he concentrated on the management of his estates from his succession to the title in 1770. He was one of the most able and energetic landlords in his day, changing the face of the land, moving populations, setting up planned villages, founding industries, and, indeed, controlling every detail in his vast estates. *See* Eric Cregeen, *Argyll Estate Instructions*, Scottish History Society, Edinburgh, 1964.

Deskford, Lord, son of 5th Earl of Findlater, *see* Ogilvy, James.

Drummond, George, (1687-1766), a strong Unionist, and six times lord provost of Edinburgh. A commissioner for improving fisheries and manufactures in Scotland in 1727, reformed the university of Edinburgh, proposed the building of New Town of Edinburgh, commissioner of the Annexed Estates in 1755, and a manager of the Edinburgh Society for the Encouragement of the Arts, Sciences, Manufactures and Agriculture. *See* T. C. Smout, *Provost Drummond*, University of Edinburgh, Extra-Mural Studies, 1978.

Duff, Alexander, of Hatton (1718-64), husband of Lady Anne Duff, dau. of William, 1st Earl Fife, and father of Jean, wife of James Grant of Grant.

Duff, George (?-1818), younger son of William, 1st Earl Fife.

Duff, James, 2nd Earl Fife (1729-1809), M.P. for the county of Banff for several years after 1754, and for the county of Elgin, 1784. By numerous purchases he nearly doubled the possessions of his family. *See* A. and H. Tayler (eds.) *Lord Fife and his factor. Being the correspondence of James, second Lord Fife, 1729-1809*, 1925.

Duff, William, 1st Earl Fife (1697-1763), purchased considerable estates in the counties of Aberdeen, Banff and Moray, and proved a careful manager of them. About 1724 he built the new castle or house of Balvenie. In 1740-45 he erected Duff House at a rumoured cost of £70,000. He married into both the Findlater and Seafield, and Grant of Grant families, first with Lady James Ogilvie, dau. of James, 4th Earl of Findlater, and secondly, Jean, dau. of Sir James Grant of Grant.

Dundas, Robert, of Arniston (1713-1787), appointed Solicitor General 1742, Lord Advocate 1754 and Lord President of the Court of

Session 1760. His second marriage was to Jean, daughter of William Grant, Lord Prestongrange.

Elliot, Sir Gilbert, of Minto (1693-1766), M.P. for Roxburgh, 1722-1726, a Lord of Session as Lord Minto, 1726, a Lord of Justiciary, 1733, and Lord-Justice-Clerk, 1763. A commissioner of Annexed Estates.

Fife, Earl, *see* Duff.
Findlater, Earl of, *see* Ogilvy, James.
Fletcher, Andrew, of Saltoun (1691-1766), advocate, made Cashier of Excise, 1718, a Lord of Session as Lord Milton, 1724, and a Lord of Justiciary, 1726. He was appointed Lord-Justice-Clerk of Scotland, 1735, and Keeper of the Signet, 1748.
Forbes, Captain John, of New (?-1775), factor on Forfeited, later Annexed Estates of Cromarty and Lovat (the latter was restored in 1774). Arbiter with Captain James of Carron as to marches between Major William Grant of Ballindalloch and James Grant of Grant in 1767. Purchaser at public roup, 17 January 1770, of part of the estate of James, Lord Forbes, with a decreet-arbitral following, 10 August 1770, by Alexander Garden of Troup and Robert Barclay of Ury as to division of purchase between Forbes of New, Lord Forbes and Jonathan Forbes of Brux (RS3/281, fo. 177).

Garden, Alexander, of Troup (?-1785), M.P. for Banff. Married Jean, sister of Sir Archibald Grant of Monymusk.
Gordon, Alexander 4th Duke of (1743-1827), succeeded his father in 1752. His mother and step-father in his name raised the 89th Regiment of Foot for Government service in 1759, disbanded in 1763. The Duke then travelled abroad for some time. His wife was the daring Duchess of so many anecdotes. To her we probably owe the new town of Fochabers.
Gordon, Cosmo, of Cluny, advocate, son of John Gordon, cashier to Duke of Gordon. Peter May acted as his factor on the estate of Buckie (George Brown followed in the same position). Cosmo Gordon and Charles Gordon, his brother, were legal advisers to the Duke of Gordon.
Grant, Sir Alexander, of Dalvey (?-1772). His family had been Jacobite and the baronetcy title had been dropped shortly after

creation, being brought out of disuse when Sir Alexander made a fortune in government contracting and West Indies trade. M.P. for the Inverness burghs 1761 to 1768, he purchased in his father's lifetime Grangehill, Morayshire, which he called Dalvey.

Grant, Sir Archibald, 2nd Bart., of Monymusk (1696-1778), advocate in 1714, who represented the county of Aberdeen in parliament from 1722 to 1732 when he was expelled for fraud. He was one of Scotland's foremost agricultural improvers pioneering many new ideas from as early as 1719. His estate in Aberdeenshire was a model of its kind. *See* H. Hamilton, *Selections from the Monymusk papers*, Scottish History Society, Edinburgh, 1945.

Grant, Sir James, of Grant (1738-1811), nephew of James Ogilvy, 6th Earl of Findlater and 3rd Earl of Seafield, M.P. for Elgin and Forres from 1761 to 1768, and on the death of his father in 1773, succeeded to the baronetcy and the chieftainship of the clan Grant. He married Jean, dau. of Alexander Duff of Hatton. His father, Sir Ludovic, made over the family estates to him in 1763, and thereafter James devoted himself to improving his estates, especially building the new town of Grantown-on-Spey. His costly projects greatly increased the family debts, which after his father's death were estimated at £130,000. Later, Peter May was to lend Sir James £2,000. To extricate himself 'from a most perilous situation' Sir James was obliged to sell large parts of his estates.

Grant, James (1733-1821), born in Cromdale, he became schoolmaster of Duthil in 1761 and later moved to Cromdale. He was used by William Lorimer (q.v.) in compiling the rental of Strathspey. He entered service as clerk with Grant of Grant in 1765. He became factor of the Strathspey estate in 1790 and retired from that post on a pension in 1807. In his later years he was known as James Grant of Heathfield from a farm near Grantown.

Grant, James, of Shewglie (1711-91), chamberlain to James Grant of Grant on Urquhart. He had been imprisoned as a suspected Jacobite in 1746.

Grant, Sir Ludovic, of Grant (1707-73), married Margaret, dau. of James Ogilvy, Earl of Findlater and Seafield; made over his estates to his son James in 1763.

Grant, William (?1701-64), Lord Prestongrange, senator of College of Justice, brother of the famous improver Sir Archibald Grant of

Monymusk (q.v.). In 1738 he was appointed commissioner for improving the fisheries and manufactures of Scotland. He introduced the bill for Annexing the Forfeited Estates and became a commissioner on that body in 1755. He was M.P. for Elgin burghs from 1747 to 1754 on his appointment to the bench.

Grant, William, manufacturer in Elgin, factor to Earl of Findlater at Elgin having succeeded his father Baillie Robert Grant in that post for Crop 1767. Peter May took over in January 1768.

Hay, Thomas, 9th Earl of Kinnoull (1710-87) succeeded to earldom in 1758 and was Lord Deskford's cousin. An enthusiastic agricultural improver who had wide experience outside Scotland; M.P. (1741-58) and recorder for Cambridge; on an embassy to Lisbon, 1759-60, during which time 5th Earl of Findlater and Lord Deskford named his Commissioners. When Peter May was factor to 7th Earl of Findlater, the Earl of Kinnoull audited his accounts.

Home, Henry (1696-1782), Lord Kames, lawyer and judge who was passionately interested in agricultural improvement. In 1755 he became a member of the Board of Trustees for the Encouragement of Fisheries, Arts and Manufacturers of Scotland, and was shortly afterwards chosen as one of the Commissioners of the Annexed Estates. During his vacations Kames improved his own estates. As an amateur agriculturalist he acquired a high reputation with his book *The Gentleman Farmer*, which ran to six editions by 1815. His greatest success was the reclamation of part of the moss of Kincardine which formed part of the Blair Drummond estate. *See* Ian S. Ross, *Lord Kames and the Scotland of his day*, Clarendon Press, Oxford, 1972.

Home, John, land surveyor, *see* Introduction, pp. xxxvii-xxxix.

Hope, John, 2nd Earl of Hopetoun (1704-81), a notable improver, living most of his life quietly on his West Lothian estate. A member of the Annexed Estates Commission in 1755. He married Anne Ogilvy, second dau. of James, Earl of Findlater and Seafield (q.v.).

Johnston, Robert, land surveyor, trained by Peter May and remained with George Brown at Linkwood. Became estate clerk to the Earl of Findlater in 1783 and later his secretary in Germany. A militia officer. The last reference to him is dated 1802.

Kames, Lord, *see* Home, Henry.
Kinnoull, 9th Earl of, *see* Hay, Thomas.

Logie, Andrew (?-1768), baillie in Aberdeen. Made a series of maps and plans of Aberdeen 1742-51 and it is possible that he employed Peter May. Later he became surveyor of customs at Montrose where he died on 19 April 1768 (SRO. Comm. Brechin testaments, vol. ii, CC3/3/11, f. 184).

Logie, John (1744-*c.* 1798), clerk to James Ross, secretary to the Duke of Gordon. In 1782 he became factor on Duffus, Dipple and the barony of Garmouth.

Lorimer, William (1717-65), adviser to James Grant of Grant. Son of William Lorimer in Dyttach, sometime Chamberlain to the Earl of Findlater. He became a bursar at Marischal College, Aberdeen, of which he was later a benefactor. On 12 November 1737 he was appointed by the Earl of Findlater to be schoolmaster at Deskford and a year later was promoted to Fordyce school. This he held until November 1747 when he became tutor to James Grant, younger of Grant. In 1758 Lorimer was in Albany, New York, probably as secretary to General James Abercromby. In 1760 Sir Ludovic Grant allowed him an annuity of £100 per annum, which he continued till his early death in January 1765 on his way by sea to Italy. Lorimer played an outstanding role formulating the initial plans for agricultural improvement on the Grant of Grant estates and much which has been attributed to the master was in fact the brain-child of the servant. James Grant was perfectly aware of his debt to an old friend for he wrote on 13 January 1769, 'And had he lived I should have remitted whatever his exigencies might have required during his stay in Italy, as I never could have done too much for that excellent man to whom I lay under the greatest obligations' (Seafield muniments SRO. GD248/177/1/93). *See* George A. Dixon, William Lorimer on forestry in the Central Highlands in the early 1760s, *Scottish Forestry*, vol. 29 No. 3, pp. 191-210; and Ian D. Grant, Landlords and land management in North-Eastern Scotland 1750-1850, unpubl. PH.D., University of Edinburgh, 1978.

Mackenzie, James Stuart (?-1800), second son of James, 2nd Earl of

Bute, who succeeded to the estates of Rosehaugh, Ross and Cromarty, according to the provisions of the will of his great-grandfather, Sir George Mackenzie, and assumed his surname and arms. He married Elizabeth, dau. of the Duke of Argyll. He represented several Scottish shires in Parliament from 1742 to 1784, and was constituted Keeper of the Privy Seal of Scotland in 1763 (often in this volume he is called Lord Privy Seal). He was deeply involved in agricultural improvement from 1755 on his extensive estates in Perthshire, Angus and Ross and Cromarty. His brother, the 3rd Earl of Bute (q.v.), effectively left the management of his Scottish estates in Mackenzie's hands until about 1784: thereafter Lord Mount Stuart played an increasing role. Mackenzie employed Peter May to do the initial surveys on his estates and was instrumental in recruiting him to serve his brother's interests on the island of Bute. *See* J. W. Barty, *Ancient deeds and other writs in the Mackenzie-Whorncliffe Charter-chest*, Edinburgh, 1906, pp. 95-99.

Maule, John, advocate, half-brother of William Maule who purchased the bulk of the forfeited family estates of Panmure from the York Building Company in 1764. John Maule, who was known as Baron Maule through his office as Baron of Exchequer, was a commissioner of the Annexed Estates.

Menzies, Archibald, of Culdares, Inspector-General for the Commissioners of Annexed Estates, later became a commissioner himself. Appointed Commissioner of Customs. He was appointed a commissioner by the Earl of Bute for management of his affairs in Scotland. He possessed an estate comprising nearly half the parish of Fortingall, Perthshire.

Milne, Alexander, became factor to the Duke of Gordon on lordships of Glenlivet and Strathavon and Barony of Kincardine in 1754, with whom he remained until 1783. At the same time he became factor to the Earl of Findlater on the Keith estate in 1766 in which position he continued until 1787 when he was succeeded by John Ross, possibly a nephew of Professor John Ross (q.v.).

Milne, Thomas, land surveyor, *see* Introduction, pp. xxviii-xxx.

Mitchell, Sir Andrew, of Thainston (?-1771), M.P. for Aberdeenshire 1747-54, Elgin burghs 1754-71.

Mitchell, Euphemia (1734-?), Peter May's wife. They were married on 18 June 1761 in Aberdeen. For family tree *see* p. xlii.

Mitchell, James (1702-73), minister in Old Machar parish, Aberdeen. Peter May's father-in-law.

Morison, James (?-1794), principal clerk to Annexed Estates Commission. Estate clerk to Earl of Findlater, he was appointed as assistant clerk to the Annexed Estates Commissioners on Findlater's 'ample recommendation'. From 1768 he acted as principal clerk and on Robert Elliot's death in 1770 took over the position. Morrison above all others appears to have been the effective executive force behind the Commissioners and this was recognised by increases in salary, which ultimately reached £200 per annum.

Morison, William (?-*c.* 1808), land surveyor who surveyed the Annexed Estates of Barrisdale in Knoydart in 1771 and in 1772 the estate of Lochiel, followed by Callart and Ardsheal. For the next few years he remained virtually a full-time employee of the Commissioners (his brother James (q.v.) was their principal clerk), but most of his work was latterly taken up in copying earlier surveys and clerical duties. He was still alive in 1808 when enquiries were being made by the Commissioners of Highland Roads and Bridges as to the conditions in the Highlands, but he was too ill and senile to explain the nature of his maps of Barrisdale made almost forty years earlier.

Mount Stuart, Lord, eldest son of the 3rd Earl of Bute, *see* Stuart, John.

Ogilvy, James, 6th Earl of Findlater and 3rd Earl of Seafield (?1714-1770), was known as Lord Deskford before succeeding his father in 1764. Patron of Peter May and one of the foremost agricultural improvers of the age. A Trustee for the Improvement of Fisheries and Manufactures, and a Commissioner of the Annexed Estates, he played a vital role in these bodies, initiating economic change. He was an enthusiastic agriculturalist and did much to introduce new methods in Banffshire: he introduced turnip husbandry and granted long leases to his tenants on condition that within a certain period they should enclose their lands and adopt improved methods of cropping. He married in 1749, Mary, dau. of 1st Duke of Atholl.

Ogilvy, James, 7th Earl of Findlater and 4th Earl of Seafield (1750-1811), was very much an absentee landlord, spending a lot of time in Brussels where in 1779 he married Christina Teresa, dau. of Joseph, Count Murray of Melgum. They had no issue.

Oliphant, Robert, of Rossie, commissioner appointed by the Earl of Bute for the management of his affairs in Scotland. He possessed the estate of Culteuchar, Forgandenny parish in Perthshire. He was deputy Post-master General of Scotland from 1764 to 1795 and a Commissioner of Annexed Estates. A close friend of Peter May. *See* A. R. B. Haldane, *Three centuries of Scottish Posts*, Edinburgh University Press, 1971.

Phinn, Thomas, a map engraver who carried on his business from 1752 to 1766, first in Parliament Square and then the east wing of the New Exchange, Edinburgh, where he sold maps, prints, water colours and artists' materials.

Prestongrange, Lord, *see* Grant, William.

Robertson, John (1731-99), merchant in Rothesay. A prominent member of Rothesay burgh council whose daughter Barbara (1754-1818) married Peter May's son Alexander.

Robertson, William (1740-1803), cashier and principal factor to Earl of Findlater. He was educated at Fordyce Grammar School, where he formed a friendship with George Chalmers, author of *Caledonia*, and at King's College, Aberdeen, where he graduated M.A. in 1756. Served part of apprenticeship to George Turner, advocate in Aberdeen, but was recommended by James Burnett of Monboddo to Lord Deskford in 1766 to be his secretary. With James Ross's departure to Gordon Castle, Robertson took over as cashier at Cullen. With the Earl's residence abroad Robertson took control of the estate under Professor John Ross and Theophilus Ogilvy, Commissioners appointed by the Earl. In 1777 Robertson was appointed joint deputy-keeper of the records of Scotland. *See DNB* for list of his published work.

Ross, Charles (1722-1806), land surveyor, began his career about 1744. Who trained him is not known, but from his style there is a large element of self-education. His map of Renfrewshire (1754) was one of the earliest county maps to be published in Scotland. He made several professional excursions to Easter Ross, the earliest in 1759 when he collaborated with Alexander Sangster. In 1763 James Grant of Grant enquired from Robert Robinson, another land surveyor, as to the possibility of employing Ross to survey his estates but Robinson observed bluntly, and one must admit honestly, that, 'Mr Ross lives near Glasgow but is now from home and I believe he is in the North Country. I must be plain enough to inform you that I have had some of Mr Ross's surveys lately through my hands which were far from being so accurate as I could wish . . .'. This judgement fell on receptive ears for Grant of Grant's clerk forwarded Robinson's words, and had the reply, 'I have no inducement to imploy Mr Ross more than any other as money laid out in that way was thrown away when the plan was not accurate and true' (SRO. GD248/250). In 1767 Ross began to advertise his nursery garden. Later he fell heir through his wife's family to part of the 'buildings at Elderslie erected for the purpose of a cotton miln' (SRO. Sasine Abridgements Renfrew No. 5968, citing PRS. vol. 43, fo. 142). He died at Greenlaw, near Paisley on 11 September 1806, aged 84.

Ross, James (1732–1782), clerk to Earl of Findlater at Cullen House until 1769 when he became principal factor on the vast Gordon Castle estates until his death. He is variously described as cashier, clerk, and factor and secretary to the Duke of Gordon, but he would be best described as Chamberlain at Fochabers. Ross took up his post for Findlater in 1761 after William Lorimer had refused the position. Ross undertook most of the correspondence which led up to Peter May taking up the factorship at Elgin. Upon going to Gordon Castle, Ross introduced the use of letter-books (these are preserved in the Gordon Castle papers (GD44) in SRO) and it was on advice he took from Peter May that the major survey of the Gordon Castle estates was undertaken by Alexander and George Taylor, Thomas Milne and George Brown from November 1769 to May 1781. He married Katherine, dau. of John Gordon of Cluny, a former cashier to the Duke of Gordon. His brother, Professor John Ross (q.v.) became one of the Commissioners to the 7th Earl of Findlater. Although a shadowy figure, James Ross was extremely significant in the spirit of change that swept over the Northeast during the 1760s and '70s; Dr Ian Grant has summed up his role, 'During his factory at Cullen significant developments of Cullen, Portsoy and Sandend villages took place, and during that at Gordon Castle the planned villages of Tomintoul and Fochabers were begun.

Estate managers trained by him included John Menzies and John Logie at Gordon Castle and James Morison of the Annexed Estates, while John Wilson, at Cullen House . . . also seems to have received his training from Ross'. (Ian D. Grant, *op. cit.*)

Ross, John (*c.* 1731-1814), professor of Hebrew and Oriental Languages at King's College, Aberdeen. He was tutor to 7th Earl of Findlater at Christ Church, Oxford, and was named his commissioner in 1771 and remained in that position until the Earl's death in 1811. His brother, James (q.v.) was factor to the Earl of Findlater and later cashier to the Duke of Gordon.

Ross, John (?-1794), factor to 7th Earl of Findlater. He was apprenticed to Andrew Thomson, factor to 1st Earl Fife. In 1769 he was a writer in Aberdeen, and was admitted in 1776 as a member of the Society of Advocates in Aberdeen. In crop 1787 he succeeded John Wilson (q.v.) as factor to the Earl of Findlater on the Cullen Collection.

Stuart, John, 3rd Earl of Bute (1713-92), one of the most powerful political figures of the eighteenth century. He spent most of the earlier part of his life on his estates in Bute where he took an interest in tree-planting and botany. He was prime minister from 1762-3. After his retirement from politics he became in 1780 the first president of the Society of Scottish Antiquaries. Improvements were begun on Bute in the middle of the 1760s but according to James Stuart Mackenzie (q.v.) and Peter May, 'We reckon that within these 15 years past there has been about £18,000 of your money absolutely thrown away on wild schemes of one sort or another, an abominable imposition and picking of your pocket'. Mackenzie recruited Peter May to look after his brother's estate and himself took an active interest in its management. Bute rarely visited Mount Stuart during May's factorship.

Stuart, John, 4th Earl and 1st Marquis of Bute (1744-1814), appears in this volume as Lord Mount Stuart. From 1779 he was British Envoy to Turin, and from March to December 1783 he held the post of Ambassador at Madrid, a post he returned to in 1795-6. After his return to Britain in 1784 he took an increasing interest in estate affairs.

Taylor, Alexander, land surveyor, *see* Introduction, pp. xxx-xxxiii.
Taylor, George, land surveyor, *see* Introduction, pp. xxx-xxxiii.

Watson, David (?1713-61), born at Muirhouse, near Edinburgh, was the son of an Edinburgh merchant and had a distinguished military career, *see DNB*. As a Lieutenant-Colonel he inaugurated the military survey of Scotland, 'Roy's Map', between 1747 and 1755. His paper on surveying an estate, read to the Commissioners of the Annexed Estates on 23 June 1755, was a major landmark in stimulating improvement in Scotland (*see* I. H. Adams, *Descriptive List of Plans in the Scottish Record Office*, H.M.S.O., Edinburgh, vol. 3, pp. vii-ix). For a definitive account of Roy's survey, *see* R. A. Skelton, *The Military Survey of Scotland 1747-1755*, Royal Scottish Geographical Society, Edinburgh, Special Publication No. 1, 1967 (reprinted from the *Scottish Geographical Magazine*, vol. 83, No. 1, April 1967).
Wilson, John (1746-1816), factor to the Earl of Findlater. From 1768 to 1770 he travelled, at the expense of the 6th Earl of Findlater, through Scotland and England examining farming methods. With the death of the 6th Earl in 1770, the 7th Earl agreed to employ Wilson as a clerk and overseer of farming business. Thereafter he rose to become the principal resident estate official at Cullen (the Earl being permanently abroad) and after 1780 he is described as factor. He was succeeded in crop 1787 by John Ross (q.v.). *See* Andrew Cassels Brown, *The Wilsons, A Banffshire Family of Factors*, Edinburgh, privately printed, 1936.

INDEX

MEMBERSHIP

Membership of the Scottish History Society
is open to all who are interested in the history of Scotland.
For an annual subscription of £5·00
members normally receive one volume each year.
Enquiries should be addressed to
the Honorary Secretary or the Honorary Treasurer,
whose addresses are given overleaf.

SCOTTISH HISTORY SOCIETY

REPORT

of the 90th Annual Meeting

The 90th Annual Meeting of the Scottish History Society was held in the Rooms of the Royal Society, George Street, Edinburgh, on Saturday, 11 December 1976, at 11.15 a.m. Professor G. W. S. Barrow, President of the Society, was in the Chair.

The Report of Council was as follows:

The issue to members of the two volumes in memory of Dr Annie I. Dunlop has unfortunately been delayed owing to editing and other difficulties. It is, however, confidently expected that both the *Calendar of Papal Letters to Scotland of Clement VII of Avignon, 1378–1394*, edited by Monsignor Charles Burns, and the *Calendar of Papal Letters to Scotland of Benedict XIII of Avignon, 1394–1418*, edited by Mr Frank McGurk, will be available early in the coming year.

At present in preparation is *Scottish Industrial History: a miscellany of documents*. This will contain four items: 'Heinrich Kalmeter's diary of his travels in Scotland, 1719–1720', edited by Professor T. C. Smout; 'The notebook of Henry Brown, woollen manufacturer, 1818–1819', edited by Dr C. Gulvin; 'Report by the committee of investigation to the shareholders of the North British Railway Company, 1866', edited by Dr Wray Vamplew; and 'The beginning and end of the Lewis Chemical Works, 1858–1874', edited by Dr T. I. Rae. These items will be preceded by a general introduction written by Professor R. H. Campbell. This miscellany will not, of course, cover all features of Scottish industry, but will include aspects of the textile industry and the development of railways, as well as the interesting and at times amusing account of an attempt to bring industry to the Highlands and Islands.

The reprints produced for the Society by the Scottish Academic Press, *The Lyon in mourning*, *The Itinerary of Prince Charles Edward Stuart*, *The Origins of the 'Forty-five'*, and *Scottish Population Statistics*, appeared early in the year. Those members who ordered copies in advance will have received them. A limited number of copies from the allocation made to the Society remains, and those members who wish to add any of these works to their collection of Society volumes are advised to apply for them as soon as possible.

As proposed in the last annual report and accepted by the last Annual General Meeting, the office of Secretary of the Society has been divided. This division necessitates an alteration in the Rules of the Society, and the opportunity has been taken to revise the Rules. Copies of the revised Rules have been circulated to members, and their adoption will be proposed to the

Annual General Meeting by the Council. In accordance with the decision to divide the secretaryship, Dr T. I. Rae, previously Secretary, has now been appointed Publication Secretary, and Dr David Stevenson has been appointed Secretary to take over the general administration of the Society. Dr Kathleen Davies has retired as Assistant Secretary.

Professor G. W. S. Barrow is now due to retire from the presidency of the Society, and Professor A. A. M. Duncan has been nominated by Council to succeed him and will be proposed to the Annual General Meeting for election.

Members of Council due to retire in rotation at this time are Dr J. M. Brown, Mr A. Fenton and Mr J. J. Robertson, In addition, a fourth vacancy on the Council has been created by the appointment of Dr Stevenson to be Secretary. The following will be proposed to the Annual General Meeting for election to the Council: Mr Patrick Cadell, Dr T. M. Devine, Mr J. B. S. Gilfillan, and Dr Annette Smith.

During the past year 6 members have died, including The Right Honourable the Earl of Crawford and Balcarres, a benefactor of the Society, 11 members have resigned and 3 have been removed from the list of members for non-payment of subscriptions. New members numbered 15. The total membership, including 234 libraries, is now 695, compared with 700 in 1975.

In presenting the Annual Report, Professor R. H. Campbell, Chairman of Council, referred with satisfaction to the reprints produced for the Society, and mentioned aspects of the new Constitution. The Hon. Treasurer reported a satisfactory balance, but also referred to the increasing costs of production.

Mr D. J. Withrington, seconded by Dr Jean Munro, moved the adoption of the Annual Report, and this was approved.

Dr R. G. Cant, seconded by Dr T. I. Rae, moved the election of Professor A. A. M. Duncan as President of the Society, and he was duly elected.

Dr Marinell Ash, seconded by Dr Frances Shaw, nominated for election as ordinary members of Council Mr Patrick Cadell, Dr T. M. Devine, Mr J. B. S. Gilfillan, and Dr Annette Smith, and they were duly elected.

Mr Stuart Maxwell, seconded by Dr Jennifer Brown, moved the adoption of the new Constitution, which was approved.

The President delivered an address entitled 'Army service in Medieval Scotland'.

Professor John MacQueen proposed a vote of thanks to the President for his paper, and for the admirable way in which he had conducted the affairs of the Society during his term of office.

ABSTRACT ACCOUNT OF CHARGE AND DISCHARGE OF THE INTROMISSIONS OF THE HONORARY TREASURER for 1 November 1975 to 31 October 1976

I. GENERAL ACCOUNT

CHARGE

I. Cash in Bank at 1st November, 1975:		
1. Sum at credit of Savings Account with Bank of Scotland		£4,731·77
2. Sum at credit of Current Account with Bank of Scotland		97·01
3. Sum at credit of Savings Account with Edinburgh Savings Bank		67·09
4. Sum at credit of Special Investment Account with Edinburgh Savings Bank		1,192·96
		£6,088·83
II. Subscriptions received		1,948·39
III. Past Publications sold		547·66
IV. Reprints sold		734·16
V. Interest on Savings Accounts with Bank of Scotland and Edinburgh Savings Bank		474·57
VI. Balance of Income Tax Refund (1973–74)		123·71
VII. Income Tax Refund (1974–75)		174·96
VIII. Donations		150·00
IX. Sums drawn from Bank Current Account	£3,630·65	
X. Sums drawn from Bank Savings Account	—	
		£10,242·28

DISCHARGE

I.	Cost of reprints		£2,000·00
	Cost of binding unbound parts		178·92
	Cost of printing Annual Report, Notices and Printers' Postages, etc.		279·45
			£2,458·37
II.	Insurance Premiums		28·13
III.	Miscellaneous Payments		224.15
IV.	Sums lodged in Bank Current Account	£3,775·89	
V.	Sums lodged in Bank Savings Account	7,386·39	
VI.	Funds at close of this account:		
	1. Balance at credit of Savings Account with Bank of Scotland	£6,013·90	
	2. Balance at credit of Current Account with Bank of Scotland	145·24	
	3. Balance at credit of Savings Account with Edinburgh Savings Bank	69·77	
	4. Balance at credit of Special Investment Account with Edinburgh Savings Bank	1,302·72	
			7,531·63
			£10,242·28

GLASGOW, *9th November, 1976*. I have examined the General Account of the Honorary Treasurer of the Scottish History Society for the year from 1 November 1975 to 31 October 1976, and I find the same to be correctly stated and sufficiently vouched.

I. M. M. MACPHAIL
Auditor

CONSTITUTION OF THE

SCOTTISH HISTORY SOCIETY

Name

1. The Society shall be known as 'The Scottish History Society'.

Objects

2. The objects of the Society are to promote interest in, and further knowledge of, the history of Scotland and, for this purpose:
   (*a*) to discover, edit, print, and issue to members unpublished documents illustrative of that history;
   (*b*) to produce reprints or new editions of published works of a similar nature which are out of print;
   (*c*) exceptionally, to commission and issue to members works of a general nature relating to Scottish history.

Membership

3. (1) The Council (mentioned in Rule 8 below), shall from time to time determine rates of subscription qualifying for membership of the Society and may determine different rates for different categories of membership.
   (2) Any person or institution may become a member of the Society on paying the appropriate subscription.
   (3) A member shall cease to be a member:
      (*a*) on resignation;
      (*b*) on failure to pay any subscription due by him.

General Meetings

4. (1) There shall be General Meetings of the members for ordinary purposes ('ordinary General Meetings') at approximately yearly intervals on dates (normally in December) to be fixed by the Council.
   (2) A General Meeting of the members for special purposes ('special General Meetings') shall be convened:
      (*a*) in accordance with any direction of the Council;

(*b*) on a requisition made in writing to the Secretary by not less than 10 members of the Society and stating the motion or motions which the said members desire to move at the meeting.

(3) Every General Meeting shall be convened by the Secretary (whom failing by any other member of the Council) by notice in writing addressed to each member of the Society and dispatched not less than 10 days before the date of the meeting.

(4) For any General Meeting a quorum shall be 10 members.

(5) At any General Meeting the Chair shall be occupied by the President of the Society if he is present; whom failing by the Chairman or any other member of the Council; whom failing by such members of the Society as may be appointed by the members present.

Procedure at General Meetings

5. Procedure at any General Meeting shall be regulated in such manner as the President or other member occupying the Chair may determine, and the person occupying the Chair:

(*a*) shall refuse to accept any motion for the alteration of the constitution or for the suspension of any provision thereof; and

(*b*) may refuse to accept any other motion;

unless notice of the motion has been given in writing by the proposer to the Secretary at least 21 days before the date of the Meeting.

President

6. There shall be a President of the Society nominated by the Council and elected by a General Meeting. A President shall normally serve for four years and preside at the General Meetings of the Society held during his term of office. He shall deliver an address to one or more of these Meetings.

Office-bearers

7. The Office-bearers of the Society shall be a Chairman, a Secretary, a Publication Secretary and a Treasurer, all of whom shall be elected by the Council for such periods as it may determine.

The Council

8. (1) Subject to any directions given by the Society in General Meeting, the affairs of the Society shall be managed by the Office-bearers and 12 other members of the Society elected by the Society in General Meeting.

(2) Apart from the Office-bearers, the members of the Council shall hold office for a term of four years and shall not be eligible for re-election until after the lapse of one year.

(3) Meetings of the Council shall be convened by the Secretary twice each year and more often if the Chairman so determines. A meeting of the Council shall also be convened by the Secretary at the request of three members of the Council.

(4) For any meeting of the Council the quorum shall be six members or office-bearers.

(5) The election of members of the Council shall be made from members of the Society nominated by two other members of the Society. Each nomination shall be delivered to the Secretary not less than seven days before the meeting at which such election is to be held.

(6) Casual vacancies occurring among the Office-bearers or other members of the Council may be filled by a member of the Society appointed by the Council.

(7) The Council shall have powers to determine:

(*a*) the number of copies of the Society's works to be presented to editors and owners of manuscripts;

(*b*) the conditions of sale to non-members of the Society's works.

Accounts

9. (1) Proper accounts of the Society's funds and financial affairs shall be kept by the Treasurer, shall be audited annually by a person appointed by the council and shall be submitted to the Society annually at a General Meeting. Copies of the accounts shall be circulated to all members with the notice calling a meeting.

(2) The financial year for the Society's financial affairs, including the annual subscription, shall run from 1 November to 31 October.

4

Publications

10. Every member of the Society who has duly paid the subscription appropriate to him in respect of any financial year shall be entitled to receive, free of charge, one copy of such of the Society's works as are issued in that year.